perspectives

Education

Academic Editor
Annette Digby
University of Arkansas

Boulder • Bellevue • Dubuque • Madison

Our mission at **coursewise** is to help students make connections—linking theory to practice and the classroom to the outside world. Learners are motivated to synthesize ideas when course materials are placed in a context they recognize. By providing gateways to contemporary and enduring issues, **coursewise** publications will expand students' awareness of and context for the course subject.

For more information on **coursewise** visit us at our web site: http://www.coursewise.com

coursewise publishing editorial staff

Thomas Doran, ceo/publisher: Journalism/Marketing/Speech
Edgar Laube, publisher: Geography/Political Science/Psychology/Sociology
Linda Meehan Avenarius, publisher: **courselinks**
Sue Pulvermacher-Alt, publisher: Education/Health/Gender Studies
Victoria Putman, publisher: Anthropology/Philosophy/Religion
Tom Romaniak, publisher: Business/Criminal Justice/Economics

coursewise publishing production staff

Lori A. Blosch, permissions coordinator
Mary Monner, production coordinator, print/online
Victoria Putman, production manager

Interior design and cover design by Jeff Storm

Library of Congress Catalog Card Number: 98-072280

ISBN 0-395-902576

Printed in the United States of America by **coursewise publishing**, Inc.
1379 Lodge Lane, Boulder, CO 80303

10 9 8 7 6 5 4 3 2 1

from the

Publisher

Sue Pulvermacher-Alt

coursewise publishing

Wanted: Teachers for the Twenty-First Century

> Applicant must be well versed in and comfortable with using many technologies. Fluency in at least two languages is required. Applicant will need to prepare, administer, and use evaluative feedback to improve learning while promoting student's positive self-image. Knowledge of developmentally appropriate practices for students and an ability to adjust teaching to the needs of each student to facilitate learning are required. Applicant must be able to organize and facilitate meetings. Experience working in a team environment is preferred. Any "sage on the stage" need not apply.

Are you ready? Could you apply and get an interview for this position? Would you be hired? If your answers are YES, I congratulate you. You can use this course to strengthen your already strong position in the job market. If your answers are NO or MAYBE, this course will help you decide if teaching is the right profession for you and will help you prepare for the education job market.

We want to help. Perhaps you're taking an introduction to education course and deciding whether or not teaching is right for you. Maybe you've made that decision and are taking a foundations course to solidify your understanding of the profession. In either case, this *Perspectives: Education* volume and the accompanying **courselinks**™ site for Education offer you readings and Internet resources to help you get ready to successfully enter the education job market of the next century.

We've tried to put together readings in this volume that help you to sort out the important issues and to become an informed educator. In Section 1, we include readings that focus on teaching as a profession. The readings in Section 2 show the relationship between history of education and education philosophy, and will help you formulate your own philosophy of education. Section 3 readings examine the diversity of the learners you'll teach. Readings in Sections 4 and 5 explore current issues and innovations and their impact on education. Finally, Section 6 offers readings that explore the likely future of educational systems and what that will mean for you.

In addition to the readings in this volume, you'll find web sites that we hope will expand your understanding of the issues. The R.E.A.L. sites you'll find throughout *Perspectives: Education* and at the accompanying **courselinks**™ site have been chosen because they are particularly useful sites. You, however, still need to be the critical consumer of the information. Read our annotations and decide if the site is worth visiting. Do the activities so you can get to know the site better. Search our **courselinks**™ site by key topic and find the information you need to be a more informed educator.

As publisher for this volume, I had the good fortune to work with Annette Digby as the Academic Editor. Annette has experience as a classroom teacher, university instructor, and now, university administrator. She cares about education. From the time and energy she put into this volume, I think she cares about you and your educational experience and training, too. She wants to give you a tool to make your college coursework more meaningful. (From what I could see, Annette did the work for this project in the evenings, on the weekends, and on flights to/from educational meetings. Seeing this project complete gives her a life back!)

We were helped by a top-notch Editorial Board. At **coursewise,** we're working hard to publish "connected learning" tools—connecting theory to practice and the college classroom to the outside world. Readings and web sites are selected with this goal in mind. Members of the Editorial Board offered some critical feedback and posed some interesting challenges. They know their content and are a web-savvy bunch. My thanks to Annette and the entire Editorial Board.

As you prepare for your twenty-first century profession and explore the issues surrounding education, I invite you to share your reactions to our materials. How'd we do in preparing you? What worked and what didn't work in this *Perspectives: Education* volume and the accompanying **courselinks**™ site? Have we helped you clarify your philosophy toward education? I'd love to hear from you—now before you take that new job.

Sue Pulvermacher-Alt, Publisher
suepa@coursewise.com

Dr. Annette Digby is the Associate Dean for Undergraduate Studies and Student Services at the University of Arkansas. She received her M.Ed. degree in English Education from Mississippi State University and her Ed.D. degree in Secondary Education from the University of Alabama. Dr. Digby has authored numerous publications on cooperative learning, middle-level education, school/university partnerships, and certification issues. Since joining the UA faculty in 1989, Dr. Digby has served in a variety of roles, including coordinator of introductory-level education courses and field placements for students.

from the Academic Editor

Annette Digby
University of Arkansas

As instructors, we face the challenge of selecting materials that will not be outdated before they arrive in campus bookstores. I agreed to edit *Perspectives: Education* because I believe that such a resource will help to meet the challenge of providing up-to-date topics for instructors and students.

Prior to proposing a table of contents for *Perspectives: Education,* I reviewed a variety of texts designed specifically for use in educational foundations classes. Not surprisingly, the most frequently used texts include discussions on curriculum, professional issues, history of American education, philosophy of education, governance, futurism, and technology. *Perspectives: Education* includes readings on these key topics, but with an emphasis on current and future implications. Designed for use either as a primary text or as a supplement to other classroom materials, the reader integrates theory with application.

Perspectives: Education allows you to assume ownership of your profession by becoming personally involved in the content, thus explaining the use of the word *our* in each of the six section titles. Section 1, "Reclaiming Our Profession: Participating in a Dynamic System," focuses on teaching as a profession. Section 2, "Examining Our Beliefs: Understanding Our Heritage and Articulating Personal Philosophies," not only illustrates the interrelationship between the history of education and educational philosophy, but also challenges you to formulate your own philosophies of education. Meeting the needs of all students in a multicultural society is the focus of Section 3, "Fulfilling Our Mission: Meeting the Needs of All Learners." Sections 4 and 5, "Assessing Our Position: Participating in Reflective Conversations on Selected Issues" and "Assessing Our Position: Participating in Reflective Conversations on Selected Innovations," lead you to think about current issues and innovations and their impact on educational systems. In conclusion, Section 6, "Shaping Our Future: Becoming Visionaries," reminds you that educational systems will continue to change, largely because of technological advances and their impact on delivery systems.

The R.E.A.L. web sites listed in *Perspectives: Education* and at the **courselinks**™ site for Education expand on the topics surrounding the six sections in the reader. The R.E.A.L. sites offer the latest information and some additional resources you can call upon in your quest to understand the issues of this profession we call teaching.

On a personal note, I have enjoyed editing *Perspectives: Education.* I appreciated the suggestions of the Editorial Board and the ongoing assistance of the **coursewise** staff, especially Sue Pulvermacher-Alt. At all times, even in the midst of challenges, Sue offered guidance, patience, and understanding. A true professional, Sue consistently demonstrated a commitment to quality, never losing sight of her vision for the *Perspectives* series.

Editorial Board

We wish to thank the following instructors for their assistance. Their many suggestions not only contributed to the construction of this volume, but also to the ongoing development of our Education web site.

Dr. Margaret Clark
University of Arkansas

Margaret Clark, Associate Professor of Curriculum and Instruction, has taught French and Secondary Education at the University of Arkansas, Fayetteville, for 29 years. She has been coordinating the sections of the Introduction to Education course for several years. Dr. Clark has organized English as a Second Language (ESL) conferences and conducted ESL workshops for area educators. She has developed and now teaches a number of ESL courses at UA (and has taught ESL methodology courses in Athens, Greece). Dr. Clark received an M.A. in French and an Ed.D. in Secondary Education from the University of Arkansas. She studied a year at the University of Paris and spent a summer at a pedagogical institute at the University of Besancon in France on a Fulbright fellowship. For her input as an Editorial Board member, we say "merci beaucoup!"

Deborah DeSimone
College of Staten Island,
City University of New York

Deborah DeSimone is an Assistant Professor of Education and Women's Studies at the College of Staten Island, City University of New York. Her area of particular interest is women in history, especially the role women have played in the history of education. She earned her Ed.D in History and Education and her M.A. in Social Studies at Teachers' College, Columbia University. She earned her BA in American History at Brown University.

Natalie Ehrlich
Oklahoma State University

Charlene Johnson
University of Arkansas

Charlene Johnson is an Associate Professor in the Department of Curriculum and Instruction at the University of Arkansas. She also served as the Director of the Center for Middle Level Education, Research, and Development. Her research interests include middle level/early adolescence, school/university partnerships, and multicultural education and issues.

Dr. Jerry Long
Emporia State University

Jerry Long is the Associate Dean at The Teachers College at Emporia State University. Dr. Long earned both his M.S.E. in Secondary Education/Social Studies and his Ed.D. in Secondary Education from Oklahoma State University. He is another web-savvy member of our Editorial Board. In his Introduction to Teaching course at Emporia, he has a technology requirement—the "successful navigation of the Internet." Prior to coming to Emporia State University, Dr. Long taught in public school and university settings in Montana, West Virginia, Arkansas, Oklahoma, and Kansas.

Dr. Kenneth Schmidt
University of Wisconsin–Eau Claire

Kenneth Schmidt is an Associate Professor in the Department of Curriculum and Instruction at the University of Wisconsin-Eau Claire. He earned his Ph.D. in Comparative Education and East Asian Studies at Syracuse University. His areas of expertise include cultural and philosophical foundations of education, curriculum, and social studies education. Dr. Schmidt published articles and made presentations on the Internet as an extension of the classroom long before it was fashionable.

WiseGuide Introduction

Critical Thinking and Bumper Stickers

Question Authority

The bumper sticker said: Question Authority. This is a simple directive that goes straight to the heart of critical thinking. The issue is not whether the authority is right or wrong; it's the questioning process that's important. Questioning helps you develop awareness and a clearer sense of what you think. That's critical thinking.

Critical thinking is a new label for an old approach to learning—that of challenging all ideas, hypotheses, and assumptions. In the physical and life sciences, systematic questioning and testing methods (known as the scientific method) help verify information, and objectivity is the benchmark on which all knowledge is pursued. In the social sciences, however, where the goal is to study people and their behavior, things get fuzzy. It's one thing for the chemistry experiment to work out as predicted, or for the petri dish to yield a certain result. It's quite another matter, however, in the social sciences, where the subject is ourselves. Objectivity is harder to achieve.

Although you'll hear critical thinking defined in many different ways, it really boils down to analyzing the ideas and messages that you receive. What are you being asked to think or believe? Does it make sense, objectively? Using the same facts and considerations, could you reasonably come up with a different conclusion? And, why does this matter in the first place? As the bumper sticker urged, question authority. Authority can be a textbook, a politician, a boss, a big sister, or an ad on television. Whatever the message, learning to question it appropriately is a habit that will serve you well for a lifetime. And in the meantime, thinking critically will certainly help you be course wise.

Getting Connected

This reader is a tool for connected learning. This means that the readings and other learning aids explained here will help you to link classroom theory to real-world issues. They will help you to think critically and to make long-lasting learning connections. Feedback from both instructors and students has helped us to develop some suggestions on how you can wisely use this connected learning tool.

WiseGuide Pedagogy

A wise reader is better able to be a critical reader. Therefore, we want to help you get wise about the articles in this reader. Each section of *Perspectives* has three tools to help you: the WiseGuide Intro, the WiseGuide Wrap-Up, and the Putting It in *Perspectives* review form.

WiseGuide Intro

WiseGuide Intro

In the WiseGuide Intro, the Academic Editor introduces the section, gives you an overview of the topics covered, and explains why particular articles were selected and what's important about them.

Also in the WiseGuide Intro, you'll find several key points or learning objectives that highlight the most important things to remember from this section. These will help you to focus your study of section topics.

At the end of the Wiseguide Intro, you'll find questions designed to stimulate critical thinking. Wise students will keep these questions in mind as they read an article (we repeat the questions at the start of the articles as a reminder). When you finish each article, check your understanding. Can you answer the questions? If not, go back and reread the article. The Academic Editor has written sample responses for many of the questions, and you'll find these online at the **courselinks**™ site for this course. More about **courselinks**™ in a minute. . . .

WiseGuide Wrap-Up

Be course wise and develop a thorough understanding of the topics covered in this course. The WiseGuide Wrap-Up at the end of each section will help you do just that with concluding comments or summary points that repeat what's most important to understand from the section you just read.

In addition, we try to get you wired up by providing a list of select Internet resources—what we call R.E.A.L. web sites because they're **R**elevant, **E**xciting, **A**pproved, and **L**inked. The information at these web sites will enhance your understanding of a topic. (Remember to use your Passport and start at http://www.courselinks.com so that if any of these sites have changed, you'll have the latest link.)

Putting It in *Perspectives* Review Form

At the end of the book is the Putting It in *Perspectives* review form. Your instructor may ask you to complete this form as an assignment or for extra credit. If nothing else, consider doing it on your own to help you critically think about the reading.

Prompts at the end of each article encourage you to complete this review form. Feel free to copy the form and use it as needed.

The courselinks™ Site

The **courselinks**™ Passport is your ticket to a wonderful world of integrated web resources designed to help you with your course work. These resources are found at the **courselinks**™ site for your course area. This is where the readings in this book and the key topics of your course are linked to an exciting array of online learning tools. Here you will find carefully selected readings, web links, quizzes, worksheets, and more, tailored to your course and approved as connected learning tools. The ever-changing, always interesting **courselinks**™ site features a number of carefully integrated resources designed to help you be course wise. These include:

- **R.E.A.L. Sites** At the core of a **courselinks**™ site is the list of R.E.A.L. sites. This is a select group of web sites for studying, not surfing. Like the readings in this book, these sites have been selected, reviewed, and approved by the Academic Editor and the Editorial Board. The R.E.A.L. sites are arranged by topic and are annotated with short descriptions and key words to make them easier for you to use for reference or research. With R.E.A.L. sites, you're studying approved resources within seconds—and not wasting precious time surfing unproven sites.
- **Editor's Choice** Here you'll find updates on news related to your course, with links to the actual online sources. This is also where we'll tell you about changes to the site and about online events.

- **Course Overview** This is a general description of the typical course in this area of study. While your instructor will provide specific course objectives, this overview helps you place the course in a generic context and offers you an additional reference point.
- **www.orksheet** Focus your trip to a R.E.A.L. site with the www.orksheet. Each of the 10 to 15 questions will prompt you to take in the best that site has to offer. Use this tool for self-study, or if required, email it to your instructor.
- **Course Quiz** The questions on this self-scoring quiz are related to articles in the reader, information at R.E.A.L. sites, and other course topics, and will help you pinpoint areas you need to study. Only you will know your score—it's an easy, risk-free way to keep pace!
- **Topic Key** The Topic Key is a listing of the main topics in your course, and it correlates with the Topic Key that appears in this reader. This handy reference tool also links directly to those R.E.A.L. sites that are especially appropriate to each topic, bringing you integrated online resources within seconds!
- **Web Savvy Student Site** If you're new to the Internet or want to brush up, stop by the Web Savvy Student site. This unique supplement is a complete **courselinks**™ site unto itself. Here, you'll find basic information on using the Internet, creating a web page, communicating on the web, and more. Quizzes and Web Savvy Worksheets test your web knowledge, and the R.E.A.L. sites listed here will further enhance your understanding of the web.
- **Student Lounge** Drop by the Student Lounge to chat with other students taking the same course or to learn more about careers in your major. You'll find links to resources for scholarships, financial aid, internships, professional associations, and jobs. Take a look around the Student Lounge and give us your feedback. We're open to remodeling the Lounge per your suggestions.

Building Better Perspectives!

Please tell us what you think of this *Perspectives* volume so we can improve the next one. Here's how you can help:

1. Visit our **coursewise** site at: http://www.coursewise.com
2. Click on *Perspectives.* Then select the Building Better *Perspectives* Form for your book.
3. Forms and instructions for submission are available online.

Tell us what you think—did the readings and online materials help you make some learning connections? Were some materials more helpful than others? Thanks in advance for helping us build better *Perspectives.*

Student Internships

If you enjoy evaluating these articles or would like to help us evaluate the **courselinks**™ site for this course, check out the **coursewise** Student Internship Program. For more information, visit:

http://www.coursewise.com/intern.html

Contents

section

Reclaiming Our Profession: Participating in a Dynamic System

section

Examining Our Beliefs: Understanding Our Heritage and Articulating Personal Philosophies

section 3

Fulfilling Our Mission: Meeting the Needs of All Learners

section 4

Assessing Our Position: Participating in Reflective Conversations on Selected Issues

section 5

Assessing Our Position: Participating in Reflective Conversations on Selected Innovations

section 6

Shaping Our Future: Becoming Visionaries

Topic Key

This Topic Key is an important tool for learning. It will help you integrate this reader into your course studies. Listed below, in alphabetical order, are important topics covered in this volume. Below each topic, you'll find the reading numbers and titles, and also the R.E.A.L. web site addresses, relating to that topic. Note that the Topic Key might not include every topic your instructor chooses to emphasize. If you don't find the topic you're looking for in the Topic Key, check the index or the online topic key at the **courselinks**™ site.

Assessment
Reading 27: Semantics, Psychometrics, and Assessment Reform: A Close Look at Authentic Assessments
Reading 29: Steps for Improving School Climate in Block Scheduling

North Central Regional Educational Laboratory Pathways to School Improvement
http://www.ncrel.org/pathways.htm

National Center for Research on Evaluation, Standards, and Student Testing
http://cresst96.cse.ucla.edu/index.htm

Block Scheduling
Reading 29: Steps for Improving School Climate in Block Scheduling

Welcome to Block Scheduling
http://curry.edschool.virginia.edu/~dhv3v/block/BSintro.html

Charter Schools
Reading 25: New Options, Old Concerns

Classroom Management
Reading 29: Steps for Improving School Climate in Block Scheduling

Commercialism
Reading 17: Making Schools Ad-Free Zones

Community Service
Reading 11: Earning an 'A' in Idealism
Reading 15: Community Service in a Multicultural Nation

Constructivism
Reading 10: Constructivist Cautions

Readings in Teaching and Education
http://www.stemnet.nf.ca/~elmurphy/emurphy/ten61939.html

Core Knowledge
Reading 19: The Core Knowledge Curriculum: What's Behind Its Success?

Curriculum
Reading 2: The Fourth Phi Delta Kappa Poll of Teachers' Attitudes toward the Public Schools
Reading 3: The 29th Annual Phi Delta Kappa/Gallup Poll of the Public's Attitudes toward the Public Schools
Reading 6: Why History of Education?
Reading 12: Living with the Pendulum: The Complex World of Teaching
Reading 19: The Core Knowledge Curriculum: What's Behind Its Success?
Reading 29: Steps for Improving School Climate in Block Scheduling

Demography
Reading 5: Population Growth Has Big Uncertainties

Putting the Bite on Planet Earth: Rapid Human Population Is Devouring Global Natural Resources
http://www.dieoff.org/page120.htm

CIESIN: Information for a Changing World
http://infoserver.ciesin.org/

Dewey, John
Reading 8: John Dewey: A Voice That Still Speaks to Us
Reading 9: The Evolution of Philosophy of Education within Educational Studies

The Center for Dewey Studies
http://www.siu.edu/~deweyctr/

The People Who Made It Happen
http://www.uwyo.edu/a&s/ams/963/amst2010/studproj/edu/people.htm

Distance Education
Reading 30: Distance Education: Does Anyone Really Want to Learn at a Distance?

Distance Education at a Glance
http://www.uidaho.edu/evo/distglan.html

Full-Service Schools
Reading 28: Full-Service Schools

Gender Equity
Multiculturalism and Gender Equity Links
http://project.ilt.columbia.edu/schools/mcs/multicultural/links.html

Expect the Best from a Girl: That's What You Get (Women's College Coalition)
http://www.academic.org/

Hirsch, E. D., Jr.
Reading 18: The Jargon Jungle

History of Education
Reading 6: Why History of Education?

Internet
Reading 33: Voices from Networked Classrooms

Assessing WWW Sites for Education
http://www.capecod.net/Wixon/wixon.htm

Learning Communities
Reading 31: Creating Intentional Learning Communities
Reading 36: Learning Networks: Looking to 2010

Multicultural Education
Reading 13: The Goals and Track Record of Multicultural Education
Reading 14: Teachers' Role in Multicultural Education: Setting the Stage for Preservice Teachers
Reading 15: Community Service in a Multicultural Nation

Multiculturalism and Gender Equity Links
http://project.ilt.columbia.edu/schools/mcs/multicultural/links.html

Parental Involvement
Reading 2: The Fourth Phi Delta Kappa Poll of Teachers' Attitudes toward the Public Schools
Reading 3: The 29th Annual Phi Delta Kappa/Gallup Poll of the Public's Attitudes toward the Public Schools

Philosophy of Education
Reading 7: Orientation to Philosophy of Education: Locating the Field of Play for New Audiences
Reading 8: John Dewey: A Voice That Still Speaks to Us

section 1

Learning Objectives

After reading the articles in this section, you will be able to:

- Identify challenges facing novice and beginning teachers.
- Discuss why a mentoring process can be effective in retaining novice teachers.
- Give examples of how public perception influences educational policy.
- List strategies that preservice and inservice teachers can use to advance the profession of education.
- Discuss the relationship between changing global demographics and the roles and expectations of teachers.

Reclaiming Our Profession: Participating in a Dynamic System

Teaching is a complex profession. Prospective teachers must address common issues and question, such as, "Why do I want to become a teacher?" On the surface, this question appears simplistic; however, as prospective teachers attempt to articulate an answer, they realize that many forces—both internal and external—must be considered.

Although each prospective teacher has a unique set of internal or personal considerations, common concerns often include compensation and opportunities for advancement commensurate with career goals. More specifically, each person must answer such questions as "Where do I want to be in 5 years? In 10 years? In 30 years?" "Will teaching allow me opportunities to achieve those goals?" and "How do I feel about entering a profession that some people view negatively or even as a nonprofession?" To answer these questions and others like them, prospective teachers need as much information as possible about the teaching profession (for example, education requirements, benefits, challenges, expectations, and influences).

Just as internal considerations impact career choices, so do external forces. Arguably, outside forces influence teaching more than any other profession: Public perception influences educational policy; changing demographics impact roles and expectations of teachers; and societal needs and expectations often guide future directions of education. Consequently, prospective teachers must recognize and accept that the profession is dynamic and responsive to a changing world.

In Section 1, the selected readings focus on education as a dynamic profession. The first reading, "Friendly Persuasion: How Do You Convince a Doubting Beginner to Remain in the Classroom," shares correspondence between a novice teacher and her mentor. The letters address many of the issues that prospective and novice teachers face (for example, career goals, public perception, compensation), and also highlight the importance of mentoring. The next two readings, "The Fourth Phi Delta Kappa Poll of Teachers' Attitudes Toward the Public Schools" and "The 29th Annual Phi Delta Kappa/Gallup Poll of the Public's Attitudes Toward the Public Schools," discuss responses on selected educational issues, such as parental involvement and strategies for increasing student achievement. The fourth reading, "Teaching as a Profession: Redefining Our Concepts," focuses on the need for using appropriate language when referring to education as a profession. The fifth reading, "Population Growth Has Big Uncertainties," does not specifically address educational issues; instead, it presents demographic data that will have a great impact on global education as we enter the year 2000.

Questions

Reading 1: What are the major issues facing prospective teachers? What are the major issues facing novice teachers? Even though experienced teachers face challenges throughout their careers, they also experience benefits that lead them to remain in the teaching profession. What are some of the benefits that teachers credit for their long-term service?

Reading 2: How are the attitudes of public school teachers and the general public similar and different toward public education? What are the trends or patterns in teachers' opinions from 1984–1997?

Reading 3: What are some of the key challenges that poll respondents believe are facing public education? What do poll respondents believe with regard to the relevancy of the public school curriculum, including specific courses?

Reading 4: What is the difference between teacher training and teacher education? Why should educators be concerned about using the appropriate language when referring to teaching as a profession?

Reading 5: What are birth rate projections for the next 50 years?

What are the major issues facing prospective teachers? What are the major issues facing novice teachers? Even though experienced teachers face challenges throughout their careers, they also experience benefits that lead them to remain in the teaching profession. What are some of the benefits that teachers credit for their long-term service?

Friendly Persuasion

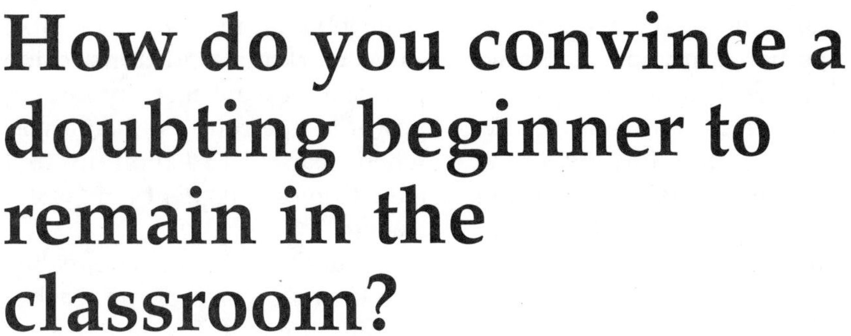

How do you convince a doubting beginner to remain in the classroom?

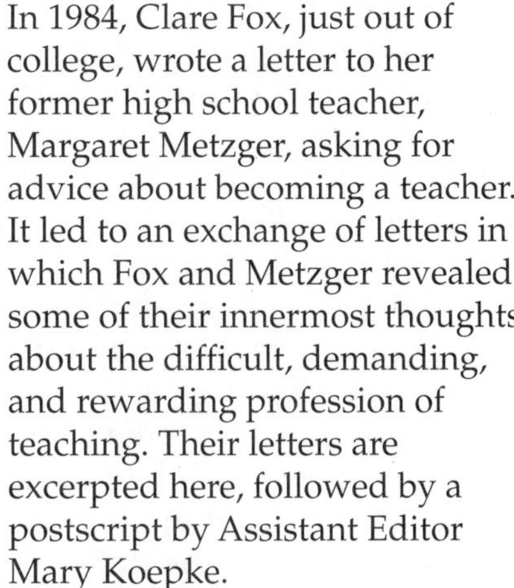

In 1984, Clare Fox, just out of college, wrote a letter to her former high school teacher, Margaret Metzger, asking for advice about becoming a teacher. It led to an exchange of letters in which Fox and Metzger revealed some of their innermost thoughts about the difficult, demanding, and rewarding profession of teaching. Their letters are excerpted here, followed by a postscript by Assistant Editor Mary Koepke.

Spring 1984

Dear Mrs. Metzger,

I am writing to you as a former student who has just graduated from Brown University and who is considering teaching English next year. I remember you as a compelling and demanding teacher who seemed to enjoy her job. At the moment, you are the only person I know who would support my career choice. Almost everyone else is disparaging about teaching in public schools.

But teaching matters. I know that. You mattered to me, and other teachers have mattered to me. I enjoyed student teaching and I look forward to next year. I have imaginary dialogues with the students in my mind. I hear myself articulating my policy on borderline grades, explaining why I keep switching the chairs from circles to rows as I flounder in my efforts to decide what's best.

But I wonder how much of teaching is actually an ego trip, a ploy to be liked, accepted, and respected by a group of people who have limited say in the matter. I also know the humiliation of a student's glare. I know there will be problems. Yet, I cannot deny the tremendous sense of worth I felt as a student teacher when students offered me their respect and when students worked hard and were proud of their effort.

I wonder where I would get this sense of worth if I were to work in a New York advertising firm or as an engineer at Bell Labs. And yet, going to work for a big corporation—whether an advertising firm, a bank, or a publishing house—impresses me. It would seem real, "grown-up," as teaching never will.

Adaptation reprinted with permission from Teacher Magazine, Vol. 11, No. 7, pp. 33–37, April 1997. Margaret Treece Metzger and Clare Fox, "Two Teachers of Letters," Harvard Educational Review, 56:4 (November 1986), pp. 349–354.

My mother doesn't want me to go into teaching. She is afraid I will get "stuck," that my efforts will not be appreciated or rewarded, and that I will not meet men. When I called home from Minneapolis after a long, productive, and exhilarating day interviewing at schools, my mother congratulated me and suggested that I spend the evening putting together a second résumé—a writing résumé—before I forgot everything else I know how to do. She suggested I spend the following day visiting television studios scouting for writing jobs, "just in case."

I write to you, Mrs. Metzger, because you were the first person to excite me about the processes of writing and because your integrity in the classroom has long been an influence on me—and on my decision to teach. You mattered. I am turning to you because you are a professional; and you continue to choose teaching after 18 years. I welcome any advice, comments, or solace you could offer me.

Sincerely,
Clare Fox

Spring 1984

Dear Clare,

I admire your courage to consider teaching. Your friends and relatives are not alone in their negative opinions about teaching. At least four blue-ribbon studies have concluded that teacher education is inadequate, that the pay is the lowest of all professions, that schools have deplorable management, and that the job is full of meaningless paperwork.

I know that much of the criticism is valid. However, the reports sensationalize and do not tell the whole truth. I appreciate your letter because you are giving me a chance to defend a profession I love.

Clare, I look forward to teaching. By mid-August, I start planning lessons and dreaming about classrooms. I also wonder whether I'll have the energy to start again with new classes. Yet, after September gets under way, I wake up in the morning expecting to have fun at work. I know that teaching well is a worthwhile use of my life. I know my work is significant.

I am almost 40 years old, and I'm happier in my job than anyone I know. That's saying a lot. My husband, who enjoys his work, has routine days when he comes home and says, "Nothing much happened today—just meetings." I never have routine days. When I am in the classroom, I usually am having a wonderful time.

I also hate this job. In March, I wanted to quit because of the relentlessness of dealing with 100 antsy adolescents day after day. I'm physically exhausted every Friday. The filth in our school is an aesthetic insult. The unending petty politics drain me.

A curious irony exists. I am never bored at work, yet my days are shockingly routine. I can tell you exactly what I have done every school day for the past 18 years at 10:15 in the morning (homeroom attendance), and I suspect I will do the same for the next 20 years. The structure of the school day has changed little since education moved out of the one-room schoolhouse. All teachers get tired of the monotonous routine of bookkeeping, make-up assignments, 20-minute lunches, and study-hall duties. I identify with J. Alfred Prufrock when he says, "I have measured out my life with coffee spoons." My own life has been measured out in student papers. At a conservation estimate, I've graded over 30,000—a mind-boggling statistic which makes me feel like a very dull person indeed.

The monotony of my schedule is mirrored in the monotony of my paycheck. No matter how well or poorly I teach, I will be paid the same amount. I am alternatively sad and angry about my pay. To the outside world, it seems that I am doing exactly the same job I did in 1996—same title, same working conditions, same pay scale (except that my buying power is 8 percent less than it was when I earned $5,400 on my first job). To most people, I am "just a teacher."

But this is the outside reality. The interior world of the teacher is quite different. I want to assure you that teachers change and grow. There is life after student teaching; there is growth after the first year. You will someday solve many of the problems that seem insurmountable during your exhilarating student teaching and your debilitating first year.

Sometimes, I am aware of my growth as a teacher, and I realize that finally, after all these years, I am confident in the classroom. On the very, very best days, when classes sing, I am able to operate on many levels during a single class: I integrate logistics, pedagogy, curriculum, group dynamics, individual needs, and my own philosophy. I feel generous and good-natured towards my students, and I am challenged by classroom issues. But on bad days, I feel like a total failure. Students attack my most vulnerable points. I feel overwhelmed by paperwork. I ache from exhaustion. I dream about going to Aruba, but I go to the next class.

I keep going because I'm intellectually stimulated. I enjoy literature, and I assign books I love and books I want to read. I expect class discussions and student papers to give me new insights into literature. As you may remember, I tell students that, in exchange for my hard work, they should keep me interested and teach me. They do.

To me, teaching poses questions worthy of a lifetime of thought. I want to think about what the great writers are saying. I want to think about how people learn. I want to think about the values we are passing on to the next generation. I am particularly interested in teaching thinking. I love to teach writing. I am working now on teacher writing as a tool for thinking. Questions about teaching are like puzzles to me; I can spend hours theorizing and then use my classroom as a laboratory.

And every year, new students require new teaching skills—Cambodian boat children who have never been in school and are illiterate even in their own language or handicapped children, such as a deaf Israeli girl who is trying to learn English without being able to hear it.

And then there are all the difficult, "normal" situations: students and parents who are "entitled," hostile, emotionally needy, or indifferent; students who live in chaotic homes, who are academically pressured, who have serious drug and alcohol problems. The list goes on and on. I received my combat training from other teachers, from myself, and mostly from the students. You will, too.

Sometimes I think I can't do it all. I don't want to be bitter or a martyr, so I am careful to take care of myself. I put flowers on my desk to offset the dreariness of an old school building. I leave school several times a week to run errands or to take walks in order to feel less trapped. Other teachers take courses at local colleges, join committees of adults, talk in the teachers' lounge, or play with computers. In order to give to others, teachers must nurture themselves.

Ultimately, teaching is nurturing. The teacher enters a giving relationship with strangers, and then the teacher's needs must give way to students' needs. I want to work on my own writing; instead, I work on students' writing. My days are spent encouraging young people's growth. I watch my students move beyond me, thinking and writing better than I have ever done. I send them to colleges I could never afford. And I must strive to be proud, not jealous, of them. I must learn generosity of heart.

I hope to love my students so well that it doesn't even matter whether they like me. I want to love them in the way I love my own son—full of respect and awe for who they are, full of wanting their growth, full of wonder at what it means to lead and to follow the next generation.

Clare, when you consider a life's work, consider not just what you will take to the task, but also what it will give to you. Which job will give self-respect and challenge? Which job will give you a world of ideas? Which job will be intellectually challenging? Which job will enlarge you and give you life in abundance? Which job will teach you lessons of the heart?

With deep respect,
Margaret Metzger

In the fall of 1984, Clare Fox took her first teaching job, in a junior high school in Tucson, Ariz. She worked there for a year and then changed jobs, dividing her time between working for a publishing company and teaching at a local inner-city high school.

Spring 1986

Dear Mrs. Metzger,

After two years of teaching, I still derive strength and vigor from the letter you wrote me so long ago. Your letter makes me remember all of the best parts of teaching. I remember lots of laughing. I laugh a lot in the classroom, more than I do in private life.

And I think a lot, too. There is no better way to learn a book than to teach it, no better way to think through a writing problem than to wrestle through the drafts of a paper, guiding the writer beyond frustration to resolution. I am at my brightest, some moments in the classroom.

And yet, I have decided to leave teaching.

I am feeling too selfish to teach, too possessive of my time and my future. I have decided to work full-time at the publishing company where I have worked afternoons this year.

After a strong, satisfying year, I left my first teaching job in June because I was afraid of the cycle that had already been established; I taught six classes a day—five writing and one advanced reading—to 7th graders. I taught at an exceptionally demanding, academically rigorous junior high. By February, I was exhausted, and by June, I had made two friends outside of teaching. Too much of my time outside of school had been spent on papers or in the library. I spent a lot of time with other teachers from the school—a smart, professional, and fun group of people. But, still, we talked about school—and our shared exhaustion.

After living for Memorial Day weekend, I found myself with no plans. I realized how completely I'd been absorbed by my job. I also saw myself years from now, a good teacher, better than I am now, but still without plans for a holiday weekend. And each year, the kids would move on.

Yet, for all my martyrdom, I have never once felt caught up. I have never passed back a set of papers without wondering whom I had disappointed, who had counted on my intuitions and my goodness and not just my editorial skills. There is no room for complacency in the classroom; we are forever judged and measured. No matter how achingly we want to do it right, there is always something that could be done better.

I hope to teach again some day, when I have more in my life and other investments to balance with teaching.

In my heart, I think I'll be back. And I think I'll be a better teacher for having stepped out and indulged my selfishness.

Thank you for your support. You have been very important to me.

Sincerely,
Clare Fox

Postscript

In February, Teacher Magazine *tracked down Metzger and Fox (now Clare Ringwall) to find out what happened after their exchange of letters:*

When Margaret Metzger got the news in the spring of 1986 that Clare Ringwall was leaving the profession, she was saddened. But the 23-year public school veteran was not convinced that her former student had abandoned the classroom forever. She hoped to find a way to lure Ringwall back into the fold.

"I thought that if Clare were given a chance to work in a school that trusted its teachers, she would love it," Metzger says. Six months after receiving Ringwall's last letter, Metzger was able to offer her that chance.

Soon after deciding to leave teaching, Ringwall took a full-time writing job with an educational materials publishing company near Boston. But she couldn't get her mind off the classroom. "I started having imaginary dialogues with students," Ringwall recalls. "And I found myself telling my friends old teaching anecdotes about the lively moments of the classroom."

Even though the then 25-year-old loved leaving the office promptly at 5 p.m. and treasured the time she was spending with friends and on her own projects, something was missing. That's when fate, with a little help from Metzger, stepped in.

Metzger was planning to go on parental leave, which meant Brookline High School would need to find someone to teach her classes for two months. When Metzger suggested to Ringwall that she take over the classes, the younger woman was flattered but reluctant to give up on her new career in publishing.

Still, she was interested enough to go for an interview when Donald Thomas, Brookline's English department chairman, called—at Metzger's suggestion. Several days after the interview, Thomas called Ringwall at work and offered her the job. Yielding to pragmatism, Ringwall said no. But not for long.

"As soon as I hung up the phone, I felt physically ill," she recalls. "Saying no made me realize how much I really did want it."

In a panic, Ringwall left her office and ran out into the dreary November rain to a phone booth on the street, where she knew no co-worker would overhear her conversation. She dialed the school's number and asked the chairman if the job was still available. After talking extensively with Thomas, she realized that she did not have to jeopardize her publishing career to take the two-month assignment. By working extra hours in the afternoons and on weekends at the publishing company, she could hold down both jobs.

In an ultimate *déjà vu,* Ringwall soon found herself in Room 347 at Brookline High School—the same room in which she, 10 years earlier, had studied the essays of E.B. White and first learned to take her writing seriously. Only now she was on the other side of the desk. "It was terrifying," she recalls. "I was stepping into Margaret's classes when her students were less than thrilled to have her leave. But also, one of the classes I had to teach was European literature, which I had been too intimidated to take as a student."

Soon after Ringwall took over Metzger's classes at Brookline, another event made her feel as if she were teaching in the twilight zone. Every year for the past 22 years, as the final assignment for an essay-writing class, Metzger has asked students to write and address letters to themselves. While her students go on to choose colleges and careers, Metzger holds the letters hostage for 10 years. Then, every New Year's Day, she slips a batch into the mail. Ringwall was standing in

Metzger's shoes when she received her decade-old missive. "A lot of the letter was about how sad I was that the class was ending," Ringwall recalls, and how much she would miss Metzger.

During her two months filling in for Metzger, Ringwall's attachment to teaching grew stronger. She enjoyed working with the 28 other teachers who made up Brookline's well-respected English department. Instead of nudging students through an adopted anthology of literature, page by page, Brookline's teachers use curricula they develop, and they choose their own books. With her strong interest in writing and curriculum development, Ringwall thrived. Her confidence increased each day in the supportive, stimulating environment. "During my first year of teaching, I was too dependent on student feedback," she admits. "If I put a huge effort into a project and kids didn't notice it, I was resentful." But at Brookline, she was learning how to trust her own judgments.

When Metzger's leave ended, Ringwall was disappointed; she was not ready to stop teaching. By coincidence, Brookline needed long-term substitutes for several other English teachers. Ringwall offered to pinch-hit for a few of them and managed to patch together a fairly full schedule that kept her teaching for the rest of the school year.

At year's end, Ringwall faced a moment of truth: teaching or publishing? "Rather than give up on teaching and try to find an alternative career that could give me a fraction of the sense of worth, challenge, and joy that teaching was giving me," she says, "I realized that I should stay and figure out how to maintain a satisfying private life." Ringwall applied for, and received, a full-time teaching job at Brookline.

Metzger no longer thinks of Ringwall as a novice. In the past few years, the younger teacher has received grants, served as a mentor teacher in a summer program at Brown University, and acquired tenure—which, at Brookline, means a lot. Metzger says she turns to Ringwall for help and ideas just as often as Ringwall turns to her.

In fact, last summer, Ringwall had the chance to give Metzger back a little of her own sweet medicine. While Ringwall was at Brown, she heard that the education department was looking for an expert teacher to offer a methods course and supervise student teachers for a year. Ringwall told them all about her older colleague. And so, this school year, Metzger is on leave from Brookline, working with 15 graduate students—and loving it.

How long Ringwall will stay in the profession is still in question. Right now, she enjoys her work; but her concerns about teaching haven't magically disappeared.

If she could custom-design her own future, Ringwall would eventually cut her load at the high school in half and spend the other half of her time studying and writing. Meanwhile, she relishes those unpredictable moments in the classroom when her intelligence, resilience, intuition, experience, sense of decency, and sense of humor all come into play at once. "Those are the things that make me feel alive and challenged," she says. "I do love teaching, and I think I do it well." Her friend and former teacher respectfully agrees.

Article Review Form at end of book.

How are the attitudes of public school teachers and the general public similar and different toward public education? What are the trends or patterns in teachers' opinions from 1984–1997?

The Fourth Phi Delta Kappa Poll of Teachers' Attitudes Toward the Public Schools

Carol A. Langdon

Carol A. Langdon is research editor for the Center for Evaluation, Development, and Research of Phi Delta Kappa International, Bloomington, Ind.

Just how good are our public schools today? If you ask public school teachers, the picture is bright. In fact, 16% more teachers give an A or a B to their local public schools than do members of the general public. More teachers rate the nation's schools higher, too. Teachers say that members of their profession are one of public education's most important assets, and they believe that the public schools where they teach are among the best. Most say their colleagues are doing a first-rate job in the classroom, and they think teachers should have the greatest voice in deciding what is taught there. These opinions were gathered in May 1997 in the Fourth Phi Delta Kappa Poll of Teachers' Attitudes Toward the Public Schools and in follow-up focus group interviews conducted in July 1997.

As was the case last year, this poll highlights similarities and differences between public school teachers' attitudes and attitudes of the public at large by asking teachers selected questions from the annual Phi Delta Kappa/Gallup Poll of the Public's Attitudes Toward the Public Schools. It also examines trends in teachers' opinions by asking selected questions from the 1984 and 1989 teacher polls conducted by the Gallup Organization for Phi Delta Kappa. The findings of this year's survey are summarized below.

- Teachers' perceptions of how often their students misbehave in the classroom have changed since 1984. Fewer teachers today say they frequently find that students are truant or absent, vandalize or steal school property, skip class, drink alcohol, or have sex at school. But 17% more elementary teachers think that children frequently disrupt class than in 1984, and 12% more say that children are often disobedient. Ten percent more high school teachers than in 1984 believe that their students frequently dress inappropriately or use drugs at school.
- Teachers are less likely to say parents will support them if they tell parents their child is disrupting the classroom than if they tell parents their child is not working hard at school. More high school teachers (63%) than elementary teachers (48%) say parents would support them if their child were not working hard. Moreover, teachers' expectations of how much support they will get from parents fall short of what parents themselves say they would do.

Reprinted with permission from PHI DELTA KAPPAN, November 1997 pp. 212–220.

- The greatest percentage of teachers say public schools have improved over the past five years, but more elementary teachers (45%) than high school teachers (29%) believe schools have improved. Fewer teachers in the East than in the South, West, or Midwest think their schools have gotten better.
- Teachers rate the schools where they teach highest (73% give them an A or a B) and their local schools second highest (62% give them an A or a B). Midwestern teachers rate their local schools higher than do teachers in the East, South, or West. Teachers grade the nation's public schools lowest; 28% give the nation's schools an A or a B. Still, teachers rate all schools higher than does the public.
- Most teachers give high marks to their colleagues: 81% give an A or a B to teachers in the local public schools. They tend to be less generous with their administrators (47% give administrators an A or a B) and even less so with local school boards and parents (35% give an A or a B to their school board, and only 18% give an A or a B to parents of students in the local public schools).
- Majorities of teachers and the public agree that higher-achieving students would be more likely to move to private schools. Teachers and the public do not agree about the effect on academic achievement of public school students who would move to private schools: 46% of teachers say their level of achievement would remain the same, whereas 65% of the public says it would improve.
- Teachers disagree with the public about the effect of parttime jobs on student achievement: 51% say it harms academic performance, whereas 32% of the public says it does so.
- Over twice as many teachers (46%) as members of the general public (20%) say there is too much emphasis on achievement testing in their schools, whereas almost twice as many public respondents (28%) as teachers (10%) say there is not enough.
- A majority of teachers (69%) are opposed to President Clinton's proposal for voluntary national assessments, whereas a majority of the public (57%) favors this plan.
- Nearly equal percentages of teachers (42%) and members of the public (43%) say they favor changing from the local property tax system for financing the nation's public schools to a local income tax system. But fewer teachers (33%) than members of the public (48%) oppose such a change.
- Teachers are more satisfied than the public with the public school curriculum: 51% say the curriculum meets the needs of students today, whereas 54% of the public says it needs to be changed.
- A majority of teachers say parents have about the right amount of influence on matters related to the allocation of school funds and the content of the curriculum, but a majority of the public in 1989 said parents should have more say in those two areas. Teachers this year were twice as likely as teachers in 1989 or 1984 to say that they themselves should have the most influence in deciding what is taught in the public schools.

Challenges Facing Public Schools

Discipline Revisited

Teachers were asked to estimate how frequently each of 18 discipline problems occurred in their classrooms in 1984 and 1989. This year's poll revisited that question to find out if teachers' perceptions have changed. The percentage of teachers who say students misbehave most of the time or fairly often has dropped over the years since 1984 for six discipline problems: truancy and absence, vandalism of school property, skipping classes, theft of school property, drinking alcohol at school, and sexual activity at school. The percentage has dropped since 1989 for five other problems: incomplete homework, sloppy dress, cheating, stealing personal property, and selling drugs at school.

The percentage of *elementary* teachers who say students disrupt the classroom and talk back to or disobey teachers most of the time or fairly often has increased since 1984. The percentage of *high school* teachers who estimate that students dress inappropriately or use drugs at school most of the time or fairly often has increased since 1984. Teachers' perceptions of the frequency of the two lowest-ranked problems—taking money or property by force/using weapons or threats and physical attacks on teachers or staff—have remained stable.

With the exceptions of cheating on tests and sloppy or inappropriate dress, a greater percentage of inner-city teachers than teachers in other settings report that students exhibit all discipline problems most of the time or fairly often. A greater percentage

The question: About how often do each of the problems listed occur at the school where you teach?

	Most of the Time/Fairly Often								
	All Teachers			**Elementary Teachers**			**High School Teachers**		
	1997	**1989**	**1984**	**1997**	**1989**	**1984**	**1997**	**1989**	**1984**
	%	%	%	%	%	%	%	%	%
Schoolwork/homework assignments not completed	71	79	76	68	76	73	78	85	80
Behavior that disrupts class	58	57	47	65	60	48	45	50	47
Talking back to, disobeying teachers	50	45	43	54	45	42	43	44	43
Truancy/being absent from school	41	45	47	35	32	29	57	67	62
Sloppy or inappropriate dress	40	45	37	36	43	33	51	49	41
Cheating on tests	27	45	40	19	33	29	47	64	51
Stealing money or personal property belonging to other students, teachers, or staff	21	32	32	21	26	25	25	40	39
Vandalizing school property	20	25	29	18	20	22	25	34	35
Skipping classes	18	29	35	9	18	16	41	59	57
Using drugs at school	15	14	17	5	5	6	39	30	29
Theft of school property	14	15	23	13	13	18	15	19	29
Selling drugs at school	9	14	13	3	1	4	26	32	24
Racial fights	6	6	4	5	5	3	6	9	5
Carrying of knives, firearms, or other weapons at school	5	4	8	3	3	5	7	8	10
Drinking alcoholic beverages at school	4	6	10	1	1	2	10	14	17
Sexual activity at school	4	6	8	1	1	3	8	13	12
Taking money or property by force, using weapons or threats	2	2	2	2	2	2	2	2	2
Physical attacks on teachers or staff	2	2	1	2	2	1	2	2	1

(Figures add to more than 100% because of multiple answers.)

of teachers in inner cities (65%) and urban areas (47%) than teachers in small towns (38%), suburban areas (36%), and rural areas (31%) estimate that students are truant or absent most of the time or fairly often. More teachers in the South (77%) than in the Midwest (48%), East (45%), or West (41%) say students talk back and disobey teachers most of the time or fairly often.

Tight Budgets, Tough Choices

When it comes to saving money, teachers favor by a margin of more than 3–1 reducing the number of administrators, an option also favored by nearly three-quarters of the public when the question was asked in 1991. Following reductions in administrative costs, 54% of both teachers and the public favor eliminating some courses. While 34% of teachers and 47% of the public favor reducing support staff, nearly seven times as many members of the public (47%) as teachers (7%) favor freezing salaries.

When teachers in focus groups were asked how they would reduce spending in their schools, a comment by a middle-school teacher reflected a common view: "Administration and bureaucracy—all that stuff could be cut out! Give it to the teachers and the students, and a lot more

The question: As you are probably aware, many states are having severe budgetary problems. If it becomes necessary to reduce spending for education in this state, would you favor or oppose the following measures in the public schools of your community?

	Teachers 1997 Favor %	Public 1991 Favor %	Teachers 1997 Oppose %	Public 1991 Oppose %	Teachers 1997 Don't Know %	Public 1991 Don't Know %
Reduce the number of administrators	74	73	21	19	5	8
Eliminate certain courses	54	54	33	34	13	12
Reduce the number of support staff members	34	47	57	45	9	8
Eliminate all extracurricular activities	24	32	70	62	6	6
Freeze all salaries	7	47	87	46	6	7
Increase class size	6	21	92	72	2	7
Reduce the number of teachers	3	15	95	78	2	7

(Figures add to more than 100% because of multiple answers.)

The question:* Suppose you reported to a parent that his or her child was misbehaving in class and disrupting other students. Whose side do you think the parent would be more likely to take—yours or the child's?

	Teachers %	Public School Parents %
My side (school's side)	41	57
The child's side	50	25
Don't Know	9	18

*The question for the public was "Suppose a teacher or principal reported that your oldest child was misbehaving and being disruptive in school. Whose side do you think you would be more likely to take—the school's or your child's?"

The question:** Suppose you reported to a parent that his or her child was not working hard enough at schoolwork. Whose side do you think the parent would be more likely to take—yours or the child's?

	Teachers %	Public School Parents %
My side (school's side)	53	70
The child's side	40	22
Don't Know	7	8

**The question for the public was "What if a teacher or principal reported that your oldest child was not working hard enough at schoolwork? Whose side do you think you would be more likely to take—the school's or your child's?"

money will be used a lot more effectively." Another teacher said, "Empower teachers. Teachers are leaders. Train them as leaders, and you won't need so many administrators."

Parent Support for Teachers

In 1984, 1989, and 1996, teachers were asked to name the biggest problem with which the schools in their communities must deal. The problem they identified most often throughout these years was lack of interest and support from parents. This year, teachers and public school parents were asked whose side they thought parents would take if a teacher told them their child was misbehaving or disrupting the class. Teachers and public school parents disagree about how much support teachers can expect from parents. If a child were misbehaving or disrupting the class, 41% of teachers say parents would back the teacher, but 57% of public school parents say they would do so. Twice as many teachers (50%) as public school parents (25%) say parents would take their child's side. No differences in attitudes were found between elementary and high school teachers or among inner-city, urban, suburban, small-town, and rural teachers.

Teachers are more likely to say parents would support them if they told parents their child was not working hard enough at school. Still, teachers' expectations of parental support fall short of what parents themselves say they would do: 53% of teachers say parents would side with the teacher, whereas 70% of public school parents say they would do so. More high school teachers (63%) say parents would support them than elementary teachers (48%).

The comments of an elementary teacher in a focus group echoed the sentiments of many teachers interviewed: ". . . if [parents] would give us their support, find their child a place to study, sign the things that need to be signed, appear at school now and then, let the child know that education is important . . . they need to back the teachers." Still, teachers agree that they have a role in engaging parental support. Another teacher said, "We need inservice training for working with parents. We need to say, 'This is what we are doing in class today, and we would like for you to do this at home to support this effort.' "

Have Schools Improved?

The greatest percentage of teachers (40%) say public schools in their communities have improved over the past five years. This image is consistent with grades teachers give their local public schools and the schools in which they teach. More elementary teachers (45%) than high school teachers (29%) believe the public schools in their communities have improved over the past five years. Fewer teachers in the East (30%) than teachers in the South (43%), West (43%), or Midwest (39%) think their public schools have improved.

The question: Would you say that the public schools in your community have improved from, say, five years ago, gotten worse, or stayed about the same?

	Teachers 1997 %
Improved	40
Gotten worse	28
Stayed about the same	29
Don't know	3

Grading the Public Schools

Local Public Schools

The question: Students are often given the grades A, B, C, D, and FAIL to denote the quality of their work. Suppose the public schools themselves, in this community, were graded in the same way. What grade would you give the public schools here—A, B, C, D, or FAIL?

	Teachers 1997 %	Public 1997 %	Teachers 1989 %	Public 1989 %	Teachers 1984 %	Public 1984 %
A & B	62	46	66	43	64	42
A	12	10	11	8	12	10
B	50	36	55	35	52	32
C	30	32	29	33	27	35
D	6	11	4	11	4	11
FAIL	2	6	*	4	1	4
Don't know	*	5	1	9	4	8

*Less than one-half of 1%.

The question: How about the public school in which you teach? What grade would you give your own school?

	1997 %	1996 %	1989 %	1984 %
A & B	73	73	75	72
A	25	27	22	21
B	48	46	53	51
C	19	22	21	20
D	6	3	3	4
FAIL	2	1	1	2
Don't know	*	1	1	2

(Not all columns add to 100% because of rounding.)
*Less than one-half of 1%.

Since 1984, when they were first asked, about 20% more teachers than members of the general public have given an A or a B to their local public schools. This year is little different, with 62% of teachers (but only 46% of the public) assigning a grade of A or B to the local public schools. Teachers in the Midwest rate their schools higher (73% A or B) than do teachers in the East (51%), South (58%), or West (60%). Only 36% of inner-city teachers assign an A or a B to their local schools, compared to 69% of teachers in schools in small towns, 67% of teachers in suburban schools, and 61% of teachers in rural schools.

The question: How about the public schools in the nation as a whole? What grade would you give the nation's public schools?

	Teachers 1997 %	Public 1997 %	Teachers 1996 %	Public 1996 %
A & B	28	22	30	21
A	1	2	1	1
B	27	20	29	20
C	52	48	49	46
D	9	15	7	18
FAIL	1	6	2	5
Don't know	10	9	12	10

The first question: What grade would you give the teachers in the local public schools?

	1997 %	1989 %	1984 %
A & B	81	83	78
A	23	20	18
B	58	63	60
C	16	15	17
D	1	1	2
FAIL	*	*	*
Don't know	2	1	3

*Less than one-half of 1%.

The second question: What grade would you give the administrators in the local public schools?

	1997 %	1989 %	1984 %
A & B	47	49	44
A	7	9	10
B	40	40	34
C	32	36	34
D	13	11	15
FAIL	7	3	5
Don't know	1	1	2

Schools Where Teachers Teach

As in years past, about three-fourths of teachers surveyed have assigned an A or a B to the school in which they teach. This year 73% give their own school an A or a B. More elementary teachers than high school teachers give their schools high-grades: 78% give an A or a B to their school, compared to 68% of high school teachers. More teachers in small towns (80%) and suburban areas (78%) give their schools an A or a B than do teachers in urban areas (73%), rural areas (72%), or inner cities (55%).

Public Schools Nationally

Both teachers and the public view the nation's public schools in a less favorable light than they do their own schools, but teachers tend to issue better grades than the public. This year, 28% of teachers give an A or a B to the nation's public schools, whereas only 22% of public respondents do so.

Five Other Ratings

In 1984, 1989, and again this year, teachers were also asked to grade local public school teachers, administrators, school boards, parents, and their own teacher training. A majority of teachers in 1997 assign high marks to their colleagues: 81% give them an A or a B. Inner-city teachers tend to rate local teachers slightly lower than others: 73% give them an A or a B, compared to 85% of suburban teachers, 84% of small-town teachers, 83% of urban teachers, and 80% of rural teachers.

When teachers in focus groups were asked what the major assets of public schools are today, many agreed with the teacher who said, "One of the most important assets [is] teachers themselves. Teachers are in that building before school, after school, hours and hours beyond their scheduled time period. All the [extracurricular activities] available to kids . . . are because there are teachers volunteering . . . on the weekend and during the summer. Teachers are teachers 24 hours a day. And they are growing and learning right along with students."

While teachers tend to rate other teachers highly, local administrators fare less well: less than 50% of teachers gave an A or a B to administrators in 1984 and 1989. This year, 47% give their local administrators an A or a B. More than 50% of elementary teachers give an A or a B to local administrators, but just 38% of high school teachers do so. Teachers in inner-city schools rate their administrators lowest: 31% give them an A or a B. Suburban teachers rate their administrators highest: 51% assign them an A or B.

Thirty-five percent of teachers give local school boards an A or a B this year, up slightly from 1984 figures. (This question was not asked in 1989.) Teachers in the East rate their school boards lowest: 24% give them an A or a B, compared to 40% in the Midwest, 35% in the South, and 33% in the West. Just 15% of inner-city teachers give an A or a B to their local school boards, compared to 41% of those in small towns, 37% of those in suburban areas, 35% of those in rural areas, and 27% of those in urban areas.

Of all the groups they were asked to grade, teachers consistently give parents the fewest A's and B's. This year just 18% give an A or a B to parents of students in the local public schools for bringing up their children. Teachers from inner-city, urban, and rural areas give no A's to parents. Only 3% of inner-city teachers give B's, compared to 12% of urban teachers and 19% of rural teachers.

Teachers give higher marks this year to their college training than they have in the past: 64% give their training an A or a B, compared to 57% in 1989 and 49% in 1984.

The third question: What grade would you give the local school board?

	1997 %	1984 %
A & B	35	29
A	7	4
B	28	25
C	32	36
D	17	19
FAIL	14	13
Don't know	2	3

The fourth question: What grade would you give the parents of students in the local public schools for bringing up their children?

	1997 %	1989 %	1984 %
A & B	18	22	21
A	1	2	2
B	17	20	19
C	43	49	45
D	27	22	24
FAIL	11	6	7
Don't know	1	2	3

(Not all columns add to 100% because of rounding.)

The fifth question: What grade would you give the teacher education training you received?

	1997 %	1989 %	1984 %
A & B	64	57	49
A	23	17	14
B	41	40	35
C	25	32	33
D	8	7	10
FAIL	2	3	6
Don't know	1	1	2

Public Versus Nonpublic Schools

Effect of a Shift to Nonpublic Schools

Cleveland's voucher program—the first to include religious schools—is entering its second year, but research on the effect of this school choice program on academic achievement has so far been inconclusive. A majority of teachers and the public agree that higher-achieving students would be more likely to move to private schools. But

The question: Suppose a large number of students in the local public schools moved to the private schools. In your opinion, who would be more likely to move to the private schools—higher-achieving students, lower-achieving students, or average-achieving students?

	Teachers %	Public %
Higher-achieving students	79	65
Lower-achieving students	5	8
Average-achieving students	9	20
No difference	–	3
Don't know	7	4

The question: In your opinion, would the academic achievement of those public school students who had moved to the private schools improve, get worse, or remain about the same?

	Teachers %	Public %
Improve	41	65
Get worse	6	4
Remain about the same	46	28
Don't know	7	3

The question: How about the students who remained in the local public schools? Would their academic achievement improve, get worse, or remain about the same?

	Teachers %	Public %
Improve	12	17
Get worse	25	11
Remain about the same	58	70
Don't know	5	2

The first question: Do you think that parents should or should not have the legal right to educate their children at home?

	Teachers 1997 %	Public 1988 %
Should	70	53
Should not	22	39
Don't know	8	8

20% of the public says that average-achieving students would be most likely to move to nonpublic schools, while only 9% of teachers say these students would be most likely to move.

There is strong disagreement between teachers and the public about the effect on academic achievement of public school students who would move to nonpublic schools. Say there achievement would improve. The greatest number of teachers (46%) say achievement would remain about the same for these students, whereas the greatest number of public respondents (65%) say their achievement would improve.

A majority of teachers (58%) and public (70%) agree that the academic achievement of students who stay in the public schools would remain about the same. But more than twice as many teachers (25%) as public respondents (11%) say students' achievement would get worse.

Home Schooling

The Home School Legal Defense Association estimates that there are approximately 1.23 million American children being taught at home.* This year's poll of teachers revisited a question asked of the public in 1988: Should parents have the legal right to educate their children at home? While 53% of the general public in 1988 said parents should have this right, 70% of teachers this year say they should. Teachers and the public were both asked this year if they thought home schools should or should not be required to guarantee a minimum level of educational quality. Ninety-five percent of teachers say home schools should be held accountable, and 88% of the public agree.

*This figure is taken from the Web site of the Home School Legal Defense Association (www.hslda.org).

Student Achievement

Part-Time Work

Teachers disagree with the public about the effect of part-time work on a student's academic performance. Only 8% say it would have a positive effect, compared to 29% of the public. Indeed, a majority of teachers (51%) say part-time work hurts academic performance.

Achievement Testing

More than twice as many teachers (46%) as members of the general public (20%) think there is too much emphasis on achievement testing in their schools. Almost twice as many members of the public (28%) as teachers (10%) say there is not enough emphasis.

In focus groups, teachers' opinions about how much emphasis is placed on testing tended to depend on the district in which they teach. Overall, teachers expressed concern about how test results are used. An elementary teachers said: "I feel there is too much emphasis on test results in my district. They are being used for teacher accountability, not student progress." Another teacher said, "The idea of testing is good, because we have to have kids come out of school with basic skills. But how do we know that without crucifying teachers and kids?"

Voluntary National Testing

Fifteen of the nation's largest school districts and a handful of states have agreed to administer voluntary national tests in reading and math, as the Clinton Administration has proposed. But the tests have stirred controversy on the floor of the U.S. House of Representatives and among conservative family and education groups. A majority of teachers (69%) are opposed to such tests; only 22% favor the President's initiative, while 57% of the public does so.

While teachers in focus groups generally agreed that they should be held accountable, they objected to the idea of the national assessment. Some teachers thought such assessment would be "impossible" to implement. An elementary teacher said, "I have a problem standardizing anything, because I think it's not possible. You cannot compare apples and oranges." A middle school teacher said, "I don't believe a national assessment is possible. Where would the funding come from? How can you have a national assessment if you don't have a national curriculum?"

Teachers also expressed concern about the purpose of a national assessment. As one teacher put it, "I don't object to having a national assessment.

The second question: Do you think that home schools should or should not be required to guarantee a minimum level of educational quality?

	Teachers %	Public %
Should	95	88
Should not	3	10
Don't know	2	2

The question: What effect do you feel having a part-time job has on the academic performance of students in the public schools in your community?

	Teachers %	Public %
Improves academic performance	8	29
Hurts academic performance	51	32
Does not affect academic performance	16	35
Don't know	25	4

The question: Academic achievement test scores are used by public schools in many ways, such as for grade promotion and for graduation. In your opinion, is there too much emphasis on achievement testing in the public schools where you teach, not enough emphasis on testing, or about the right amount?

	Teachers %	Public %
Too much emphasis	46	20
Not enough emphasis	10	28
About the right amount	41	48
Don't know	3	4

The question: President Clinton has proposed that the performance of the nation's public schools be assessed according to how well students score on achievement tests at two different grade levels. In general, do you favor or oppose this proposal?

	Teachers %	Public %
Favor	22	57
Oppose	69	37
No opinion	9	6

The question: At the present time, local property taxes are the main source for financing the nation's public schools. Thinking about your own community, would you favor or oppose changing the local property tax system to a local income tax system as the principal way to finance the local public schools?

	Teachers %	Public %
Favor	42	43
Oppose	33	48
No opinion	25	9

The question: Do you think the curriculum in the public school where you teach needs to be changed to meet today's needs, or do you think it already meets today's needs?

	Teachers %	Public %	Public School Parents %
Needs to be changed	47	54	53
Meets today's needs	51	39	46
Don't know	3	7	1

(Not all columns add to 100% because of rounding.)

The problem is the tool and how it would be used. Once you have test results for a school district, figures lie and liars figure. You can use them against people, and you can draw conclusions that are probably incorrect."

Teachers also expressed concern about the consequences of a national assessment. A high school teacher said, "If you have national testing, you have a national curriculum, and you will teach to the test in order to look good when the scores are printed in the newspaper."

Financing the Public Schools

Like the public, teachers are divided about changing the system of financing public education from one based on local property taxes to one based on a local income tax. Nearly equal percentages of teachers (42%) and public respondents (43%) say they favor such a change, but fewer teachers (33%) than public respondents (48%) are opposed.

An East Coast elementary teacher observed in a focus group, "We have schools located very close to each other that are very unequal in what they can provide for students. People get upset about their high taxes because the person who lives across the street ends up paying less than half. That happens on the street where I live. There has to be a restructuring of the tax base. It's so unfair, and we see it very vividly where we live."

The Curriculum

Teachers are slightly less likely to agree with the public or with public school parents that the curriculum in their local public schools needs to be changed. While majorities of the public (54%) and of public school parents (53%) say the curriculum in their local public schools needs to be updated, a majority of teachers (51%) say they are satisfied with the curriculum in their schools.

When teachers were asked in focus groups to identify weaknesses in their school curriculum, a general concern was whether the curriculum meets the needs of students who are not college-bound. As one elementary teacher noted, "Sometimes I think in education we focus on those people who were going to go places, and we forget that somebody's got to work at McDonald's."

School Governance

Parental Control of Public Schools

The 1990 Kentucky Education Reform Act mandated school-based decision making by means of councils of administrators, teachers, and parents, but studies of these councils indicate that in many instances parents actually play a limited role.* In Rochester, New York, contract negotiations between the local teacher union and the school district were held up last summer over a proposal to give parents a voice in evaluating teachers' job performance.

The extent to which parents should be involved in local school governance continues to be debated. When the public was asked a question on this issue in 1989, more than 50% said parents should have more say about allocations of school funds and the content of the curriculum, and more than 40% said parents should have more say about selecting and hiring teachers and administrators and selecting books and instructional materials.

In this year's poll, teachers were asked the same question the public was asked in 1989. Fifty percent or more think parents have about the right amount of say about fund allocations, about the curriculum, and about the selection of books and instructional materials, and more than 40% believe parents have about the right amount of say with regard to selecting and hiring teachers and administrators, setting teacher and administrator salaries, and selecting school library books.

*See, for example, Institute on Education Reform, *The Implementation of Kentucky's School-Based Decision-Making Program* (Lexington: University of Kentucky, 1995); Patricia J. Kannapel et al., "School-Based Decision Making in Rural Kentucky Schools: Interim Findings of a Five-Year, Longitudinal Study," paper presented at the annual meeting of the American Educational Research Association, New Orleans, April 1994; Jane L. David, "School-Based Decision Making: Linking Decisions to Learning; Third-Year Report to the Prichard Committee," paper presented at the annual meeting of the American Educational Research Association, San Francisco, April 1995; and Eddy J. Van Meter, "Implementing School-Based Decision Making in Kentucky," *NASSP Bulletin*, vol. 78, 1994, pp. 61–70.

The question: Do you feel that parents of public school students should have more say, less say, or do they have about the right amount of say regarding the following areas in the public schools?

	More Say		Less Say		Right Amount	
	Teachers 1997 %	Parents 1989 %	Teachers 1997 %	Parents 1989 %	Teachers 1997 %	Parents 1989 %
Allocation of school funds	23	59	18	10	54	27
Curriculum (i.e., the courses offered)	25	53	21	9	52	36
Selection and hiring of administrators	23	46	28	14	44	37
Books and instructional materials	14	43	34	13	50	41
Selection and hiring of teachers	11	41	38	17	47	38
Teacher and administrator salaries	11	39	42	17	43	39
Books placed in the school libraries	15	38	35	15	47	44

(Columns do not add across to 100% because "Don't Know" responses are not included.)

The question: In your opinion, who should have the greatest influence in deciding what is taught in the public schools of your community?

	1997 %	1989 %	1984 %
Teachers	70	36	33
Local school board	11	15	19
State government	10	18	17
Parents	3	11	2
Federal government	2	4	3
Principals and other administrators	—	9	—
Don't know	4	7	26

Control of the Curriculum

Teachers consistently say they should have the most influence in deciding what is taught in the public schools. This attitude is stronger this year than in the past: nearly twice as many teachers (70%) say so this year as in 1989 (36%) or 1984 (33%). Teachers rank local school boards second in influence, followed by state government, parents, and the federal government. (Principals and other administrators appeared only in the 1989 poll.)

The curriculum in our public schools is "stuffed," as one high school teacher put it in a focus group. Teachers mentioned the "hidden curriculum" that enables teachers to "place the emphasis in the best ways they can and still get around all of those standards and requirements and mandates that have to be there."

Research Procedure

The Fourth Phi Delta Kappa Poll of Teachers' Attitudes Toward the Public Schools was developed and implemented by the Phi Delta Kappa Center for Evaluation, Development, and Research. The mail survey consisted of 25 questions—13 from the 1997 Phi Delta Kappa/Gallup Poll of the Public's Attitudes Toward the Public Schools, two from the 1988 public opinion poll, one from the 1989 public opinion poll, one from the 1991 public opinion poll, and eight from the 1984 and 1989 polls of teachers' attitudes conducted for Phi Delta Kappa by the Gallup Organization. A random sample of 4,000 public school teachers throughout the United States was provided by Market Data Retrieval. The sample was stratified proportionately by the Gallup Organization's four regions and by grade level taught.

The survey, cover letter, and a return envelope were mailed on 6 May 1997. A follow-up postcard was mailed on 10 May 1997. Five surveys were returned as undeliverable.

Completed surveys were sorted by zip code into the four geographic regions established by the Gallup Organization. The response rate was 17.8%, with 714 respondents returning completed surveys. This sample has a margin of error estimated to be plus or minus 4% at the 95% confidence level. A margin of error plus or minus 4% at the 95% confidence level means that sample responses would differ by no more than plus or minus 4% from the true values. Reported differences in responses between elementary and secondary teachers; among inner-city, urban, suburban, small-town, and rural teachers; and among teachers from the East, South, Midwest, and West are statistically significant at the 95% confidence level.

Focus group interviews were conducted three times during July 1997 to amplify quantitative data for specificity, depth, and personal context. Participants were drawn from public school teachers enrolled in professional development seminars at Phi Delta Kappa. In all, 26 teachers took part. They represented the states of Illinois, Indiana, Kentucky, Maryland, New Jersey, New York, Ohio, Pennsylvania, and Tennessee, as well as British Columbia, Canada. Comments from focus group participants reported in this article are not generalizable to all public school teachers.

Composition of the Sample

Demographic information provided by respondents indicates that 75% are female, and 25% are male. The mean age of respondents is 44 years. Racial/ethnic background information indicates that 91% are white, 6% are black, 1% are Asian or Pacific Islander, 2% are "other." Of all persons answering the survey, 2.4% indicated that they are of Hispanic origin.

Respondents indicated that their highest degree earned was a bachelor's (39%), master's (55%), specialist's (5%), or doctorate (1%). They have taught an average of 17 years. Fifty percent indicated they teach at the elementary level, 21% at the middle/junior high school level, and 29% at the high school level. Twelve percent teach in inner cities, 13% in urban areas, 27% in suburban areas, 31% in small towns, and 17% in rural areas.

Article Review Form at end of book.

What are some of the key challenges that poll respondents believe are facing public education? What do poll respondents believe with regard to the relevancy of the public school curriculum, including specific courses?

The 29th Annual Phi Delta Kappa/Gallup Poll of the Public's Attitudes Toward the Public Schools

Lowell C. Rose, Alec M. Gallup, and Stanley M. Elam

Lowell C. Rose is executive director emeritus of Phi Delta Kappa International. Alec M. Gallup is co-chairman, with George Gallup, Jr., of the Gallup Organization, Princeton, N.J. Stanley M. Elam, who was Kappan *editor from 1956 through 1980, is contributing editor of the* Phi Delta Kappan.

Place a computer in every classroom. Move persistent "troublemakers" into alternative schools. Establish national standards for measuring the academic performance of the public schools. Let parents and students choose which public schools the students will attend. Group students in classes according to ability level. Establish a national curriculum. Use standardized national tests to measure the academic achievement of students. Provide health-care services in schools. These are all measures that the public believes would improve student achievement in the public schools. Probing attitudes about improving achievement was a major focus of the 1997 Phi Delta Kappa/Gallup Poll of the Public's Attitudes Toward the Public Schools, conducted by the George H. Gallup International Institute.

Why do some public schools achieve better academic results than others? The public believes that three factors are important: 1) strong support from parents, 2) the amount of money spent, and, to a lesser extent, 3) the kinds of students in attendance.

This year's poll data make it clear that public schools continue to enjoy strong public support. Most respondents give good grades to the schools in their own communities, and parents of public school students express even stronger satisfaction. While there is an obvious desire for improvement, almost three-fourths (71%) of those surveyed believe that this improvement should come through reforming the existing system rather than through seeking an alternative system.

Reprinted with permission from PHI DELTA KAPPAN, Vol. 79, No. 1, September 1997 pp. 42–56.

At the same time, however, the public seems more willing than in earlier years to approve government financial support for students who wish to attend nonpublic schools. This continues a trend tracked by these polls for nearly three decades. As recently as 1993, only 24% of respondents favored "allowing students and parents to choose a private school to attend at public expense." Seventy-four percent were opposed. In 1997, 44% favor this and 52% oppose it. When the words "public expense" are changed to "government expense," the public is exactly divided (48% in favor, 48% opposed).* On the basic "voucher question," asking respondents to indicate whether they would support allowing parents and students to choose a public or nonpublic school to attend with the government paying "all or part of the tuition," this poll shows a virtual deadlock, for the first time, with 49% favoring and 48% opposing. While this is good news to advocates of nonpublic schools, the conditions the public would impose on such support suggest that proposals of this kind are certain to be controversial.

The public expresses the strong belief that any nonpublic school that accepts public funds should be required to enroll students from a wider range of backgrounds and academic ability than is now the case. This popular conviction would seem to invite the kind of government regulation that has led some proponents of nonpublic schools to oppose the voucher idea.

This year's poll reflects a strong public belief in the important role parents can and should play in the education of their children. Respondents regard the amount of support provided by parents of public school students as a major factor in determining why some schools are better than others; they also believe strongly that parents should be notified if their children have a substance abuse problem or suffer from a sexually transmitted disease.

Other findings in the 1997 Phi Delta Kappa/Gallup poll include the following.

- Majorities in all demographic groups believe that the problems faced by the public schools in urban areas are more serious than those affecting nonurban schools.
- Lack of discipline and inadequate financing are the local school problems most frequently mentioned by respondents. The use of drugs and "fighting, violence, and gangs" are not far behind.
- Forty-six percent of those surveyed give the public schools in their community an A or a B. Fifty-six percent of public school parents give them a grade of A or B, and almost two-thirds (64%) of public school parents give the school their eldest child attends an A or B.
- The public believes that, if given the opportunity, the students most likely to move from public schools to private schools under a voucher system would be the high-achieving students. Furthermore, the public believes that the academic achievement of these students would *improve* as a result of the move, while the academic achievement of the students remaining in the public schools would stay about the same.
- The public believes the home school movement is a bad thing for the nation; however, fewer respondents hold this belief today than when this question was asked in 1988 and 1985. Moreover, the public feels strongly that home schools should be required to guarantee a minimum level of educational quality.
- The public does not believe that state takeover of failing schools will improve academic achievement. Indeed, a strong majority (69%) believes that achievement would remain the same or get worse.
- Do the public schools overemphasize achievement testing? Approximately half (48%) believe the current emphasis is appropriate; the remaining half are divided between "too much" (20%) and "not enough" (28%).
- There is no consensus regarding the effect on academic achievement of lowering a school's starting age for children. However, a majority (75%) of the public would have students start school at age 5 or under.
- People divide almost equally in assessing the way a part-time job outside of school affects students' academic performance: one-third say it lowers performance, one-third say it improves performance, and one-third say it has no effect.
- The public supports President Clinton's main education initiatives. The President would assess performance of the nation's public schools according to how well students score on achievement tests at two different grade levels; he proposes a five-year, two-billion-dollar program to place

*Although on the borderline of statistical significance, this difference reminds us of the need for very careful wording of questions that assess opinion on sensitive issues.

a computer with access to the Internet in every classroom; and he seeks a tax credit for each first-year college student in a family with an annual income of $100,000 or less.

- Seven out of 10 respondents (71%) reject the idea that the local public schools are infringing on the right of parents to direct their children's education.
- Children today are getting more parental help with their homework than in earlier years, and Americans in general report an increased willingness to work as unpaid volunteers in their local public schools.
- A majority of public school parents (57%) say they would be more likely to take the school's side than their child's if a teacher or principal reported the child misbehaving or being disruptive in school.
- A majority of the public (60%) indicates that a C is the lowest grade a child of theirs could bring home on a report card without causing them to be upset or concerned.
- Fifty-four percent of Americans believe that the curriculum in their local schools needs to be changed to meet today's needs, while 39% believe it already does so.
- Majorities define curriculum "basics" as including mathematics and English. Pluralities would add history/U.S. government and science to the list.
- A small majority (52%) of the public believes that gifted and talented students should be placed in separate classes. Moreover, 66% believe that grouping students by ability in classrooms improves student achievement overall.
- Almost two-thirds of Americans (63%) believe that extracurricular activities are very important. Another 27% believe they are fairly important. The importance assigned to these activities is substantially greater today than when the question was last asked in 1985.
- A small majority (53%) of the public believes that the emphasis placed on sports such as football and basketball is about right. However, 39% believe there is too much emphasis.
- Ninety-six percent of respondents would require an average grade of C or better for interscholastic athletic eligibility.
- Americans are divided as to whether public schools should be financed through local property taxes, state taxes, or federal taxes. They are also divided as to whether local property taxes or local income taxes should be the main source of school funding.
- A small majority of the public (53%) is at least somewhat satisfied with the steps being taken to deal with the use of drugs in the local schools. Fifty-two percent of respondents believe an educational approach is the best way to deal with the problem; 42% believe severe penalties are best.
- The public gives strong support to "zero tolerance" policies that call for automatic suspension for drug and alcohol possession in school and for carrying weapons of any kind into school.

Improving the Public Schools and Student Achievement

Since some of the proposals being considered for improving student achievement call for alternatives to the public schools, the initial question, in effect, asked whether people would prefer reform or revolution. The answer is clear: 71% of those responding believe that reform should come through the existing system. This response is uniform across demographic categories.

Improving Student Achievement

The question most directly aimed at discovering what the public believes will improve student achievement offered respondents the opportunity to evaluate 10 proposals. A majority of the pub-

The question: In order to improve public education in America, some people think the focus should be on reforming the existing public school system. Others believe the focus should be on finding an alternative to the existing public school system. Which approach do you think is preferable—reforming the existing public school system of finding an alternative to the existing public school system?

	National Totals %	No Children In School %	Public School Parents %	Nonpublic School Parents %
Reforming existing system	71	70	72	67
Finding alternative system	23	23	24	32
Don't know	6	7	4	1

The question: Here is a list of measures that have been proposed for improving the academic achievement of public school students. As I read each one, would you tell me whether you believe that measure would improve the achievement of the students in the local public schools a great deal, quite a lot, not very much, or not at all?

	A Great Deal or Quite a Lot %	A Great Deal %	Quite A Lot %	Not Very Much %	Not Much At All %	Don't Know %
Placing a computer in every classroom	81	50	31	13	5	1
Establishing national standards for measuring the academic performance of the public schools	77	41	36	15	6	2
Moving persistent "troublemakers" into alternative schools	75	43	32	14	9	2
Allowing parents and students to attend the public school of their choice	73	39	34	18	7	2
Using standardized national tests to measure the academic achievement of students	67	36	31	23	8	2
Grouping students in classes according to ability level	66	34	32	19	13	2
Establishing a national curriculum	66	35	31	20	10	4
Providing health-care services in schools	61	35	26	25	12	2
Lengthening the school year	38	18	20	33	27	2
Lengthening the school day	25	12	13	38	35	2

The question: Some states have taken over the administration of schools in local school districts where the public schools were considered to be doing a poor job. What effect do you think takeover by the state would have on the academic achievement of students in a public school in your community? Do you think their academic achievement would improve, get worse, or do you think it wouldn't have much effect on their academic achievement?

	National Totals %	No Children In School %	Public School Parents %	Nonpublic School Parents %
Would improve	25	24	25	46
Would get worse	26	25	27	27
Wouldn't have much effect	43	45	42	25
Don't know	6	6	6	2

lic assigns either a great deal or quite a lot of importance to eight of them. However, two frequently mentioned reform proposals—lengthening the school year and lengthening the school day—could garner support from only 38% and 25% of respondents respectively.

With relatively few exceptions, there is little difference in the way subgroups in the national population view these measures. However, 75% of blacks (compared to 50% for the national population) feel that placing a computer in every classroom would improve student achievement a great deal. In addition, 59% of blacks and 51% of nonwhites believe that allowing parents and children to attend the public school of their choice would improve student achievement a great deal; the corresponding figure for the nation as a whole is just 39%.

Indeed, blacks favor many of the national reforms proposed in recent years to a much greater extent than does the general population. For example, blacks are more likely to believe that student achievement will be improved a great deal by establishing national standards (58% to 41%), by establishing a national curriculum (58% to 35%), by using standardized tests to measure achievement (52% to 36%), and by providing health-care services in the public schools (65% to 35%).

State Takeovers

In some states the administration of faltering or failing schools is taken over by the state. People were asked what effect they thought such a move would have on student achievement in the schools in their community. The public is split on this question; 43% believe such a takeover would have no effect, and the rest are evenly divided on whether achievement would improve or get worse.

School-Starting Age and Part-Time Work

The current poll probed people's beliefs about the effect on student achievement of starting school a year earlier and of holding a part-time job. There is no consensus on either question. Thirty-seven percent of respondents believe that starting school a year earlier would improve student achievement, 24% disagree, and 37% believe it would make no difference. Blacks are more than twice as likely as whites (75% to 31%) to believe that starting school earlier would improve student achievement.

On the question of starting age, three-fourths of Americans would have students start school at age 5 or under. Twenty-six percent would have them start at age 4 or under. Groups in the national population that most strongly support having children start school at age 4 or under include blacks (64%), nonwhites (59%), 18- to 29-year-olds (40%), and urban residents (35%).

Data on public school parents reveal a pattern similar to that for the national population. Sixty-four percent of black parents would prefer a school starting age of 4 or under (compared to 30% for all parents), as would 57% of 18- to 29-year-old parents and 61% of nonwhite parents.

The first question: In your opinion, what effect would starting a child a year younger than is now generally the case have on the child's academic achievement in elementary and in high school? Do you think starting a year younger would improve the child's achievement, make it worse, or wouldn't it make much difference?

	National Totals %	No Children In School %	Public School Parents %	Nonpublic School Parents %
Improve achievement	37	35	40	37
Make it worse	24	22	25	39
Not much difference	37	40	33	23
Don't know	2	3	2	1

The second question: At what age do you think students should start school?

	National Totals '97 %	National Totals '86 %	No Children In School '97 %	No Children In School '86 %	Public School Parents '97 %	Public School Parents '86 %	Nonpublic School Parents '97 %	Nonpublic School Parents '86 %
4 years (or under)	26	29	24	29	30	27	27	29
5 years	49	41	50	40	47	44	44	42
6 years	21	18	22	18	19	20	16	23
7 years (or over)	3	2	3	1	3	2	11	*
Don't know	1	10	1	12	1	7	2	6

*Less than one-half of 1%

The third question: What effect do you feel having a part-time job outside of school has on the academic achievement of students in the public schools in this community? Generally speaking, do you feel having a part-time job improves their academic achievement, hurts their academic achievement, or do you feel it does not affect their academic achievement one way or the other?

	National Totals %	No Children In School %	Public School Parents %	Nonpublic School Parents %
Improves achievement	29	31	28	16
Hurts achievement	32	32	30	44
Does not affect achievement	35	34	37	37
Don't know	4	3	5	3

Improving Schools

People frequently ask, "Why are some schools better than others?" This year poll respondents were asked to rate the importance of three factors sometimes offered to explain such differences. The public considers the amount of support from parents of students in the local public schools to be the most important factor in making a school better. However, the amount of money spent on the local public schools is a close second. The kinds of students attending the local public schools is regarded as either quite important or very important by two-thirds of

The question: Here are some factors that are sometimes mentioned to explain why the public schools in some places are better than those in others. As I read off each one, would you tell me whether you think that factor is very important, quite important, not very important, or not at all important in determining the quality of the local public schools?

	Very Important %	Quite Important %	Not Very Important %	Not at All Important %	Don't Know %
Amount of support from parents of students in the local public schools	86	11	3	*	*
Amount of money spent on the local public schools	62	29	6	2	1
Kinds of students attending the local public schools	41	26	20	9	4

*Less than one-half of 1%.

	Percentage Responding "Very Important"			
	National Totals %	No Children In School %	Public School Parents %	Nonpublic School Parents %
Amount of support from parents of students in the local public schools	86	84	88	92
Amount of money spent on the local public schools	62	59	67	63
Kinds of students attending the local public schools	41	39	45	52

The first question: President Clinton has proposed a tax credit for families with an annual income of $100,000 or less for each first-year college student. The $1,500 tax credit would also apply to the second year if the student maintained a B average and had no conviction for drugs. In general, do you favor or oppose this proposal?

	National Totals %	No Children In School %	Public School Parents %	Nonpublic School Parents %
Favor	82	79	87	88
Oppose	17	20	12	12
Don't know	1	1	1	*

*Less than one-half of 1%.

the public but is not considered as important as the other two factors.

President Clinton's Proposals

President Clinton has offered three proposals designed to improve schools, enhance student achievement, or provide incentives for students to succeed in school. These proposals are currently before Congress and may or may not become law.

While all the proposals made by President Clinton attract majority support, the strongest support (82%) is the proposed tax credit for the parents of first-year college students. This proposal has already been debated in Congress, with the Administration indicating a willingness to compromise on the need for a B average as a condition for second-year aid. Support for the proposal is strong among all groups in the poll.

Two-thirds of the public (66%) favor the proposal for placing a computer with access to the Internet in every public school classroom. Groups strongly in favor of the proposal include blacks (85%), nonwhites (83%), 18- to 29-year-olds (78%), and those in the $50,000 and over income range (78%).

The President's testing proposal has the least support and, based on past experience, is likely to generate the most controversy.

Achievement Testing

Testing and its role in school improvement is a frequent subject of debate. Respondents this year were asked their opinion of the level of emphasis on testing in their local public schools. Forty-eight percent responded that the emphasis is about right. The rest were divided between too much and too little. These responses were consistent among all demographic groups.

Biggest Problems Facing Local Schools

Efforts at school improvement must, of course, address the problems the public schools face. In all recent polls the public has been asked to indicate the biggest problem facing the local public schools. This year a follow-up question was asked to determine whether the public feels the problems faced by urban schools are more serious than those faced by their nonurban counterparts. Sixty-nine percent said they believe the problems that urban schools face are either much more serious or somewhat more serious.

This year "lack of discipline" and "lack of financial support" were mentioned by 15% of the respondents respectively as the most serious problems facing local public schools. Use of drugs, designated the number-one problem in last year's poll, was mentioned by 14% of respondents this year, and fighting/violence/gangs was mentioned by 12%. These four problems were the only ones to reach double figures.

One caution needs to be offered relative to the findings reported. The question requires respondents to identify a problem, and they do not have a list from which to choose. That is undoubtedly why so many different problems are mentioned and why the percentage of mentions is so small. (Eleven other problems were mentioned by 2% of respondents.)

The second question: President Clinton has proposed a five-year, two-billion-dollar program that would place a computer with access to the Internet in every public school classroom in the nation. In general, do you favor or oppose this proposal?

	National Totals %	No Children In School %	Public School Parents %	Nonpublic School Parents %
Favor	66	64	70	73
Oppose	32	34	29	26
Don't know	2	2	1	1

The third question: President Clinton has proposed that the performance of the nation's public schools be assessed according to how well students score on achievement tests at two different grade levels. In general, do you favor or oppose this proposal?

	National Totals %	No Children In School %	Public School Parents %	Nonpublic School Parents %
Favor	57	56	59	53
Oppose	37	37	37	42
Don't know	6	7	4	5

The question: In your opinion, is there too much emphasis on achievement testing in the public schools in this community, not enough emphasis on testing, or about the right amount?

	National Totals %	No Children In School %	Public School Parents %	Nonpublic School Parents %
Too much emphasis	20	20	19	24
Not enough emphasis	28	28	26	42
About the right amount	48	46	54	32
Don't know	4	6	1	2

Grading the Schools

Since 1974 respondents to the Phi Delta Kappa/Gallup education polls have been asked to grade the public schools in their communities on a scale of A to F. In 1981, people were first asked to rate the "nation's public schools" on the same scale. Then, beginning in 1985, parents were asked to grade the public school their oldest child was attending.

One significant generalization derived from responses to these questions over the years is the fact that the closer respon-

The first question: What do you think are the biggest problems with which the public schools in this community must deal?

	National Totals '97 %	National Totals '96 %	No Children In School '97 %	No Children In School '96 %	Public School Parents '97 %	Public School Parents '96 %	Nonpublic School Parents '97 %	Nonpublic School Parents '96 %
Lack of discipline/ more control	15	15	15	16	12	12	22	18
Lack of financial support/ funding/money	15	13	15	14	14	13	4	7
Use of drugs/dope	14	16	14	17	14	14	9	12
Fighting/violence/gangs	12	14	12	14	12	15	16	17
Overcrowded schools	8	8	6	6	10	11	17	15
Concern about standards/ quality of education	8	4	7	4	8	4	10	9
Pupils' lack of interest/poor attitudes/truancy	6	5	6	5	6	6	3	4
Difficulty getting good teachers/quality teachers	3	3	3	3	4	3	*	3
No problems	2	3	2	2	3	7	*	3
Miscellaneous	9	9	9	8	8	10	13	11
Don't know	10	13	13	15	6	9	4	10

*Less than one-half of 1%

The second question: Just your impression, are the problems faced by the public schools in urban areas much more serious, somewhat more serious, somewhat less serious, or much less serious than those faced by the public schools in nonurban areas?

	National Totals %	No Children In School %	Public School Parents %	Nonpublic School Parents %
Much more serious	40	40	40	43
Somewhat more serious	29	29	30	32
Somewhat less serious	16	16	17	16
Much less serious	7	6	7	5
Don't know	8	9	6	4

dents are to the public schools, the higher the grades they give them. Thus people give the schools in their own community much higher grades than they give the nation's schools. Parents give the schools in the community much higher grades than do those who do not have children in the public schools. By the same token, public school parents, when asked to grade the school their oldest child attends, give that school higher grades than they give to schools in the community as a whole. Current poll findings reinforce the basic generalization: familiarity with the public schools breeds respect for them.

The differences are impressive. Over the last nine years the differences between the percentage of A's and B's given to the nation's public schools and to the local schools have averaged about 23 points. Even more startling is the difference between the percentage of A's and B's parents give to the school their oldest child attends and the percentage of A's and B's given to the nation's schools. Here the difference over the last nine years has averaged 47 percentage points.

Taken together, these items suggest a second generalization: the low grades given the nation's public schools are primarily media-induced. Whereas people learn firsthand about their *children's* schools, they learn about the *nation's* schools primarily from the media.

Local Public Schools

As has been the case for two decades, over four Americans in 10—46% this year—award a grade of A or B to the public schools in their own communities. And almost eight in 10—78% this year—award them at least a grade of C. An even higher percentage of public school parents (56%) assign an A or a B to the schools in their community.

Public Schools Nationally

As has been the case since this question was first asked in 1981, about half as many Americans give a grade of A or B to the nation's public schools as give these grades to the local public schools. This year the figures are 22% and 46% respectively. The groups assigning unusually high percentages of A's and B's to the nation's public schools include blacks (44%) and nonwhites (35%).

Public School Oldest Child Attends

The parents of public school children are likely to be among the best-informed citizens about the public schools. Since 1985, this poll has asked parents to grade the school their oldest child attends. This year almost two-thirds (64%) of public school parents assign the school their oldest child attends an A or a B. Another 23% assign this school a C, bringing to 87% the proportion of parents giving the school their oldest child attends at least a passing grade of C. The parents who are most likely to give the school their oldest child attends an A or a B include college graduates (75%), parents who live in the East (74%), and those parents whose children are at the top of their class or above-average academically (74%).

Public Versus Nonpublic Schools

The current poll featured the usual questions regarding attendance at public, private, or church-related schools with the government paying all or part of the costs. The first question dealt with choosing a private school to attend at public expense. In the past, when this question has been asked, some critics have suggested that the results would be different if the words "government expense" were used in place of "public expense." With this in

The question: Students are often given the grades A, B, C, D, and FAIL to denote the quality of their work. Suppose the public schools themselves, in this community, were graded in the same way. What grade would you give the public schools here—A, B, C, D, or FAIL?

	National Totals		No Children In School		Public School Parents		Nonpublic School Parents	
	'97 %	'96 %	'97 %	'96 %	'97 %	'96 %	'97 %	'96 %
A & B	46	43	42	38	56	57	26	24
A	10	8	8	6	15	15	9	2
B	36	35	34	32	41	42	17	22
C	32	34	33	36	30	29	35	43
D	11	11	11	12	10	9	21	13
FAIL	6	6	7	6	3	4	13	13
Don't know	5	6	7	8	1	1	5	7

The question: How about the public schools in the nation as a whole? What grade would you give the public schools nationally—A, B, C, D, or FAIL?

	National Totals		No Children In School		Public School Parents		Nonpublic School Parents	
	'97 %	'96 %	'97 %	'96 %	'97 %	'96 %	'97 %	'96 %
A & B	22	21	23	20	23	26	24	8
A	2	1	3	1	2	2	2	1
B	20	20	20	19	21	24	22	7
C	48	46	49	47	46	43	38	57
D	15	18	15	19	16	14	15	21
FAIL	6	5	6	5	4	7	6	3
Don't know	9	10	7	9	11	10	17	11

The question: Using the A, B, C, D, FAIL scale again, what grade would you give the school your oldest child attends?

	Public School Parents '97 %	Public School Parents '96 %
A & B	64	66
A	26	23
B	38	43
C	23	22
D	7	6
FAIL	4	5
Don't know	2	1

mind, a split-sample design was used in this year's poll. That is, the sample was divided, and the question was asked both ways. The customary question dealing with the use of vouchers was also asked, along with a question designed to determine whether the public believes any changes in admission policies should be required for nonpublic schools that accept public funds.

Providing for parents and students to attend nonpublic school at public expense has been strongly opposed in past years. In 1993, for example, the percentage opposing allowing students and parents to choose a private school to attend at public expense was 74%, with only 24% in favor. In 1994 allowing parents to send their school-age children to any public, private, or church-related school of their choice with the government paying "all or part of tuition" was opposed 54% to 45%. However, with each succeeding year, the opposition has lessened. This year the public can be described as almost equally divided on this issue.

The first question: Do you favor or oppose allowing students and parents to choose a private school to attend at public expense?

	National Totals				No Children In School				Public School Parents				Nonpublic School Parents			
	'97	'96	'95	'93	'97	'96	'95	'93	'97	'96	'95	'93	'97	'96	'95	'93
	%	%	%	%	%	%	%	%	%	%	%	%	%	%	%	%
Favor	44	36	33	24	44	33	30	21	45	39	38	27	52	60	44	45
Oppose	52	61	65	74	54	63	68	76	50	59	59	72	44	38	51	55
Don't know	4	3	2	2	2	4	2	3	5	2	3	1	4	2	5	*

*Less than one-half of 1%

The second question: Do you favor oppose allowing students and parents to choose a private school to attend at government expense?

	National Totals		No Children In School		Public School Parents		Nonpublic School Parents	
	Gov't. Exp. %	Public Exp. %	Gov't. Exp. %	Public Exp. %	Gov't. Exp. %	Public Exp. %	Gov't. Exp. %	Public Exp. %
Favor	48	44	51	44	43	45	50	52
Oppose	48	52	45	54	54	50	44	44
Don't know	4	4	4	2	3	5	6	4

Choosing Private Schools at Public Expense

The current poll is the fourth (starting in 1993) to ask the public its attitude toward allowing parents to choose a private school to attend at public expense. The opposition has been consistent, though it dropped from 74% in 1993 to 65% in 1995 to 61% in 1996. This year the poll shows that 52% oppose such choice while 44% approve it.

The group most likely to oppose this form of choice is the 18- to 29-year-olds (62% opposed, 38% in favor). Groups most likely to support this form of choice include nonwhites (51% in favor, 46% opposed) and urban residents (53% in favor, 45% opposed).

A second form of the question was also asked this year with the words "government expense" substituted for "public expense." When asked in this way, the public is equally divided, with 48% in favor and 48% opposed. Those most likely to support this choice include blacks (72%), nonwhites (68%), 18- to 29-year-olds (70%), professional and business persons (53%), and urban residents (59%).

The question most directly associated with vouchers was asked in 1994 and repeated in 1996. When it was first asked in 1994, 45% favored the idea. Support was virtually the same (43%) in 1996; however, this year's poll shows the public equally divided, with 49% in favor and 48% opposed. Both public school parents (55%) and nonpublic school parents (68%) favor allowing parents to send their school-age children to any public, private, or church-related school they choose, with the government paying part or all of the cost.

This issue divides men and women. Women favor permitting the choice by 52% to 45%; men oppose it by 51% to 47%. Other groups in support include blacks (62% to 34%), nonwhites (61% to 36%), 18- to 29-year-olds (55% to 43%), 30- to 49-year-olds (53% to 45%), those who live in the South (56% to 42%), those in the $20,000 to $30,000 income group (55% to 43%), those in the $10,000 to

$20,000 income group (53% to 42%), and manual laborers (53% to 44%). Groups in opposition include those 50 years of age and older (56% to 40%), those living in the West (54% to 45%), those in the $50,000 and over income group (57% to 41%), and suburban residents (51% to 45%).

The question: A proposal has been made that would allow parents to send their school-age children to any public, private, or church-related school they choose. For those parents choosing nonpublic schools, the government would pay all or part of the tuition. Would you favor or oppose this proposal in your state?

	National Totals '97 %	National Totals '96 %	National Totals '94 %	No Children In School '97 %	No Children In School '96 %	No Children In School '94 %	Public School Parents '97 %	Public School Parents '96 %	Public School Parents '94 %	Nonpublic School Parents '97 %	Nonpublic School Parents '96 %	Nonpublic School Parents '94 %
Favor	49	43	45	46	38	42	55	49	48	68	70	69
Oppose	48	54	54	51	59	57	43	49	51	31	28	29
Don't know	3	3	1	3	3	1	2	2	1	1	2	2

Obligations of Private Schools Accepting Public Funds

One of the issues that comes up in any debate over public funds going to nonpublic schools is the extent to which those schools should be bound by the same obligations that fall on public schools. This year's poll asked whether such schools should be required to accept students from a wider range of backgrounds and levels of academic ability than is now generally the case. The public is strongly in agreement that they should. Seventy-eight percent of the public holds this view. This response is consistent across all demographic groups.

The question: Do you think nonpublic schools that receive public funding should or should not be required to accept students from a wider range of backgrounds and academic ability than is now generally the case?

	National Totals %	No Children In School %	Public School Parents %	Nonpublic School Parents %
Should be required to accept a wider range	78	78	80	76
Should not	18	17	17	22
Don't know	4	5	3	2

Effects of a Shift to Nonpublic Schools

Another concern raised by those opposing the use of public funds for nonpublic schools is that the students and parents with the financial means to do so might opt for private schools, leaving the public schools to serve the poor and underprivileged. Three of the questions in this year's poll addressed this concern. The responses offer some indication that the concern is warranted.

The first question: Suppose a large number of students in your local public schools moved to private schools. Just your opinion, who would be most likely to move to the private schools—the higher-achieving students, the lower-achieving students, or the average-achieving students?

	National Totals %	No Children In School %	Public School Parents %	Nonpublic School Parents %
Higher-achieving students	65	67	62	56
Lower-achieving students	8	8	8	10
Average-achieving students	20	19	21	28
No difference	3	3	5	2
Don't know	4	3	4	4

Almost two-thirds of those surveyed (65%) believe that it would be the higher-achieving students who would take the opportunity to attend private schools. The same percentage believe the result for these students would be improved academic achievement. As for the students remaining in the public schools, 70% of the public believes that their achievement would remain about the same.

Responses to these three questions vary little across the subgroups in the poll.

The second question: Again, just your opinion, how would the academic achievement of those public school students who had moved to the private schools be affected? Do you think their academic achievement would improve, get worse, or remain about the same after moving to private schools?

	National Totals %	No Children In School %	Public School Parents %	Nonpublic School Parents %
Improve	65	68	58	80
Get worse	4	4	4	*
Remain about the same	28	25	35	19
Don't know	3	3	3	1

*Less than one-half of 1%.

The third question: How about the students who remained in the local public schools? Do you think their academic achievement would improve, get worse, or remain about the same?

	National Totals %	No Children In School %	Public School Parents %	Nonpublic School Parents %
Improve	17	16	19	10
Get worse	11	11	11	10
Remain about the same	70	70	68	80
Don't know	2	3	2	*

*Less than one-half of 1%.

Home Schooling

The Phi Delta Kappa/Gallup poll first addressed the home-school movement in 1985, asking respondents whether the fledgling move toward home schooling was a good thing or a bad thing for the nation. At that time, 73% said they thought it was a bad thing, while 16% said they thought it was a good thing. When the question was repeated in 1988, the proportion who said it was a bad thing had fallen to 59%, and the proportion who said it was a good thing had risen to 28%. Given a continuing increase in the number of students being schooled at home, poll planners deemed it important to revisit the issue this year. While the public still feels that the home-school movement is a bad thing, the margin has now shrunk to just 21 percentage points.

It is interesting to note that nonpublic school parents, who thought the home-school movement was a bad thing in 1985 (by a margin of 71% to 22%), now favor it by 52% to 41%. This is the only group sampled that believes the movement to home schooling is a good thing.

This year's poll also asked respondents whether home schools should or should not be required to guarantee a minimum level of educational quality. Almost nine in 10 respondents (88%) felt that they should. This response is consistent among all groups.

The first question: Recently, there has been a movement toward home schools—that is, situations in which parents keep their children at home to teach the children themselves. Do you think this movement is a good thing or a bad thing for the nation?

	National Totals			No Children In School			Public School Parents			Nonpublic School Parents		
	'97 %	'88 %	'85 %	'97 %	'88 %	'85 %	'97 %	'88 %	'85 %	'97 %	'88 %	'85 %
Good thing	36	28	16	34	27	16	38	29	14	52	29	22
Bad thing	57	59	73	59	59	72	56	61	75	41	56	71
Don't know	7	13	11	7	14	12	6	10	11	7	15	7

The second question: Do you think that home schools should or should not be required to guarantee a minimum level of educational quality?

	National Totals %	No Children In School %	Public School Parents %	Nonpublic School Parents %
Should be required	88	88	91	80
Should not be required	10	10	8	19
Don't know	2	2	1	1

Parents and Their Relationship to the Public Schools

This poll went further than most recent Phi Delta Kappa/Gallup polls in exploring the relationship between the public schools and the parents who send students to those schools. That seems to have been an appropriate decision, given the fact that 86% of the public cites the amount of support from parents of students in the local public schools as the most important factor in determining why schools in some places are better than others.

Infringing on Rights of Parents

One of the charges heard from some critics is that the public schools are infringing on the right of parents to direct their children's education. This seems to be part of a more general feeling among some Americans that the government has too much control over their lives. However, more than seven in 10 respondents (71%) said they do not believe that the public schools are infringing on the rights of parents. Only nonpublic school parents differ.

Help with Homework

The 1986 poll asked parents how much help they gave their oldest child with his or her homework. At that time, 34% said that they provided no help—a figure that fell to 13% when the question was repeated in this year's poll. It also appears that parents who help their children are spending more hours doing so than they did in 1986. Forty-seven percent of this year's respondents say that they help with homework four or more hours a week, compared to 14% who said they spend that much time in the earlier poll. Thirty-nine percent of all public school parents report that they help their children five or more hours per week.

The question: People in some communities say the local public schools are infringing on the rights of parents to direct their children's education. In your opinion, are the public schools in your community infringing on the rights of local parents to direct their children's education?

	National Totals %	No Children In School %	Public School Parents %	Nonpublic School Parents %
Yes, infringing	24	20	28	50
No, not infringing	71	73	70	44
Don't know	5	7	2	6

The question: During the school year, on average, about how many hours a week do you help your oldest child with his or her homework?

	'97 %	'86 %
None	13	34
Up to 1 hour	5	13
1–1:59 hours	12	17
2–2:59 hours	12	10
3–3:59 hours	9	7
4–4:59 hours	8	5
5–5:59 hours	14	4
6 hours or more	25	5
Undesignated	2	5

Willingness to Volunteer

Much has been made recently of the importance of persons being willing to serve as unpaid volunteers in addressing problems the nation faces. Television recently featured pictures of past U.S. Presidents working at sprucing up inner-city areas. Gen. Colin Powell heads a Presidential task force to promote volunteerism. Given this backdrop, poll planners thought it important to repeat the 1992 question in which participants were asked about their willingness to serve as unpaid volunteers in the public schools. At that time 59% said that they would be willing to do so. In this year's poll that figure rose to 69%.

Parental Support for Teachers and Principals

One of the complaints heard from teachers and principals is that they no longer have the parental support they once enjoyed. Two questions were asked in this poll to explore the support parents give to school personnel.

Parental Expectations Regarding Achievement

By a 2-1 margin (60% to 28%) respondents in the 1996 Phi Delta Kappa/Gallup poll said that, if forced to choose, they would prefer their sons or daughters to make C grades and be active in extracurricular activities rather

The question: If you were asked, would you be willing to work as an unpaid volunteer in any of the public schools in this community or not?

Willing to Work as Unpaid Volunteer	'97 %	'92 %		'97 %	'92 %
NATIONAL TOTALS	69	59	50–64 years	56	54
Sex			65–and over	57	36
Men	64	54	**Education**		
Women	73	64	College graduate	73	70
Race			High school graduate	63	57
White	68	61	High school incomplete	63	45
Nonwhite	74	49	**Children in School**		
Age			No children in school	65	51
18–29 years	72	65	Public school parents	78	72
30–49 years	76	65	Nonpublic school parents	60	49

The first question: Suppose a teacher or principal reported that your oldest child was misbehaving and being disruptive in school. Whose side do you think you would be more likely to take—the school's or your child's?

	Public School Parents %	Nonpublic School Parents %
The school's side	57	73
Your child's side	25	16
Don't know	18	11

The second question: What if a teacher or principal reported that your oldest child was not working hard enough at schoolwork? Whose side do you think you would be more likely to take—the school's or your child's?

	Public School Parents %	Nonpublic School Parents %
The school's side	70	70
Your child's side	22	25
Don't know	8	5

The question: Regardless of whether you have children in public school, what would be the lowest grade a child of yours could bring home on a report card without upsetting or concerning you?

	National Totals %	No Children In School %	Public School Parents %	Nonpublic School Parents %
A	1	1	*	2
B	21	20	21	22
C	60	58	63	64
D	13	15	11	9
FAIL	3	3	4	1
Don't know	2	3	1	2

*Less than one-half of 1%.

than make A grades and not be active. This response led poll planners to ask on this year's poll about the lowest grade a student could bring home without causing the parent to the upset or concerned. A majority (60%) said their child could bring home a report card with a C without raising concern. This response is consistent among all groups in the poll.

Parental Expectations on Communication

Given today's concern for privacy, one of the important dilemmas for school personnel is how much information regarding student problems should be reported to parents. This is an area, however, where parental expectations are quite clear. Ninety-eight percent of all respondents believe that public schools should be required to notify the parents if their child is found to have a substance abuse problem, and 90% felt that parents should be notified if their child is found to have a sexually transmitted disease. These responses are consistent across all groups surveyed.

The Curriculum

One question that quickly surfaces in any discussion of school reform is the extent to which the curriculum needs to be changed to meet today's needs. This question was explored in the 1982 poll. At that time a plurality (42%) expressed the view that the curriculum did meet the needs of the day. Fifty percent of public school parents agreed. In this year's poll, however, 54% of respondents say they think the curriculum needs to be changed. Public school parents now call for change by a 53% to 46% margin. Groups most likely to feel the need for change include nonwhites (65%), 18- to 29-year-olds (64%), and clerical and sales personnel (65%).

Curriculum 'Basics'

In every public school forum conducted by Phi Delta Kappa during the 1996–97 academic year, there was agreement that the schools should teach the "basics." The ensuing discussions, however, suggested that there might be a difference of opinion as to what the "basics" included. This year's poll asked respondents to define the term. The responses indicate that mathematics (named by 90%) and English (named by 84%) constitute the heart of the "basics." This seems close to the traditional three R's. Large percentages of respondents would also add science (44%) and history/U.S. government (38%).

A word of caution is required here. The fact that the public wants the basics taught and defines them narrowly should not be interpreted to mean that people do not value other subjects and other parts of the curriculum. In fact, the public assigns great importance even to extracurricular activities (as a later question shows). What seems clear is that, while the public sees teaching the so-called basics as a central mission, it has many other expectations of its public schools as well.

The first question: Do you think that the public schools in your community should or should not be required to notify the parents of a student who is found by school authorities to have a substance abuse problem?

	National Totals %	No Children In School %	Public School Parents %	Nonpublic School Parents %
Should be required	98	98	98	100
Should not be required	1	1	2	*
Don't know	1	1	*	*

*Less than one-half of 1%.

The second question: How about a sexually transmitted disease? Do you think the public schools in your community should or should not be required to notify the parents of a student who is found by school authorities to have a sexually transmitted disease?

	National Totals %	No Children In School %	Public School Parents %	Nonpublic School Parents %
Should be required	90	89	92	89
Should not be required	9	10	7	10
Don't know	1	1	1	1

The question: Do you think the curriculum in the public schools in your community needs to be changed to meet today's needs, or do you think it already meets today's needs?

	National Totals '97 %	National Totals '82 %	No Children In School '97 %	No Children In School '82 %	Public School Parents '97 %	Public School Parents '82 %	Nonpublic School Parents '97 %	Nonpublic School Parents '82 %
Needs to be changed	54	36	54	33	53	42	65	46
Already meets needs	39	42	36	38	46	50	30	44
Don't know	7	22	10	29	1	8	5	10

Dealing with Drugs and Weapons in School

The public continues to believe that drugs and weapons in school are major problems for the public schools. Although school personnel in most situations do not believe these problems are as severe as the public does, schoolpeople must nonetheless deal with the public's concern. The first of three drug-related questions in this poll sought to find out how satisfied people are with steps being taken to deal with the drug problem in their local schools. Perhaps surpris-

The question: People have different ideas as to what constitutes the so-called basic subjects in school. Would you name the school subjects that you consider to be the basics?

	National Totals %	No Children In School %	Public School Parents %	Nonpublic School Parents %
Mathematics	90	89	91	93
English	84	84	84	91
Science	44	41	49	53
History/U.S. government	38	36	40	50
Geography	8	9	8	4
Computer training	8	8	8	12
Physical education	7	7	9	11
Art	5	6	5	8
Social studies	5	4	7	4
Foreign language	5	4	6	13
Music	3	3	3	1
Health education	2	2	4	4
Vocational training	1	2	1	*
Career education	1	1	1	*
Business	1	1	1	2
Other	8	8	7	7
Don't know	1	2	1	2

*Less than one-half of 1%.

The first question: How satisfied are you yourself with the steps being taken to deal with the use of drugs in the public schools in your community—very satisfied, somewhat satisfied, not very satisfied, or not at all satisfied?

	National Totals %	No Children In School %	Public School Parents %	Nonpublic School Parents %
Very satisfied	17	13	25	11
Somewhat satisfied	36	35	40	35
Not very satisfied	22	24	17	32
Not at all satisfied	20	21	17	17
Don't know	5	7	1	5

The second question: Some public schools have a so-called zero-tolerance drug and alcohol policy, which means that possession of any illegal drugs or alcohol by students will result in automatic suspension. Would you favor or oppose such a policy in the public schools in your community?

	National Totals %	No Children In School %	Public School Parents %	Nonpublic School Parents %
Favor	86	84	89	93
Oppose	13	15	10	7
Don't know	1	1	1	*

*Less than one-half of 1%.

ingly, 53% indicate they are either very or somewhat satisfied. The level of satisfaction rises to 65% for public school parents and to 60% for rural residents. However, it falls to 45% for urban residents.

The second question dealt with "zero tolerance" policies calling for automatic suspension of students carrying drugs or alcohol into school. Support for such policies is strong. Eighty-six percent say they support such policies, and this level of support is consistent among all groups.

Respondents were also asked whether they feel an educational approach or severe penalties offer the best means of dealing with the drug problem. A small majority (52%) prefers an educational approach, while 42% favor severe penalties. These percentages vary little across groups.

Many schools also have "zero tolerance" policies that call for automatic suspension of students who bring weapons to school. Such policies garnered media attention when authorities suspended a student for bringing a nail file to school. Regardless of difficulties in application, support for such policies is very strong. Ninety-three percent of poll respondents express support, and that support is consistent among all groups.

Financing the Public Schools

From time to time, the Phi Delta Kappa/Gallup polls have surveyed public attitudes regarding school finance. The first question on that topic this year repeated one asked in 1986 concerning the source of taxes used to finance the public schools. In findings remarkably similar to those in the 1986 poll, 27% expressed a preference for local property taxes, 34% for state taxes, and 30% for taxes from the federal government. There is certainly no consensus. The two groups that do take a majority position in favor of federal funding are blacks (56%) and nonwhites (54%).

In a second question respondents were reminded that the local property tax is the main source for financing the public schools and were asked whether they would prefer to change to a local income tax system as the principal source of public school funds in their community. Once again, there is no consensus: 43% favor changing to a local income tax system, while 48% oppose it. This lack of consensus characterizes all groups surveyed.

The third question: In your opinion, which is more effective for dealing with a drug problem in the public schools in your community—an educational approach, pointing out the consequences of drug use, or severe penalties for those violating the school drug policy?

	National Totals %	No Children In School %	Public School Parents %	Nonpublic School Parents %
Educational approach	52	52	53	44
Severe penalties	42	41	43	49
Don't know	6	7	4	7

The fourth question: Some public schools have so-called zero tolerance weapons policy, which means that students found carrying weapons of any kind in school will be automatically suspended. Would you favor or oppose such a policy in the public schools in your community?

	National Totals %	No Children In School %	Public School Parents %	Nonpublic School Parents %
Favor	93	92	95	91
Oppose	5	6	4	9
Don't know	2	2	1	*

*Less than one-half of 1%.

The first question: There is always a lot of discussion about the best way to finance the public schools. Which do you think is the best way to finance the public schools—by means of local property taxes, by state taxes, or by taxes from the federal government in Washington?

	National Totals '97 %	National Totals '86 %	No Children In School '97 %	No Children In School '86 %	Public School Parents '97 %	Public School Parents '86 %	Nonpublic School Parents '97 %	Nonpublic School Parents '86 %
Local property taxes	27	24	30	22	22	28	32	22
State taxes	34	33	35	34	32	32	28	36
Federal taxes	30	24	26	23	37	28	36	22
Don't know	9	19	9	21	9	12	4	20

The second question: At the present time, local property taxes are the main source for financing the public schools in most states. Thinking about your own community, would you favor or oppose changing the local property tax system to a local income tax system as the principal way to finance the local public schools?

	National Totals %	No Children In School %	Public School Parents %	Nonpublic School Parents %
Favor	43	42	47	39
Oppose	48	49	44	51
Don't know	9	9	9	10

Research Procedure

The Sample. The sample used in this survey embraced a total of 1,517 adults (18 years of age and older), including 1,017 parents of public school children. The sample of public school parents was increased to 1,017 interviews this year from the 500 interviews customarily used. The increased sample size permits analysis and reporting of findings for subgroups within the national public school parent population. A description of the sample and methodology can be found at the end of this report.

Time of Interviewing. The fieldwork for this study was conducted during the period of 3 June to 22 June 1997.

The Report. In the tables used in this report, "Nonpublic School Parents" includes parents of students who attend parochial schools and parents of students who attend private or independent schools.

Due allowance must be made for statistical variation, especially in the case of findings for groups consisting of relatively few respondents, e.g., nonpublic school parents.

The findings of this report apply only to the U.S. as a whole and not to individual communities. Local surveys, using the same questions, can be conducted to determine how local areas compare with the national norm.

Composition of the Sample

Adults	%
No children in school	64
Public school parents	33*
Nonpublic school parents	7*

*Total exceeds 100% because some parents have children attending more than one kind of school.

	National	**Public School Parents**
Gender	%	%
Men	46	43
Women	54	57
Race		
White	85	83
Nonwhite	13	15
Black	9	11
Undesignated	2	2
Age		
18-29 years	22	12
30-49 years	44	75
50 and over	33	12
Undesignated	1	1
Education		
Total college	56	47
College graduate	23	16
College incomplete	33	31
Total high school	44	53
High school graduate	31	33
High school incomplete	13	20
Undesignated	*	*
Income		
50,000 and over	30	32
40,000 and over	42	48
$30,000-$39,999	14	14
$20,000-$29,999	16	13
Under $20,000	20	20
Undesignated	8	5
Region		
East	24	22
Midwest	25	20
South	30	38
West	21	20
Community size		
Urban	28	26
Suburban	48	49
Rural	24	25
Undesignated	*	*

*Less than one-half of 1%.

Design of the Sample

For the 1997 survey the Gallup Organization used its standard national telephone sample, i.e., an unclustered, directory-assisted, random-digit telephone sample, based on a proportionate stratified sampling design.

The random-digit aspect of the sample was used to avoid "listing" bias. Numerous studies have shown that households with unlisted telephone numbers are different in important ways from listed households. "Unlistedness" is due to household mobility or to customer requests to prevent publication of the telephone number.

To avoid this source of bias, a random-digit procedure designed to provide representation of both listed and unlisted (including not-yet-listed) numbers was used.

Telephone numbers for the continental United States were stratified into four regions of the country and, within each region, further stratified into three size-of-community strata.

Only working banks of telephone numbers were selected. Eliminating nonworking banks from the sample increased the likelihood that any sample telephone number would be associated with a residence.

The sample of telephone numbers produced by the described method is representative of all telephone households within the continental United States.

Within each contacted household, an interview was sought with the youngest man 18 years of age or older who was at home. If no man was home, an interview was sought with the oldest woman at home. This method of respondent selection within households produced an age distribution by sex that closely approximates the age distribution by sex of the total population.

Up to three calls were made to each selected telephone number to complete an interview. The time of day and the day of the week for callbacks were varied so as to maximize the chances of finding a respondent at home. All interviews were conducted on weekends or weekday evenings in order to contact potential respondents among the working population.

The final sample was weighted so that the distribution of the sample matched current estimates derived from the U.S. Census Bureau's Current Population Survey (CPS) for the adult population living in telephone households in the continental U.S.

As has been the case in recent years in the Phi Delta Kappa/Gallup poll series, parents of public school children were oversampled in the 1997 poll. This procedure produced a large enough sample to ensure that findings reported for "public school parents" are statistically significant (see Research Procedure).

Conducting Your Own Poll

The Phi Delta Kappa Center for Professional Development and Services makes available PACE (Polling Attitudes of the Community on Education) materials to enable nonspecialists to conduct scientific polls of attitude and opinion on education. The PACE manual provides detailed information on constructing questionnaires, sampling, interviewing, and analyzing data. It also includes updated census figures and new material on conducting a telephone survey. The price is $55. For information about using PACE materials, write or phone Phillip Harris at Phi Delta Kappa, P.O. Box 789, Bloomington, IN 47402-0789. Ph. 800/766-1156.

Sampling Tolerances

In interpreting survey results, it should be borne in mind that all sample surveys are subject to sampling error, i.e., the extent to which the results may differ from what would be obtained if the whole population surveyed had been interviewed. The size of such sampling error depends largely on the number of interviews.

The following tables may be used in estimating the sampling error of any percentage in this report. The computed allowances have taken into account the effect of the sample design upon sampling error. They may be interpreted as indicating the range (plus or minus the figure shown) within which the results of repeated samplings in the same time period could be expected to vary 95% of the time, assuming the same sampling procedure, the same interviewers, and the same questionnaire.

The first table* shows how much allowance should be made for the sampling error of a percentage.

*Table 1 in this publication.

The table would be used in the following manner: Let us say that a reported percentage is 33 for a group that includes 1,000 respondents. We go to the row for "percentages near 30" in the table and across to the column headed "1,000."

The number at this point is 4, which means that the 33% obtained in the sample is subject to a sampling error of plus or minus four points. In other words, it is very probable (95 chances out of 100) that the true figure would be somewhere between 29% and 37%, with the most likely figure the 33% obtained.

In comparing survey results in two samples, such as, for example, men and women, the question arises as to how large a difference between them must be before one can be reasonably sure that it reflects a real difference. In the tables below,* the number of points that must be allowed for in such comparisons is indicated. Two tables are provided. One is for percentages near 20 or 80; the other, for percentages near 50. For percentages in between, the error to be allowed for lies between those shown in the two tables.

Here is an example of how the tables would be used: Let us say that 50% of men respond a certain way and 40% of women respond that way also, for a difference of 10 percentage points between them. Can we say with any assurance that the 10-point difference reflects a real difference between men and women on the question? Let us consider a sample that contains approximately 750 men and 750 women.

Since the percentages are near 50, we consult Table B, and, since the two samples are about

*Table 2 in this publication.

Table 1 Recommended Allowances for Sampling Error of a Percentage

In Percentage Points (at 95 in 100 confidence level)* Sample Size

	1,500	1,000	750	600	400	200	100
Percentages near 10	2	2	3	3	4	5	8
Percentages near 20	3	3	4	4	5	7	10
Percentages near 30	3	4	4	5	6	8	12
Percentages near 40	3	4	5	5	6	9	12
Percentages near 50	3	4	5	5	6	9	13
Percentages near 60	3	4	5	5	6	9	12
Percentages near 70	3	4	4	5	6	8	12
Percentages near 80	3	3	4	4	5	7	10
Percentages near 90	2	2	3	3	4	5	8

*The chances are 95 in 100 that the sampling error is not larger than the figures shown.

Table 2 Recommended Allowance for Sampling Error of the Difference

In Percentage Points (at 95 in 100 confidence level)* Sample Size

TABLE A Size of Sample	Percentages near 20 or percentages near 80 1,500	1,000	750	600	400	200
1,500	4					
1,000	4	5				
750	5	5	5			
600	5	5	6	6		
400	6	6	6	7	7	
200	8	8	8	8	9	10

TABLE B Size of Sample	Percentages near 50 1,500	1,000	750	600	400	200
1,500	5					
1,000	5	6				
750	6	6	7			
600	6	7	7	7		
400	7	8	8	8	9	
200	10	10	10	10	11	13

*The chances are 95 in 100 that the sampling error is not larger than the figures shown.

750 persons each, we look for the number in the column headed "750," which is also in the row designated "750." We find the number 7 here. This means that the allowance for error should be seven points and that, in concluding that the percentage among men is somewhere between three and 17 points higher than the percentage among women, we should be wrong only about 5% of the time. In other words, we can conclude with considerable confidence that a difference exists in the direction observed and that it amounts to at least three percentage points.

If, in another case, men's responses amount to 22%, say, and women's to 24%, we consult Table A, because these percentages are near 20. We look in the column headed "750" and see that the number is 5. Obviously, then, the two-point difference is inconclusive.

How to Order the Poll

The minimum order for reprints of the published version of the Phi Delta Kappa/Gallup education poll is 25 copies for $10. Additional copies are 25 cents each. This price includes postage for delivery (at the library rate). Where possible, enclose a check or money order. Address your order to Phil Delta Kappa, P.O. Box 789, Bloomington, IN 47402. Ph. 800/766-1156.

If faster delivery is desired, do not include a remittance with your order. You will be billed at the above rates plus any additional cost involved in the method of delivery. Persons who wish to order the 664-page document that is the basis of this report should contact Phi Delta Kappa, P.O. Box 789, Bloomington, IN 47402. Ph 800/766-1156. The price is $95, postage included.

Article Review Form at end of book.

What is the difference between teacher training and teacher education? Why should educators be concerned about using the appropriate language when referring to teaching as a profession?

Teaching as a Profession

Redefining our concepts

There is a massive difference between teacher training and teacher education. This article reminds us to distinguish between the two perceptions and be mindful of the language we use.

G. Patrick O'Neill

G. Patrick O'Neill is a Professor of Education at Brock University, St. Catharines, Ontario, Canada.

Introduction

A profession, if indeed it is a profession, must be "socially defined" (Berg, 1983, p. 176). In other words, its status must be sanctioned by society-at-large. Failure to obtain this recognition will affect, to some extent, how members perceive themselves (Lasley and Galloway, 1983); that is, nonprofessional, semi-professional or professional. As well, it is maintained that this image, whether internal or external, is conveyed, in part, by one's choice of words. In short, if we employ terms that convey a nonprofession, then, despite protests to the contrary, we could be perceived, by and large, as a nonprofession. This scenario has direct implications for teaching as its claim to professional status is continually being challenged (Covert, 1982, 1987; Ornstein, 1981; Shanker, 1985; Shumate, 1987).

Consequently, this article draws a critical distinction between two conflicting concepts that have impaired perceptions of teaching as a profession for decades; namely, that between "teacher training," on the one hand, and "teacher education" on the other. Specifically, it is held that, presently, teacher training has a nonprofessional or, at best, a semi-professional connotation, while teacher education has a professional connotation. This position is based on the fact that, since the mid-1960s, training colleges formerly known as normal schools have been increasingly absorbed by university faculties or colleges of education (Gordon and Lawton, 1984). In turn, it could, or should, be assumed that teacher preparation programs have become more academically and professionally oriented. Therefore, it is argued that the expression teacher training should no longer apply, rather the primary reference should be to teacher education. Evidence to support this thesis is taken from the literature.

Literature Review

Beginning as early as 1943, Rivlin, in the following quotation, calls for a clear distinction between the two concepts.

> Teacher education refers to the *whole* range of activities that constitute preparation for, and improvement of members of, the teaching profession. It includes pre-service education for those who have not had teacher experience and in-service education for those who are actually engaged in teaching. The elevation of quantitative and qualitative standards for the profession is reflected in the use of the term "teacher education" rather than the older term "teacher

From THE JOURNAL OF THE ASSOCIATION OF TEACHER EDUCATORS, Vol. X, No. 2, Summer 1988, pp. 5–10. Reprinted with permission of Association of Teacher Educators.

> training." Whereas teacher training suggests the development of a rather *narrow* proficiency in the skills or methods of classroom teaching, teacher education connotes the *broad* professional preparation needed for the highly complex task of teaching in the modern world. (Italics added) (Rivlin, 1943, p. 793)

Seven years later, Monroe (1950) likewise notes that

> "teacher education" refers to the *total* educative experiences which contribute to the preparation of a person for a teaching position in schools, but the term is more commonly employed to designate the program of courses and other experiences offered by an educational institution for the announced purpose of preparing persons for teaching and other educational service and for contributing to their growth in competency for such service. (Italics added) (p. 1374)

In both instances, teacher education is seen as the major concept. Terms like "whole," "broad," and "total" suggest that it pertains to both the theoretical and practical components of a teacher preparation program. In contrast, teacher training has a "narrow" interpretation in that it refers only to the teaching act itself. Hence, teacher training is seen as part of the larger process, but it is not synonymous with it.

In 1955, the *Education Index* adopted this view. As a result, "TEACHER training" ceased to be employed as a major heading in the June, 1953 to May, 1955 edition of the *Index* (Carpenter, 1955, p. 1257). In June, 1955, "TEACHER education," became the major heading (Carpenter, 1957, p. 1339) and has remained so throughout the years, the latest edition included (Hewitt, 1987). Moreover, the expression teacher education has been the only term of reference in three successive editions of the *Encyclopedia of Educational Research* (Ebel, 1969; Harris, 1960; Mitzel, 1982).

Recent sources reiterate this distinction. For instance, Rowntree (1981) claims that teacher education

> is wider than TEACHER-TRAINING in that it includes not simply a teacher's vocational training (whether INITIAL, PRE-SERVICE TRAINING or subsequent IN-SERVICE TRAINING) but also whatever general POST-SECONDARY EDUCATION he has that contributes to his growth as a person regardless of his future profession. Thus, teacher education courses include the study of one or more ACADEMIC DISCIPLINES as well as educational subjects and SUPERVISED TEACHING PRACTICE. (p. 313)

Elaborated, education is

> The process of successful LEARNING (usually, but not necessarily, aided by teaching) of KNOWLEDGE, SKILLS AND ATTITUDES, where what is learned is worthwhile to the learner (in the view of whoever is using the term) and usually (in contrast with TRAINING) where it is learned in such a way that the learner can express his own individuality through what he learns and can subsequently apply it, and adapt it flexibly, to situations and problems other than those he considered in learning it. (Rowntree, 1981, p. 75)

Conversely, training is

> The *systematic* development in a person of the KNOWLEDGE, ATTITUDES and SKILLS necessary for him to be able to perform adequately in a job or task whose demands can be reasonably *well identified* in advance and that requires a fairly *standardized* performance from whoever attempts it. (Italics added) (Rowntree, 1981, p. 327)

As before, the phrase teacher education is seen as having a wider application than that of teacher training. The term training is restricted more to "well identified" instructional activities which require "systematic" or "standardized performance."

And finally, Hawes and Hawes (1982) reaffirm this distinction by defining teacher education as

> The very *broad* field of study and instruction concerned with professional preparation for careers in teaching, administration, or other specialties in education, particularly in the levels of preschool, elementary, and secondary education. Also called professional teacher education. (Italics added) (p. 225)

Interestingly, but not surprisingly, the expression "professional teacher education" appears as well within the term education which includes:

> 1. Any process, formal or informal, that helps develop the potentialities of human beings, including their knowledge, capabilities, behavior patterns, and values. 2. The developmental process provided by a school or other institution that is organized chiefly for instruction and learning. 3. The *total development* acquired by an individual through instruction and learning . . .
> 5. The area of study concerned with teaching and learning, including *professional teacher education.* (Italics added) (p. 73)

Once again, the phrase "total development" would suggest that education is indeed the major concept. Reference to training is separate from education in that training is confined to:

> 1. Instruction in carrying out *specific* functions. 2. Supervised practice to develop functional skills and knowledge as in *on-the-job* training. (Italics added) (p. 234)

Conclusion

In summary, teacher training is limited to specific, relatively standardized, well identified, job related practices. As the above definition reveals, such skills are frequently obtained through "on-the-job" internships. In teaching, these internships might best equate with certain activities related to the practicums. For example, supervisory duties, classroom management and certain administrative functions would typically fall within this domain. Hence, training involves activities that relate to the mechanical, technical and vocational aspects of teaching; activities that might be aptly labelled rote, ritualistic or repetitive.

Contrarily, teacher education is more complex than teacher training in that it includes both the philosophical and pedagogical components of a teacher preparation program. And since it is complexity, in particular, that separates the professional from the nonprofessional (Medley, Coker and Soar, 1984), then plainly, if teaching is a profession, our primary reference should be to teacher education, not teacher training. The phrase teacher training may have been appropriate at a time when teachers were viewed as technicians, but surely that era has passed.

Discussion

It is now well over 40 years since Rivlin (1943) first distinguished between teacher education, on the one hand, and teacher training on the other. Yet, despite numerous reaffirmations, the expressions continue to be used synonymously and interchangeably throughout the literature. The question, of course, is why? Why do scholars and practitioners alike fail to make this crucial distinction? The answer, in part, lies, no doubt, in the fact that, at times, the authorities themselves have fostered confusion. For instance, Deighton (1971) uses the following titles indiscriminately: "Professional training" (p. 70), "Teacher education in universities and colleges" (p. 78), "IN-SERVICE TRAINING" (p. 79), "Sources of training" (p. 80), and "Types of in-service education" (p. 81). In addition, Knowles (1977) mixes the phrases "TEACHER EDUCATION" (p. 4063), "TEACHER EDUCATION AND TRAINING" (p. 4069) and "TEACHER TRAINING" (p. 4070) while Page and Thomas (1977) define the word "training" as:

> 1. Systematic practice in the performance of a skill. 2. Industrial training. 3. Teacher education. (p. 346)

Too, some distinctions have been contradictory. For example, Good (1973) distinguishes correctly between the terms education and training, but then proceeds to treat the expressions teacher education and teacher training as synonyms. Expanded, education is defined as:

> (1) the aggregate of *all* the processes by means of which a person develops abilities, attitudes, and other forms of behavior of positive value in the society in which he lives; . . . (3) ordinarily, a general term for the so-called "technical" or more specifically classified professional courses offered in higher institutions for the preparation of teachers and relating directly to educational psychology, philosophy and history of education, curriculum, special and general methods, instruction, administration, supervision, etc.; broadly, the *total* pattern of preparation, formal and informal, that results in the professional growth of teachers: see teacher education: . . . (Italics added) (p. 202)

Alternatively, training is purportedly limited to:

> (1) the special kind of teaching and instruction in which the goals are clearly determined, are usually readily demonstrated, and call for a degree of mastery which requires student *practice* and teacher guidance and appraisal of the student's improved performance capabilities; . . . (3) in a derogatory sense, a process of helping others to acquire skills or knowledge by *rote,* without reference to any greater framework of knowledge or comprehension. (Italics added) (Good, 1973, p. 613)

Obviously, these definitions parallel those noted earlier in that education is defined as the major concept while training is defined as the minor concept. The discrepancy, however, arises with the definition of teacher education which supposedly includes

> (1) *all* the formal and informal activities and experiences that help to qualify a person to assume the responsibilities of a member of the educational profession or to discharge his responsibilities more effectively; (2) the program of activities and experiences developed by an institution responsible for the preparation and growth of persons preparing themselves for educational work or engaging in the work of the educational profession. Syn. teacher training. (Italics added) (Good, 1973, p. 586)

And, herein lies the paradox. Teacher education is defined in terms of education, not training, but Good 1973) insists that the two concepts are synonymous. This view is further reinforced on pages 587 and 619 where teacher training is again equated with teacher education. To say the least, such subtle contradictions are confusing, especially for those planning a career in education.

A Final Comment

Surely, by now, the expression "teacher training" is an antiquated concept. We no longer say teacher trainer, but rather teacher educator. Moreover, the phrase "training college" has been widely accepted as an anachronism for some time (Blishen, 1969; Good, 1973; Gordon and Lawton, 1984; Page and Thomas, 1977). Yet ironically, the expression, teacher training, continues to be employed when referring to present-day teacher preparation programs.

Ultimately, of course, the distinction between teacher education and teacher training is germane if, and only if, teaching is perceived, by and large, as a profession rather than a nonprofession. And, assuredly, this statement strikes at the heart of the matter. The contemporary educator will have to decide shortly, either teaching is a profession or it is a nonprofession. If it is a profession, then the established vernacular should correspond accordingly which, in this case, would be teacher education, not teacher training. If, on the other hand, teaching is a nonprofession, the most apt descriptor is, in all likelihood, teacher training.

So, which one is it? A consensus is long overdue. The confusion must cease, there must be agreement among the shareholders and that includes teacher educators, researchers, classroom teachers, and school administrators. To date, the membership has slipped badly in this regard, and unless there is a concerted effort to promote unanimity, in word as well as action, teaching will remain an uncertain profession.

References

1. Berg, G. (1983). Developing the teaching profession: Autonomy, professional code, knowledge base. *Australian Journal of Education,* 27, 173–186.
2. Blishen, E. (Ed.) (1969). *Blond's encyclopedia of education.* London, England: Blond Educational Ltd.
3. Carpenter, D. R. (Ed.) (1955). *The Education Index,* Vol. 9, New York, N.Y.: The H. W. Wilson Co.
4. ——— (1957). *The Education Index.* Vol. 10, New York, N.Y.: The H. W. Wilson Co.
5. Covert, J. R. (1982). The professional status of teachers: An unattainable goal. *Teacher Education,* 20, 42–55.
6. Covert, J. R. (1987). The profession of teaching: A reply to Professor Foster. *Canadian Journal of Education,* 12, 214–217.
7. Deighton, L. C. (Ed.) (1971). *The Encyclopedia of Education.* Vol. 9, New York, N.Y.: The MacMillan Co. & The Free Press.
8. Ebel, R. L. (Ed.) (1969). *Encyclopedia of Educational Research,* 4th Edition. London, England: The MacMillan Co., 1969.
9. Good, C. V. (Ed.) (1973). *Dictionary of Education,* 3rd Edition. New York, N.Y. McGraw-Hill Book Co.
10. Gordon, P. and Lawton, D. (1984). *A Guide to English Educational Terms.* New York, N.Y.: Schocken Books.
11. Harris, C. W. (Ed.) (1960). *Encyclopedia of Educational Research,* 3rd Edition. New York, N.Y.: The MacMillan Co.
12. Hawes, G. R. and Hawes, L. S. (1982). *The Concise Dictionary of Education.* New York, N.Y.: Van Nostrand Reinhold Co.
13. Hewitt, M. (Ed.) (1987). *Education Index.* Vol. 37. New York, N.Y.: The H. W. Wilson Co.
14. Knowles, A. S. (Ed.) (1977). *The International Encyclopedia of Higher Education,* 1st Edition, Vol. 9. Washington, D.C.: Jossey-Bass Publishers.
15. Lasley, T. J. and Galloway, C. M. (1983). Achieving professional status: A problem in what teachers believe. *Clearing House,* 57, 5–8.
16. Medley, D. M., Coker, H. and Soar, R. S. (1984). *Measurement-based evaluation of teacher performance: An empirical approach.* New York, N.Y.: Longman Inc.
17. Mitzel, H. E. (Ed.) (1982). *Encyclopedia of Educational Research,* 5th Edition, Vol. 4, New York, N.Y.: The Free Press.
18. Monroe, W. S. (Ed.) (1950). *Encyclopedia of Educational Research,* Rev. Edition. New York, N.Y.: The Macmillan Co.
19. Ornstein, A. C. (1981). The trend toward increased professionalism for teachers. *Phi Delta Kappan,* 63, 196–198.
20. Page, G. T. and Thomas, J. B. (1977). *International Dictionary of Education.* New York, N.Y.: Nichols Publishing Co.
21. Rivlin, H. N. (Ed.) (1943). *Encyclopedia of Modern Education.* New York, N.Y.: The Philosophical Library of New York City, Inc.
22. Rowntree, D. (1981). *A Dictionary of Education.* New York, N.Y.: Harper and Row, Publishers.
23. Shanker, A. (1985). In support of teachers: The making of a profession. *NASSP Bulletin,* 69, 93–99.
24. Shumate, N. E. (1987). One teacher's profession. *Clearing House,* 60, 409–410.

Article Review Form at end of book.

What are birth rate projections for the next 50 years?

Population Growth Has Big Uncertainties

High birth rates in developing countries are still causing concern.

Robert Schley

Birth rates have fallen globally in the past 20 years, and most projections assume they will continue falling. However, demographers are still concerned that birth rates may not fall far enough and fast enough to prevent massive population growth over the next century, especially in the poorest developing nations.

In 1997, the world's developing countries accounted for 98% of the global population increase. In sub-Saharan Africa, women averaged about six births during their lifetimes, according to the *1997 World Population Data Sheet* published by the Population Reference Bureau in Washington, D.C. While it is expected that these birth rates will decrease, it is difficult to predict just when or how fast that may happen.

Demographers have good information about the current situation, much better than they did 20 years ago, says Carl Haub, co-author of the data sheet. Demographers can confidently predict that world population will total 6.1 billion by century's end. All longer-range projections assume that birth rates will decline and that virtually all growth will take place in developing countries.

Most projections assume that birth rates will come down in these poorer countries as they develop, simply because, historically, these rates fell as today's developed countries industrialized and urbanized. The key uncertainty, according to Haub, is how quickly the birth rates will fall—how far and how fast.

The projections used most often are from the United Nations, which produces medium, high, and low projections, based on different variables and situations. The media and the public largely ignore both extremes and pick the middle of the road, Haub explains.

The developing countries now have about 4.7 billion people, and, in the medium projections, will have over 10 billion by 2100. That assumes that all countries in the developing world will average two children per woman no later than 2040–2045. The countries where that is expected to happen last are in Africa; in other countries it will happen sooner.

In a "high" projection, the birth rate comes down, but to a somewhat higher level. If it stabilizes at 2.5 per woman, for example, then developing countries could reach 25 billion people. That level of population may not really be sustainable, according to Haub, but it's possible mathematically.

If the birth rate in developing nations goes to European levels—around 1.7 per woman—in the distant future, then the total would become about 4 billion in developing countries. Many demographers have trouble visualizing that African countries will ever come down to 2.1 or 2.5 children per family, much less in the next 40 years, so this "low" scenario seems unlikely.

However, the rationale for thinking that such a drastic cut could happen is that, in Thailand and Taiwan and even Cuba, birth rates have fallen to below two children per woman in the last 30 years. Thailand's birth rate in the late 1960s was at six per family; it's now below two. Still, coun-

Originally appeared in the November/December 1997 issue of THE FUTURIST. Used with permission from World Future Society, 7910 Woodmont Avenue, Suite 450, Bethesda, Maryland 20814, 301/656-8274; http://www.wfs.org/wfs.

tries in Latin America remained at nearly three per woman for quite some time, despite economic development. Clearly, birth rates are influenced by culture as well as economics.

The medium projections, and uncertainty about the complex variables at play over the next 40–50 years, have led the media and public perception into a state of complacency, Haub worries. "Family planning can be quite successful in developing countries, and many couples are willing to take the necessary steps. However, if we feel we don't have to worry any more about global population growth, we're wrong," he says. "The real story is that the average birth rate in all developing countries is about four per person, down from six per person, but that rate needs to go to two per person to be stable, so we're halfway there."

The next 10 years will give a really good indication of where things are headed, Haub believes. India and Pakistan are huge wild cards, and so is Africa. A key question is how soon the birthrate revolution is going to take root in Africa.

"The present demographic situation makes a large increase in numbers a mathematical certainty; that is something we know," says Haub. "The great unknown is how large that increase will be."

Source: *1997 World Population Data Sheet* and interview with demographer Carl Haub. Population Reference Bureau, 1875 Connecticut Avenue, N.W., Suite 520, Washington, D.C. 20009. Telephone 1-202-483-1100; fax 1-202-328-3937; e-mail popref@prb.org; Web site www.prb.org/prb.

Article Review Form at end of book.

WiseGuide Wrap-Up

- Being aware of and understanding the challenges facing novice and beginning teachers will help prospective teachers make appropriate career choices.
- Effective mentoring is key to retaining effective teachers.
- Sufficient understanding of issues important to the general public can assist teachers in their efforts to advance the education profession.
- Public perception influences educational policy.
- The education profession has changed significantly during the past 20 years.
- Roles and expectations of teachers will continue to change as global demographics change.

R.E.A.L. Sites

This list provides a print preview of typical **coursewise** R.E.A.L. sites. There are over 100 such sites at the **courselinks**™ site. The danger in printing URLs is that web sites can change overnight. As we went to press, these sites were functional using the URL provided. If you come across one that isn't, please let us know via email to: webmaster@coursewise.com. Use your Passport to access the most current list of R.E.A.L. sites at the **courselinks**™ site.

Site name: U.S. Department of Education

URL: http://www.ed.gov/index.html

Why is it R.E.A.L.? This site includes a comprehensive review of current news, frequently asked questions and answers about the activities of the Department of Education, funding opportunities, press releases, and key speeches and testimonies. The site has links to federal resources, library resources, state agencies and resources, general information, educational organizations, curricular resources, and networking opportunities.

Key topics: curricular resources, federal funding, professional organizations, federal educational initiatives

Activity: Write a position statement on your opinion of the role of the federal government in public education.

Site name: CIESIN: Information for a Changing World

URL: http://infoserver.ciesin.org/

Why is it R.E.A.L.? This site provides information on global network development, science data management, training, education, and technical support. It has links to interactive applications, resources, information cooperatives, and education/training ideas.

Key topics: global demographics

Activity: All too often, we view our world from a narrow perspective. Working in pairs, write and deliver a 60-second public service announcement on the importance of global education initiatives.

section 2

Examining Our Beliefs: Understanding Our Heritage and Articulating Personal Philosophies

Learning Objectives

After reading the articles in this section, you will be able to:

- Discuss the importance of studying the history of education.
- Discuss the relationship between philosophical beliefs and actions.
- Discuss the impact that John Dewey and other key philosophers have had on American educational systems.
- Articulate a personal philosophy of education.

To understand the context of and rationale for modern educational systems, teachers must have a basic knowledge of the historical and philosophical foundations of education. Although the areas of emphasis may be different, historical and philosophical foundations of education are interrelated and mutually supportive. A study of historical foundations identifies trends and patterns of change, whereas a study of philosophical foundations attaches meaning to those trends and changes through logic and reason.

Preservice teachers have the potential to become leaders and agents of change in the education profession. Knowledge and understanding of past events enhance their ability to make judgments about present and future directions. Reflections on the past can lead to effective solutions to today's questions and can facilitate making accurate future projections. Specifically, a study of the history of education helps teachers to identify the origins of today's educational purposes, institutions, beliefs, and practices.

Just as a study of historical foundations helps teachers put into context the "what" (that is, current beliefs and practices), a study of philosophical foundations helps them to understand the "why" (reasons and rationale). This understanding, in turn, leads to a realization that beliefs affect actions. Thus, teachers base decisions about curriculum, classroom management, and instructional strategies on their personal philosophies of teaching and learning.

Readings in Section 2 will help preservice teachers to understand the historical and philosophical foundations of education and to utilize that knowledge to give contextual meaning to their own professional milieu. The first reading, "Why History of Education?," outlines numerous reasons for studying historical foundations and discusses goals of modern educational systems through a historical perspective. The next four readings—"Orientation to Philosophy of Education: Locating the Field of Play for New Audiences," "John Dewey: A Voice That Still Speaks to Us," "The Evolution of Philosophy of Education within Educational Studies," and "Constructivist Cautions"—summarize principles of key philosophers and selected philosophies representing diverse beliefs and contributions. The last reading, "Earning an 'A' in Idealism," illustrates the relationship between belief and action by discussing the design and implementation of community service projects.

Questions

Reading 6: Why should preservice teachers study the history of education? What are at least three objectives of today's modern educational systems?

Reading 7: What are four instructional strategies for helping preservice teachers to understand educational philosophy?

Reading 8: What was Dewey's concept of a democracy? Why has there been a resurgence of interest in Dewey's life and contributions to philosophy of education in the 1990s?

Reading 9: Briefly summarize the beliefs of one of the following philosophers: Isocrates, John Dewey, Montaigne, Bacon, Locke, R. S. Peters, Leo Strauss.

Reading 10: What is constructivism? Describe a constructivist classroom.

Reading 11: What are school-based service programs? What are some of the benefits that students who participate in community service programs experience? What are two or three obstacles that often hinder schools from implementing community service programs?

Why should preservice teachers study the history of education? What are at least three objectives of today's modern educational systems?

Why History of Education?

Herbert M. Kliebard
University of Wisconsin-Madison

History of education has become more or less entrenched as part of the professional education of teachers and school administrators. At one level, that inclusion makes a certain amount of sense. We are told vaguely that education professionals need a historical background or a historical perspective on their work, and these grounds are sometimes sufficient to justify the admittance of such a course into a professional program of study. But if we push that justification a step further and ask of what real value is that background or that perspective, we are sometimes hard pressed to find a persuasive answer. We are also told that we ought to study history because, as we all know, history repeats itself and, therefore, a knowledge of the subject will somehow guide our professional behavior in the right direction and thereby keep us from repeating old mistakes. Upon examination, however, that rationale leaves something to be desired as well. If history is supposed to guide us, how exactly does it provide such guidance?

When the renowned sociologist Emile Durkheim began to teach a required course for future secondary schoolteachers at the University of Paris in 1904–1905 titled History of Education in France, he felt obliged in his opening lecture to provide a rationale for why anyone should study history in the first place. Rejecting the idea that the function of any course in professional education is "a question of simply instructing our future teachers in how to apply a number of sound recipes," Durkheim developed his course around the nature of school culture and how it evolved over time. Deriving lessons from that approach, however, was no easy task. There is, he noted, the commonsensical assumption that because the past consists of a series of old mistakes anyway, a study of the past can keep us from repeating those mistakes. In rejecting that rationale, Durkheim argued:

> Since the realm of errors knows no bounds error itself can appear in an infinite variety of forms; a knowledge of the past made in the past will enable us neither to foresee nor to avert those which will be made in the future. (1977, pp. 8–9)

At best, historical awareness will keep us from repeating only a relative handful of that infinitude of mistakes.

Therefore, just as educational psychologists are not able to provide useful recipes for how to teach on the basis of their investigations into the nature of learning or human development, so historians of education can offer no guarantees against committing all sorts of pedagogical errors on the basis of their historical inquiries. Nevertheless, Durkheim (1977) promised his class of future teachers that, as a result of their explorations into history of education, they would be able ultimately "to get away from the prejudices both of neophobia and neophilia: and this is the beginning of wisdom" (pp. 8–9).

Theoretical training in education (pedagogie), for which history is the best vehicle, (Durkheim, 1977), should provide the capability to analyze one's own pedagogical context with wisdom and insight, not with

THE JOURNAL OF EDUCATIONAL RESEARCH, Vol. 88, No. 4, March/April 1995, pp. 194–199. Reprinted with permission of the Helen Dwight Reid Educational Foundation. Published by Heldref Publications, 1319 Eighteenth St., N.W., Washington, D.C. 20036-1802.

a shoe box full of ready-made solutions. Such training teaches us neither to fear the new and contemporary (neophobia) nor to delight in it uncritically (neophilia), and, conversely, it teaches us that although some ideas and practices of the past may have had some merit after all, certain commonly held assumptions that we have inherited from our professional and intellectual forebears need to be studied mainly as a way of getting rid of them. Unfortunately, there is no foolproof way of knowing which is which. Certainly, however, examining the way these ideas played themselves out in various historical contexts helps.

Perhaps, more than anything, what the study of the history of education can provide is not so much specific lessons pertaining to such matters as how to construct a curriculum or how to run a school as it is the development of certain habits of thought. Principal among these is the habit of reflection and deliberative inquiry, which is holding up the taken-for-granted world to critical scrutiny, something that usually can be accomplished more easily in a historical context than in a contemporary one. Ideas and practices that seem so normal and natural in a contemporary setting often take on a certain strangeness when viewed in a historical setting, and that strangeness often permits us to see those ideas and practices in a different light.

In the end, then, much of the value of studying the history of education lies not in providing us with answers, but in daring us to challenge the questions and the assumptions that our intellectual forebears have bequeathed to us. The key problem, often, is not to find an answer to a question but to get past it. John Dewey (1910) touched on this point in one of his most brilliant essays:

> Old ideas give way slowly; for they are more than abstract logical forms and categories. They are habits, predispositions, deeply ingrained attitudes of aversion and preference. Moreover, the conviction persists—though history shows it to be a hallucination—that all the questions that the human mind has asked are questions that can be answered in terms of the alternatives the questions themselves present. But, in fact, intellectual progress usually occurs through sheer abandonment of questions together with both of the alternatives they assume—an abandonment that results from their decreasing vitality and a change of urgent interest. We do not solve them: we get over them. (p. 19)

Conceivably, some of the questions that are most imbedded in contemporary thinking may be the very ones that are meaningless and need to be abandoned.

What follows is a small sample of these frequently taken-for-granted truths expressed as questions that, according to conventional wisdom, need answering. Locating them, however briefly, in their historical contexts may serve the purpose not of answering them but of casting as problematic the nature of the questions. These are three examples of questions, in other words, that we probably need to "get over."

What should be the goals that define the curriculum of schools?

Defining the goals of schooling has become a kind of cottage industry in the United States and in many other countries of the world. All of the 50 states, for example, have adopted an official list of such goals, and the recently enunciated national goals for the year 2000 have attracted an enormous amount of attention. Behind such goal stating is the widely held assumption that it is an indispensable first step to improving educational practice generally and in developing a curriculum in particular. Perhaps the most visible and most significant historical precedent for the practice of goal stating in education is the Cardinal Principles Report of the Commission on the Reorganization of Secondary Education (1918), with its immortal seven aims—health, command of fundamental processes, worthy home membership, vocation, civic education, worthy use of leisure, ethical character—set a pattern that has been much emulated and admired. Yet, if we ask ourselves in what ways has the educational enterprise been forwarded by that statement in its own time as well as by the many statements of aims that followed over the years, we would be hard pressed to find a good concrete example.

To be sure, all sorts of school practice have been justified by lists of intent of that sort, but, in all likelihood, those practices would have gone on anyway, even in the absence of such goals. The goals seem to function not so much as ideals to be achieved in a never-attained future, but as convenient justifications for what we would be doing anyway. The goal of "worthy use of leisure," for example, gives us license in school to teach everything from poetry to television watching. It does not give direction, however, as to how to distinguish between the commendable and the undeserving or how to differentiate between the worthy or the unworthy. Taking the list as a whole, the aims of the Cardinal Principles Report excludes practically nothing. Nevertheless, the ritual of goal stating is so well entrenched that it has become difficult even to imagine how we could proceed to develop a curriculum without goals. The process of goal stating may even become a surrogate for taking action. The goal of eradicating drugs from schools by the year 2000, for example, does not tell us anything about how that task could possibly be accomplished.

Instead of beginning the enterprise of curriculum making with the time-honored but essentially ritualistic process of stating goals to be achieved, we could begin simply by educating children in the best way we know how and proceed from there to build our understanding of what it means to educate them. To take a different historical example, one would search in vain for any formal statement of goals of the Laboratory School at the University of Chicago, which Dewey ran from 1896 to 1904. Dewey set forth his ideas on what should be accomplished not as laundry lists of goals but in ordinary (or perhaps not so ordinary) prose. His works of that period, such as *School and Society* and *The Child and the Curriculum,* are not filled with high-sounding declarations of intent but with serious efforts to untangle and address significant educational problems. These issues included such matters as the nature of the resources that children bring with them to school and how the school can adapt its structure and organization to those resources. They included as well such concerns as how the immediate and spontaneous interests of children can be transmuted over time into disciplined and sophisticated thought. They also took into account the relationship between the school as a social institution and society at large.

Contrary to popular belief, Dewey did not view activity as a good in itself. Neither did he believe that activity should be governed by predetermined goals. Appropriately designed activity, however, can provide the context from which goals may eventually emerge. Dewey, in other words, did not reject goals as such; he rejected the idea of goals as external to ongoing activity. According to Dewey, goals emerge and function within activity, making the activity richer and more educative. A goal is something that gives direction to present activity, not something enunciated prior to the activity and imposed from without. Once we engage in an activity, we can begin to foresee the probable consequences of that activity and make choices as to the direction in which that activity should be taken. Those directions *within* activity are, in effect, our goals, and only activity that is pointed in an appropriate direction can properly be deemed an educative activity.

Dewey commonly referred to goals not as ends or objectives but as ends-in-view; that is, for Dewey, goals insofar as they functioned at all were never fixed. As activities proceed, it is often desirable, indeed necessary, to change direction. To hold onto goals stated, as they often are, at the outset of a venture even when these goals prove to be unworkable or unworthy in the light of experience is contrary to ordinary common sense. (The curriculum of the Dewey school was substantially revamped after 2 years.) As we sail toward a distant point on the horizon, we begin to see something worthy of attainment beyond that point, and this frequently necessitates a change of course. If the experience of the Dewey school is any guide, we may properly understand goals, then, almost literally as "in view"; that is, they are what we *see* given our present vantage point, but we would be foolish if we did not change direction in line with the new vistas that emerge as we progress to that initially foreseen point on the horizon.

Stating precise and clearly defined goals at the outset of a venture is frequently defended on the ground that one needs such yardsticks against which to measure the success of the enterprise. This turns out to be a dangerous half-truth. In that context, Dewey (1939, pp. 40–43) once paraphrased Charles Lamb's story of the discovery of roast pork. According to Lamb's account, certain villagers were accustomed to keeping pigs in their homes. When one of the houses burned down, a villager touched one of the scorched pigs and, upon bringing his fingers to his lips, discovered how tasty roast pig was. Thereupon, the villagers burned down their houses to achieve their goal of roast pork.

The history of American education is replete with examples of educators burning down their educational houses to reach their announced goals, however trivial they may have been or whatever the devastation created by achieving them. The success of any educational enterprise is to be judged not in terms of whether the ends were accurately anticipated at the outset, but in terms of the worthiness of *all* the consequences of the activity including, or perhaps especially, the unintended ones.

Historically, then, we can look at two kinds of precedents

with respect to this issue. The Cardinal Principles precedent points in the direction of goal stating as a necessary, or at least desirable, prelude to curriculum decision making, but it may merely be in reality one of many empty rituals of schooling. The Dewey school alternative may have less appeal because it is more ambiguous, but it may in the end rest on sounder assumptions.

What educational experiences should be provided by schools to prepare children for the adult activities that they will one day be required to perform?

The common assumption that education is simply and inevitably a preparation for what lies ahead is related to the notion that stated goals are indispensable to curriculum planning. Both are a legacy from the period roughly of the 1920s when so-called scientific curriculum making was reaching its peak. Major leaders of that movement, such as Franklin Bobbitt, W. W. Charters, and David Snedden, proceeded from the assumption that a commendable curriculum could be devised by creating a comprehensive catalog of human activity and then, in effect, performing those activities successfully in school. In this respect, the curriculum became a rehearsal for a putative future, and it became important to know in fairly precise detail what that future held.

The mathematics curriculum, therefore, was built on mathematical activities that children would presumably perform in their adult lives. Thus, checkbook balancing virtually became the sine qua non of school mathematics because it was, presumably, a widespread mathematical activity in the adult world. For example, Snedden (1924, p. 11) stated that because only about 2% of the adult population actually performed algebraic operations, that subject should be reserved for only those few who were destined to use it. The same could be said for the study of foreign languages or poetry. A prediction as to what one would do in the future became the basis for what one would study in school.

To the modern ear, this sounds silly and stupid (or ought to), but many of the assumptions that are implicit in those practices of yesteryear are, curiously enough, also imbedded in modern thinking about the curriculum. The justification commonly given for why we should require all children to study computer science, for example, is that it will prepare them for a future world. In the present context as well as in the recent past, we perceive children as preparing for what lies ahead. The role of the computer in the society of the future, however, is unknown and probably unknowable. Computers are important in modern education not because of the need to train present-day children in how to use them for future use but, at least in part, to stimulate and refine children's cognitive processes and to give them a sense of efficacy in the world they now inhabit. At its best, computer science as a school subject is valuable because the computer represents a splendid instrument for enlarging understanding and engaging children in sophisticated intellectual activities here and now. To quote Dewey (1938, p. 51) once more:

> We always live at the time we live and not at some other time, and only be extracting at each present time the full meaning of each present experience are we prepared for doing something in the future. This is the only preparation which in the long run amounts to anything.

In my opinion, the most pervasive educational problem that schools face today is the rejection of school knowledge on the part of schoolchildren. Surely a good part of that problem derives from the time-honored assumption, first enunciated by the so-called scientific curriculum makers, that the knowledge that schools purvey is for a remote point in the future. Even the better students, in an academic sense, are not fooled by such promises. They simply tolerate what schools offer rather than rebel openly.

Bobbitt (1924, p. 8) once claimed that education is for the 50 years of adulthood, not for the 20 years of childhood and youth; and in the nearly 70 years since Bobbitt made that pronouncement, educators have tacitly assumed that schooling is something that children and youth have to endure on their way to becoming full-fledged, functioning adults. Dewey (1938) characterized this position as conceiving of the educational process as getting children ready for a remote world and, as a result, expelling them from social membership in the community. "They are looked upon as candidates," he said; "they are placed on the waiting list" (p. 63). For most of this century, schoolchildren have in effect been put on a waiting list to become adults, and the result has been their profound alienation and disaffection from schooling.

Reexamining the commonly accepted notion of education as preparation prompts us to begin to think that a good curriculum is one that purveys knowledge and understanding to enrich children's lives and that allows them to act effectively in the time and place they now occupy. Children will begin to see knowledge as important if the knowledge they get in school is of consequence to them in the immediate world in which they live, not in an imagined, distant, and often fanciful world of the future. It is in this way, not by surveying or anticipating adult activities, as the scientific curriculum makers of the 1920s and their ideological heirs believed, that the curriculum can bridge the gap between school knowledge and the world of affairs. Paradoxically, enabling children and youth to function effectively in the world they now inhabit by equipping them with the intellectual tools to make sense of that world may turn out to be, as Dewey (1916) suggested, the best preparation for that unknowable future.

Once again, examining an issue in the light of our historical experience casts a somewhat different light on issues of great moment. In particular, the idea that education is invariably and inevitably a preparation for what lies ahead seems somewhat less normal and natural, especially when seen in the light of the Deweyan alternative. Ironically, although Dewey is often cast as the quintessential American philosopher, his ideas on education seem curiously out of step with prevailing beliefs and doctrines. The ideas of the relatively obscure Bobbitt seem to resonate more directly with the way Americans then and now perceive the role and function of schooling.

How can schools meet the common and individual needs of children and youth?

One of the great historical confrontations of relatively recent times was the one that emerged in the 1950s between proponents of life-adjustment education and academic critics, such as the historian Arthur E. Bestor. With the best of intentions, life-adjustment reformers sought to deemphasize academic subject matter and to introduce into the curriculum a far more encompassing range of school activities, particularly those that were believed to function directly within people's lives. Bestor's favorite example of such an activity, how to bake a cherry pie, came to symbolize, over time, the anti-intellectual implications of life adjustment as a reform movement.

The even deeper issue that lay behind Bestor's often vitriolic and, as it turned out, effective criticisms of life-adjustment education was the role and function of the school itself. Does the school, as the life adjusters believed, exist to meet the common and individual needs of youth, including how to bake a cherry pie, or does it have a distinctive function to perform that no other social institution can perform successfully? In their zeal to break the bonds of what they saw as an inert and ineffective education, many educational reformers of that time failed to see the school as embedded in a nexus of other social institutions, all with their distinctive functions to perform. As a result, many of them tended to overestimate both the power and the responsibility of schooling.

The obvious implications of an overestimation of the power of schools lie mainly in the common tendency to ascribe to the school functions that it cannot realistically perform. In their eagerness to demonstrate the omnipotence of schooling, state legislatures, state departments of education, and even educators have indiscriminately assigned to schools responsibilities that cannot even remotely be accomplished by one social institution among many. Nevertheless, social problems of all sorts become incorporated willy-nilly as the responsibility of the schools; the result is a curriculum without direction, coherence, or purpose. It is in this sense that questions relating to "meeting the needs of children and youth" operate not so much as legitimate questions to be answered, but as slogan systems functioning to attract allegiances and build constituencies.

At best, the schools' assuming responsibility for correcting genuine and urgent social evils affirms American optimism about the power of education. It may also serve as a public relations function. At worst, however, that exaggerated conception of what schools can or should accomplish detracts from what they can reasonably be expected to do. It may even deflect criticism about the absence of genuinely constructive action regarding the social problems that schools have been assigned to address.

At the same time that American schools have become the focus for drug and alcohol abuse and unwanted pregnancies, critics have pointed to American schools' failure to teach science, literature, history, mathematics, and foreign languages as successfully as other industrialized nations. Yet, many of those critics fail to see the connection between a diffuse and indefinitely expanded curriculum on one hand and the failure to teach academic subjects successfully on the other. To give Bestor his due, this is precisely what his criticism of American schools was about. Baking a cherry pie and doing chemistry are not exactly incompatible; but time and effort consumed in doing one thing in practice takes away from the other, and Americans have traditionally been unwilling to make a choice. Whatever excesses Bestor may have been guilty of, he deserves credit for defining the function of schools in terms of a single overarching purpose rather than a potpourri of half-cooked ingredients. The distinctive and distinguishing purpose of schooling as he saw it was intellectual development, and that is not such a bad starting point after all.

Several recent studies have perceptively called attention to the glaring absence of purpose in American schools (Boyer, 1983; Goodlad, 1984). Surely, some of that absence is the result of such a diffusion of purposes that any guiding direction cannot emerge. This lack of focus results in what Dewey (1966) once called "a congestion in the curriculum" (p. 185). In one recent examination of the modern American high school, for example, Powell, Farrar, and Cohen (1985) noted that over 400 courses were being offered in a single high school. The report drew attention to the self-conscious neutrality that governs the matter of what to study.

In part, this state of affairs is the result of the tendency to overestimate and therefore to overstate what schools can actually do. A likely consequence of this situation is the diminution, and perhaps even the subverting, of the power that schools do have: the raising up of a new generation ready to address the problems they and their society face, equipped with the intellectual resources that lie imbedded in the disciplines of knowledge to deal with those problems. Another consequence of a lack of focus in the curriculum is the failure to see the role of the school in relation to other socializing agencies. Families, law enforcement officials, social work agencies, health clinics, and care providers of all sorts share in the socializing of the young. Sharing and even subordinating the schools' role with respect to many urgent matters of social concern may bring to the fore the schools' special role in intellectual development.

Recognizing intellectual development as the overarching purpose of schooling, however, is only the barest first step. As astute as Bestor was in recognizing the deficiencies of life-adjustment education, he stopped short of interpreting what an intelligent command of the modern world really means. It is that task that still needs to be pursued, not a well-meaning but inevitably futile attempt to make American schools the supreme socializing agency. Seen in this light, "meeting the needs of youth" as a way of defining the function of schooling is probably the most pernicious slogan ever to enter into curriculum discourse. A far more benign one would be Theodore Sizer's (1984) dictum "Less is more."

In one respect, the annals of American history in the 20th century at least help to document a movement in the direction of an indefinite expansion of the school curriculum. On a case-by-case basis, each of the claimants for a place in the curriculum can appear to make a plausible argument that the needs and interests of students will somehow be met. In retrospect, the cumulative effect of such a policy has been disastrous. The American curriculum has become so diffuse and incoherent that any sense of a central mission has become obliterated.

All three of the questions discussed here are so imbedded in modern curriculum thought that we rarely stop to examine their salience or worthiness. Questions such as what the objectives of schooling are or how to prepare children for their adult lives or how to meet their needs have acquired over the years such a taken-for-granted quality that we almost automatically proceed to try to answer them rather than hold them up to critical examination. Somehow seeing those questions played out in a different time and under different social circumstances serves the purpose of casting them as something less than normal and natural. As Dewey argued, real advances are rarely made by doggedly pursuing the answers to questions that in effect have no answers; and one effect of casting those questions in historical perspective is to begin to see them in a fresh light, leading, perhaps, even to abandoning them.

In the end, we might as well admit that historical inquiry will not provide a solution to any urgent educational problem. The lessons of the history of education are obviously not lessons in the ordinary sense. Instead, history invites us to reinterpret old questions and sometimes to cast them aside in order to pave the way for new ones. At its best, history provides us with a record of our cumulative experience and suggests how that experience may be interpreted. The renditions of certain traditional questions provided here are undoubtedly subject to other interpretations that may lead to quite different conclusions; nevertheless, if the study of the history of education unearths old and often-buried assumptions imbedded in the questions we ask and thereby exposes them to critical scrutiny, it could be of some real use after all.

References

Bobbitt, F. (1924). *How to make a curriculum.* Boston, MA: Houghton Mifflin.

Boyer, E. L. (1983). *High School: A report on secondary education in America* (pp. 43–57). Carnegie Foundation for the Advancement of Teaching. New York: Harper & Row.

Commission on the Reorganization of Secondary Education (1918). *The cardinal principles of secondary education.* Bulletin No. 35. Washington, DC: U.S. Printing Office.

Dewey, J. (1910). The influence of Darwin on philosophy. *The influence of Darwin on philosophy and other essays in contemporary thought.* New York: Holt.

Dewey, J. (1916). *Democracy and education.* New York: Macmillan.

Dewey, J. (1938). *Experience and education.* New York: Macmillan.

Dewey, J. (1939). Foundations of the unity of science (No. 4). In *International encyclopedia of unified science* (Vol. 2, pp. 40–43). Theory of Valuation, 2(4). Chicago, IL: University of Chicago Press.

Dewey, J. (1966). *Lectures in the philosophy of education: 1899* (R. D. Archambault, Ed.). (Vol. 85). New York: Random House.

Durkheim, E. (1977). *The evolution of educational thought: Lectures on the formation and development of secondary education in France* (P. Collins, Trans.). London: Routledge & Kegan Paul.

Goodlad, J. I. (1984). *A place called school.* New York: McGraw-Hill.

Powell, A. G., Farrar, E., & Cohen, D. K. (1985). *The shopping mall high school: Winners and losers in the educational marketplace.* Boston, MA: Houghton Mifflin.

Sizer, T. R. (1984). *Horace's compromise: The dilemma of the American high school.* Boston, MA: Houghton Mifflin.

Snedden, D. (1924, November 1). Education for a world of team-players and team-workers. *School and Society, 20*(11).

Article Review Form at end of book.

What are four instructional strategies for helping preservice teachers to understand educational philosophy?

Orientation to Philosophy of Education

Locating the field of play for new audiences

David P. Ericson

David P. Ericson is Professor and Chair, Department of Educational Foundations, University of Hawaii at Manoa, 1776 University Ave., Honolulu, HI 96822. His primary area of scholarship is philosophy of education.

Introducing students to the field of philosophy of education can be a vexing problem for even the most experienced philosopher of education. Most students, whether in preservice teacher education programs or in graduate programs in schools and colleges of education, come to the field with little preparation and background in philosophy as a discipline of inquiry. Consequently, they lack even a rudimentary starting point that might allow them to begin engagement with the issues, problems, and ideals that have occupied the attention of philosophers of education in this and previous centuries. In addition, students in preservice teacher education programs are especially difficult to engage. Typically, they are concerned most about simple survival in classrooms and schools. Thus, they are likely to approach foundational courses in philosophy of education with a mixture of apprehension and disdain. The apprehension is a result of having to deal with a subject that is arcane to them, while the disdain emanates from a vague preconception that philosophy, whatever it is, is impractical and useless in helping them to master the nuts and bolts of classroom survival.

A variety of pedagogical strategies are current in introducing students to philosophy of education—strategies adopted by both professors of philosophy of education as well as authors of materials for use in introductory philosophy of education courses. The first strategy is to treat philosophy of education as the *history* of the philosophy of education. Here, there may be no special attempt to motivate the field as being particularly relevant to the nuts and bolts of classroom survival. Rather, such courses are often surveys of what particular historical thinkers thought about education. Students are simply left to their own devices in making application of the ideas and arguments presented to their own practice. It is not surprising that few students make these connections, and so the preconception is strengthened that philosophy of education has little or nothing to offer practicing educators.

The second strategy, which often draws on the historical record as well, is to present philosophy of education as a clash of *isms:* realism, idealism, empiricism, rationalism, pragmatism, existentialism, and so on. Such an approach takes issues concerning the nature of reality, human beings (persons), and human learning and knowing and attempts to deduce implications for educational practice. The "isms" approach takes the relevance problem seriously and tries to establish why philosophy of education, in this guise, is of great

"Orientation to Philosophy of Education: Locating the Field of Play for New Audiencies" by David P. Ericson from *Educational Theory,* Fall 1997, Vol. 47, No. 4, pp. 501–511, © 1997 Board of Trustees, University of Illinois.

importance to practitioners. While authors and teaching faculty often have their favorite "ism" and try to convince students of its worthiness, it is a great distance, indeed, from the metaphysical and epistemological assumptions of the "ism" to prescriptions for classroom practice. There is a lot of room for dubious premises to be smuggled in, and that is often a royal invitation for loose and fuzzy thinking that an earlier generation of analytic philosophers of education often took great pains to expose. While students were often invited to adopt an "ism" of their own, a personal guide to their own practice, such adoption need not reflect a further adoption of the critical spirit or a reflective attitude, something (whatever else one's intellectual commitments) we might hope is stimulated in philosophy of education courses. The problem of distance from practice, as well, might easily raise questions of whether the journey from metaphysical assumptions is worth it. Finally, the whole grand systems approach is only as strong as the initial assumptions themselves. Strong anti-foundationalist arguments have made the "isms" approach seem as sturdy as a house of cards.[1]

The third pedagogical strategy often resembles the first approach, the historical approach, but with a critical twist. Rather than simply laying out historical philosophers' views on education, the author or professor engages in critical dialogue with their views and arguments presented, an approach that appraises strengths and probes weaknesses. This strategy has the virtue of attempting to stimulate in students a critical spirit. But, as with the first approach, when confronted with students who care only about mastering the nuts and bolts of classroom practice, it has the weakness of often failing to address the question of relevance. Why should students bother learning what this or that philosopher said—especially when they never seem to really get it right? What real import, after all, might it have for my teaching? In trying to respond to these questions, we often point out that for every adopted classroom practice there are implicit philosophical assumptions—assumptions typically examined by many of these historical figures. By explicitly testing them, we thereby come to understand that our own teaching practice requires reason and moral justification. While this kind of response should make sense to us, as purveyors of the critical spirit, it may only appeal to the already-committed. And there's the rub.

The fourth and final pedagogical strategy to be outlined here is generally nonhistorical in approach. Rather, it tends to be problem- or concept-oriented. Historical figures are mentioned only when their views and analyses bear importantly on the issue or concept under discussion. Typically, it does address the issue of relevancy in two ways. First, by using a problem or concept format, it is able to elicit student interest because of its focus upon deep and perennial problems and concepts in education that *any* committed student in education *should* be interested in. Second, because this kind of approach tries to get students to grapple seriously with the conundrum or concept, including taking issue with the author or professor, it seeks to give students a feel for what it is to think in a forthright philosophical manner. It is an attempt to get students to engage, from the inside, in the activities of philosophy. Often this kind of approach presupposes no special interest on the part of students in philosophy of education. Rather, it proffers a promissory note to the effect that if students are willing to struggle toward doing philosophy, they will come to appreciate the power of philosophical methods of analysis, not merely for self-consciously doing philosophy but also as a *way* of thinking that can be usefully applied to all facets of life. As a result, many authors and teachers of philosophy of education, in this vein, are themselves self-consciously methodological in their approach. By discussing and dissecting the elements of philosophical method, they attempt to ease the way for students to do philosophy on their own.[2]

The books under review here—F. Raymond McKenna's *Philosophical Theories of Education*, Nel Noddings's *Philosophy of Education*, and Francis Schrag's *Back to Basics*—exemplify varying degrees of these four pedagogical strategies.[3] In what follows, then, I would like to trace out these books to show how these strategies fall into place and to discern what is unique and valuable to each of them.

1. See, for example, Frederick S. Ellett, Jr. and David P. Ericson, "In Defense of Public Reason: On the Nature of Historical Rationality," *Educational Theory* 47, no. 2 (Spring 1997): 133–61.

2. See, for example, Thomas F. Green, *The Activities of Teaching* (New York: McGraw-Hill, 1971) and Jonas F. Soltis, *An Introduction to the Analysis of Educational Concepts* (Reading, Mass.: Addison-Wesley, 1968).

3. F. Raymond McKenna, *Philosophical Theories of Education* (Lanham, Md.: University Press of America, 1995); Nel Noddings, *Philosophy of Education* (Boulder, Colo.: Westview Press, 1995); and Francis Schrag, *Back to Basics* (San Francisco: Jossey-Bass, 1995). These works will be referred to as *PTOE*, *POE*, and *BTB* with page numbers in the text for all subsequent citations.

McKenna's Orientations

McKenna's *Philosophical Theories of Education* is explicitly designed for "people preparing to teach" (*PTOE,* preface). While McKenna's own orientation to philosophy of education appears to be a throwback to the isms approach rarely seen today in professional circles of philosophy of education, he expressly eschews that pedagogical strategy. As he says,

> The thing to do, then, is to back far enough away from all "isms" until one can see basic differences and similarities. At that place, one can locate the three basic starting places from which all "isms" originate (*PTOE,* p. 30).

The "three basic starting places" are *Milieu* (one's natural and social surroundings), *Self* (the knowing, organizing power), and *Reality* (that which cannot be reduced to either of the foregoing and sometimes transcends them) (*PTOE,* p. 30). McKenna uses each of these three "intellectual orientations" to organize the predominant parts of his book. Each orientation, then, is further subdivided into three aspects: (1) a historical survey of pertinent intellectual movements in philosophy, axiology, politics, and religion; (2) educational theorists exemplifying a dominant orientation to milieu, self, or reality; and (3) what he calls "professional theories" for education implied by each of the three intellectual orientations.

Professional theories for education, themselves, contain two aspects: (1) organizing premises derived from philosophy, science, or both, and (2) tested practices derived from experienced practitioners (*PTOE,* p. 29). McKenna passes over any discussion of tested practices, while preferring to concentrate on the organizing premises aspect of professional theory. In doing so, he attempts to show how the organizing premises exemplified in the historical intellectual movements and thinking of particular educational theorists of each orientation respond to the why, how, and what of the teaching/learning encounter (*PTOE,* p. 30).

While the pedagogical strategy selected by McKenna disfavors the "isms" approach, it is clearly reliant upon it. Intellectual and social movements and educational theorists are set side-by-side historically and discussed in terms of their "ism" orientation. Yet, predominantly, this is a work located within the first category of pedagogical strategies: the historical one. McKenna is content to describe each intellectual movement and the thought of each historical educational theorist in their own terms. He notes when they agree or disagree, when they compare or contrast, but he does little to engage in critical dialogue with any of them. His more ultimate concern is to show how they eventuate in implications for the development of professional theory for education. Each intellectual orientation yields a partial perspective for this development. It is clear that through a dialectic among milieu, self, and reality McKenna believes that we can make, at the very least, progress toward the prize of a professional theory of education.

As McKenna notes, teacher education programs are often criticized for the ambiguity of their goals and for what passes for "theory." Much of this "is a jumble of opinions, beliefs, knowledge, tested and untested practices—often incompatible—and derived from common sense, business practices, politics, remnants of the Progressive Education movement, and a smattering of philosophy, psychology, and sociology" (*PTOE,* p. 5). What it lacks and what it needs are the "organizing premises" that he believes will emerge out of the philosophic (and scientific) dialectic among milieu, self, and reality. Noting that a professional theory of education, like law and medicine, is not as scientific as theories found in physics or engineering, given the differing nature of the subject matter, McKenna claims that such "lifebased" theories still will enable practitioners ". . . who have mastered it to outperform consistently those practitioners lacking such mastery" (*PTOE,* pp. 13–14).

This, then, is the heart of McKenna's project: to shed light on the organizing premises for a professional theory of education that can be taught to students in teacher preparation programs. But how well does McKenna's project measure up against this goal? And how reachable is the goal itself?

First, because of McKenna's method of simply surveying the historical record of what philosophers have said about education, he does not take us far toward elucidating which *particular* premises should comprise a professional theory of education. He would have fared far better by attempting to elucidate such principles themselves and dispensing with the thumbnail sketches of the educational theorists. But here he really has little to say. Second, there is a serious ambiguity in his own aims in this book. While the intended audience is students in preservice teacher education programs, his overall project is actually more suitable for practicing philosophers of education who already possess the historical background knowledge in far greater depth than he develops here. Thus, while he might impress preservice teachers with the need for a professional theory of education, the fact that he fails to develop one that would be useful to novice practitioners is a weakness that counts against using this book in a preservice teacher education program. In my judgment, preservice students will at best be bewildered by this book, while practicing philosophers of education, because of the elementary level of treatment, will not be much impressed. The fact, too, that McKenna does not seem to be very familiar with the recent literature in philosophy of education—only a handful of philosophers and philosophers of education writing after 1950 are mentioned—does not inspire much confidence in McKenna's command of the field. The notion of organizing premises is an interesting one, however, that should be developed at a far more sophisticated level than offered here.

Finally, in response to the question of whether this project is even feasible, I have some serious reservations. While, doubtless, a professional theory of education would be a wonderful thing to have, I am less confident than McKenna about what it would look like. As he notes, it would be a combination of settled philosophy and science (especially social science) that elucidate the organizing principles or premises brought together in conjunction with the practical wisdom of experienced practitioners. McKenna recognizes that neither sociology or psychology of education has been able to stand up to the task of developing a good set of principles based upon empirical knowledge (*PTOE*, pp. 14–15).[4] And controversy in philosophy of education is a constant, even though the field is more amenable to developing the kind of organizing premises that McKenna calls for. Would it do, even as a pilot project, to extract organizing premises from John Dewey's mature thinking on education? Apparently not, according to McKenna. Even though Dewey offers, arguably, one of the most comprehensive educational theories, McKenna cites him as predominantly a milieu theorist, while a professional theory of education, in his terms, requires organizing premises drawn from all three intellectual orientations. If Dewey's thought is partial in perspective, what hope do we have of even beginning to approach McKenna's lofty goals?

A Philosophical Primer on Education

In her excellent work, *Philosophy of Education,* Noddings takes a very different stance toward introductory philosophy of education. Whereas McKenna only briefly forayed into the twentieth century, Noddings's prime concern is twentieth century philosophy of education. There is a brief nod, in the form of a single chapter, to pre-twentieth century developments, but even here she tries to relate earlier philosophers and movements to contemporary thinkers and issues. *Philosophy of Education* is published as part of the Dimensions of Philosophy Series, under general editors Norman Daniels, Lehrer, and Noddings, joins such illustrious company as Elliott Sober on philosophy of biology, Peter van Inwagen on metaphysics, Keith Lehrer on epistemology, and Clark Glymour on philosophy of science, to name just a few. The series is meant to be accessible to students in the various branches and areas of philosophy, yet also reflect current debate on prominent issues by contemporary thinkers in the various fields.

In *Philosophy of Education,* Noddings adopts a pedagogical strategy that lies halfway between our third and fourth approaches: critical history of philosophy of education and an issues and concepts strategy. While the book is aimed at a level that is, perhaps, too elementary for graduate students in philosophy of education, it may serve as a good source book for summarizing some of the current debates in philosophy of education and so be useful as a background reference work. Just how suitable it is for non-philosophy of education graduate students in education and preservice teacher education students is something that I shall take up below.

In exemplifying a hybrid approach, Noddings spends the first four chapters out of a total of ten on a mildly to fairly critical discussion of (1) pre-twentieth century philosophers of education, (2) Dewey's philosophy of education, (3) analytic philosophy of education that centers on the analysis of "teaching," and (4) a brief characterization of approaches to philosophy of education arising out of the continental tradition (existentialism, phe-nomenology, critical theory, hermeneutics, and postmodernism in continental guise). The next five chapters concern

4. Though McKenna states that they are simply immature sciences, I believe that the reasons for their failure are more deep-seated and complex.

themselves with major branches of philosophy—logic, epistemology, philosophy of social science, ethics, and social and political philosophy—and how they might be usefully applied to problems, concepts, and issues of widespread interest to educators. The final chapter, in a more personal vein, is devoted to feminist perspectives and critiques of philosophy, philosophy of education, and educational practices. This arises out of Noddings's own well-known work in arguing for a feminist perspective on moral education.[5]

As an example of Noddings's manner of approach in *Philosophy of Education,* consider her discussion in Chapter 7 entitled "Philosophy of Social Science and Educational Research." In the previous chapter on epistemology and education, Noddings rehearses the "justified-true-belief" conception of knowledge, problems concerning the concept of truth, foundationalism, and non-foundationalist theories of knowledge that have resulted from criticisms of foundationalist accounts. She closes with a critical discussion of constructivist views in mathematics and science education. Chapter 7 then picks up on these strands and shows how they apply to contemporary accounts of the nature and growth of scientific knowledge and educational research.

Here she begins the discussion with Karl Popper's falsificationism as an alternative to confirmational theories and shows how it may be applied to the contemporary debate in psychology over the subject of repressed and recovered memories in alleged abuse victims (usually women). In showing how this scientific debate occurs within a context of wider social, political, legal, and ethical beliefs concerning abuse victims, Noddings relates that any application of falsificationism and the requirement that accusations arising out of "recovered" memories be subjected to strict scrutiny can lead to "blaming the victim" and subsequent counterclaims that science in this mode "protects males" and even exemplifies "a system of corrupt science."

While such politically—and ethically—infused charges might be made of an insensitive use of strict falsification, Noddings does not question whether there might be other (and perhaps better) grounds for rejecting Popper's account (namely, the truth status of observational statements used to falsify knowledge claims). But failing a full discussion, she proceeds to examine Imre Lakatos's views on the growth of scientific knowledge as an improvement on Popper, one that takes "research programs," rather than individual knowledge claims, to be the object of philosophical and scientific analysis and one that provides a better understanding of the relation of political views and values to the growth of science. She then relates how a Lakatosian treatment might be applied to the recovered memory debate, but does not critically assess its strengths and weaknesses.

Instead, Noddings shows how, alternatively, the recovered memory debate might be viewed as a Kuhnian paradigm clash. In exploring what this means, she notes that Kuhn argues that such disputes between differing schools sometimes are indicative of incommensurable assumptions held by each. Here she states that Kuhn (apparently) holds that there are no rational standards or criteria by which we might evaluate the claims (or programs) of each; instead, Kuhn allows for resolution of such revolutionary periods of science on only extra-rational grounds of politics and values.[6] At any rate, while Noddings's own explicit leanings are to the view that science (whether natural or social) is suffused with values such that political or moral bias is unavoidable, she moderates such claims with the observations that such bias can be mitigated and that (through meta-languages) rational comparison of clashing paradigms is possible. This would seem to indicate that Noddings believes that clashing paradigm disputes can be resolved on rational grounds either by proclaiming one paradigm to be rationally preferable or by showing how such clashes result in a rationally superior new paradigm that arises out of the dispute between the old ones. And this despite her view that science cannot escape the domain of values. (She takes up this view in greater depth in her final chapter on feminism, philosophy, and education.)

In the final section of this chapter, Noddings attempts to illustrate how a new paradigm may emerge out of the clash between two older ones by exploring the hoary quantitative vs. qualitative dispute in educational and social science research. She recognizes that it may be stretching it to call this debate a clash of paradigms that are in some senses incommensurable with one another. In this I think she is right to be cautious, for arguably it might better be perceived as a debate based on ram-

5. See, for example, Nel Noddings, *Caring: A Feminine Approach to Ethics and Moral Education* (Berkeley, University of California Press, 1984).

6. I think it can be shown that this is a misconstrual of Kuhn.

pant conceptual confusion, since it just is true that phenomena have properties or attributes (qualities) that can be quantified and measured. At this level, at least, the dispute is just plain silly.

However, Noddings connects the quantitative vs. qualitative dispute to a more interesting one: naturalistic social science vs. nonnaturalistic social science. Should educational and social science research be modeled on the natural sciences or is there something about the nature of social and educational phenomena that dictate a different kind of treatment from natural phenomena? And while the natural sciences may yield us truth about the natural world, is it the case that we have to settle for something like "plausibility" (or "likely stories" as Plato would derisively put it in another context) in social inquiry? These issues have to do with ontology, truth, rationality, and realism in natural and social inquiry.

Noddings basically skirts the deep issues here, while letting the reader know that it makes sense to ask radical narrative researchers who have seemingly abandoned all rational standards for assessing their claims whether their stories are "true." She does, however, indicate that a *rapprochement* is in the offing between less radical quantitative and qualitative theorists in educational and social science research, at least on a surface level. But even if quantitative researchers admit the usefulness of qualitative methods and qualitative researchers finally discover that it is sometimes sensible to want to count and measure things in education, this is not a very interesting example of a "paradigm shift" in Kuhnian terms. For here the deeper issues beckon and on these Noddings has little to say. In all fairness, however, I should note that any thorough discussion of these would go well above the introductory reader's head.

Finally, in this chapter, as in all others, Noddings provides a list of summary questions that usefully probe for understanding. They also serve as an excellent place to begin classroom inquiry.

In her treatment of the work of philosophers of education and current debates in philosophy of education, Noddings is balanced and judicious. The prose itself is clear, so that the reader is not left in a position of having to make inferential leaps in order to follow the exposition of a position, yet sufficiently lively that his or her intelligence is not underestimated by belaboring a point or issue. In the more critical aspects of Noddings' presentation, the reader is carried along to see the crux of an issue or argument and she uses a fairly wide range of sources (including her own) in exploring inadequacies of arguments and pointing the way to more promising directions. This is a fine textbook approach to philosophy of education in this century.

The question that remains is whether the work is likely to appeal to a broad range of non-philosophy of education graduate students in education and to preservice teacher education students. While there is no substitute for learning from experience in using the book, I project that the results will be mixed. Despite her attempts to make it lively and interesting by sometimes alluding to contemporary debates on age-old problems in education, I believe that Noddings's book will be least successful in engaging these students when she adopts the historical approach and simply elucidates what philosophers of education have said or what this or that philosophical school of thought comes to. On the other hand, where the book is most likely to be successful on this criterion is when she shows how philosophy can be applied to contemporary problems and issues in a way that yields new perspectives on them. She does this most effectively in the chapters on critical thinking, philosophy of social science and educational research, social and political philosophy, and on feminist views concerning philosophy and education. But these are only four chapters out of ten and they all come in the second half of the book. Here students have the opportunity, if they are willing to struggle, to join in the debate along with Noddings. Even so, preservice teacher education students may find that the content goes over their heads, since my experience tells me that they have not in the past thought very deeply about these issues, if they have thought of them at all.

Thus, in the final analysis, I believe that Noddings has written an excellent textbook that does a fine job of covering most of the contemporary perspectives on philosophy of education. But on my view that is a problem. It reads too much like a textbook, given over to too much exegesis and not enough grappling with the issues. And while it is probably not sufficiently sophisticated for a graduate level seminar in philosophy of education, except as a background resource book, it is probably too sophisticated for undergraduate preservice teacher education courses. Perhaps my experience is idiosyncratic in not having a great deal of success in using textbooks of this sort—even in graduate level introduction to philosophy of education courses—others may find it an extremely valuable direct instructional resource. But I just do not think that it goes far enough or fast enough in getting students on the inside of the activities of philosophy of education.

Schrag's Fundamentals

Schrag's slim volume entitled *Back to Basics* most successfully meets the test of relevance and speed of introduction into the activities of philosophy of education of the books under review here. It will not be without controversy among philosophers of education about just exactly what he has accomplished here, however. For some may argue that he is not really doing philosophy of education at all, but rather is engaged in some other project. That remains to be seen.

The title of the book is a bit of mischief on Schrag's part. He plays on the standard conservative call for a return to an educational emphasis on basic skills, good old phonics instruction, the celebration of "traditional" American values, and the memorization of historical facts and figures, while he clearly locates himself squarely in the middle of the progressive tradition in American thought and Deweyan pragmatism. Since progressivism and Dewey are *bêtes noir* among traditional conservatives, Schrag's title selection is certain to raise their hackles, if not get their goat. Schrag, however, clarifies his project in the preface to the book: "My title refers not to the three R's, but to the basic educational questions our society, indeed any society, must grapple with" (*BTB*, p. xi). And after acknowledging his partial indebtedness to Dewey, he states clearly, "I hope it reads neither like a conventional textbook nor like a work designed to impress learned colleagues at tenure time" (*BTB*, p. xi). Here only part of his hope is fulfilled. It clearly does not read as a conventional textbook. On the other hand, despite Schrag's avowal, and despite the fact that the book is clearly designed to appeal to a broad lay audience of nonspecialists in philosophy of education—including preservice teacher education students—the lucid writing and the keen insights of the book *should* impress learned colleagues at tenure or any other time. This is the recipe for Schrag's success: unconventionality, while at the same time making it irresistible to join battle with Schrag's arguments in such a way that you do not even realize that you are doing philosophy of education.

Schrag's fundamental questions for education form the basis for his book and lead to a chapter-by-chapter division of labor on such concepts in education as educational aspirations, curriculum, teaching, accountability, authority, inequality, and change. While he is clear on his philosophy of education, his target is mainly what the schools in our society—especially the public schools—should be about. And in keeping with his progressive philosophy, he early on takes issue with educational conservatives who stress what students should know or be able to demonstrate:

> Isn't our adult concern with the next generation ultimately a concern with the kind of people they will *be* and with what they will or will not *do?* What finally determines people's character and their actions is not what they could demonstrate at some earlier point or what they once understood, but what they can learn to do, what they're disposed to do, and what they care about (*BTB*, p. 6).

Though the entire book pushes this rhetorical line, Schrag sets the preliminary basis for his view in a Rawlsian-type thought experiment in which individuals with all types of belief and ideology come together to prescribe principles for the education of successive generations. Without knowing what society will look like in the future or of their descendants' powers and place within it, Schrag initiates the argument that, despite all of their differences, they could settle only on the following three principles or aspirations:

1. Our descendants should care about arguments and evidence bearing on any course of action or conclusion they are contemplating.
2. They should be disposed to continue their own learning.
3. To the extent possible, they should have developed the capacity to continue that learning (BTB, pp. 9–11).

The remainder of the book involves the attempt to flesh out how these principles would underwrite and operate in the various aspects of schooling mentioned above. Schrag considers and rejects alternative perspectives and arguments that would push in a different direction—especially those representing the conservative tradition in American life, but also religious fundamentalists, more radical leftists, religious and other communitarians, and ethnic separatists. He does so with admirable clarity, accessibility to nonphilosophers, and verve, and he is terribly unapologetic about trying to make the case. Some of the claims he makes are so baldly stated that at times I found myself nearly infuriated. But that is part of the fun in this book. It does not merely beguile you into taking up issue or argument with Schrag no matter what your sympathies are—and I am on the whole sympathetic with his basic position—it impels you right into the thick of things. If any introduction to philosophy of education is likely to grab the attention of preservice teacher education students and nonphilosophy graduate students in education, then I don't think that we can do better than with this little book. But—and this is the kicker—is this really a work in philosophy of education?

Noddings, in the introduction to *Philosophy of Education*, raises precisely this issue. In choosing to concentrate on the traditional content of philosophy and philosophy of education, she states:

> Some of the liveliest contemporary [introductory] treatments [by philosophers of education] have all but abandoned what might be called the *content* of philosophy and concentrate instead on applying a clarity of thought (characteristic of philosophical method) to serious problems of education (*POE*, p. 2).

This is a most apt description for what Schrag is up to in *Back to Basics*. For instance, in examining the book's index, the reader will find no entry on epistemology, moral philosophy or ethics, metaphysics or logic, philosophy of science or philosophy of mind, or social and political philosophy. In terms of individuals cited, beyond Dewey, there are only a few other philosophers or philosophers of education. Most of the citations are to empirical studies needed to help substantiate a large number of clearly empirical claims that Schrag uses in his overall argument. Schrag himself makes no bones about what he is doing, for he begins the book with this question, "What's a philosopher of education good for, if not to help people think about education in a deeper and clearer way than they otherwise would?" (*BTB*, p. xi). Though Schrag does not drag into his arguments the heavy machinery or philosophical vocabulary that we would expect in a book written by a philosopher of education for other philosophers of education, and though he is not self-conscious on the matter of philosophical method in the way that Jonas Soltis or Tom Green are, he defends his approach as a work in philosophy of education in this way:

> Philosophers concentrate on asking fundamental questions and try to defend them by means of persuasive argumentation. . . . When it comes to education, philosophers ask general questions about the proper aims of education, the most reasonable basis for selecting what students ought to study, and the way in which and the extent to which schools ought to be responsive to demands from the broader society, among many other topics. Philosophers of education see as their primary mission posing and answering the most basic questions (*BTB*, p. 1).

Whatever else it is, *Back to Basics* is about asking and answering some fundamental questions in education. While it does not have the scope and survey to philosophy of education nor the greater sophistication to be found in Noddings's treatment, I believe that Schrag makes the case that it is undeniably a work within philosophy of education proper. Moreover, it proffers the additional bonus of appeal to specialists and nonspecialists alike. As a springboard to deeper and more trenchant reflection and argumentation, I would not hesitate to use it in graduate seminars in philosophy of education. But imagine, too, my surprise and delight to see *Back to Basics* being used by my colleagues in their own undergraduate teacher education courses—colleagues who are anything but specialists in philosophy of education. Schrag has accomplished a major service to the field by amply showing the relevance of philosophy to education. And that is no mean feat.

Article Review Form at end of book.

What was Dewey's concept of a democracy? Why has there been a resurgence of interest in Dewey's life and contributions to philosophy of education in the 1990s?

John Dewey

A voice that still speaks to us

David Halliburton

David Halliburton is Professor of English, Modern Thought and Literature, and Comparative Literature at Stanford. He also is the founder of both the Center for Teaching and Learning and the Program for Faculty Renewal.

In a recent *AAHE Bulletin* article, a university administrator echoed John Dewey by calling for closer ties between the academy and the larger community, while on the same page a senior professor uttered a Deweyan call "to create ways of reconnecting with one another that fit the way we now live." In these as in many other instances, Dewey's still-timely voice is reaching listeners who are either new to his ideas or newly receptive to them.

A surge of scholarly interest, beginning in the 1980s, has led major presses to publish several ambitious studies of Dewey; this decade, his *Democracy and Education* is being read in 25 languages. The similarity between our 1990s and his 1890s is another factor in our growing sense of Dewey's timeliness. Now, as then, the hungry and the homeless challenge social resources; crime, drugs, and poverty plague overcrowded cities; and school systems struggle to provide immigrant children with the education they need to survive. In that period and ever since, Dewey, speaking as our most public and intellectual of public intellectuals, has left us a host of ideas on which to reflect.

The Public Intellectual

For advice, our forebears hearkened to the voices of Enlightenment shapers of opinion like Montesquieu, Adam Smith, and Jefferson, who exemplified the public intellectual of that time. Emerson—Dewey's "philosopher of democracy"—assumed that role in the 19th century, to be followed in the 20th by Walter Lippmann, Lewis Mumford, and Hannah Arendt. But above all, educators (and many others) remember Dewey himself; and what this current revival is about is how best to comprehend his contributions to education and the larger public interest and how best to make use of them.

Born in 1859, Dewey belonged to the first generation of American professors of philosophy who were not clergymen. But Dewey was always much more than a professor or philosopher. Early on he praised T. H. Green for integrating the roles of philosopher, teacher, and public moralist. After following Green's lead for 40 years, Dewey wondered why so few other thinkers had done the same:

> Philosophers in general, although they are themselves usually teachers, have not taken education with sufficient seriousness for it to occur to them that . . . philosophizing should focus about education as the supreme human interest in which, moreover, other problems, cosmological, moral, logical, come to a head.

Dewey played a highly visible role on the national stage for a half-century and more. In the words of political scientist Alan Ryan, "As a public intellectual he felt a duty to communicate with a wide public and became strikingly good at doing so." Dewey tirelessly answered the public call for an intellectual leader who could speak with authority on the issues of the day. To reach that public, he employed every mode of communication available: the lecture, the magazine article, the scholarly essay, the book, the leaflet, the radio broadcast, the encyclopedia

CHANGE, January/February 1997, pp. 24–29. Reprinted with permission of the Helen Dwight Reid Education Foundation. Published by Heldref Publications, 1319 Eighteenth St., N.W., Washington, D.C. 20038-1801.

entry, the interview, the pamphlet, the public letter, and testimony before Congress. Moreover, he delivered his many messages to every kind of audience: student associations, parent associations, teachers' groups, and union locals, political and social organizations, and scholarly societies.

For upwards of 20 years, Dewey contributed to the *New Republic,* whose editors, in the words of historian Robert Westbrook,

> laid out the task of public intellectuals in terms very similar to those Dewey used to characterize the intervention of the philosopher in the problems of men. That task—"social education" or "opinion formation"—was distinguished from the work of both those Dewey termed manipulative "accelerators" of public sentiment and the Olympian detachment of the scholar.

Speaking to an American Federation of Labor local that he helped to launch, Dewey worried "about the effort of the big power trusts to control education both in public and private schools. We know that the instructions that went out to the publicity agents were to get hold of two things specially, the press and the schools." This was evidently one reason why he backed a federal cabinet post for education, even while urging that its functions be diffused "all along the line" to avoid the risk of too much central control.

As a sort of publicist himself, Dewey took an interest in the rise of public opinion. The modern state, he observed, "rests upon . . . that impalpable thing called public opinion," the control of which "is the greatest weapon of anti-social forces" and which only an "informed publicity" could effectively resist. Unfortunately, informed public opinion is often in short supply, and "where there is not public opinion . . . our affairs remain very largely in the hands of bosses. . . ."

Informed public opinion presupposes, in turn, success in public education; but the image of education that Dewey envisaged when these remarks were made was largely negative. To illustrate bad teaching, he told the true story of a man who taught swimming without letting any pupils into the pool. One maverick plunged in anyway, and when asked what had happened, the teacher replied that the student had sunk. In the majority of schools things weren't necessarily better. Reliance on rote learning, recitation, and discipline—in these and other ways education had gone so wrong that Dewey imagined students suing their schools for educational malpractice.

The particular job of the educational community, as Dewey saw it, was to overcome ever-competitive individualism with interactive cooperation, and this presupposed participation.

By 1916, Dewey felt that the country had reached "a turning point . . . where we need a more carefully thought out constructive policy regarding public education and the duties and responsibilities that fall upon it in connection with our national life." To construct such a policy, leadership was needed. But Dewey speculated about the wisdom of bringing in specialists, for "a crucial question for our democracy is whether we can develop and utilize experts."

Lippmann would answer that such experts were a must in a civil society; otherwise the masses would continue to be led by symbols that were not much more than chimeras. What Dewey wanted was not this elite of unelected technocrats but social science experts, serving in effect as circuit-riders, who would deliver the "best advice" on everything from school buildings to new courses, asking, "Why should not the locality have these things at arm's length?"

Following a much-publicized visit to the Soviet Union a dozen years after the 1917 October Revolution, Dewey made explicit the fact that education there had already become what we would call a multimedia affair. To uproot popular faith, the Russian rulers employed "all means of education—the schools, the press, poster-pictures." The growing use of publicity in the United States led Dewey to speak of "a kind of newspaper government" here that was similarly unreliable.

On the American educational scene, confusion reigned: "Every important educational dispute . . . gives evidence of our weakness in respect to the incoherent, uncertain, and haphazard way in which educational questions arise and are settled, because of the lack of any means of adequate publicity to reach even the educational force, the teaching force, to say nothing of reaching the parents and the taxpayers and others concerned."

Reluctantly, Dewey concluded that "in default of a central authority to take care of such matters, I see no recourse but an organization of publicity to illuminate and direct public opinion." The country could bear the burden of more bureaucracy-building and red tape because it had already "achieved a vigilant, enlightened, cooperative spirit in the community."

The philosopher of education was also the philosopher of change. Fixity may exist in the realm of ideals, he conceded, but every instance of fixity in the real world occurs "in a state of continuous if obscure change." Recognition of this state of affairs represents in itself a marked change in our understanding of our environment and its things; "It signifies nothing less than that the world or any part of it as it presents itself at a given time is accepted or acquiesced in only as *material* for change."

Such is the viewpoint of the carpenter, who, unlike the philosopher, does not merely contemplate things. The carpenter sees things in terms of what he can do with them; looking at his materials, he imagines how they can be changed into a house. As Dewey saw it: "His attention is directed to the changes they [the materials] undergo and the changes they make other things undergo so that he may select that combination of changes which will yield him his desired results." In contemporary education, Dewey saw a shift from traditional hit-or-miss practices toward a scientific perspective, the latter enriched by a recognition of the paradigmatic role of art and the aesthetic.

With these perspectives in mind, let us examine some key issues that Dewey addressed in his campaign to bring educational ideals closer to reality.

Educating for Democracy

In a celebrated essay called "My Pedagogic Creed," Dewey held forth on these and related issues.

Participation

Dewey believed "that all education proceeds by the participation of the individual in the social consciousness of the race." In addition to reinforcing the concept of participation, this statement underlines the connection between civil society and the individual, a connection that Herbert Hoover's "rugged individualism," for example, endeavors to erase or hide. Dewey's individual is, to borrow from his colleague G. H. Mead, an essentially social individual.

Environment

"I believe that the only true education comes through the stimulation of the child's powers by the demands of the social situations in which he finds himself," wrote Dewey. Situation is a synonym for milieu or environment, the social medium by means of which education takes place—its background, or surroundings. But it is much more: "Human nature exists and operates in an environment. And it is not 'in' that environment as coins are in a box, but as a plant is in the sunlight and soil. It is of them, continuous with their energies, dependent upon their support, capable of increase only as it utilizes them, and as it gradually rebuilds from their crude indifference an environment genially civilized."

In a sense, this environment is like the air we breathe. Thus, Dewey speaks of it as "circumambient atmosphere" to which we become unconsciously habituated, as residents of a city become habituated to their neighborhood. It is "that underlying intangible thing which we call atmosphere and spirit," something in which we become "saturated."

Service

Sounding a contemporary note, Dewey suggested that education, "the art of thus giving shape to human powers and adapting them to social service, is the supreme art. . . ." Further, he believed "that every teacher . . . is a social servant set apart for the maintenance of proper social order and the securing of the right social growth." Reverting to the sermon mode, Dewey avowed "that in this way the teacher always is the prophet of the true God and the usherer in of the true Kingdom of God."

In a more down-to-earth vein, Dewey argued during World War I that American youngsters could help the national effort more by working on farms than by military training. Farm work "enables the teacher to help evolve in the growing generation the idea of universal service in the great battle of man against nature. . . . It gives a chance for the expression of the idea of service to one's country which is not of the destructive kind."

Experience

In 1897, the year of the pedagogic creed, Dewey was more explicit about action than experience, but the importance of experience is everywhere assumed in this and many other texts. By the time of *Democracy and Education* (1916), experience is rarely, if ever, out of sight. It is crucial to the learning process, as Dewey explained, because "the initial stage of that developing experience which is called thinking is experience." Experience brings people together in civic association and participation to the degree that when we speak of the life of a community we are speaking of its experience: "The continuity of any experience, through renewing of the social group, is a literal fact. Education . . . is the means of this social continuity of life."

Community

The school, the family, the political party, and the general public all constitute communities. The particular job of the educational community, as Dewey saw it, was to overcome ever-competitive individualism with interactive cooperation, and this presupposed participation. "Mere instruction that is not accompanied with direct participation in school affairs upon a genuine community basis will not go far . . .," wrote Dewey. "This participation should extend beyond the school and include an active part in some phases of the larger community life."

Cooperative learning in a school environment might involve working with your hands, interpreting experiences, or teaming up on a class project. But in-school activities represented only one part of the picture, since education owes much to the larger community: "the level and style of the arts of literature, poetry, ceremony, amusement, and recreation which obtain in a community . . . do more than all else to determine the current direction of ideas and endeavors in the community."

Dewey omitted reference to religious implications, presumably because community no longer fell clearly within the spiritual domain: "the office of religion as sense of community and one's place in it has been lost." In the broadest sense, community is ultimately what religion is, namely, a sense of a meaningful whole, and belief in such a whole is not without its compensations: "Within the flickering inconsequential acts of separate selves dwells a sense of the whole which claims and dignifies them. In its presence we put off mortality and live in the universal. The life of the community in which we live and have our being is the fit symbol of this relationship."

Activity

Since "only action really unifies," Dewey once observed that "expressive or constructive activities" should integrate various educational functions. More plainly, "every educative process should begin with doing something," that is, "cooking, sewing, manual training. . . ." Educational activity is a hands-on affair and happens interactively, face to face.

Communication

"Of all affairs," Dewey declared, "communication is the most wonderful. That things should be able to pass from the plane of external pushing and pulling to that of revealing themselves to man, and thereby to themselves; and that the fruit of communication should be participation, sharing, is a wonder by the side of which transubstantiation pales."

Communication is the medium through which our words work in formative ways on today's agenda of needs. Communicating enables us to reconstruct: "When communication occurs, all natural events are subject to reconsideration and revision; they are re-adapted to meet the requirements of conversation, whether it be public discourse or that preliminary discourse termed thinking."

Character

In educational terms, how you learn is who you are, and vice versa. For Dewey, character is "that body of active tendencies and interests in the individual which make him open, ready, warm to certain aims, and callous, cold, blind to others, and which accordingly tend to make him acutely aware of and favorable to certain sorts of consequences, and ignorant of or hostile to other consequences."

Of the three types of character traits a student must have, as examined by Dewey, the first is force, or "efficiency in education," meaning roughly the right stuff to get the job done. The second, more intellectual trait is the capacity to judge; although force may be efficient willy nilly, if it is to achieve anything really worthwhile, the person exercising it must have good sense. Besides force and execution, a third, more affective trait is responsiveness: "there must also be a delicate personal responsiveness—there must be an emotional reaction. Indeed, good judgment is impossible without this susceptibility."

Complementing the psychological with the social, Dewey noted that any educational approach worthy of the name must develop "a love of active doing and effective executive capacity. The social aspect of character training is exhibited in the demand that education shall prepare students for an intelligent choice of a calling in which they may be most serviceable to the community."

Equilibrium and Integration

In *Art as Experience,* Dewey argued the need to maintain equilibrium or balance while attempting to integrate the issues listed above. In living together within an environment, human beings, like other organic entities, keep adjusting themselves to their surroundings as a way of adjusting their surroundings to themselves. When this tension is resolved, a state of equilibrium obtains unless or until some desire or need supervenes, whereupon the organism makes new adjustments to close the gap between itself and its surroundings, and so on. But the result is now an *active* equilibrium. In nature, "form is arrived at whenever a stable, even though moving, equilibrium is reached. Changes interlock and sustain one another. . . . Because it is active . . . order itself develops."

The entire process, in which Dewey saw a parallel with artistic creativity, is one of participation: "For only when an organism shares in the ordered relations of its environment does it secure the stability essential to living. And when the participation comes after a phase of disruption and conflict, it bears within itself the germs of a consummation akin to the esthetic."

Higher Education

Although Dewey emphasized the public school rather than the college or the university, in many ways he personified higher education. He was a product of the Johns Hopkins graduate program, which became the model for post-secondary research and instruction, and he taught at Michigan, Minnesota, Chicago, and Columbia. His Laboratory School, as its name implies, was instituted not only to educate the young but to legitimize experience-based teaching, learning, and curriculum as topics of university research. Dewey trained a host of graduate students and had much to say in particular about teacher training in the university.

As a political activist, he supported professional attempts to participate more fully in university governance. When civil liberties of professors were threatened at Columbia and Ohio State, he rallied to the defense of the accused. He criticized War Department attempts to silence pacifists and protested when university officials cracked down on liberal clubs and publications. Though not a Communist himself, he opposed the barring of Party members from university teaching. Finally, as an active union member, he urged teacher-training institutions to compensate for the absence of a centralized governmental department of education by becoming leaders themselves. And he repeatedly urged his teaching colleagues to organize and become intelligently militant.

Dewey believed the university to be a kind of organic whole. Indeed, the term *university* derives from *universe*—literally a turning into one. Fittingly, the first universities were cooperative, participatory ventures in which faculty and students effectively acted as one. Dewey carried the sense of wholeness over into his thinking about the relation of his experimental school to the university: "The problem is to unify, to organize, education, to bring all its various factors together, through putting it as a whole into organic union with everyday life."

Dewey sought, though he never managed to supply, a working model of the ways in which learners from the age of four right up to the college and university years could be brought together. As he put it, "We want to bring all things educational together . . . so that it shall be demonstrated to the eye that there is no lower and higher, but simply education."

The Democratic Ideal

James Marsh, a founder of American philosophy, convinced Dewey that American pioneering was not an achievement of loners but a stage in advancement toward a more nearly ideal civil society and democratic community. Noting how Marsh referred continually to the *community* of individuals, Dewey argued that "the essence of our earlier pioneer individualism was not non-social, much less anti-social; it involved no indifference to the claims of society, its working ideal was neighborliness and mutual service."

Hazarding a working definition of the ideal, Dewey stipulated two essential elements, the first being that democracy should entail "not only more numerous and more varied points of shared common interest, but greater reliance upon the recognition of mutual interest as a factor in social control." The second element of the ideal, he reasoned, required "not only freer interaction between social groups . . . but change in social habit—its continuous readjustment through meeting the new situations produced by varied intercourse. And these two traits are precisely what characterize the democratically constituted society."

To Dewey the ideal was never fanciful, but "has its roots in natural conditions; it emerges when the imagination idealizes existence by laying hold of the possibilities offered to thought and action." Ideals operate concretely in real persons: Florence Nightingale and other philanthropists "have modified institutions. Aims, ideals, do not exist simply in 'mind'; they exist in character, in personality and action." Moreover, he noted that in the United States "there has been the appeal to idealism in the initiation of every significant American political movement. . . ."

Democratic Culture

Dewey held that "the problem of the relation of mechanistic and industrial civilization to culture is the deepest and most urgent problem of our day." By civilization, he seemed usually to mean a society's stage of overall development, with particular respect to material features of that society. Culture also relates to a particular society, but with a nearer sense of education, improvement, and refinement. This understanding of culture secured, Dewey sought a way "of making the material an active instrument in the creation of the life of ideas and art." For "the unique fact about our own civilization," he observed, "is that if it is to achieve and manifest a characteristic culture, it must develop, not on top of an industrial and political substructure, but out of our material civilization itself."

When he glanced around at public behavior, Dewey saw little of the original thinking or acting that citizens were capable of in democratic theory. He concluded that democracy "is still so immature that its main effect is to multiply occasions for imitation." For that matter, education, too, stood in need of further development; he considered it "one of the great opportunities for present-day pioneering."

Existing institutions, ironically, could have an inhibiting effect on the development of democratic culture. To put such a culture together, people would need an open arena in which to experiment, but the public domain was already filled with legislatures, town councils, political parties, and other collective entities. What was needed was an assimilation of democratic aims into the social and moral environment until it became the very atmo-sphere we breathe.

In his optimistic way, Dewey believed that this would actually occur as "the new ideas" of reconstruction and reform gradually gained hold:

> As the new ideas find adequate expression in social life, they will be absorbed into a moral background, and the ideas and beliefs themselves will be deepened and be unconsciously transmitted and sustained. They will color the imagination and temper the desires and affections. They will not form a set of ideas to be expounded, reasoned out and argumentatively supported, but will be a spontaneous way of envisaging life. Then they will take on religious value.

For Dewey, any democracy worthy of the name must not only embrace all comers, it must help them to participate in its processes and institutions.

Dewey, however, was by no means promoting doctrinal or sectarian value. He was reminding his readers of "the religious devotion to education which has characterized . . . the American republic." At the same time he was playing the prophet, as he sometimes liked to do, and what he prophesied was, to borrow the title of the book most relevant to this context, a common faith: "The ideal ends to which we attach our faith are not shadowy and wavering. They assume concrete form in our understanding of our relations to one another and the values contained in these relations."

Localism and Regeneration

Although Dewey's observations on democratic culture apply on a national scale, culture begins at home and remains grounded in the local community. Community is something that happens face to face. For evidence of this in education, one needs only to note the strong support for local self-government found almost everywhere in the nation. In sum, community—if it is to be national—must first be local.

It also must be generational, a Jeffersonian idea to which Dewey, who edited a Jefferson reader, subscribed. In the words of the main author of the Declaration of Independence, "the generation which commences a revolution can rarely compleat [*sic*] it." In the words of Dewey, "Democracy has to be born anew every generation, and education is its midwife." That is, each generation must regenerate. Education alone provides the necessary conditions for understanding and sympathizing with others; in a complex industrial civilization like ours, people "will not see across and through the walls which separate them, unless they have been trained to do so."

Diversity

Dewey's common faith was in part a faith in cultural pluralism. For Dewey, any democracy worthy of the name must not only embrace all comers, it must help them to participate in its processes and institutions. Dewey rejected outright the proposition that immigrants should abandon their traditions. Rather than serve as a melting pot, he contended that the nation should welcome and even nurture diversity. Rather than drill the population into faceless conformity—the likely consequence of a proposal for universal military service—he advocated a viable institution of national service that should "see to it that all get from one another the best that each strain has to offer from its own tradition and culture."

In a word, Dewey's credo was that everyone should be free to be democratic in his or her own way; and if that means, in civic terms, the right to speak and to vote as one sees fit, it also means, in educational terms, the right to freedom of thought and inquiry. Putting the matter in even more general terms, Dewey observed that "a progressive society counts individual variations as precious since it finds in them the means of its own growth. Hence a democratic society must, in consistency with its ideal, allow intellectual freedom and the play of diverse gifts and interests in its educational measures."

A final reason for more active participation in educational development is that education, like democracy, is greatly in need of reform, and is thereby an opportunity for "present-day pioneering." Readers may yet pioneer, for that matter, in Deweyan thinking itself. There are many volumes of it, and the best of them beckon like a new frontier.

Article Review Form at end of book.

Briefly summarize the beliefs of one of the following philosophers: Isocrates, John Dewey, Montaigne, Bacon, Locke, R.S. Peters, Leo Strauss.

The Evolution of Philosophy of Education within Educational Studies

J.R. Muir
University of Oxford

A number of educationists have recently advocated a broadened conception of philosophy of education, which incorporates the history of educational ideas. As a component of this wider discussion, the history of educational philosophy within educational studies has become the subject of study and evaluation. One potentially fruitful debate has been between Kevin Harris and James Kaminsky. Kaminsky argues that:

> . . . the discipline of educational philosophy has a definite beginning date: Sunday, February 24, 1935, when a group of school superintendents and academics met in Atlantic City and established the John Dewey Society.
>
> (Kaminsky 1992, p. 179)

Yet Harris points out that by defining educational philosophy in terms of formal societies devoted to it, Kaminsky fails to account for thinkers, from Plato to Rousseau, who engaged in educational philosophy without the formality of, say, the Plato Society (Harris 1988, p. 51). As this disagreement suggests, a better appreciation of the origins and evolution of the philosophy of education within educational studies is needed.

Although Kaminsky and Harris adopt opposed opinions concerning the history of philosophy of education, they share a more fundamental and unselfconscious opinion. Both regard Kaminsky's history of educational philosophy as a radically new one. Yet Kaminsky has merely reiterated presuppositions which have been dominant within educational studies for at least thirty years. J.W. Tibble, for example, writing in 1966, expressed what had been, and is, a universally, if often tacitly, held opinion among educationists:

> The study of education has developed piecemeal from its first beginnings towards the end of the nineteenth century.
>
> (Tibble 1966, pp. vii-viii. Cf. Kaminsky 1986; Kaminsky 1992)

This astonishingly narrow—and quite unsubstantiated—view was to become still more parochial by 1971 when Tibble wrote that 'the study of education is of very recent origin', becoming fully developed 'only within the last decade [1960–1970]' (Tibble 1971). As Tibble acknowledges, and as Kaminsky reiterates, the impetus for this study of education was not the pursuit of the truth, or even of a wider perspective, but the pursuit of 'relevance' within the political imperatives of the current educational institutions (Tibble 1966, p. ix; Kaminsky 1992, p. 180). One of the consequences of this profoundly narrow and parochial view of philosophy and the study of education has been a devastating loss of historical and philosophical learning, as has been observed for some time (Wilson & Cowell 1989, pp. 44, 52. Cf. Commission on the Humanities 1980, pp. 52–53; Darling 1993, pp. 36–38; Proctor 1988, p. xv). If philosophy of education within educational studies is to have a worthwhile future, then a more self-conscious appreciation of the increasing narrowness and loss of learning that define the evolution of the discipline in this century will be necessary. The intention of this paper is to provide neither an exhaustive nor a definitive discussion of this most difficult problem. On the contrary, it is intended only to show that widespread presuppositions about the evolution of educational philosophy are dubious, and to provide a point of departure for debates within educational studies which are now long overdue.

An Illustration: Isocrates

Classicists have described Isocrates as 'the educator of Europe' (Newman 1975, p. 358), and 'one of the greatest educationalists of history' (Knowles 1962, p. 60). Medievalist David Knowles has shown that:

> Great and permanent, even in this field, as was the influence of the two philosophers [Plato and Aristotle], the victory and the future lay with Isocrates.
>
> (Knowles 1962, p. 61)

While classicist historians of education such as Hubbell, Burk, Jaeger, Marrou, Finley and others disagree about the philosophical profundity of Isocrates, particularly in comparison with Plato, all agree that Isocrates was by far the more influential in the history of educational thought (Hubbell 1914; Burk 1923, pp. 199–224; Jaeger, 1947, Vol. 3, p. 46; Marrou 1948, 1984; Finley 1975. Cf. Beck 1964; Scolnicov 1988, pp. 11–12). As the distinguished classicist and historian of education, Henri-Irenee Marrou argued, as early as 1948:

> The importance of this fact must be emphasized from the beginning. On the level of history Plato had been defeated: he had failed to impose his educational ideal on posterity. It was Isocrates who defeated him, and who became the educator first of Greece, and subsequently of the whole of the ancient world.
>
> (Marrou 1948, p. 292. Cf. p. 128)

This is not to suggest that Isocrates is of merely antiquarian interest. Contemporary practical problems in schooling such as class inequality, gender inequality and the specialisation (or 'vocationalisation') of schooling have been traced *directly* to the continuing influence of Isocrates (e.g. Finley 1975). The continuity of the dominant influence of Isocrates in Western educational thought, from classical Greece until the present day, was once again reiterated by Marrou, in an essay published in 1984:

> Isocrates' ideas and the system of education which put them into practice reigned virtually unchallenged in Western Europe almost to our own generation.
>
> (Marrou 1984, p. 200. Cf. Kimball 1986, p. 11; Power 1962, p. 102)

Finally, the conclusions of the past four generations of classicist research into the history of education, as summarised by Moses Hadas, give an indication of the pervasive and well-established influence of Isocrates.

> It was the program of Isocrates which has shaped European education to this day, which has kept humanism alive, and which has given Western civilization such unity as it possesses.
>
> (Hadas 1969, p. 129. Cf. Laistner 1957, p. 447)

Yet in spite of ample historical evidence, and the classical scholarship of the past four generations, educationists remain unaware that Isocrates ever existed. Standard reference works in the history of education and educational ideas, such as Rusk's *The Doctrines of the Great Educators*, Curtis and Boultwood's *A Short History of Educational Ideas* (1965), Hirst's remarkably inaccurate 'Liberal education' in *The Encyclopedia of Education* (1971), Nakosteen's *The History and Philosophy of Education*, and Nodding's *Philosophy of Education* (1995) do not even mention Isocrates, while Boyd's *History of Western Education* merely mentions Isocrates without discussing either his ideas or his influence. More generally, as I demonstrated elsewhere with reference to these texts, 'the histories of education and educational ideas upon which educationists and training teachers have been dependent for the greater part of this century are wholly inaccurate in almost every important respect' (Muir 1995, Conclusion). Isocrates will be alluded to throughout this article as an illustration of some of the consequences of the evolution of philosophy of education within educational studies.

The Victorian Revival

Victorian educational scholars believed that they were recovering educational scholarship after a period of neglect. As R.H. Quick ruefully observed:

> There has been much talk about education of late years; and at length people are beginning to

perceive that some thought about it and study of it may be desirable.
(Quick 1980 [1880], pp. xv–xvi)

To say that people are beginning to perceive that others in the past thought and wrote about education is to recognise that a tradition of educational thought exists, and Quick sought to study that tradition. A primary concern of the Victorian educational scholars was a recovery of the history of educational ideas and philosophy.

Quick observed that academic study of the history of educational thought was dominated by German scholars 'who hitherto have had the history of education in their own hands' (Quick 1980 [1880], p. xvi. Cf. Myers 1960, p. vii). The Germans argued that Locke was the source of 'modern pedagogy' (Quick 1980 [1880]), and so motivated Quick to publish a new edition of Locke's *Some Thoughts Concerning Education* in 1880. The irony of German scholars arguing for the importance of Locke's book when it was out of print in England did not escape Quick and, furthermore, hints at the marginal status the history of educational ideas has always had in English-language universities.

Quick's pioneering efforts in Locke textual scholarship were matched by other scholars. Nettleship published a study of Plato's educational ideas (Nettleship 1935 [1880]), Davidson published a study of Artistotle's educational ideas (Davidson 1904), and Laurie published a study of Renaissance educational thought (Laurie 1903). William Heinemann Publishers issued *The Great Educators* series, which featured books by classical and medieval scholars on the educational ideas of Loyola, Alcuin, Abelard and others. Throughout the Victorian revival, however, the status and purpose of such historical study was far more limited than in Germany.

The study of education in Germany was regarded as an academic subject in its own right, comparable with political science or philosophy, as Quick observes. The Anglo-American model was profoundly narrower, and the subject correspondingly accorded lower status. Specifically, education was defined in terms of a single, proportionately very small, aspect of the subject as a whole, namely, (state) schooling. Quick issued his edition of Locke hoping that 'there will be some young teachers who find it useful to read the chief English classic connected with their profession' (Quick 1880, p. xvi), a sentiment shared by Laurie (Laurie 1903, p. v). Education had become merely 'a practical activity' and the study of it reduced to an 'applied' discipline, though only among educationists.

The Victorian revival of educational scholarship included a renewed interest in the educational ideas of Isocrates. Classicists such as Jebb (Jebb 1893), Dobson (Dobson 1913), Hubbell (Hubbell 1913) and Freeman (Freeman 1922) wrote extensively on Isocrates. Classically educated educational scholars such as Adamson (Adamson 1922, p. 96) and Gwynn (Gwynn 1964 [1926], p. 46) wrote of Isocrates's unequalled importance in educational thought, the last educationists to do so in this century (Beck 1961, p. 7; Kimball 1986, p. 2).

Subsequent to the Victorian revival, Isocrates scholarship became exclusively the domain of classicists, who published continuously on the subject until the present day (e.g. Burk 1923; Jaeger 1947, Vol. II; Marrou 1948; Finley 1975; Kennedy 1980; Marrou 1984; Pangle 1992). By 1965, on the other hand, educationists such as Hirst (Hirst 1971) or Curtis and Boultwood (Curtis & Boultwood 1965) could offer remarkably inaccurate historical discussions of education in which Isocrates simply does not appear, while their classicist contemporaries were extensively discussing his educational ideas and influence (e.g. Marrou 1948; Finley 1975). From the Victorian period until the present, the loss of any knowledge of Isocrates's educational legacy has been one of the defining features of educationist philosophy of education.

John Dewey

Although educationists portray John Dewey as the originator of philosophy of education as a new academic subject (Kaminsky 1986, p. 42; Kaminsky 1992, p. 179; Peters 1983, p. 30), he, in fact, perpetuated the Victorian emphasis on (state) schooling, while radically narrowing the historical and philosophical perspectives the Victorians had recovered. We shall examine each of these issues in turn.

Like most writers in the history of educational thought, Dewey was aware that agencies other than schools, such as the family and the community as a whole, can contribute towards 'education' in important ways (Dewey 1916, p. 4). Nevertheless, a close reading of his works reveals that Dewey's conception of philosophy of education was limited to the study of contemporary schooling, and that this is a continuous presupposition in his writings (Dewey 1964 [1899], pp. 295–310; Dewey 1913b, pp. 697–703; Dewey 1916, pp. 8–9).

Dewey's contemporaries and students were well aware that he regarded schooling as the primary focus of philosophy of education (e.g. Bruner 1966, pp. 211, 226; Cremin 1966; Adler 1988, p. xxv). Reginald Archambault, for example, when editing the 1964 edition of Dewey's *John Dewey on Education*, placed Dewey's conception of the study of education explicitly within the confines of the school:

> Education, then, must promote creativity and stability, individuality and social consciousness. The chief means for this were to be found in the environment of the school in general, and in the method of instruction in particular.
>
> (Dewey 1964, p. xxvii)

It should be emphasised that the 'environment of the school' refers to the environment *within* the school, and that there is no mention of other agencies, such as the family or community. Dewey's focus on schooling continues to be recognised by contemporary scholars. As Kaminsky has observed,

> In the hands of Dewey and his colleagues at the University of Chicago and Columbia University, educational philosophy became the device for the realisation of the fact and promise of the public school.
>
> (Kaminsky 1992, p. 180. Cf. Ravitch 1983, p. 47; Hirsch 1987, p. 122)

Dewey's conception of educational philosophy merely conformed to the Victorian emphasis on current 'practice' and, particularly, on state schooling. The primary evidence for this conclusion is found most clearly in those works in which Dewey sought to define his conception of the philosophical study of education.

Dewey's pamphlet, 'My Pedagogic Creed' (1987) (in Dewey 1958), set out the conception of educational philosophy he was to follow for the remainder of his career (Bruner 1966, p. 211). The first article, 'What education is,' provides a very broad definition of education in social, psychological, sociological and political terms. Nevertheless, the second article, 'What the school is,' unambiguously places the study of 'education' firmly within the context of the school. Although the contribution made to education by the family and the community is recognised, that contribution is studied within the context of the school (Dewey 1964, pp. 431, 437). The remaining three articles are concerned with the subject matter of education, educational method and social reform, though once again in terms of the contribution which education can make *through the schools* social progress (Dewey 1964, pp. 427–439). As Dewey says:

> . . . it is the business of everyone interested in education to insist upon the school as the primary and most effective interest of social progress and reform in order that society may be awakened to realise what the school stands for, and aroused to the necessity of endowing the educator with sufficient equipment properly to perform his task.
>
> (Dewey 1964, p. 438)

Dewey's belief that the philosophical study of education was essentially the study of schooling in the service of political ends is a common and continuous feature of his subsequent writings, as his 'My Pedagogic Creed' would lead us to expect.

The book by Dewey most widely read in his day was given the unambiguous title, *Schools for Tomorrow* (Hirsch 1987, p. xv). His best known book today is probably *Democracy and Education* and it, too, continuously focuses its philosophical and practical discussion on the schools, and not on any other agency (Dewey 1916, e.g. pp. 22, 40, 51, 53, 233, 360. Cf. Dewey 1958, e.g. pp. 30, 36, 47–49, 63, 66–69, 76–78, 88–92). The chapter of *Intelligence in the Modern World* devoted to philosophy of education is entitled 'The schools and social welfare', and throughout is focused on schooling (Dewey 1939, Ch. 12).

Finally, in his article 'The need for a philosophy of education' (1934), a later statement of his program for philosophy of education, Dewey once again limits the philosophical study of education to the study of schooling. This limitation is clear in both the structure of the article, and its concrete educational proposals. Dewey argues that philosophy of education is needed if education is to respond to social and political problems in a productive way. After discussing a number of these problems, Dewey turns to schooling as the educational context within which they will be addressed:

> Unless the schools of the world can engage in a common effort to rebuild the spirit of common understanding, of mutual sympathy and good will among all people and races, to exorcise the demons of prejudice, isolation and hatred, the schools themselves are likely to be submerged by the general return to barbarism, which is the sure outcome of present tendencies if they go unchecked by the forces which education alone can evoke and fortify.
>
> (Dewey 1964, p. 14)

Throughout Dewey's career, however broadly he sometimes

defined education in the abstract, he limited the philosophical study of education to the prevailing institutions, (state) schools.

While Dewey perpetuated the Victorian focus on schooling, he turned away from the Victorian revival of the history of educational philosophy and ideas. In a sense, his lack of interest in serious historical study was a consequence of his belief in 'progress'. Dewey believed that he and his contemporaries had:

> . . . finally reached a point where learning means discovery, not memorising traditions.
>
> (Dewey 1913b, p. 702)

Accordingly, Dewey abandoned any systematic examination of the history of educational ideas. The inevitable consequence of such an abandonment is that Dewey proves to be systematically ignorant of even the elementary features of his own discipline and isolated from those scholars who are concerned with its traditions.

We will consider first the question of the extent to which Dewey showed any real knowledge of, or concern for, the educational ideas of the philosophers that make up the history of educational thought. If we are to deal with this question productively, and without being intimidated by Dewey's fame, we must begin with a simple but important distinction. When examining Dewey's many mentions of thinkers of the past, we must ask whether they reveal any evidence of serious scholarly engagement, or whether they are mere rhetorical devices, august names mentioned in the hope of making Dewey's argument appear to be more authoritative than it is. What we find, repeatedly, is that Dewey attributes his own views to older thinkers. The brevity and inaccuracy of Dewey's mentions of the educational thinkers of the past suggest that they are rhetorical devices of this kind, and cannot be regarded as evidence of any interest in their ideas.

As an illustration of Dewey's lack of interest in, and ignorance of, the history of educational philosophy, consider first the case of Rousseau. It is often assumed that Dewey's educational ideas were derived from, or were elaborations of, the educational thought of Rousseau (e.g. Hirsch 1987, p. xv). This assumption can be dispatched with Dewey's own hand. In the words of William Kilpatrick, his long-time associate:

> As to the origin of Dewey's educational ideas, some thought he had derived these from Rousseau and Froebel. I once asked him about this and he told me explicitly that he had not read either one until after he had formed his educational outlook.
>
> (quoted in Dewey 1964, p. 5)

In this context, Dewey's 'discussions' in *Democracy and Education* suggest that he used the authority of Rousseau as a rhetorical prop for the educational outlook he had already formulated, without any serious engagement with Rousseau's texts. For example, Dewey makes the following assertion:

> Educational concern with the early years of life—as distinct from inculcation of useful arts—dates almost entirely from the time of the emphasis by Pestalozzi and Froebel, following Rousseau, of the natural principles of growth.
>
> (Dewey 1916, p. 116)

The assertion is, of course, false. Educational concern with the early years of life is an explicit and continuous concern of educational thinkers from Isocrates and Plato, through Quintilian, and beyond (e.g. Isocrates *To Demonicus*, pp. 11–12, *Nicocles*, pp. 57; Plato *Laws* Bk. 7; Quintilian 1.1, pp. 4–12). Moreover, it is Dewey himself who was concerned with 'growth', and he provides neither evidence nor argument to show that this concern was shared by Rousseau. Rousseau is mentioned in three other places in this text, though no reference is made to his works (Dewey 1916, pp. 60, 91, 93 n.1). These passing mentions of Rousseau's name do not constitute discussion of his educational ideas. Dewey had not studied Rousseau in any substantive sense, but rather employed the authority of Rousseau's name to lend specious authority to his own educational opinions, which he had formulated long before.

Consider, as a second example, Dewey's 'discussion' of the sophists, which is contained entirely in a short paragraph. It should be noted that no sophist is named, and no ancient or contemporary source is mentioned. Dewey merely asserts, without evidence or argument, that:

> . . . the travelling teachers, known as the Sophists, began to apply the results and the methods of the natural philosophers to human conduct.
>
> (Dewey 1916, p. 330)

First, it is Dewey, not 'the sophists', who sought to apply natural science to the problems of human conduct (e.g. Dewey 1910, pp. 8–9. Cf. Bloom 1987, pp. 194–195). As the distinguished classicist, John Burnet, had argued two years earlier, 'the "age of the Sophists" is, above all, an age of reaction against science' (Burnet 1962, p. 109). Second, Dewey treats 'the sophists' as an historical abstraction, and attributes the same vague educational concerns to a group notorious for the diversity of its educational ideas (Gomperz 1964 [1901], Vol. I, Bk. 3; Burnet 1962, p. 107; Romilly 1988, Ch. 1, Ch. 3). To mention only a single example, it is well known that the sophists Gorgias and Protagoras sought to develop the Sicilian tradition of rhetorical education originating with Tisias and Corax and not, as Dewey claims, the unspecified 'methods' of unidentified 'natural philosophers' (e.g. Bowen 1972, p. 87). Dewey's brief discussion of the sophists consists entirely of vague and improbable assertions, unsubstantiated by argument or evidence. His discussion provides no evidence to support the view that he devoted any serious study to these thinkers, while the superficiality and elementary errors in his discussion suggest that he did not.

Dewey also mentions Mill, Montaigne, Locke, Bacon and Spencer (Dewey 1916, pp. 339, 293, 221). To take one of these mentions as a typical example, Dewey asserts, without evidence or argument, that after the sixteenth century:

> . . . mind, the source and possessor of knowledge, was thought of as wholly individual. Thus upon the educational side, we find educational reformers, like Montaigne, Bacon, Locke, henceforth vehemently denouncing all learning which is acquired on hearsay, and asserting that even if beliefs happen to be true, they do not constitute knowledge unless they have grown up in and been tested by personal experience.
>
> (Dewey 1916, p. 293)

The sentence in which the names Montaigne, Bacon and Locke appear constitutes Dewey's 'discussion' of them in its entirety, and as such is no different from his 'discussions' of these thinkers in other works (e.g. Dewey 1958, pp. 106, 296, 283; Dewey 1939, pp. 246, 850, 895, 965). No reference is made to their works, and no evidence is presented to show they adhered to anything like the *educational* ideas Dewey attributes to them. Indeed, these thinkers rejected the view that all learning must be and/or ought to be verified by personal experience, particularly in moral and political education.

Montaigne, who developed ideas derived from Isocrates, explicitly argued that book learning can be an effective substitute for personal experience. Montaigne regarded practical judgement as the proper aim of education, and did not share the epistemological concern with 'knowledge' that Dewey attributes to him (e.g. Montaigne 1957, 'Of pedantry'). In Montaigne's view, the study of historical texts allows the student to:

> . . . inquire into the conduct, the resources, and the alliances of this prince and that. These are things very pleasant to learn and very useful to know.
>
> In this association with men I mean to include, and foremost, those who live only in the memory of books. He will associate, by means of histories, with those great souls of the best ages.
>
> (Montaigne 1957, p. 115)

Similar educational ideas were advocated by Francis Bacon, who also held a much more elaborate conception of the relationship between education and knowledge than that attributed to him by Dewey. In *The Advancement of Learning*, for example, Bacon divides knowledge into two kinds, understanding and reason on the one hand, and will, appetite and affection on the other. These correspond to propositions and action respectively. In part continuing the Isocratic tradition of rhetorical education, Bacon recommends learning based on rhetoric, and consisting of the development of moral and political judgement through inspirational narrative rather than personal experience (Bacon 1861, pp. 120–121). To come finally to Locke (1980), we read the following in his *Some Thoughts Concerning Education*:

> The Lord's Prayer, the Creeds, and the Ten Commandments, 'tis necessary he should learn perfectly by heart, but I think, not by reading them himself in his Primer, but by somebody's repeating them to him, even before he can read.
>
> (Locke 1980 [1880], Sec. 157)

Contrary to Dewey's assertion, Locke also in part recommends learning which is not based on personal experience, a recommendation which is reiterated and emphasised in his discussions of political and moral education particularly (e.g. Locke 1968, pp. 397, 399–400, 403, 422). The brevity and inaccuracy of Dewey's one sentence 'discussion' of Montaigne, Bacon and Locke supports the view that Dewey had little knowledge of their works, and provides no evidence of any serious engagement with their educational thought.

We come now to our final example of both Dewey's limited familiarity with the history of educational thought, and his isolation from mainstream educational scholarship. This example is particularly relevant to my broader concern with the decline of educational philosophy because it is taken from Dewey's contribution to a basic reference work that has been used by educationists for many years. In an article in Monroe's *Cyclopedia of Education*, Dewey asserts that the school, defined as 'a public institution with a regular curriculum' (Dewey 1913a, p. 723), was invented by Plato, and that the Academy was the first such institution. Yet the schools of the Pythagoreans existed for a century before Plato (Cohen 1913, p. 687), while Isocrates's school opened several years before the Academy (Beck 1964, p. 290). Dewey tells us that the idea of a fixed curriculum originates with Plato's *Laws* (Dewey 1913a, p. 723), apparently unaware that the Pythagoreans, Hippias of Elis, Gorgias, Isocrates and others developed fixed curricula well before the *Laws* was written. Dewey asserts that the medieval quadrivium, composed of arithmetic, geometry, astronomy and music, was passed to the medieval universities through the *Laws* and the *Republic* (Dewey 1913a, p. 723). Yet it is well known that the quadrivium is a medieval innovation, based on the Isocratic liberal arts (Marrou 1984, p. 190; Clarke 1971, p. 4), and that Plato's *Laws* or *Republic* could not have had such influence on medieval education because medieval Europe did not possess these texts. The only Platonic text known in Europe prior to the Renaissance was a Latin translation of the *Timaeus* (Reynolds & Wilson 1974, p. 106; Rashdall 1936 [1895], Vol. I, p. 38). Finally, Dewey asserts that it is 'generally recognised' that Plato's Academy was, somehow, the origin of the medieval university. If Dewey had not been so entirely isolated from educational scholarship he might have known that the Academy was closed in 529 AD by Justinian, and that it was in fact 'generally recognised' that the medieval universities were modelled on Arabic institutions, medieval in origin, and owed little directly to the classical world (Wieruszowski 1966, p. 5; Haskins 1957a [1923], pp. 1–2; Haskins 1957b [1927], p. 371; Rashdall 1936, Vol. I, pp. 1–24).

Dewey's legacy to philosophy of education within educational studies is the perpetuation of the narrow Victorian focus on schooling, combined with both a loss of learning in the history of educational thought and isolation from the contemporary educational scholarship of classicists and others. It is only in this sense that educational philosophy originated with John Dewey.

Interlude on the Analytic 'Revolution' in Philosophy

The evolution of philosophy of education (among educationists) between Dewey and the R.S. Peters era cannot be understood without reference to the 'revolution in philosophy' (O'Connor 1957, p. 3; Peters 1966b, p. 59; Moore 1982, p. 3), and the analytic philosophy deriving from it.

From the point of view of its influence on educational studies, it is most important to recognise the exceptionally dogmatic and parochial nature of the 'revolution in philosophy', as sympathetic academics have observed:

> Analytic philosophy in the twentieth century has become a too small and self-contained circle, one too comforted by the myths of current wisdom; one which lacks a sense of historical perspective on itself; one whose chief vice is intellectual arrogance.
>
> (Hudson 1986, p. xv)

As philosophers with less absolutist methodological commitments have long argued, analytic philosophy has always been characterised by its isolation, and by the loss of learning which was among its causes, and its legacy (Aron 1975, p. xv; Bloom 1990, pp. 344–345; Strauss 1968, Ch. 3; Proctor 1988, p. xv; MacIntyre 1981, pp. 2–3).

The parochialism of the 'revolution in philosophy' is difficult to discuss without seeming to exaggerate. Although Collingwood has argued that Moore and Russell merely refuted propositions which they attributed to F.H. Bradley (Collingwood 1944, pp. 22–23), it was widely believed that their refutation was sound. What is most astonishing, however, is that the refutation of one Oxbridge academic by two others is presented as, and believed to be, the elimination of metaphysics as a philosophical enquiry (Ayer 1946, Ch. 1; Ryle *et al.* 1956, p. 4, Ch. 1). The fact was, of course, that Continental philosophers such as Henri Bergson, Heidegger, Herman Cohen and others, as well as Middle Eastern philosophers such as Shlomo Pines, perpetuated the traditions of metaphysics beyond the narrow horizons of the notoriously insular Oxbridge academic philosophers. It was not a revolution in *philosophy*, but in one section of English language academic philosophy.

From the inception of the movement, analytic philosophers subjectively defined philosophy as whatever they themselves were doing. As Santayana remarked, in 1913, Bertrand Russell's *The Problems of Philosophy:*

> . . . hardly deserves its title; it treats principally, in a somewhat personal and partial way, of the

> relation of knowledge to its objects, and might rather have been called 'The problems which Moore and I have been agitating lately'.
>
> (Santayana 1913, p. 112)

Later, just as Santayana suggested a more modest title for Russell's book, Todd suggested a less absolute title for Ayers's *The Central Questions of Philosophy* (1973): 'It is not a typographical error, but *The* in the title should be *Some*' (Todd 1976, p. 59).

Similarly, as Copleston observed, Russell's quite unreliable *A History of Western Philosophy* was hardly 'historical' at all, and 'should have been given some such title as "My Reactions to a Number of Philosophers"' (Copleston 1979, p. 35). Only twenty years after Santayana's comment, however, the subjective parochialism of the analytic school had become active and dogmatic.

In his manifesto, *Language, Truth and Logic* (1936), A.J. Ayer asserts that his own analytic conception of the nature of philosophy is absolutely and universally correct, and that no other conception should be permitted:

> One of the main objects of this treatise has been to show that there is nothing in the nature of philosophy to warrant the existence of conflicting philosophical parties or 'schools' . . . Accordingly, we who are interested in the condition of philosophy can no longer acquiesce in the existence of party divisions among philosophers.
>
> (Ayers 1936, p. 133. Cf. Aron 1975, p. xv; Todd 1976)

Of course philosophical schools are distinguished by their differing conceptions of the nature of philosophy. Ayer insists, however, that we ought not to 'acquiesce' to such diversity. As late as 1980, members of the analytic school could continue to assert—though still without argument—that analytic philosophy 'remains the only real philosophy there is' (Williams 1980, p. 75. Cf. Berlin 1980, p. 115).

Analytic philosophy is unique among contemporary philosophical schools for its dismissive, and consequently uninformed, attitude toward the history of the subject. As MacIntyre observed:

> One of the most important aspects of British philosophy when it was strongly influenced by positivism was a belief that the history of philosophy was a mere addendum, a source-book of problems.
>
> (MacIntyre 1971, p. 193)

It must be emphasised that the positivists devoted little serious study to the works of the philosophers of the past. On the contrary, they began with an absolute commitment to the imperatives of positivist (and later analytic) methodology, and engaged only with selected fragments of older philosophy insofar as they could be rhetorically ridiculed from the perspective of that commitment. As Leszek Kolakowski concluded in his examination of early positivist and analytic philosophers, including A.J. Ayer specifically:

> The judgements passed by positivists on the philosophical systems of the past as well as on contemporary metaphysical speculation usually have the character of summary condemnations; they are not based on study of the condemned doctrines, but on ridiculing single statements chosen at random.
>
> (Kolakowski 1972, pp. 236–237)

Although Kolakowski's observation is a useful one, it could be said that he overestimates the extent to which the analytic philosophers engaged with the philosophical thought of those outside their school. Ayer, for example, condemned theology not on the basis of statements chosen at random from the work of philosophical theologians, but on the basis of simplistic theological propositions entirely of his own invention, and attributed by him to unidentified 'metaphysicians' (e.g. Ayer 1946, pp. 114–120). D. J. O'Connor's *An Introduction to the Philosophy of Education* (1957) perpetuates these attitudes and procedures, and helped introduce them into educational studies.

O'Connor asserts *without argument* that G.E. Moore and B. Russell were the first philosophers in history to understand the true nature of the subject (O'Connor 1957, p. 3), and that anyone adhering to a different view holds 'a false and confused idea of philosophy' (O'Connor 1957, p. 141. Cf. Quinton 1967, p. 1). One cannot help balancing O'Connor's enthusiasm with Wittgenstein's reported description of G.E. Moore as an illustration of 'how far a man can go who has absolutely no intelligence whatever' (Leavis 1982, p. 130). Turning to the history of philosophy, O'Connor asserts that:

> In the past, both philosophers and their critics made the mistake of assuming that philosophy was a kind of superior science that could be expected to answer difficult and important questions about human life and man's place and prospects in the Universe.
>
> (O'Connor 1951, p. 4)

Note, first, that O'Connor offers neither evidence nor argument to show that any philosopher ever held this opinion *as O'Connor formulates it*. Second, O'Connor wrongly asserts that this opinion was 'assumed', and neither presents nor addresses the arguments that have been made for the much more elaborate classical version (e.g. Maimonides 1963). On the contrary, O'Connor's assertions are wholly unestablished analytic dogmas, mere elaborations of Ayer's original refusal to 'acquiesce' to the existence of any non-analytic conception of philosophy, past or present.

The fate of political philosophy illustrates the self-referential isolationism of the analytic school. In 1956, Laslett famously proclaimed that 'political philosophy is dead' (Laslett 1956, p. vii), and the assertion is repeated by analytic philosophers for decades afterwards (Quinton 1967, p. 19; Pettit 1980, p. ix). It must be emphasised, once again, that no argument is provided to substantiate this proclamation. Indeed, it is difficult to see how any argument could support such a counter-factual claim. Throughout the philosophical world, political philosophy was not merely alive but thriving in the form of Leo Strauss, Critical Theorists, Habermas, Hayek, Popper, Oakeshott, McPherson, Kojeve, Gadamer, Arendt, Wolin (and 'The Berkeley School') and many others, both in Europe and the Middle East (e.g. Strauss and Cropsey 1987; Berstein 1976; de Crespigny & Minogue 1976). Laslett's assertion is merely an echo of Ayer's authoritarian parochialism: if Anglo-American academic analytic philosophers are not doing political philosophy, then political philosophy does not exist.

The R.S. Peters Myth

The analytic approach to philosophy of education, although perhaps first seen in Hardie's *Truth and Fallacy in Educational Theory,* became popular within educational studies through the works of Israel Scheffler in the U.S. and R.S. Peters in England. We shall concentrate here on R.S. Peters, for reasons best understood as components of what Kevin Harris has rightly described as 'The R.S. Peters myth' (Harris 1988, p. 55). As others have observed, Peters's work has been difficult to discuss in any productive way because he and his supporters attribute any substantial disagreement with his ideas to a failure to understand either the ideas or the ('applied') analytic method (Harris 1988, p. 56). Be that as it may, there are two reasons for concentrating on Peters's branch of applied analytic philosophy of education. First, as recent commentators have emphasised, the Peters school did not merely perpetuate the neglect of the history of educational thought consolidated by Dewey, but added to this neglect the doctrinaire historical parochialism of the analytic school (see Darling 1992). Secondly, and more importantly, are the exaggerated and evangelical claims that have been made concerning Peters's originality and influence.

The historical parochialism of the analytic school, and the closely related isolation of that school from educational scholarship as a whole, requires a more extensive and specific discussion than I will provide here. I intend to publish a discussion shortly which examines the way in which ignorance of the history of educational philosophy has undermined the philosophical value of 'applied' philosophy of education. In the present paper I will briefly mention, in general terms, the neglect of the history of educational philosophy within educational studies, and concentrate on the exaggerations that constitute the R.S. Peters myth.

The educationist case against study of the history of educational ideas as a prerequisite of philosophy of education was first presented by R.S. Peters in 1964 (Peters 1964, p. 142), presented again by Peters in 1966 (Peters 1966, pp. 64–66), repeated, uncritically and almost verbatim, by Dearden in 1971 (Dearden 1971, pp. 92–93), presented once again by Peters in 1983 (Peters 1983, p. 31) and by Hirst in 1986 (Hirst in Cooper 1986, p. 8). This now orthodox educationist opinion was rhetorical rather than argued, and inadequate on several grounds.

First, these educationists adopted the self-referential isolationism of the analytic school. Ayer and Laslett, for example, passed judgement upon metaphysics and political philosophy defined without qualification, while such criticism as they offer referred only to their own propositions, or to their own colleagues or immediate predecessors. Likewise, when Peters, Dearden or Hirst criticise the history of educational philosophy and ideas, they discuss only their own definitions of the subject, or courses taught to training teachers in colleges of education in England (Peters 1966, p. 64), by instructors with little competence in the subject (Peters 1966, pp. 62, 65; Dearden 1971, p. 93; Peters 1983, p. 31). Although the criticisms of these definitions or courses may be valid, the conclusions drawn concerning the value of the study of the history of educational thought could not, and did not, in any way apply to any of the research and teaching in the history of educational ideas being provided at that time by political philosophers, classicists and historians (e.g. Marrou 1948; Johnson 1959a; Beck 1964; Strauss 1967; Lord

1982). The fact that historical scholarship in educational philosophy existed outside the charmed circle of their own education departments seems never to have occurred to these educationists.

In addition to drawing general conclusions based solely on peculiar and local examples, the conclusions were often insinuated rather than stated explicitly, and 'supported' by nothing more than an appeal to the authority of 'general' philosophers. For example, Peters asserted that *unidentified* philosophers are:

> . . . aghast when they learn that students [of philosophy of education] are very often brought up on an antiquated diet of Plato, Rousseau and Froebel—perhaps with a dash of Dewey to provide a final obfuscation of the issues.
>
> (Peters 1964, p. 142. Cf. Peters in Tibble 1966, p. 66)

Perpetuating the historical parochialism of the analytic school, Peters insinuates that philosophers rightly object to any philosophy of education which precedes his own. No evidence is presented to show that any philosopher held this view. No argument is presented to show that any philosopher would have been justified in objecting to such an antiquated diet. Indeed, Peters made this assertion at a time when an increasing number of classicists, political philosophers, and historians, many of them explicitly aghast at the lack of learning among educationists, were arguing that a return to such an 'antiquated diet' was necessary in educational philosophy (e.g. Freeman 1922; Marrou 1948; Barzun 1954; Barzun 1959; Strauss 1968; Frankena 1965; Koerner 1965; Beck 1964; Johnson 1959a; Kennedy 1980; Knowles 1962; Blanshard 1973; Clarke 1971; Klein 1960; Gadamer 1980, Ch. 4; Finley 1975; Brann 1979). Peters's assertion was not an argued evaluation of the state of research in educational thought, but an artifact of his isolation from the educational scholarship outside his personal circle. It is only in the context of such historical parochialism and academic isolation that estimations of Peters's influence and originality can be credibly evaluated.

With regard to Peters's influence, P.H. Hirst could claim, without evidence or argument, that:

> Richard Peters has revolutionised philosophy of education and as the work of all others now engaged in that area bears witness, there can be no going back on the transformation he has brought about.
>
> (Hirst 1986, pp. 37–38)

It must be emphasised that Hirst is not estimating Peters's influence in English departments of education in the 1960s. He is claiming that all those engaged in the philosophy of education *as of 1986* were influenced by the 'revolution' Peters is alleged to have brought about. This assertion is an absurd exaggeration. Even within educational studies, many philosophers were not influenced by Peters, or were actually opposed to him. Harris demonstrates this quite clearly in the case of Australia, and one need only look to followers of John Dewey and Lawrence Kohlberg, or advocates of variations of Critical Theory such as Henry Giroux, to see that the same is true in the United States (see also Noddings 1995).

Much more importantly, if we look outside educational studies to the work of classicists and political philosophers who account for most philosophy of education, we see that Peters had no influence at all (e.g. Arendt 1968; Blanshard 1973; Minogue 1973; Ackerman 1980, Ch. 5; Walzer 1983, Ch. 8; Bloom 1990; Habermas 1989; Oakeshott 1990; Pangle 1992). Political scientist Amy Gutmann, for example, explicitly dissociated herself from Peters's approach to the philosophy of education (Gutmann 1987, p. 7). Perhaps the most telling example, however, is the political philosopher, Leo Strauss. As Strauss had explained, in a paper first published in 1962, 'I own that education is in a sense the subject matter of my teaching and my research' (Strauss 1968, p. 9). Strauss was explicitly identified as an alternative to R.S. Peters by Anthony Quinton as early as 1967 (Quinton 1967, p. 195). Some thirty years later, Strauss's widely recognised eminence as a political and educational philosopher continued to be acknowledged even by his critics, one of whom observed that Strauss:

> . . . gave more thought to the subject of liberal education than did any other major political thinker of the twentieth century.
>
> (Schram 1991–92, p. 201)

A number of Strauss's students wrote studies in educational philosophy which were very well and widely reviewed outside educational studies and only a few years before Hirst made the pronouncement quoted above (e.g. Lord 1982; Tarco 1984. Cf. Pangle 1992; Pangle & Pangle 1993). From this perspective, Hirst's assertion ceases to be a credible estimation of Peters's influence, but is exposed as an unintentional measure of the increasing parochialism and conformism that defined the evolution of philosophy of education within educational studies (cf. Muir 1996).

If claims about Peters's influence have been extremely exaggerated, similar claims concerning his originality are equally unfounded. Three claims have been made concerning the 'revolutionary' originality of Peters's philosophy of education. These claims are reiterated in Professor White's discussion of 'the Peters revolution' (White 1987, p. 156), and the current state of educationist philosophy of education. White mentions, first, Peters's 'cartography of educational concepts' (White 1987, p. 160). In light of the fact that White himself provides us with good reason to doubt the significance of this achievement (White 1987, pp. 156, 157, 160), we shall concentrate on the remaining two.

It is suggested that Peters has some claim to originality in philosophy of education on the grounds that he demonstrated the 'application of philosophy to the felt problems of practitioners' (White 1987, p. 160). As the preceding sections in this paper show, however, the application of philosophy to the felt problems of educational practitioners had been an explicit intention of academic educationists since before the turn of the century. So, far from originating this 'applied' relationship between philosophy and education (schooling), Peters at most perpetuated the view of this relationship that had been effectively compulsory within the departments of education for nearly a century (Schrag 1994).

White describes Peters's third claim to originality in the following terms:

> Peters has been drawn throughout his career towards fundamental reflection on the nature of human beings, the foundations of morality, and the place of reason in human life. His abiding legacy to philosophy of education will be, in my opinion, not his cartography, but his showing how first-order practical issues have their roots in such reflections as these.
>
> (White 1987, p. 160)

It is difficult to take seriously the claim that such reflection constitutes Peters's 'abiding legacy' to philosophy of education. R.M. Hare has observed that for Plato, 'philosophy was the philosophy of education' (Hare 1970, p. 15), and Plato showed that serious educational thought has its roots in reflection on such questions as the nature of human beings or the place of reason in human life. The same is certainly true of other educational thinkers, from Isocrates through Martianus Capella and Alcuin, to Locke and Rousseau, Leo Strauss, and even John Dewey or Lawrence Kohlberg. Rather than being Peters's abiding legacy to the subject, his awareness of such questions once again at most perpetuates what has always been a defining characteristic of the subject.

Peters may have been influential in educational philosophy within educational studies in England during the 1960s and 1970s. Yet, from the broader perspective of educational scholarship as a whole, Peters was never more than a marginal figure of little originality and of no broad or lasting influence. On the contrary, he represents the culmination of nearly a century of decline of educational philosophy within educational studies, and the unfounded estimations of his originality and influence are nothing more than examples of what Peters himself knew to be the consequent 'narrowness and orthodoxy' of such philosophy (Cooper 1986, p. 4). He seemed to educationists to be original and influential because, divorced from the history of their discipline and isolated from mainstream educational scholarship, they had no basis for comparison. The Peters myth is no longer believable, even within educational studies, and the time has come when educationist philosophers of education no longer have any choice but to look elsewhere for a more substantial and enduring conception of their discipline.

A Glance at the Future

Educational philosophy is one of the oldest and richest features of the Western intellectual tradition, and it has never ceased to thrive among political philosophers, classicists, and historians of ideas. Unfortunately, the introduction of philosophy of education into educational studies, and the subsequent evolution of this 'new' academic discipline, was defined above all by its divorce from the traditions that preceded it, its increasing narrowness, orthodoxy, and isolation (Cooper 1986, pp. 4–5), and by a consequent—and devastating—loss of learning and intellectual credibility (e.g. Smith 1995. Cf. Wilson & Cowell 1989, pp. 44, 52; Commission on the Humanities 1980, pp. 52–53; Grafton & Jardine 1986, p. xi).

Although a few educationists have advocated a more historically informed approach to educational philosophy (e.g. Darling 1993, pp. 36–38; Jonathan 1993, p. 177), such advocacy is undermined by an insufficient awareness of the consequences of the recent evolution of the discipline. Ruth Jonathan, for example, has advocated 'a radical broadening' of educational philosophy, understood in terms of the incorporation of the history of educational ideas into the discipline. It seems to me, however, that educationist philosophers must be less self-congratulatory about their new (and still quite uninformed) enthusiasm for history, and honest enough to acknowledge that they are merely beginning to rectify the 'radical narrowing' they themselves have inflicted on the discipline in the first place. After all, this supposedly 'radical' broadening of educationist philosophy can accomplish nothing more than bringing the discipline in line with the way in which it has always been pursued, and still is, outside the tightly closed world of the education departments.

Although educationists have also begun to wonder whether arguments might be made which will support the advocacy of a more historically informed approach to educational philosophy, such arguments were made and accepted more than a hundred years ago and have been refined and reiterated, over the past fifty years in particular, by classicists, political philosophers, historians of ideas and others devoted to educational scholarship (e.g. Burk 1923; Jaeger 1947; Marrou 1948; Meyers 1960; Finley 1975; Arendt 1968; Strauss 1968; Lord 1982; Kimball 1986; Proctor 1988; Tarcov 1984; Pangle 1992; Pangle & Pangle 1993). A return to the fundamental *educational* questions, firmly grounded in serious study of the philosophical traditions comprised of attempts to formulate and answer them, is probably the only means by which a worthwhile future for our discipline may be secured. I say 'probably', not because I doubt the necessity of historically informed educational philosophy, but because the migration of serious educational philosophy into departments of philosophy, political science or classics is continuing to accelerate, and we can no longer assume that educational philosophy has any future at all within educational studies.

References

Ackerman, B.A. (1980). *Social Justice and the Liberal State*, New Haven: Yale University Press.

Adamson, J.W. (1922). *A Short History of Education*, Cambridge: University of Cambridge Press.

Adler, M.J. (1988). *Reforming Education: Opening the American Mind*, New York: Macmillan.

Arendt, H. (1968). 'The crisis in education', *Between Past and Future*, New York: The Viking Press.

Aron, R. (1975). *History and the Dialectic of Violence*, tr. B. Cooper, Basil Blackwell: Oxford.

Ayer, A.J. (1936). *Language, Truth and Logic*, New York: Dover.

Ayer, A.J. (1973). *The Central Questions of Philosophy*. Harmondsworth: Penguin.

Bacon, F. (1861). *The Advancement of Learning*, London: J.M. Dent & Sons.

Beck, F.A.G. (1964). *Greek Education, 450–350 B.C.*, London: Methuen & Co.

Berlin, I. (1980). *Personal Impressions*, London: The Hogarth Press.

Bernstein, R.J. (1976). *The Restructuring of Social and Political Thought*, London: Methuen & Company.

Blanshard, B. (1973). *The Uses of a Liberal Education*, LaSale: Alcove Press.

Bloom, A. (1987). *The Closing of the American Mind*, New York: Simon & Schuster.

Bloom, A. (1990). *Giants and Dwarfs*, New York: Simon & Schuster.

Bowen, J. (1972). *A History of Western Education, Vol. I: The Ancient World*, London: Methuen.

Boyd, W. (1966). *The History of Western Education*. 8th edn. London: Adams & Co.

Bruner, J.S. (1966). 'After John Dewy, what?', in R.D. Archambault (ed.), *Dewey on Education*, New York: Random House.

Burk, A. (1923). *Die Padagogik des Isokrates als Grundlegung des humanistischen Bildungsideals, im Vergleich mit den zietgenossischen und den modernen Theorien dargestelt*, Wurzburg: Studien zur Geschichte und Kultur des Altertums.

Burnet, J. (1962) [1914]. *Greek Philosophy: Thales to Plato*, London: Macmillan & Co.

Clarke, M.L. (1971). *Higher Education in the Ancient World*, London: Routledge & Kegan Paul.

Cohen, M.R. (1913). 'Philosophy', in P. Munroe (ed.) *Cyclopedia of Education*, Vol. 4, New York: Macmillan Co.

Collingwood, R.G. (1944). *An Autobiography*. Harmondsworth: Penguin.

Commission on the Humanities (1980). *The Humanities in American Life*, Berkeley: University of California Press.

Cooper, D.E. (ed.) (1986). *Education, Values and Mind*, London: Routledge & Kegan Paul.

Copleston, F. (1979). *On the History of Philosophy and Other Essays*, London: Search Press.

Cremin, L.A. (1966). 'John Dewey and the progressive-education movement, 1915–1952', in R.D. Archambault (ed.), *Dewey on Education*, New York: Random House.

Curtis, S.J. & Boultwood, M.E.A. (1965). *A Short History of Educational Ideas*, London: University Tutorial Press.

Darling, J. (1992). 'Rousseau as progressive instrumentalist', *Journal of Philosophy of Education*, 27, 1: 27–38.

Davidson, T. (1899). *Aristotle and Ancient Educational Ideals*, New York: Charles Scribner's Sons.

Dearden, R.F. (1971). 'The philosophy of education', in J. W. Tibble, (ed.), *An Introduction to the Study of Education*, London: Routledge & Kegan Paul.

de Crespigny, A. & Minogue, K. (eds) (1976). *Contemporary Political Philosophers*,London: Methuen & Co.

Dewey, J. (1910). *The Influence of Darwin on Philosophy*, New York: Henry Holt & Co.

Dewey, J. (1913a). 'Plato', in P. Monroe, (ed.) *Cyclopedia of Education*, Vol. 4, New York: Macmillan Co.

Dewey, J. (1931b). 'Philosophy of education', in P. Monroe, (ed.) *Cyclopedia of Education*, Vol. 4, New York: Macmillan Co.

Dewey, J. (1916). *Education and Democracy*, New York: The Macmillan Co.

Dewey, J. (1939). *Intelligence in the Modern World*, ed. J. Ratner, New York: The Modern Library.

Dewey, J. (1958). *Philosophy of Education*, Totowa: Littlefields, Adams & Co.

Dewey, J. (1964) [1899]). *John Dewey on Education*, ed. R.D. Archambault, New York: Modern Library.

Dobson, J.F. (1913). *The Greek Orators*, London: Methuen & Co.

Finley, M.I. (1975). 'The heritage of Isocrates', in *The Use and Abuse of History*, London: Chatto & Windus.

Frankena, W.K. (1965). *Three Historical Philosophies of Education*, Glenview: Scott, Foresman & Co.

Freeman, K.J. (1922). *Schools of Hellas: An Essay on the Practice and Theory of*

Ancient Greek Education, London: Macmillan & Company.
Gomperz, T. (1964) [1901]. *The Greek Thinkers*, 4 vols, London: John Murray.
Grafton, A. & Jardine, L. (1986). *From Humanism to Humanities*, Cambridge: Harvard University Press.
Gutmann, A. (1987). *Democratic Education*, Princeton: Princeton University Press.
Gwynn, A. (1964 [1926]). *Roman Education From Cicero to Quintillian*, New York: Russell & Russell.
Habermas, J. (1989). *The New Conservatism*, New York: Polity Press.
Hadas, M. (1969). *The Living Tradition*, New York: Meridian Books.
Harde, C.D. (1942). *Thruth and Fallacy in Educational Theory.* Cambridge: Cambridge University Press.
Hare, R.M. (1970). 'General introduction', in *The Dialogues of Plato*, tr. B. Jowett, London: Sphere Books.
Harris, K. (1988). 'Dismantling a deconstructionist history of philosophy of education', *Educational Philosophy and Theory*, 20, 1: 50–58.
Haskins, C.H. (1957a [1923]). *The Rise of the Universities*, Ithaca: Cornell University Press.
Haskins, C.H. (1957b) [1927]). *The Renaissance of the Twelfth Century*, Meridian Books, New York.
Hirsch, Jr. E.D. (1987). *Cultural Literacy. What Every American Needs to Know*, Boston: Houghton Mifflin Co.
Hirst, P.H. (1971). 'Liberal education', in L. C. Deighton (ed.), *The Encyclopedia of Education*, Vol. 5, New York: Macmillan.
Hirst, P.H. (1986). 'R.S. Peters's contribution to the philosophy of education' in D. E. Cooper (ed.), *Education, Values and Mind*, London: Routledge & Kegan Paul.
Hubbell, H.M. (1914). *The Influence of Isocrates on Cicero, Dionysius and Aristides*, New Haven, NY: Yale University Press.
Hudson, S.D. (1986). *Human Character and Morality: Reflections from the History of Ideas*, Boston: Routledge & Kegan Paul.
Jaeger, W. (1947). *The Ideals of Greek Culture*, Oxford: Blackwell.
Jebb, R.C. (1893). *The Attic Orators from Antiphon to Isaeus*, London: Macmillan & Co.
Jonathan, R. (1993). 'Education, philosophy of education and the fragmentation of value', *Journal of Philosophy of Education*, 27, 2: 171–178.
Kaminsky, J.S. (1986). 'The first 600 months of philosophy of education—1935–1985: A deconstructionist history', *Educational Philosophy and Theory*, 18, 2:42–47.
Kaminsky, J.S. (1992). 'A pre-history of educational philosophy in the United States: 1861–1914', *Harvard Educational Review*, 62, 2:179–198.
Kennedy, G. (1980). *Classical Rhetoric and Its Christian and Secular Tradition from Ancient to Modern Times*, Chapel Hill: University of North Carolina Press.
Kimball, B.A. (1986). *Orators and Philosophers: A History of the Idea of Liberal Education*, New York: Teachers College Press.
Knowles, D. (1962). *The Evolution of Medieval Thought*, London: Longman's, Green & Co.
Kolakowski, L. (1972). *Positivist Philosophy*, Harmonsworth: Penguin.
Laslett, P. (ed.) (1956). *Philosophy, Politics and Society*, New York: Macmillan.
Laurie, S.S. (1903). *Studies in the History of Educational Opinion from the Renaissance*, Cambridge: Cambridge University Press.
Leavis, F.R. (1982). *The Critic as Anti-Philosopher*, G.H. Singh (ed.), Athens, Georgia: University of Georgia Press.
Locke, J. (1968). *Locke's Educational Writings*, (ed. J. L. Axtell), Cambridge: Cambridge University Press.
Locke, J. (1980 [1880]), *Some Thoughts Concerning Education*, ed. R. H. Quick, Cambridge: Cambridge University Press.
Lord, C. (1982). *Education and Culture in the Political Thought of Aristotle*, London: Cornell University Press.
MacIntyre, A. (1971). 'Philosophy and social theory', in B. Magee, (ed.) *Modern British Philosophy*, London: Secker & Warburg.
MacIntyre, A. (1981). *After Virtue*, Notre Dame: University of Notre Dame Press.
Maimonides, M. (1963). *The Guide of the Perplexed*, tr. S. Pines, Chicago: University of Chicago Press.
Marrou, H.I. (1948). *Histoire de l'education dans l'Antiquite*, Paris: Editions du Seuil.
Marrou, H. I. (1984). 'Education and rhetoric', in M.I. Finley (ed.), *The Legacy of Greece*, Oxford: Oxford University Press.
Minogue, K.R. (1973). *The Concept of a University*, London: Weidenfeld & Nicolson.
Montaigne, M. (1957). *The Complete Essays of Montaigne*, (trans. D.M. Frame), Stanford: Stanford University Press.
Moore, T.W. (1982). *Philosophy of Education: An Introduction*, London: Routledge & Kegan Paul.
Muir, J.R. (1995). The Relationship Between Education and Political Doctrine: The Isocratic Heritage and a Socratic Alternative. Doctoral Thesis, Oxford: University of Oxford.
Muir, J.R. (1996). 'The strange case of Mr. Bloom', *Journal of Philosophy of* Education, 30, 2: forthcoming.
Myers, E.D. (1960). *Education in the Perspective of History*, New York: Harper & Brothers.
Nakosteen, M. (1965). *The History and Philosophy of Education*. New York: The Ronald Press.
Nettleship, R.L. (1935[1880]). *The Theory of Education in Plato's Republic*, Oxford: Oxford University Press.
Newman, K. (1975). 'Without vision, the people perish', *The Listener*, 20 March, pp. 358–359.
Noddings, N. (1995). *Philosophy of Education*, Boulder: Westview Press.
Oakeshott, M. (1990). *The Voice of Liberal Learning*, New Haven: Yale University Press.
O'Conner, D.J. (1957). *An Introduction to the Philosophy of Education*, London: Routledge & Kegan Paul.
Pangle, T.L. (1992). *The Ennobling of Democracy: The Challenge of the Postmodern Era*, Baltimore: The Johns Hopkins University Press.
Pangle, L.S., Pangle, T.L. (1993). *The Learning of Liberty: The Educational Ideas of the American Founders*, Lawrence, University of Kansas Press.
Peters, R.S. (1964). 'The place of philosophy in the training of teachers', *Education and the Education of Teachers*. London: Routledge & Kegan Paul.
Peters, R.S. (1966). 'The philosophy of education', in J.W. Tibble (ed.), *The Study of Education*, London: Routledge & Kegan Paul.
Peters, R.S. (1983). 'Philosophy of education', in P.H. Hirst, (ed.), *Educational Theory and its Foundation Disciplines*, London: Routledge & Kegan Paul.
Pettit, P. (1980). *Judging Justice*, London: Routledge & Kegan Paul.
Power, E.J. (1962). *Main Currents in the History of Education*, New York: McGraw-Hill.
Proctor, R.E. (1988). *Education's Great Amnesia: Reconsidering the Humanities from Petrarch to Freud*, Bloomington: Indiana University Press.
Quick, R.H. (1980 [1880]). 'Introduction', in J. Locke, *Some*

Thoughts Concerning Education, ed. R.H. Quick, Cambridge: Cambridge University Press.

Quinton, A. (ed.) 1967. *Political Philosophy*, Oxford: Oxford University Press.

Rashdall, H. (1936 [1895].) *The Universities of Europe in the Middle Ages*, eds F.M. Powicke & A.M. Emden, Oxford: Oxford University Press.

Ravitch, D. (1983). *The Troubled Crusade*, Basic Books, New York.

Reynolds, L.D. & Wilson, N.G. (1974). *Scribes and Scholars: A Guide to the Transmission of Greek and Latin Literature*, Oxford: Clarendon Press.

Romilly, J. (1988). *Les Grands Sophists dans l'Athenes de Pericles*, Paris: Editions de Fallois.

Rusk, R.R. (1962). *The Doctrines of the Great Educators*. London, Macmillan & Co.

Ryle, G. *et al.* (1956). *The Revolution in Philosophy*, London: Macmillan & Company.

Santayana, G. (1913). *Winds of Doctrine: Studies in Contemporary Opinion*, London: J.M. Dent & Sons.

Schrag, F. (1994). 'A view of our enterprise', *Educational Theory*, 3, 2.

Schram, G. N. (1991–1992). 'The place of Leo Strauss in a liberal education', *Interpretation: A Journal of Political Philosophy*, 19, 2:201–216.

Scolnicov, S. (1988). *Plato's Metaphysics of Education*, London: Routledge.

Smith, R. (1995). 'Editorial', *Journal of Philosophy of Education*, 29, 3:293.

Strauss, L. (1968). *Liberalism Ancient and Modern*, New York: Basic Books.

Strauss, L., Cropsey, J. (eds) (1987). *History of Political Philosophy*, Chicago: University of Chicago Press.

Tarcov, N. (1984). *Locke's Education for Liberty*, London: University of Chicago Press.

Tibble, J.W. (ed.) (1966). *The Study of Education*, London: Routledge & Kegan Paul.

Tibble, J.W. (ed.) (1971). *An Introduction to the Study of Education*, London: Routledge & Kegan Paul.

Todd, T.D. (1976). 'Ayer's the central questions of philosophy', *Philosophy and Rhetoric*, 9, 1:55–59.

Walzer, M. (1983). *Sphere of Justice*, New York: Basic Books.

Weatherford, W.D. (ed.) (1960). *The Goals of Higher Education*, Cambridge: Harvard University Press.

White, J. (1987). 'The medical condition of philosophy of education', *Journal of Philosophy of Education*, 21, 2:155–162.

Wieruszowski, H. (1966). *The Medieval University*, New York: Van Nostrand.

Williams, B. (1980). 'Politics, philosophy and the analytic tradition', in M. Richter (ed.), *Political Theory and Political Education*, Princeton: Princeton University Press.

Wilson, J. & Cowell, B. (1989). *Taking Education Seriously*, London, Ontario: Althouse Press.

Article Review Form at end of book.

What is constructivism? Describe a constructivist classroom.

Constructivist Cautions

The authors point out the difference between the theory of constructivism and its practical application, and they argue that the consequences of implementing constructivism in the classroom will be considerably more challenging than might be anticipated from the simple slogans that advocates repeat.

Peter W. Airasian and Mary E. Walsh

Peter W. Airasian and Mary E. Walsh are professors in the School of Education, Boston College, Chestnut Hill, Mass.

Recently, the concept of "constructivism" has been receiving a great deal of attention. At the conceptual level, constructivists debate such questions as, What is knowledge? What is teaching? What is learning? And is objectivity possible?[1] At the practical level, these complex issues have, in many cases, been reduced to catch phrases such as "Students construct their own knowledge" or the slightly narrower "Students construct their own knowledge based on their existing schemata and beliefs." Many efforts are under way to translate constructivist epistemology into classroom practices that will enable students to become "constructors of their own knowledge." While readily acknowledging that constructivism has made and will continue to make a significant contribution to educational theory and practice, we wish to sound a cautionary note about the euphoria surrounding constructivism.

What Is Constructivism?

Constructivism is an epistemology, a philosophical explanation about the nature of knowledge. Although constructivism might provide a model of knowing and learning that could be useful for educational purposes, at present the constructivist model is descriptive, not prescriptive. It describes in the broadest of strokes the human activity of knowing and nowhere specifies the detailed craft of teaching. It is important to understand at the outset that constructivism is not an instructional approach; it is a theory about how learners come to know. Although instructional approaches are typically derived from such epistemologies, they are distinct from them. One of the concerns that prompted us to undertake this discussion is the rush to turn the constructivist epistemology into instructional practice with little concern for the pitfalls that are likely to ensue.

Constructivism describes how one attains, develops, and uses cognitive processes. Multiple theories, such as those of Piaget and Vygotsky, have been proposed to explain the cognitive processes that are involved in constructing knowledge. While constructivism provides the epistemological framework for many of these theories, it is not itself an explanation for the psychological factors involved in knowing.

In general, constructivists compare an "old" view of knowledge to a "new," constructivist view. In the old view, knowledge is considered to be fixed and independent of the knower. There are "truths" that reside outside the knower. Knowledge is the accumulation of the "truths" in a subject area. The more "truths" one acquires, the more knowledge one possesses. In sharp contrast, the constructivist view rejects the notion that knowledge is independent of the knower and consists of accumulating "truths." Rather, knowledge is produced by the knower from existing beliefs and experiences. All knowledge is constructed and consists of what

"Constructivist Cautions" by Peter W. Airasian and Mary E. Walsh in PHI DELTA KAPPAN, Vol. 78, No. 8, Feb. 1997, pp. 444–449. Reprinted by permission.

individuals create and express. Since individuals make their own meaning from their beliefs and experiences, all knowledge is tentative, subjective, and personal. Knowledge is viewed not as a set of universal "truths," but as a set of "working hypotheses." Thus constructivists believe that knowledge can never be justified as "true" in an absolute sense.

Constructivism is based on the fundamental assumption that people create knowledge from the interaction between their existing knowledge or beliefs and the new ideas or situations they encounter. In this sense, most constructivists support the need to foster interactions between students' existing knowledge and new experiences. This emphasis is perceived to be different from the more traditional "transmission" model, in which teachers try to convey knowledge to students directly.

These fundamental agreements among constructivists are tempered by some important areas of difference about the process of constructing knowledge. These differences are reflected in two versions of constructivist theories or cognition: developmental and sociocultural. Developmental theories, such as Piaget's, represent a more traditional constructivist framework. Their major emphasis is on describing the universal forms or structures of knowledge (e.g., prelogical, concrete, and abstract operations) that guide the making of meaning. These universal cognitive structures are assumed to be developmentally organized, so that prelogical thinking occurs prior to concrete logical thinking in a developmental sequence. Within this framework, the individual student is considered to be the meaning maker, with the development of the individual's personal knowledge being the main goal of learning.

Critics of developmental theories of cognition point out that this perspective does not take into account "how issues such as the cultural and political nature of schooling and the race, class, and gender backgrounds of teachers and students, as well as their prior learning histories, influence the kinds of meaning that are made in the classroom."[2] Cognitive-developmental theories, it is claimed, divorce meaning making from affect by focusing on isolating universal forms of knowledge and thus limiting consideration of the sociocultural and contextual influences on the construction of knowledge.[3]

A second version of constructivism is reflected in the social constructivist or situated social constructivist perspective. As its name suggests, this type of constructivism puts its major emphasis on the social construction of knowledge and rejects the individualistic orientation of Piagetian theory. Within the sociocultural perspective, knowledge is seen as constructed by an individual's interaction with a social milieu in which he or she is situated, resulting in a change in both the individual and the milieu. Of course, it is possible for an individual to "reside" in many milieus, from a classroom milieu through a much more general cultural milieu. The point, however, is that social constructivists believe that knowledge has a social component and cannot be considered to be generated by an individual acting independently of his or her social context.[4] Consequently, recognition of the social and cultural influences on constructed knowledge is a primary emphasis. Because individual social and cultural contexts differ, the meanings people make may be unique to themselves or their cultures, potentially resulting in as many meanings as there are meaning makers. Universal meanings across individuals are not emphasized.

Critics of this perspective have pointed to the chaos that might be inherent in a multiplicity of potential meanings. While the social constructivists' concern with particular contextual or cultural factors that shape meaning enhances their recognition of differences across meanings, it limits their recognition of the universal forms that bring order to an infinite variety of meanings. Arguably, the critics of each version of constructivism exaggerate the positions espoused by these theories; however, they do set into relief the relative emphasis of each theory on the individual or the context.

This brief overview of constructivism omits many of the nuances and issues that characterize the debate over constructivist theory. However, our purpose is not to provide an in-depth portrait of constructivism, but rather to identify fundamental tenets that most constructivists would endorse and to point out that constructivism is not a unitary viewpoint. This latter fact is often overlooked in practice-oriented activities that derive from the slogan "Students are constructors of their own knowledge." The conflict between the two versions of constructivism is not merely "a matter of theoretical contemplation. Instead, it finds expression in tensions endemic to the act of teaching."[5] The particular version of constructivism one adopts—developmental or social constructivist—has important implications for classroom practices,[6] for the definition of knowledge,[7] for the relative emphasis on individual versus social learning,[8] for the role of the teacher,[9] and for the definition of successful instruction.[10]

Why Is Constructivism So Readily Accepted?

In the broad sense, constructivism represents a shift in the perspective of the social sciences and humanities from a view in which truth is a given to a view in which it is constructed by individuals and groups. There has been an inevitable spillover of this view from the social sciences and the humanities to education.

However, most educational theories and innovations are adopted with high levels of uncertainty. The wisdom of their adoption and the range of their impact are rarely known in advance of their implementation. Thus the justification for adopting a theory or innovation must come from outside the theory or innovation per se.[11] Typically, the justification is supplied by the existence of a pressing need or problem that requires quick amelioration or by the moral symbolism inherent in the theory or innovation. This is as true for constructivism as it has been for all educational theories and innovations that have sought to make their way into practice. However, it is very important to emphasize that there is a crucial difference between evidence that documents the need for change and evidence that documents the efficacy of a particular strategy of change. The specific strategy selected to produce change must seek its own validation, independent of the evidence of the need for change of some kind.

To understand its rapid acceptance, we must examine both present educational needs and the symbolic aspects of constructivism. The pressing educational need that fuels interest in constructivism is the perception that what we have been doing in schools has failed to meet the intellectual and occupational needs of the majority of our students; schools seem not to be promoting a sufficiently broad range of student outcomes. In particular, "thinking" or "higher-order" skills are not receiving sufficient instructional emphasis. A large part of the explanation for the perceived deficiency in pupil learning is thought to be an emphasis on "reductionist" or rote outcomes and forms of instruction. Reorienting instruction to nonrote outcomes makes such skills as generalizing, analyzing, synthesizing, and evaluating very important. From an instructional point of view, it puts much more of the onus on the student to construct personal meanings and interpretations. There is a link, then, between an epistemology that focuses on students' constructing their own knowledge and an education system that seeks to promote higher-level learning outcomes.

Constructivism seems to pass the onus of creating or acquiring knowledge to the student.

Also linking constructivism and educational need is the current emphasis on bottom-up as opposed to top-down approaches to reform. Thus recent reforms have increasingly allocated discretion for reforming the educational process to individual schools, teachers, students, and parents. In particular, teachers are given more discretion to construct their own meanings and interpretations of what will improve classroom teaching and learning. Moreover, because constructivism is an epistemology of how people learn, its focus is logically on classroom practice. The increased teacher discretion over teaching and learning, combined with the classroom orientation and higher-level focus of constructivism, has sparked teachers' interest in the potential of constructivism for classroom practice.

Of course, it is not just increased teacher discretion and the classroom focus of constructivism that prompt interest. Constructivism is also appealing for other, more symbolic reasons. First, the rhetoric that surrounds constructivism is seductive. It plays off the metaphor of "lighting the flame" of student motivation (constructivism) against that of "filling the bucket" of students' heads with facts (present methods).[12] Constructivists claim that they emphasize autonomy as opposed to obedience, construction as opposed to instruction, and interest as opposed to reinforcement.[13] The implication is that, if one is opposed to constructivism, one is opposed to student autonomy, construction of meaning, and interest. Thus opponents are viewed as being against lighting the flame of student motivation. Such rhetoric plays a potent role in the reception of all innovations, including constructivism.

Second, since knowledge consists of what is constructed by the learner and since attainment of absolute truth is viewed as impossible, constructivism makes the implicit assumption that all students can and will learn—that is, construct knowledge. The vision of the constructivist student is one of activity, involvement, creativity, and the building of personal knowledge and understanding. This is an appealing symbol in an education system that is perceived to be inadequate for meeting the learning needs of many students. However, our consideration of constructivism should extend beyond process to an examination of the nature of the knowledge actually constructed.

Third, in a variety of ways and with a variety of potential consequences, constructivism symbolizes emancipation. From one perspective, constructivism can be interpreted as a symbol of the emancipation of teachers from the primary responsibility for student learning, since constructivism passes the onus of creating or acquiring knowledge from the teacher to the student. This notion is mistaken. The teacher will no longer be a supplier of information, but he or she will remain very much involved in the learning process, coordinating and critiquing student constructions, building his or her own knowledge of constructivism in the classroom, and learning new methods of instruction. Constructivism can also be interpreted as a symbol of the emancipation of teachers from the burden of dealing with the difficult issue of motivation, since many constructivists view the student's sense of ownership of and empowerment over the learning process as providing its own intrinsic motivation.[14]

Constructivism certainly is emancipatory and dovetails well with the agendas of many interest groups through its social constructivist emphasis on context as a critical feature of knowledge construction. When context becomes an important aspect of knowledge construction, it is logical to conclude that involvement in different contexts will lead to the construction of different knowledge, even if the same set of "data" is presented in the different contexts. Given a problem or an issue, a context—which is often designated in social, economic, racial, and gender terms—will influence the interpretations, conclusions, motives, and attitudes of individuals in that context. When confronted with the same problem or issue, individuals in different milieus may construct different interpretations and conclusions. In this case, "truth" becomes what those in a given milieu construct. And since different milieus vary in their constructions and since there is no absolute truth to search for, knowledge becomes relative to the milieu one inhabits.

This view is certainly symbolically emancipatory for many disempowered groups, but with what effect on the classroom? It would be naive to ignore the sociopolitical agendas and potential consequences for education that constructivism can evoke, particularly those emanating from the social constructivist version of constructivism.

Thus there are strong forces that underlie the growing interest in and acceptance of the constructivist epistemology. These forces stem from the perceived need to alter educational practice from an associational approach to one that emphasizes the higher-level knowledge construction needed to cope with the rapid expansion of information. They also stem from symbolic features of constructivism, particularly the symbols associated with the rhetoric of constructivism.

Cautions

Despite the persuasiveness of the above forces, it is important to be aware that the application of constructivism in classrooms is neither widespread nor systemic. This is not to suggest that there are no successful applications of constructivism. In fact, a number of writers have described approaches to constructivist teaching in special education classrooms, in largely African American classrooms, and in after-school programs.[15] With the exception of Ann Brown's Community of Learning schools, however, most applications of constructivism have tended to be recent, narrowly focused pilot studies. In discussing her ongoing work, even Brown indicates that, "for the past 10 years or so, my colleagues and I have been gradually evolving learning environments [to foster grade school pupils' interpretive communities]."[16] Accentuating the need for gradual development is important, because in simultaneously mounting constructivist teaching and endeavoring to remain faithful to constructivist tenets, teachers and administrators will be confronted with a number of obstacles and issues.

We turn now to some cautions that need to be kept in mind as teachers attempt to implement constructivism in their classrooms. Some of these cautions are pertinent to any classroom innovation. Others are specific to constructivism.

Do not fail to recognize the difference between an epistemology of learning and a well-thought-out and manageable instructional approach for implementing it. We do not have an "instruction of constructivism" that can be readily applied in classrooms. There are suggestions for methods that are likely to foster student construction of knowledge, primarily those that emphasize nonrote tasks and active student participation in the learning process (e.g., cooperative learning, performance assessments, product-oriented activities, and "hands-on" learning, as well as reciprocal teaching and initiation-reply-evaluation methods). However, it is not clear how such methods relate to learning in different content areas or whether these methods will be equally successful across all subject areas.[17]

It is even more important to recognize that the selection of a particular instructional strategy represents only part of what is necessary in the constructivist approach. Selection of a strategy does not necessarily lead to appropriate implementation or to the provision of individual feedback to students regarding their constructions. Implementing constructivism calls for a "learn as you go" approach for both students and teachers; it involves many decisions and much trial and error. Commenting on the relevance of this theory for contemporary practices and procedures in education, Kenneth Gergen writes:

> There is no means by which practical derivatives can simply be squeezed from a theory of knowledge. As has been seen, theories can specify neither the particulars to which they must be applied nor the contexts in which they may be rendered intelligible. There are no actions that follow necessarily from a given theory. . . . Thus, rather than seeking clear and compelling derivatives of constructionist theory, we should explore the kinds of practices that would be favored by the perspective within current conventions of understanding.[18]

Do not fall into the trap of believing that constructivist instructional techniques provide the sole means by which students construct meanings. This is not the case. Students construct their own knowledge and interpretations no matter what instructional approach is implemented and no matter what name is given to it. What teacher has not taught a didactic, rote-oriented topic or concept only to find that the students constructed a variety of very different meanings from those anticipated by the teacher? Thus no single teaching method ought to be used exclusively. One of the leading advocates of constructivism in education has compellingly argued that, from a constructivist point of view, it is a misunderstanding to consider teaching methods such as memorization and rote learning useless. "There are, indeed, matters that can and perhaps must be learned in a purely mechanical way."[19] One's task is to find the right balance between the activities of constructing and receiving knowledge, given that not all aspects of a subject can or should be taught in the same way or be acquired solely through "hands-on" or student-centered means.

Because students always make their own meaning from instruction, the important curricular and instructional choice is not a choice between making and not making personal meaning from instructional activities, but a choice among the ideas, concepts, and issues that we want our students to construct meaning about. It is in this area that states such as Kentucky, California, and Vermont, among others, are redefining the expectations for student learning and reinforcing those expectations through statewide assessments. Similarly, it is in this area that such organizations as the National Council of Teachers of Mathematics are promulgating and advocating newer, more performance-oriented goals in their subject areas. The issues addressed by states and professional organizations are much more focused on the outcomes than on the means of instruction.

Do not assume that a constructivist orientation will make the same demands on teaching time as a nonconstructivist orientation. Time is an extremely important consideration in implementing constructivist education in two regards.

1. *Time is needed for teachers and pupils to learn and practice how to perform in a constructivist classroom.* If criticisms of "reductionist" education are valid, then substituting another approach, whether in part or in toto, will call for redefinition of both teachers' and students' roles. In a constructivist approach, teachers will have to learn to guide, not tell; to create environments in which students can make their own meanings, not be handed them by the teacher; to accept diversity in constructions, not search for the one "right" answer; to modify prior notions of "right" and "wrong," not stick to rigid standards and criteria; to create a safe, free, responsive environment that encourages disclosure of student constructions, not a closed, judgmental system.

   Students will also have to learn new ways to perform. They will have to learn to think for themselves, not wait for the teacher to tell them what to think; to proceed with less focus and direction from the teacher, not to wait for explicit teacher directions; to express their own ideas clearly in their own words, not to answer restricted-response questions;

to revisit and revise constructions, not to move immediately on to the next concept or idea.

It is easy to *say* that constructivist teachers must create an open, nonjudgmental environment that permits students to construct, disclose, and expose their constructions to scrutiny. But listening and responding to student constructions will be difficult and time-consuming.[20] Teachers will have to become accustomed to working with quite different and more general goals, since the instructional emphasis will be on the viability of varied, idiosyncratic student constructions. Teachers will need to serve as initiators of activities that will evoke students' interests and lead to new constructions and as critics of the constructions that students produce. In a sense, much of the responsibility for learning will be turned over to the students through "hands-on" experiences and activities designed to spur their constructions of meaning. The more teachers become engaged in this process, the more the resulting constructions will be theirs, not the students'.

Finding a balance between teacher involvement or noninvolvement in the process of learning will be a challenge. It is legitimate to ask how well—and how soon—teachers will be able to create such an environment and reorient their practice. In this regard it is noteworthy that, with few exceptions,[21] there is considerably less discussion about the role and activities of the *teacher* in constructivist education than there is about the role and activities of the *students.* But changes in orientation for both teacher and students will not occur immediately, especially for those who have had a long time to become accustomed to the current norms of classroom practice. New ways of thinking, acting, organizing, and judging will always take time to develop.

2. *In the shift to constructivist teaching, considerable time will be required for responding to the individual constructions of students.* Student constructions have two important properties: 1) they are complex in form, and 2) they differ from student to student. Because constructions represent understandings and connections between prior and new knowledge, they cannot be conveyed in a word or a phrase. To convey one's construction of meaning will require an in-depth presentation about one's knowledge and how one arrived at or justifies that knowledge. If constructions are reduced to multiple-choice items or to some other truncated representational form, the richness and meaning of constructivism will be lost. Hence, to review, understand, and respond to student constructions will require substantial teacher time and perhaps the involvement of parents and community members as well.

Moreover, different students are likely to produce quite different constructions, making it difficult to apply the same frame of reference to the review of their constructions. Each construction and its underlying logic will need to be examined, understood, and reviewed. Hence, the amount of time needed to respond to these constructions will be further increased. Responding to student constructions will be more like reading essays or viewing oral reports than like scoring multiple-choice or short-answer tests.

Implicit in the need for increased time are other important time-related issues, such as the tradeoff between coverage and depth. It is likely that the quality of students' knowledge constructions will depend in part on the time they are given to construct. More time will mean richer and deeper constructions. Teachers and schools will have to face the question of whether it is better to cover a large amount of content at a rather shallow level or to cover a smaller amount of content in great depth. The constructivist approach fits much better with the latter choice, since it aims for personal meaning and understanding, not rote associations.

Do not believe that the opposite of "one-right-answer" reductionism is "anything-goes" constructivism. Implicit in any form of classroom instruction guided by any theory of learning is the need for standards and criteria of judgment. This matter is both important and challenging in constructivist thought and application. Among the questions that constructivist teachers will have to confront regarding standards and criteria are: On what basis should students have to justify their constructions? Can the teacher who facilitates the constructions also be an objective evaluator of them? What constitutes a "reasonable" or "acceptable" student construction?

Should the teacher try to avoid transmitting standards and criteria that end up influencing or controlling the nature of student constructions? If so, how? Are evaluation standards and criteria independent of context or are they contextually bound?

A teacher who accepts the constructivist tenet that knowledge is constructed by individuals and that knowledge and experience are subjective must inevitably face the relationship between truth and meaning. In practical terms, the teacher must decide how much emphasis will be placed on the relative "truthfulness" of students' constructions or on their "meaningfulness" to the student. Since there is no one best construction and since people must construct their own meanings from personal experiences and understandings, there are many viable constructions.[22] Further, if it is assumed that knowledge is ego- and context-specific, the likelihood of agree-ing on common standards of evaluation is diminished greatly. This perspective could create many problems when applied in classrooms.

A rejoinder to this view argues that the lack of one best construction does not mean that some constructions cannot be deemed better than others. Moreover, sole reliance on personal meaning to justify constructions leads to rampant relativism and potentially biased, self-serving, and dishonest constructions.[23] In this view, the role of the teacher is to challenge students to justify and refine their constructions in order to strengthen them.

At the opposite end of the spectrum from meaningfulness is truthfulness. Absolute certainty is alien to the tenets of constructivism. However, there can be intermediate positions between absolute and relative truthfulness. Thus it is possible to evaluate some constructions as being more truthful (i.e., reasonable) than others. If a position of modified or relative truthfulness is adopted, as it inevitably will be in real classrooms, the teacher is directly confronted by the need to establish standards and criteria for evaluating the merits of students' constructions.

However, in facing this need, the teacher also faces an issue that should be approached with awareness and caution. In evaluating some constructions as being better than others, the teacher will find that the more explicit the evaluation standards and criteria, the greater the likelihood that they will be transmitted to and adopted by the students. When standards and criteria are constructed jointly by teachers, students, and parents, transmission and adoption become desirable. However, if the teacher is the sole determiner of standards and criteria, he or she is likely to have the primary influence on the nature of classroom constructions. Students may not construct meaning on their own, for they know that high grades derive from meeting the teacher's standards and criteria. Constructivism is thus compromised. The problem of guiding and evaluating students without undermining their constructivist activities is a thorny one. The development of standards and criteria that are clear but that allow variance in evaluation is paramount, and each teacher will have to find his or her appropriate balance, given that few external guidelines for defining such standards and criteria exist.

In the preceding discussion we have pointed out the difference between the theory of constructivism and its practical application. In particular, we have argued that the consequences of implementing constructivism in the classroom will be considerably more challenging than might be anticipated from the simple slogans that advocates repeat. But our comments and cautions should not be taken as criticisms of the constructivist viewpoint. Indeed, we recognize and appreciate the positive role that this orientation can play in changing educational practice. Rather, our comments are meant to illuminate and anticipate important issues that will inevitably arise in attempts to implement constructivism in practical, classroom settings. These are not reasons to avoid trying to implement constructivism: they are efforts to help readers know something about what they are adopting at a more substantive level. Knowing some of the nuances and problems of a theory or innovation makes one better able to move beyond rhetoric to consider the implications for one's own practice.

1. Richard S. Prawat. "Teachers' Beliefs About Teaching and Learning: A Constructivist Perspective," *American Journal of Education,* vol. 100, 1992, pp. 354–95; Carl Bereiter, "Constructivism, Socioculturalism, and Popper's World 3," *Educational Researcher,* October 1994, pp. 21–23; Rosalind Driver et al., "Constructing Scientific Knowledge in the Classroom," *Educational Researcher,* October 1994, pp. 5–12; and Neil M. Agnew and John L. Brown, "Foundations for a Model of Knowing: II. Fallible but Functional Knowledge," *Canadian Psychology,* vol. 30, 1989, pp. 168–83.
2. Michael O'Loughlin, "Rethinking Science Education: Beyond Piagetian Constructivism Toward a

Sociocultural Model of Teaching and Learning," *Journal of Research in Science Teaching,* vol. 29, 1992, p. 792.
3. Martin L. Hoffman, "Development of Moral Thought, Feeling, and Behavior." *American Psychologist,* vol. 34, 1979, pp. 958–66.
4. Kenneth J. Gergen, "Exploring the Postmodern: Perils or Potentials," *American Psychologist,* vol. 49, 1994, pp. 412–16; and James V. Wertsch and Chikako Toma, "Discourse and Learning in the Classroom: A Sociocultural Approach," in Leslie P. Steffe and Jerry Gale, eds., *Constructivism in Education* (Hillsdale, N.J.: Erlbaum, 1995), pp. 159–74.
5. Paul Cobb, "Where Is the Mind? Constructivist and Sociocultural Perspectives on Mathematical Development," *Educational Researcher,* October 1994, p. 13.
6. Deborah L. Ball, "With an Eye on the Mathematical Horizon: Dilemmas of Teaching Elementary School Mathematics," *Elementary School Journal,* vol. 93, 1993, pp. 373–97.
7. Virginia Richardson, "Constructivist Teaching: Theory and Practice," paper presented at the annual meeting of the American Educational Research Association, New Orleans, 1994; and Bereiter, op. cit.
8. Driver et al., op. cit.
9. Ibid.
10. Ginnette Delandshire and Anthony J. Petrosky, "Capturing Teachers' Knowledge: Performance Assessment," *Educational Researcher,* June/July 1994, pp. 11–18.
11. Peter W. Airasian, "Symbolic Validation: The Case of State-Mandated, High-Stakes Testing," *Educational Evaluation and Policy Analysis,* vol. 4, 1988, pp. 301–13.
12. David Elkind, "Spirituality in Education," *Holistic Education Review,* vol. 5, no. 1, 1992, pp. 12–16.
13. Rhete DeVries and Lawrence Kohlberg, *Constructivist Early Education* (Washington, D.C.: National Association for the Education of Young Children, 1987).
14. Aire W. Kruglanski, *Lay Epistemics and Human Knowledge* (New York: Plenum Press, 1989): Penny Oldfather, "Sharing the Ownership of Knowing: A Constructivist Concept of Motivation for Literacy Learning," paper presented at the annual meeting of the National Reading Conference, San Antonio, 1992; and O'Loughlin, op. cit.
15. Ann Brown, "The Advancement of Learning," *Educational Researcher,* November 1994, pp. 4–12; Richardson, op. cit.; Gloria Ladson-Billing, *The Dreamkeepers: Successful Teaching of African-American Children* (San Francisco: Jossey-Bass, 1994); and Wertsch and Toma, op. cit.
16. Brown, "Advancement of Learning," p. 7.
17. Susan S. Stodolsky, *The Subject Matters* (Chicago: University of Chicago Press, 1988); and Cobb, op. cit.
18. Kenneth Gergen, "Social Construction and the Educational Process," in Steffe and Gale, pp. 17–39.
19. Ernst von Glaserfeld, "A Constructivist Approach to Teaching," in Steffe and Gale, p. 5.
20. Peter W. Airasian, "Critical Pedagogy and the Realities of Teaching," in Henry Perkinson, *Teachers Without Goals, Students Without Purposes* (New York: McGraw-Hill, 1993), pp. 81–93.
21. See, for example, Brown, "The Advancement of Learning"; and Ladson-Billing, op. cit.
22. Geraldine Gilliss, "Schön's Reflective Practitioner: A Model for Teachers?" in Peter Grimmett and Gaalen Erickson, eds., *Reflection in Teacher Education* (New York: Teachers College Press, 1988), pp. 47–54.
23. Bereiter, op. cit.; and Karl Popper, *Objective Knowledge: An Evolutionary Approach* (Oxford: Clarendon, 1972).

Article Review Form at end of book.

What are school-based service programs? What are some of the benefits that students who participate in community service programs experience? What are two or three obstacles that often hinder schools from implementing community service programs?

Earning an 'A' in Idealism

Schools are giving student idealism a gentle nudge with community service curricula.

Donna Harrington-Lueker

Donna Harrington-Lueker is an associate editor of The American School Board Journal.

In Minneapolis, junior high students shovel snow for the disabled, read to the blind, and help nursing-home residents balance their checkbooks. In Philadelphia, high school students operate an official monitoring station for the Environmental Protection Agency. And in Ellington, Conn., high school students serve on the town's rescue squad.

They're all part of a groundswell effort among schools nationwide to incorporate community service into students' everyday lives. All across the U.S., in fact, schools are experimenting with mandatory community service programs and elective courses in service and citizenship. Some schools are offering service-based intervention programs for at-risk youngsters, and some are developing K-12 curricula that weave community service into every subject at every grade level.

The goal is to use the community as a classroom where students can learn important lessons in responsibility and citizenship—lessons, some say, that the Me Generation might not learn otherwise. And along the way, proponents of community service programs point out, the experience can bolster students' self-esteem, improve their academic achievement, and perhaps revive flagging interest in school.

The idea of such school-based initiatives isn't entirely new—some schools have had Key Clubs, food drives, and Honor Society service requirements for years. But school-based community service as a national goal is at a crossroads, say experts who spoke with *The American School Board Journal.*

"Right now, youth service is basically a lot of grass-roots efforts that rely on the vitality and energy of some intense individuals," says Catherine A. Rolzinski, director of education for Youth Service America, a Washington, D.C., advocacy group for youth service opportunities. In fact, Rolzinski continues, "Nobody would even have called [school-based service] a movement until the last couple of years."

That might be changing, though, as school-based service programs grow in number and sophistication. During the past year, the idea of a student service requirement received considerable attention from Congress and the President. That national attention, combined with increased interest in school restructuring, leads advocates to predict, tentatively, that school-based youth service programs just might be primed to move from the margins of education to the mainstream.

The Status of Service

What's school-based service like on the margins? Figures are muddy. Generally, though, private schools are more likely to require community service than public schools are, and by a wide margin: According to the National Association of Independent Schools, 25 percent of private schools require service for gradu-

Reprinted with permission from *The American School Board Journal,* March 1990, pp. 36–37.

ation. According to researchers Fred Newmann and Robert Rutter, only 4 percent of public schools do.

Reasons for the low numbers are easy to find: Many schools worry that service will divert time from academics, while others are reluctant to use youngsters to do work that state and local governments should be doing. Still others are legitimately wary of the hidden costs: The youngsters' time might be freely given, but administrative costs for a good service program can mount up.

Whatever the obstacles, though, more schools seem to be turning to community service if not as a requirement, at least as an option. And they cite some persuasive reasons for doing so: Proponents of school-based service—including former Maryland State Superintendent of Schools David W. Hornbeck—note that students who participate in community service develop responsible attitudes toward others, gain self-esteem, and improve attendance and behavior. They also learn important lessons about the work ethic and develop a feeling of belonging—no small accomplishment for youths who might be isolated or self-absorbed.

Consider the following examples:

- In Atlanta, high school students must volunteer at least 75 hours of their time and earn half a credit in community service before they graduate. The five-year-old program, brainchild of former Atlanta Superintendent Alonzo Crim, has served as a model for other school systems as well. The Detroit and Cherry Creek, Colo., schools already have similar requirements for their high school students, and in Washington, D.C., the school board has voted to require students to complete 100 hours of service before graduating, effective in 1991.
- In Minneapolis, more than 400 youngsters in the city's 12 junior high schools currently participate in Fresh Force, an innovative community service program that provides $500 grants for projects in the students' own neighborhoods. Students plan the projects—anything from cleaning up neighborhood parks to shoveling snow for the elderly—and work on them during school, after school, or on weekends, while a student board of directors dispenses funds. "Kids just learn through service," says Mary Spindler, director of student activities for the Minneapolis public schools. "They learn leadership and self-esteem, and they just do better in school. . . . And it happens whether the youngster comes from a low socioeconomic background or a high one."
- In Pittsburgh, eighth-graders identified as being at risk because of attendance problems, low grades, or poor behavior can take part in a school system program called OASES (Occupational and Academic Skills for Employment of Students). Youngsters spend half their school day in the classroom and half in the community, working on projects they've voted to complete. One OASES class, for example, built a playhouse for the Pittsburgh School for the Blind. Some 20 percent of the youngsters in the program reportedly make the honor roll, and virtually all improve their attendance, grades, and attitude toward school.
- In San Antonio, the Valued Youth Partnership program identifies Hispanic youths who are in danger of dropping out and trains them to serve as peer tutors for elementary youngsters. Both groups benefit from the eight hours a week of required service: The younger students get a boost with their studies, while the older kids improve their own grades and attendance records. Most important, the older youths are more likely to stay in school. The dropout rate among Hispanic students hits 65 percent nationwide and reaches 44 percent in San Antonio, but the dropout rate in the Valued Youth Partnership program is only 6 percent.
- Springfield, Mass., has taken what many youth service advocates consider the next step: weaving service into the curriculum in every grade, from kindergarten to grade 12, in each of the city's 40 schools. The "service by immersion" approach begins with a schoolwide project, such as providing a free lunch for as many as 100 needy people. Kindergartners might bring canned food from home, while second-graders make place mats in art class and third-graders learn about sanitary procedures for making sandwiches. "By the time these youngsters leave school," says Ann Southworth, assistant superintendent of instruction, "we want service to be a part of their lives."
- At the state level, Minnesota and Pennsylvania both provide state funds for school-based service programs, and Maryland requires local school systems to offer community service as a high school elective. (The Maryland State

Board of Education adopted the requirement for elective community service in 1985—three years after it spurned an attempt by former State School Superintendent David W. Hornbeck to require that all students perform 100 hours of community service to graduate.)

- A fourth state—Vermont—has a privately funded program called SerVermont, which provides grants for student service projects.

What's Next?

So why, despite these gains, isn't the idea of school-based service whipping across the country like a prairie fire before a west wind?

"Nothing new happens without strong advocacy," observes Kathleeen Kennedy Townsend. The eldest daughter of Robert F. Kennedy, Townsend has directed the Maryland Student Service Alliance for a little over a year and has stumped the state to build support for the state-mandated high school elective and for school-based youth service in general.

It takes time. Only 40 of the state's 234 high schools (in 16 of Maryland's 24 school systems) offer elective credits in community service, despite the fact that the state board of education passed the service regulation almost five years ago. Townsend aims to jack up both of those numbers and have all high schools and all 24 school systems participating next year.

Even in Pennsylvania, where Governor Robert P. Casey has been a strong advocate of youth service and where schools can apply for $5,000 grants for school-based service, the number of schools lining up to come on board isn't a long one yet. This year, in fact, only 59 Pennsylvania high schools applied for youth service grants, despite the efforts of PennServe, the governor's office of volunteer programs, and a public relations blitz in the state school board magazine.

The reason? "If you do [service learning] right in school, you don't run the school the same way," contends John Briscoe, a former Peace Corps volunteer and current director of PennServe, Pennsylvania's state office of volunteer programs. PennServe provides $5,000 grants for school-based service.) In fact, according to Briscoe and other advocates, school-based community service, done well, involves a commitment to experimental learning and a revision of the teacher's role in the classroom (the teacher lectures less and involves youngsters more).

Using this line of argument, many community service advocates look hopefully at school restructuring: Given similar ends and means, community service just could piggyback on the drive toward professionalism, site-based management, and school reform, they say.

Other hurdles—transportation, insurance, scheduling, and general administrivia—deter some schools, though these are easily surmounted, advocates and school people alike maintain. The Springfield public schools, for example, put a service elective in place within a month and revamped the K-12 curriculum between January and September; in fact, the first year the program operated, says Ann Southworth, every school in the system did a community service project.

"It's a question of priorities," maintains Townsend, who fields questions about funding and logistics as she travels to schools throughout Maryland. "If it's important to be an effective citizen, then you just do it." Some schools have; many haven't.

A Federal Infusion

So school-based community service remains just that: a local effort to meet local needs. At the national level, though, both Congress and President George Bush are working to turn a spotlight on community service. President Bush's program, unveiled just after Christmas, asks Congress for $25 million annually to fund a private foundation (called the Points of Light Initiative Foundation) that would encourage local community service—including school-based service—but would not provide federal funds.

Also on Capitol Hill, though, is Senator Edward M. Kennedy's (D-Mass.) ServeAmerica bill, which calls for a five-year program that would provide $100 million annually in start-up grants for youth service programs. Sixty-five million of that money—"no inconsiderable sum," in the words of Frank Slobig, codirector of Youth Service America—is earmarked for K-12 service programs, to be divvied up among the states according to traditional funding formulas. The aim, says Slobig, is to provide the funds needed to build a school's community service infrastructure: its capacity to coordinate and administer school-based service projects.

Kennedy's bill, which Slobig says has "strong bipartisan support," was reported out of committee last term and was expected to come before the full Senate in late February or early March.

Federal money alone won't move service-learning into the

How to Get High Marks in Effectiveness, Too

Mandatory or voluntary? During school or after? For academic credit, or just for goodwill? Schools that are about to embark on community service programs are asking the same questions and often coming up with different answers. "There's no one successful model," says Catherine A. Rolzinski, who's spent more than a year surveying U.S. community service programs as director of education for Youth Service America. "There are as many models as there are communities and schools."

But as Rolzinski and others point out, effective programs do not have some traits in common:

1. *Effective programs encourage students to reflect on what they're doing and what they have learned.* Schools can't simply send youngsters out to shovel snow or serve as candy stripers. Students need the chance to reflect on what they're doing. In Atlanta, for example, students submit a paper, which is not graded, describing their experience and how it affected them. In Maryland, schools are encouraged to adopt a series of readings from the Great Books—Socrates, Montesquieu, Thomas Jefferson, and others. "We want to give youngsters the language they need to talk about service," explains Kathleen Kennedy Townsend, director of the Maryland Student Service Alliance. Some service programs ask students to keep journals, encouraging them to get beyond the perfunctory "Went to the nursing home. Read. Came back to school"; and still others (like Minneapolis's Fresh Force) train teachers, college interns, or other adults to lead group discussions.
2. *Effective programs forge close links with the community at large.* Students must be primed for service, and community groups must be primed for students. In other words, the more contact you have with advocates for the elderly, public parks and recreation, or whatever, the more likely your program is to succeed. Take transportation, for example. Getting youngsters from Central Middle School to a service project miles away can seem an insurmountable hurdle. Ditto matching individual students with service projects that meet their needs. But if you work your community service network effectively and stay in touch with groups needing aid, you're likely to find appropriate service opportunities close by, says Minneapolis' Mary Spindler.
3. *Effective programs build in incentives and recognition.* T-shirts, awards banquets, the chance to serve on a planning committee with adults—successful programs find many ways to bill youth service as positive and inviting, to students and community alike.
4. *Effective programs involve institutional commitment.* Top-notch community service programs are sustained and structured, not one-shot deals put together on the fly. Teachers must be trained, schedules developed, and students matched with the best service opportunities for them—all tasks that cry out for a supervisor, if the school system can afford one. Programs should be poised to grow, too, notes Mary Spindler. Now that the first of Fresh Force's young recruits have graduated from junior high, for example, the Minneapolis public schools are looking at ways the program can be extended or adapted in the high schools. The youngsters, Spindler explains, have come to expect service to be part of going to school.

Finally, should a service program be mandatory or voluntary? No firm consensus exists on this point, though the scales might tip slightly in favor of voluntary programs. "The program should be so exciting and interesting that everyone will want to do it," maintains Rolzinski. "You want to keep that vital energy going, not shrink service down to some common denominator." —D.H.-L.

---

mainstream, though. As Catherine Rolzinski of Youth Service America points out, educators must have solid research—not just anecdotal evidence—showing that community service produces cognitive, social, and academic gains. And if youth service is to become a national movement, Rolzinski observes, it will need to identify and build on the best existing programs, develop a good national clearinghouse, and put together an effective national network for sharing ideas and expertise. Little of that kind of national coordination exists, yet.

Until it does, and even when it does, local school boards like yours will remain at the center of the youth service movement. And for good reason: Not only do you make policy, but you're in the citizenship business.

"Look at a school's mission statement," says Rolzinski. "It includes citizenship building. Now we need to start looking at the community as a laboratory for citizenship."

Article Review Form at end of book.

WiseGuide Wrap-Up

- Preservice teachers can benefit from studying the history of education.
- Preservice teachers should begin forming a personal philosophy of education that they revise or expand as professional growth dictates.
- Awareness of key philosophers and their contributions to educational philosophy helps preservice teachers to understand the development of philosophical thought during the last century.
- Personal philosophies influence action. For example, a teacher's personal philosophy of education will influence her or his selection of instructional strategies.

R.E.A.L. Sites

This list provides a print preview of typical **coursewise** R.E.A.L. sites. There are over 100 such sites at the **courselinks**™ site. The danger in printing URLs is that web sites can change overnight. As we went to press, these sites were functional using the URL provided. If you come across one that isn't, please let us know via email to: webmaster@coursewise.com. Use your Passport to access the most current list of R.E.A.L. sites at the **courselinks**™ site.

Site name: Readings in Teaching and Education

URL: http://www.stemnet.nf.ca/~elmurphy/emurphy/ten61939.html

Why is it R.E.A.L.? This site contains the text of N. Postman's "The End of Education," as well as a bibliography of key works related to selected educational issues. The site also has links to readings on constructivist philosophies, educational choice, educational technology, and purpose of schooling.

Key topics: constructivism, educational philosophy, John Dewey, purpose of schooling

Activity: Write a reaction paper in response to the summary of Postman's "The End of Education."

Site name: NOEMA: The Collaborative Bibliography of Women in Philosophy

URL: http://billyboy.ius.indiana.edu/WomeninPhilosophy/WomeninPhilo.html

Why is it R.E.A.L.? This site provides a database of more than 15,000 records, representing the works of more than 5,000 women. Included are works on the history of philosophy; philosophy of the mind, of science, and of art; ethics; and logic.

Key topics: philosophy of education, women in education

Activity: For the purpose of learning to use an electronic database, locate works by Jane Addams, Maria Montessori, and Emma Willard. Then write a brief summary of the contributions or beliefs of one of the women as expressed in the works located.

Site name: The Center for Dewey Studies

URL: http://www.siu.edu/~deweyctr/

Why is it R.E.A.L.? This site provides comprehensive information about the life of John Dewey, including a chronology of important events. Also available are lists of resources and recommended readings for in-depth research into Dewey's life and educational philosophies.

Key topics: John Dewey, educational philosophy

Activity: Compose a time line of key events in John Dewey's life, including his contributions to the field of educational philosophy.

section 3

Learning Objectives

After reading the articles in this section, you will be able to:

- Discuss the relationship between theory and practice.
- List characteristics of effective multicultural education programs.
- Discuss the importance of preservice teachers' attitudes toward multicultural education.
- Discuss the classroom teacher's role in developing and implementing an effective multicultural education program.
- Explain why community service projects promote multicultural education.
- Discuss the best ways to link community service projects to academic content.

Fulfilling Our Mission: Meeting the Needs of All Learners

One of the most challenging aspects of the teaching profession is answering the question, "How do I structure my classroom and plan activities to ensure that all students have equal opportunities to learn?" To be effective, classroom teachers must demonstrate proficiency in content-area knowledge. This, however, is not enough. They must also recognize and accept the uniqueness of each student. This acceptance, in turn, leads to classroom activities designed to be effective with the diverse learning styles evident in today's public school classrooms.

In discussions about the instructional needs of students, limitless topics arise that cannot be dealt with sufficiently in one volume. For this reason, the readings in this section lead preservice teachers to focus on integrated multicultural education as one strategy for meeting the needs of a diverse student body. Teacher preparation programs should include opportunities for preservice teachers to identify characteristics of and best practices indicative of model multicultural education programs. More importantly, however, teachers should be encouraged to (1) identify personal attitudes and dispositions indicative of teachers who have been successful in meeting the needs—instructional and emotional—of all students and (2) reflect on how their own beliefs and actions mirror these attitudes and dispositions.

Readings in Section 3 describe effective classroom activities and exemplary programs to help preservice teachers become aware of and understand the unique needs of each student. The first reading, "Living with the Pendulum: The Complex World of Teaching," includes a brief history of curricular reforms, personal experiences of the author, and strategies for integrating theory and application to ensure the success of all students. The next two readings—"The Goals and Track Record of Multicultural Education" and "Teachers' Role in Multicultural Education: Setting the Stage for Preservice Teachers"—focus on the characteristics of effective education initiatives and on attitudes, knowledge, and skills that enhance teacher effectiveness in designing and implementing multicultural education initiatives. The last reading, "Community Service in a Multicultural Nation," presents a specific example of how to integrate multicultural education concepts throughout the curriculum and describes how community service projects promote interconnectedness among people, respect for one another, and commitment to conflict resolution.

Questions

Reading 12: What are the two ideological extremes that classroom teachers often confront when making curricular and instructional decisions? What should be the relationship between theory and practice? What does Jeanette Throne mean when she says that preservice teachers should create a vision of learning and teaching as a multidimensional world?

Reading 13: Historically, what have been the goals of an effective multicultural education program? What are at least two reasons why multicultural education should be integrated into the general education curriculum, instead of being delivered as discrete concepts?

Reading 14: Why are the attitudes of preservice teachers toward multicultural education so important? What is the teacher's role in developing and implementing an effective multicultural education program?

Reading 15: How can community service projects promote understanding of multiculturism? What are characteristics of effective community service projects? To be effective, community service projects must be integrated into the academic curriculum. How can this integration be accomplished?

What are the two ideological extremes that classroom teachers often confront when making curricular and instructional decisions? What should be the relationship between theory and practice? What does Jeanette Throne mean when she says that preservice teachers should create a vision of learning and teaching as a multidimensional world?

Living with the Pendulum

The complex world of teaching

Jeanette Throne

Mercer School, Shaker Heights, Ohio

In this article, Jeannette Throne describes how educational reforms seem to swing from one opposing ideology to another, while teachers confront the complex nature of the classroom, where different needs exist simultaneously. Throne looks at this problem from two perspectives: a historical look at curricular reforms and her own classroom practice. Examining the evolution of her kindergarten language arts curriculum, she questions whether the learning needs of individual students can be met within the bounds of a single theoretical framework. Throne reflects on and analyzes the learning processes of her students, focusing on both their successes and challenges as they begin to read and write. She then describes the ways her students' learning has informed her teaching and prompted her to integrate several theoretical perspectives into her curriculum in order to ensure their success. She concludes by stressing that educators must look beyond either/or choices in order to see solutions that reflect the realities of the classroom, and emphasizes the importance of creating ongoing dialogue between teachers and theorists, researchers, and policymakers in order to foster a more comprehensive view of students and their learning needs.

As a classroom teacher, every time the educational pendulum swings from one opposing ideology to another, I feel that once again I have been hit by a moving object. Schools are either going back to basics or going beyond them, with little examination as to why these either/or choices have not been more effective. One side of the pendulum has teachers imparting knowledge to students through direct, systematic instruction with an emphasis on skills and content. The other side encourages children to take a more active role in constructing their own knowledge with less explicit teaching of skills. In math, the opposing sides may be computation versus problem-solving; in science, they may be content versus process; and in the reading/language arts area, they may be phonics versus whole language. In this article, I look at this problem from two perspectives: that of history and that of my kindergarten language arts program. Curriculum reforms examined through a historical lens provide a reference point for analyzing current reform promises and challenge educators not to repeat the excesses of the past. Analyzing these reforms from my classroom practice, I have found that these either/or choices conflict with the complex nature of the classroom, where different needs exist simultaneously.

These reform movements create a great deal of controversy in the language arts curriculum, especially in the primary grades (kindergarten through second grade), where learning to read is the main focus. In the primary grades, "the basics" usually refers to the skills needed to use the alphabetic code and the conventions of print (i.e., letters of the

Reprinted with permission from the HARVARD EDUCATIONAL REVIEW, Vol. 64, No. 2, Summer 1994, pp. 195–208. Copyright © by President and Fellow of Harvard College.

alphabet, sound-symbol relationships, decoding, spelling, handwriting, punctuation, and grammar). Current educational research on teaching young children to read places those educators who believe that the alphabetic code and the conventions of print should be directly taught into one ideological camp (Chall, 1989; Delpit, 1988; Stanovich, 1993/1994). In the other camp are whole language proponents, who believe children will naturally acquire these skills within the contexts of language and literacy experiences that focus primarily on meaning, process, problem-solving, creativity, and the interests of each child (Goodman, 1992; Watson, 1989). Classroom teachers may try to resolve these ideological differences by adopting an eclectic approach—a little bit of one method and a little bit of another—without always understanding that there is a complementary relationship between the theories and practices represented by opposing viewpoints. The paradox is that no one approach works for all children—which is why the pendulum never stops swinging.

Debating an issue by standing firmly on one side causes polarization, which prevents educators from seeing the whole picture. Educators therefore see the solution as an either/or decision rather than one in which both approaches have the potential to complement one another. Many educators find accepting both ideologies difficult. Such polarization is not a new problem for educational reform. In 1938, John Dewey, concerned about the excesses he saw in both traditional practices and the progressive movement, wrote:

> It is the business of an intellectual theory of education to ascertain the causes for the conflicts that exist, and then, instead of taking one side or the other, to indicate a plan of operations proceeding from a level deeper and more inclusive than is represented by the practices of the contending parties. (Dewey, 1938/1965, p. 5)

When theory does not reflect the realities of the classroom, classroom teachers working directly with children have difficulty finding common ground from which to discuss these conflicts with educators whose main responsibilities lie outside the classroom. Dewey (1929) attributed this difficulty to theory's quest for certainty when, in fact, "uncertainty is primarily a practical matter" (p. 223). In practice, theory's quest for certainty often leads to unfulfilled promises.

Children's literature and a language-experience approach (Van Allen & Allen, 1969) have been an important part of my curriculum since the beginning of my teaching career.[1] At various times in my career, I have also been responsible for teaching commercial reading programs that relied on a systematic phonics approach (Boston Educational Research Company, 1971; Lindamood & Lindamood, 1975). When I taught these commercial programs, I had students who easily learned to read and students who struggled. When I was introduced to big books (Holdaway, 1979), process writing (Graves, 1983), and invented spelling (Temple, Nathan, & Burris, 1982) through the educational literature, I integrated them into my curriculum. I minimized the amount of phonics I taught and no longer used a commercial reading program. Again, I had students who learned easily and students who struggled. I found that the promise made by proponents of all of these approaches—that is, that all children will become successful readers and writers—did not hold true. I stopped believing in the certainty of this promise and began to see that no one program or approach held all the answers for all children.

The Quest for Certainty

Currently, teachers are criticized when they rely too much on basal readers and the step-by-step lesson plans provided in most teachers' manuals.[2] Basals were originally advocated, however, as a way of improving reading instruction. In the 1920s, reading experts promoted the use of basals and teachers' manuals in order to render reading instruction more standard and scientific. In his book, *Broken Promises,* Patrick Shannon (1989) writes of this history:

> The problem facing these and other reading experts since the late 1920s was how to induce teachers, who were already using textbooks according to their own ideas, to follow the scientific directions

[1]The current whole language philosophy has some similarities to the language-experience approach. Important components of both are the integration of all language experiences (speaking, listening, writing, and reading) and teaching skills within the context of these experiences. Another similarity is the reading aloud of children's books and poetry and integrating children's literature into units that focus on a common theme. One of the fundamental differences between the two is the methods and the materials used for teaching writing and reading. The language-experience approach uses children's dictation, written down by the teacher, as the primary method for teaching writing and reading. Language-experience charts, class books, and individual stories and books are generated by children's personal and classroom experiences. The whole language philosophy puts more emphasis on children doing their own writing and using trade books for teaching reading.

[2]A basal reading program is a series of graded readers organized by reading levels, starting with a kindergarten readiness program or a first-grade preprimer and extending to the middle school grades.

> included in the teacher's guidebooks. . . . And over the next sixty years, the control of reading instruction passed from teachers' hands to those of the reading experts and commercial publishers as basal use became more and more prevalent in elementary schools across America—so prevalent, in fact, that it often seems that the materials are using teachers rather than teachers using the materials. (p. 29)

Knowing where the promises of the past have led gives teachers a reference point from which to examine today's promises. When they analyze and articulate the uncertainties, struggles, and triumphs that reflect their daily experiences and philosophies, they add another dimension to the debates that challenge all educators. The role of a classroom teacher thus expands from one who implements theory to one who also creates, tests, questions, and informs theory within the context of his or her classroom. Teachers are able to move beyond what they have often done to cope with bureaucratic certainty—that is, to quietly shut their doors and teach.

By entering into the educational dialogue as active participants, teachers construct a deeper understanding of what they do and why. This dialogue begins among colleagues. Exchanging activities and procedures is part of the traditional dialogue among classroom teachers, but conversations that clarify a teacher's thinking and generate new knowledge can also be part of this exchange. Knowledge generated from inside the classroom is not only useful for teachers, it also challenges the assumption that knowledge about teaching and learning should be generated only by theorists working outside the classroom (Cochran-Smith & Lytle, 1993). If the classroom door is to be kept open, teacher inquiry should challenge and inform theory just as theory challenges and informs practice.

In the following sections of this article, I take a closer look at my own classroom. A teacher since the late 1960s, I currently teach all-day, every-day kindergarten in an integrated, suburban school district. I have no glorious success stories to tell—stories of how I or a particular instructional program achieved success while all others failed. Instead I offer an in-depth look at the strengths and needs of one child's learning within the broader context of my classroom. I also focus on my language arts curriculum and how it facilitates each student's need to comprehend the meaning and the conventions of print. Woven throughout is an examination of my role as teacher and as learner. Although these stories are told from the perspective of a kindergarten language arts teacher, I hope other teachers will see themselves in my stories and make connections that help them analyze and articulate their experiences, concerns, and insights. Perhaps as teachers look more closely at their own classrooms, all educators—those working inside and outside the classroom—will see that the quest is not one for certainty or single answers, but a quest for understanding the many influences that bear upon a child's learning and a teacher's teaching.

Matthew: Insights into One Child's Learning

Whenever I think I have found "The Answer" (the one that solves every problem, every dilemma), I meet a child who reminds me to keep looking. Matthew was one of these children. Matthew entered my kindergarten with special needs in both written language and math. Matthew spent two years in my classroom because both his mother and I felt that he would benefit from a second year in kindergarten in order to give him more time to develop a better understanding of written language and mathematics. Matthew was a young kindergartner; he had a September birthday where, in Ohio, the cut-off date for school entrance is October 1. In addition to being young relative to his peers, Matthew needed more individual help than could be provided in the regular classroom. Thus, during his first year in my classroom, he received additional language support from the speech and language teacher, and he received help in the areas of reading and math from the basic skills tutor. In January of Matthew's second year in kindergarten he was placed in an afternoon kindergarten class specifically designed for children with special needs, while he remained in my classroom in the morning.

Matthew's greatest success was drawing. The first pictures he drew consisted of a mass of circles and lines. These circles and lines, however, gradually changed into people drawn with two eyes placed in a circle with two lines protruding from the bottom for legs. Crayons and markers were his favorite media, green was his favorite color, and people were his favorite subject. Matthew was a quiet child and, unlike some other children, did not verbally communicate what his pictures represented unless I asked him to dictate a story about his drawing. His first drawings were generally about his mom or himself. These pictures held meaning for Matthew, but neither I nor the other children knew what they represented unless Matthew told us.

In the two years Matthew was in my kindergarten classroom, he added more detail to his people until everyone had arms, hands, fingers, legs, feet, and hair. Faces had eyes and mouths but no noses; the males in his pictures wore shirts and pants, and the females wore dresses. Matthew spent a lot of time on these pictures, and the pages were always full; he drew wherever there was empty space. His progress with drawing continued and his pictures became more organized (Gardner, 1980). In the spring of his second year in kindergarten, Matthew began to arrange the people in his drawings into rows, and the meaning of his pictures could be better understood by others. A picture depicting Matthew's preference for drawing people in rows showed ten of his cousins and friends riding skateboards with a car drawn among them. They were skateboarding in two rows across consecutive pages in his writing book. Each boy was wearing sunglasses, and all had numbers written on their shirts. This was one of my favorite pictures.

Although Matthew's use of symbolic representation grew through his drawing, he struggled to learn the symbols of written language. Learning to write his name was difficult for Matthew. Teaching him to write his name was difficult for me. I felt Matthew wanted to learn to write his name, but he resisted because neither he nor I could find a way to begin. Both letter formation and putting letters in the correct sequence were a challenge for him. My biggest challenge was teaching him to write the first letter in his name. No matter how many times he traced over or copied the letters in his name using a variety of media such as plastic letters, sandpaper letters, clay, markers, crayons, chalk, or pencils, he could not retrieve the letters from memory. Nothing worked until I brought in a paper bag from a McDonald's restaurant, and we talked about how the golden arches represented the letter M. I am not sure if Matthew understood that the golden arches were intended to represent the first letter in the McDonald name and could also represent the first letter in his name, but the familiar shape of the arches seemed to help him to remember how the M is formed. This seemed an important breakthrough, but every letter in this name continued to be a struggle for him. Matthew's success in writing the letter M gave him more confidence in his ability to learn how to write his name. This confidence led to less resistance from Matthew, and the activities and materials that I introduced previously were more effective in helping him attend to and remember the visual features of print.

As Matthew began to write the letters in his name, he still was unable to write them in the correct sequence. This difficulty persisted into his second year of kindergarten. We both persevered, however, and by the end of that year he was able to write his first and last names, recognize letters, and use seemingly random letters in the stories he wrote. Although Matthew could write his name and use letters in this writing, he had not yet internalized the abstract nature of an alphabetic writing system and how it is organized to represent thoughts and speech. This came later. For Matthew, progress with symbolic representation in one area did not naturally lead to use and understanding in another. His progress using pictorial symbols came from his own initiative and motivation. His progress with written symbols came from the direct instruction he received from others and me.

I had to let Matthew teach me so I could learn how best to teach him. What I learned from Matthew enriched my teaching for all children. Watching him struggle with written language and flourish with drawing helped me to better understand the symbolic nature of art and to see how different symbol systems (oral language, written language, the arts, mathematics, etc.) are vehicles through which humans create and communicate meaning (Gardner, 1982). From Matthew's difficulty with putting the letters in his name in the correct sequence, I learned that serial order is important to young children's understanding of written language (Clay, 1991). I also came to see that my role as teacher was not just to provide my students with direct, explicit instruction or to provide opportunities for them to learn naturally; it was also to weave the two together to meet the strengths and needs of each child.

A Community of Learners

Children learn and acquire knowledge long before they enter kindergarten. They are not empty vessels to be filled with equal amounts of knowledge. The complexity of teaching—working with young children and deciding how to guide and support them in their language learning—confronts me from the first day my kindergartners enter my classroom. Giving each child a writing book filled with empty sheets of paper elicits a diverse range of responses that emerge from each child's individual understanding of how humans use language and symbol systems to create meaning.

Some children enter kindergarten reading, and others are learning to write their names. Some enjoy expressing ideas through writing, and others prefer to express themselves through play or the arts. Some write or dictate stories with a narrative style, and others label each picture with a sentence beginning with "This is" or "There's a." Some talk their way through a story with friends nearby, some make running commentaries to themselves, and others work quietly.

One child writes independently using invented spellings, another fills the page by copying friends' names from their name cards, and yet another dictates long stories to me. Some children who already have a good knowledge of print can spell words phonetically and put space between words, but they write only limited stories without encouragement. For them, invented spelling is not "real spelling," and they want to use only words they can spell correctly. Other children may have a limited knowledge of print, but confidently start to write. One child draws elaborate, detailed pictures, but struggles with understanding how print works, and another child has original ideas but struggles with the physical aspects of using crayons or holding a pencil. And, there are some children who can put it all together—their ability to draw, write, and create stories challenges me to build on all their strengths.

Teaching would be easier for me if I adopted an either/or perspective—to teach letters and sounds or to encourage self-expression. Viewing my role from the first perspective, my job would be to impart the conventions of print that our society uses; the application of these skills would come later. From the second, more creative perspective, my role would be to provide encouragement and materials for my students to express their ideas through talking, drawing, and writing.

This either/or position is not a comfortable one for me. I have always enjoyed teaching the alphabet and introducing young children to its power to make sense of written language. This interest has been balanced with my love of children's art, children's play, and literature for children. I want my students to explore and begin to understand how books, poetry, the arts, mathematics, science, and play can expand their worlds and take them into new ones. Children who come to me with different strengths, needs, interests, behaviors, and backgrounds challenge me to see beyond these either/or choices.

The Child, the Book, the Teacher

Reading aloud to my kindergartners is an important part of my language arts curriculum. It provides the best way I know to enhance young children's enjoyment and comprehension of literature before they become readers themselves. The interaction between the child, the book, and the teacher is influenced by many factors, such as a child's interest, the difficulty of a book, or how a teacher chooses to use it. Children bring their own experiences (both literary and life) to their understanding of text, and these experiences are part of the transaction between them and the text (Rosenblatt, 1938/1976). When I read aloud with a child, three voices interact to bring meaning to the text—the author's, the child's, and mine—and the illustrations provide a visual interpretation of the story. Meaning is shaped and reshaped as the child and I build on each other's understanding of the book. Our conversations help me to understand a child's thinking about a story as well as my own. Without this exchange of ideas, further understanding of the story would be limited for both the children and me. We learn from the book and from each other. Practices that emphasize one part of this reciprocal relationship over another (such as if only the teacher asks the questions) limit what a child learns and how a teacher teaches.

My kindergartners select books to read with friends, to read alone, and to read with me. They make their choices during book choosing times and during free-choice times when other choices are available, such as puzzles, math, blocks, sand, paints, or computer. I choose books to read with the class during story times or to have a child read with me during our free-choice times. When a child reads with me, we may read the book together or the child may choose to read alone, which involves retelling a story, reciting the memorized text while pointing to the words on a page, or reading in the conventional sense. Repetition, rhyme, predictable language patterns, or a controlled vocabulary support beginning readers, but it is the story that engages their feelings and imaginations.

Knock Knock Who's There? (1988), written by Sally Grindley and illustrated by Anthony Browne, evoked lots of "ooo's" and "eee's" as I read it to my class. In this story, a little girl is in bed when she hears a knock at her door. When the door is first opened, the reader is introduced to a gorilla standing in the doorway. The refrain "Knock Knock Who's There?" is repeated throughout the story, when a witch, a ghost, a dragon, and a giant knock at her door. She does not let anyone in until her daddy knocks with a story to tell and a mug of hot chocolate. She tells him about the previous visitors and how she knew it was him all along . . . "really." The drawings show that each character who knocks on the door is wearing the same bedroom slippers.

The slippers sparked a lively discussion among my kindergartners. Some children wondered, were they the gorilla's shoes or daddy's shoes? The gorilla-shaped shadow drawn behind the father added more fuel to their debate. This book stretched my children's imaginations just as the knock on the door stretched the little girl's imagination. Their questions and comments reflected their feelings, perceptions, and search for meaning as they tried to answer the question of who was at the door. This question did not have the same answer for every child—some were convinced it was the gorilla and others were convinced it was the daddy. No one proposed that it could have been any of the other characters pictured knocking at the door. Several children suggested it was the little girl's daddy because she recognized his voice, but this hypothesis did not provide the proof needed for everyone to agree.

When Carmella chose to read this book with me, she questioned whether the main character was a girl or a boy. When I asked her what she thought, she answered, "I think the kid is a girl." She also thought the witch was the girl who married the gorilla and said, "Then she got all the children. All these children in these books." She looked through the book showing me the ghost, the dragon, and the giant. Her interpretation did not hold up when we got to the page showing the daddy. I realized this when she looked at me and said, "Daddy's not the children. He turned into a gorilla." When I asked her how he turned into a gorilla, she told me she thought he had a costume. Carmella's questions and comments indicated to me that the imaginative play taking place during the little girl's game of "knock knock" was not always clear to her. I am not sure it was clear to the other children either, but Carmella questioned it more as she tried to distinguish real from make-believe and to use both to explain the book to herself. I tried to give her support by asking questions, answering her questions, or by helping her answer her own.

When I first read this book to my class, I did not realize how important the bedroom slippers would be to the children's understanding of the story. Their response to these slippers strengthened my belief that the child, the book, and the teacher work together to enhance children's enjoyment and comprehension of literature. Focusing on the debate over the superiority of a child-centered versus a teacher-directed curriculum or a content-based curriculum (knowing children's literature is knowing content) blocks educators from seeing how each complements the other.

The Challenge of Embracing Both Sides of the Debate

Learning the alphabet and the phonetic structure of print are key parts of learning to read and write, but these skills are the object of great controversy when educators debate how and when to teach them. Much of the extensive research in this debate is confusing because the researchers' points of view are positioned oppositionally and rarely integrated. There are many questions in this debate, but the ones that most affect me as a kindergarten teacher are 1) what is the optimum age to introduce children to these skills? and 2) should these skills be directly taught in isolation from meaningful contexts, or should children learn them naturally within a print-rich environment?

Observing my students has shown me that the alphabetic code is important for children to learn. Children who struggle to understand the relationship between speech sounds and the letters they represent struggle with learning to read. Most children who understand sound-symbol relationships and use them to spell words phonetically (the letters a child writes closely match the sounds in a word) learn to read successfully. Although I feel the alphabetic code is important for children to learn, how to teach it so all children are successful is not an easy question to answer. Many basal reading readiness programs adopted by school districts focus primarily on teaching sound-symbol relationships and phonics. These programs conflict with educational organizations' recommendation for a whole language philosophy that focuses mainly on language development, children's literature, and children's writing (Bredekamp, 1987; Early Childhood and Literacy Development Committee, 1985; Strickland & Morrow, 1989). Both approaches have limitations. In my experience, the first approach focuses too much on teaching phonetic skills in isolation and not enough on the contexts in which they are used. The second approach may not focus enough on phonetic skills for children who need more direct, explicit instruction in order to apply these skills to their reading and writing.

Finding ways to incorporate the alphabet and phonetic skills into a balanced language arts curriculum in order to meet the strengths and needs of every child is a question I still work toward answering. My goal is to provide my kindergartners with a variety of literacy experiences so they will attend to print, talk about it, and use it. Each week I introduce a new letter and its sound to the whole class. I provide objects that correspond to the weekly sound, along with related pictures and words, a children's letter book for each sound (Randell, 1970), plastic letters, and environmental print (for example, McDonald's and M&M bags for "M" week). I place these materials on a table along with markers, colored pencils, and paper for the children to look at and use throughout the week. I also display self-portraits of those children whose first or last names start with the letter being highlighted. This area is a popular choice during our free-choice periods. Another popular activity is substituting the first sound of each child's name with the weekly letter-sound. Other phonetic-related activities that may not always relate to the weekly letter are clapping the syllables in our names and other words, reading alphabet and rhyming books, playing alphabet and letter-sound games, or analyzing the sequence of sounds we hear in words as the children or I write down the corresponding letters.

Even though the "sound-of-the-week" activities to which I refer focus primarily on teaching letters and sound-symbol relationships, I use this format because it gives me an organized structure to introduce letters and sounds. This structure, in turn, allows for an openness that fosters many spontaneous discoveries as children investigate and talk about print. Furthermore, this provides me with opportunities to expand my understanding of how my students are thinking about print. I listen to children's questions and comments to build on their thinking and clarify my own. Their observations move into new directions as they build on the ideas and information that I have presented to them. For example, while sharing pictures for "D" week, Jacqueline insisted I remove the picture of a dress because the word dress started with "jr" not "d," which is how she heard the /dr/ blend. This observation led to a discussion of how the sounds heard in words are sometimes different from the letters seen. There may be a time when I eliminate the sound-of-the-week, but not until I find another approach that gives me both the structure and the flexibility to meet different needs, both the children's and mine.

In over twenty-five years of teaching, I have yet to find one single approach that meets all children's needs. What I have learned, however, is that whatever method or approach I use, its problems must be examined along with its advantages. For this reason, I use the sound-of-the-week approach with caution. Just as any method or theory can be misused, so can this one. Because this approach focuses primarily on phonetic skills, I integrate it into my language arts curriculum that provides children with many opportunities to talk about and apply this knowledge within the context of stories, poetry, big books, writing, and other meaningful experiences with print. I am careful that the total curriculum does not center around the weekly letter and that worksheets are not used as the primary means for introducing my students to letter-names and letter-sound relationships. Just as important, I try to be aware of the times when a word or a word activity is confusing to a child. Understanding Jacqueline's confusion with the word "dress" from her perspective enabled me to help her try to resolve it. There may also be times when children who learn English as a second language may have difficulty hearing or saying sounds that are not in their native language, and children with cultural or regional dialects may also experience difficulty with particular sounds.

Examining both the advantages and the problems of different approaches helps teachers to critique and evaluate how the programs they create and those they are required to implement affect children's learning. Searching for the single, correct answer that has no problems or limitations takes classroom teachers from one curriculum reform to another and back again. A dialogue between teachers and theorists that reflects the advantages, problems, and limitations of different approaches and theories would benefit teachers more than a dialogue that pushes the pendulum from one opposing viewpoint to another. When the role of classroom teachers becomes more than the implementation of curriculum, teachers may find themselves questioning the experts. Such repositioning can lead to a deeper understanding of what teachers do and why, and it brings the teacher's voice into the dialogue that challenges all educators.

Building on Children's Thinking

Research into the phonetic bases of nonstandard spellings by young children (Bissex, 1980; Read, 1975; Temple et al., 1982) has given educators many insights into children's thinking about print. My kindergartners apply their phonetic knowledge more readily to writing than to reading. Just as children construct and use their own system of rules when they first learn to speak (Brown, 1973), they construct and use a system of rules for writing that is different from conventional writing. My students form and test new hypotheses as they adapt their theories of how print works to the information and language (both oral and written) that others and I have shared with them.

I build on my kindergartners' understanding of how the alphabetic code works by helping them work out the discrepancies between their hypotheses and conventional print. I give support during whole class sessions as we discuss the letters and sounds we see and hear in words. I may sit with a small group of children working in their writing books, answering their questions about letter formation, letter-sounds, or words. When I transcribe children's stories, I work with them individually on a variety of writing skills. For example, I help the child who uses letter-like marks or writes only the letters she knows in her name to form letters and to learn the alphabet. I encourage the child who hears beginning consonants in words to use more letter-sounds in his writing. Some children may need guidance hearing the sequence of sounds in words, while others are encouraged to write left-to-right across the page or to put space between words. I introduce the spellings of high-frequency words to children who mix conventional spelling with invented spelling. I also help them to understand the use of silent letters or when a word does not "play fair" phonetically.

Writing gives children many opportunities to experiment with print, and it gives me a better sense of their thinking about written language. Meaning, however, often gets lost to children's intense concentration in putting letter, sounds, and words down on paper. Because these skills are not yet automatic for kindergartners, the conscious attention they must give to the mechanics of writing as they write makes it difficult for them to give their full attention to meaning. Therefore, I encourage my students to write what they can independently (or with my support to write more than they think they can) and to dictate the rest to me. Dictation fosters self-expression and extends children's writing. As I write what they tell me, we talk and think our way through a story together. I ask questions and offer suggestions to encourage them to clarify an idea, expand an imaginative thought, tell the reader more about an experience, or to pursue a new idea.

As teachers try to understand all that is involved in learning to read and write and how they can best help children become confident readers and writers, they must also look at how children perceive and respond to their teaching practices. To know when a child may need direct, explicit instruction or when a child would benefit from exploration and discovery, a teacher relies on his or her knowledge of a child's thinking and learning, knowledge of the curriculum, and knowledge of his or her own teaching.

Seeing Beyond "Either/Or" Choices

I used to believe educators could stop the swinging pendulum; now I am not sure it can be stopped, or even if it should be. Curriculum reforms that put educators into opposing camps, such as direct teaching versus discovery learning, phonics versus whole language, or a child-centered curriculum versus a content-based or teacher-directed curriculum, move the field of education back and forth to the extreme ends of the pendulum. The educational debates that often ensue promote one ideology or the other and prevent educators from engaging in the back-and-forth dialectic that could help them better understand teaching and learning. The question educators should be asking is not how to stop the pendulum, but how to stop the ideological wars that block the effectiveness of the reforms represented by the different ideologies. These debates inhibit communication and too often take on a critical, patronizing, or elitist tone based primarily on the ideology being opposed or promoted. Mandates, policies, standards, and curricula based on either/or choices often rectify one problem and create another, thereby moving educators from one opposing reform to another. The power to mandate change (regardless of which side of the pendulum it is on) is not the same as the power to be effective.

Teachers are often caught in the middle of these changes. Teachers' voices as authorities are heard when they agree with or accept the changes; their voices are less likely to be heard by administrators, theorists, researchers, or policymakers when they question changes or express concern based on their knowledge and experience. Teachers do not have all the answers, nor can they do their job without support from the entire education community. Further, the exclusion of classroom voices (children's and teachers') pushes teachers from one opposing reform to another with little inquiry into understanding where they have been, where they are, or the consequences of where they are going. Communication based on a reciprocal relationship among teachers, parents, administrators, curriculum specialists, researchers, theorists, teacher educators, commercial publishers, and policymakers, rather than a hierarchical relationship, allows educators to see teaching and learning in new ways and gives them a more comprehensive view.

When I look at a child like Matthew, I see a child who not only challenges me, his teacher, but a child who challenges all educators to work together to see beyond either/or choices. Such choices limit the support teachers give to children, and they limit the support educators give to each other. Understanding children's strengths and needs, their difficulties and triumphs; designing a curriculum that focuses on meaning and the conventions of print; and teaching both directly and indirectly requires a vision that may encompass opinions on both sides of the pendulum. It is this perspective that enables educators to learn from each other to seek effective interventions.

Devising a language arts program for kindergartners is only one of the many issues that currently challenge teachers. Teachers are also challenged by issues inherent in subject areas that affect students differently at different grade levels. They are challenged by assessment, standards, mainstreaming, discipline, class size, at-risk students, and many other demands on their time. These challenges face all educators—those who work primarily with children as well as those who work with teachers. If educators are to meet these challenges, they must look beyond either/or choices in order to see solutions that reflect the realities of the classroom.

This article began with the image of a swinging pendulum; I would like to end with the metaphor of my grandmother's stereoscope. As a child in an age of television and movies, I was enchanted by the stereoscope's simplicity. A postcard-size picture with two photographs of the same scene taken from slightly different viewpoints was placed into the front slot, and when I peered through both lenses, I could see up close a three-dimensional world of faraway places. The realism and depth of these photographic scenes were recreated by looking through both lenses simultaneously, and my mind fused the two pictures into one.

When teachers look at what is in front of them with both eyes, the depth and breadth of their vision is clearer. When they look at the questions and the answers—the possibilities and the limitations—they see new opportunities for themselves and the children they teach. These opportunities merge with their beliefs, knowledge, experiences, and concerns as they begin to create a vision of learning and teaching as a multidimensional world that connects the values and needs of a democratic society, the interactive nature of a diverse classroom community, and the uniqueness of each child. This is the complex world of teaching.

References

Bissex, G. (1980). *Gyns at work: A child learns to read and write.* Cambridge, MA: Harvard University Press.

Boston Educational Research Company. (1971). *Beginning to read, write and listen.* Philadelphia: J. B. Lippincott.

Bredekamp, S. (Ed.). (1987). *Developmentally appropriate practice in early childhood programs serving children from birth through age 8.* Washington, DC: National Association for the Education of Young Children.

Brown, R. (1973). *A first language: The early stages.* Cambridge, MA: Harvard University Press.

Chall, J. S. (1989). Learning to read: The great debate 20 years later—A response to debunking the great phonics myth. *Phi Delta Kappan, 70,* 521–538.

Clay, M. M. (1991). *Becoming literate: The construction of inner control.* Portsmouth, NH: Heinemann.

Cochran-Smith, M., & Lytle, S. L. (1993). *Inside/outside: Teacher research and knowledge.* New York: Teachers College Press.

Delpit, L. (1988). The silenced dialogue: Power and pedagogy in educating other people's children. *Harvard Educational Review, 58,* 280–298.

Dewey, J. (1929). *The quest for certainty: A study of the relation of knowledge and action.* New York: Minton Balch.

Dewey, J. (1963). *Experience and education.* New York: Macmillan. (Original work published 1938)

Early Childhood and Literacy Development Committee. (1985). *Literacy development and pre-first grade* [pamphlet]. Newark, DE: International Reading Association.

Gardner, H. (1990). *Artful scribbles: The significance of children's drawings.* New York: Basic Books.

Gardner, H. (1982). *Art, mind, and brain: A cognitive approach to creativity.* New York: Basic Books.

Goodman, K. S. (1992). I didn't found whole language. *Reading Teacher, 46,* 188–199.

Graves, D. H. (1983). *Writing: Teachers and children at work.* Portsmouth, NH: Heinemann.

Grindley, S. (1988). *Knock knock who's there?* London: Methuen Children's Books.

Holdaway, D. (1979). *The foundations of literacy.* Sydney, Australia: Ashton Scholastic.

Lindamood, C. H., & Lindamood, P. C. (1975). *The A.D.D. program: Auditory discrimination in depth.* Boston: Teaching Resources.

Randell, B. (1970). *PM listening skillbuilders.* Wellington, New Zealand: Price Milburn.

Read, C. (1975). *Children's categorization of speech sounds in English.* Urbana, IL: National Council of Teachers of English.

Rosenblatt, L. (1976). *Literature as exploration.* New York: Noble and Noble. (Original work published 1938)

Shannon, P. (1989). *Broken promises: Reading instruction in twentieth-century America.* New York: Bergin & Garvey.

Stanovich, K. E. (1993/1994). Romance and reality. *Reading Teacher, 47,* 280–291.

Strickland, D. S., & Morrow, L. M. (Eds.). (1989). *Emerging literacy: Young children learn to read and write.* Newark, DE: International Reading Association.

Temple, C., Nathan, R., & Burris, N. (1982). *The beginnings of writing.* Boston: Allyn & Bacon.

Van Allen, R., & Allen, C. (1969). *Language experiences in early childhood: A teacher's resource book.* Chicago: Encyclopedia Britannica.

Watson, D. J. (1989). Defining and describing whole language. *Elementary School Journal, 40,* 129–141.

Article Review Form at end of book.

Historically, what have been the goals of an effective multicultural education program? What are at least two reasons why multicultural education should be integrated into the general education curriculum, instead of being delivered as discrete concepts?

The Goals and Track Record of Multicultural Education

Paying attention to the varied learning styles of all students will do more to accomplish the goals of multicultural education than misguided programs that often divide children.

Rita Dunn

Rita Dunn is Professor, Division of Administrative and Instructional Leadership, and Director, Center for the Study of Learning and Teaching Styles, St. John's University, Grand Central and Utopia Parkways, Jamaica, NY 11439. She is the author of 17 books, including ASCD's How to Implement and Supervise Learning Style Programs *(1996).*

Because multicultural education is a volatile political issue—one with articulate proponents and antagonists on both sides—the research on this topic needs to be examined objectively. Many practices that schools promote make little sense in terms of how multiculturally diverse students learn. Thus, we need to examine the data concerning how poor achievement has been reversed among culturally diverse students in many schools.

What Is Multicultural Education?

Multicultural education originated in the 1960s as a response to the longstanding policy of assimilating immigrants into the melting pot of our dominant American culture (Sobol 1990). Over the past three decades, it has expanded from an attempt to reflect the growing diversity in American classrooms to include curricular revisions that specifically address the academic needs of students. In recent years, it has been distorted by some into a movement that threatens to divide citizens along racial and cultural lines (Schlessinger 1991). Generally, multicultural education has focused on two broad goals: increasing academic achievement and promoting greater sensitivity to cultural differences in an attempt to reduce bias.

Increasing Academic Achievement

Efforts intended to increase the academic achievement of multicultural groups include programs that (1) focus on the research on culturally based learning styles as a step toward determining which teaching styles or methods to use with a particular group of students; (2) emphasize bilingual or bicultural approaches; (3) build on the language and culture of African- or Hispanic-American students; and (4) emphasize math and science specifically for minority or female students (Banks 1994). Programs in each of these categories are problematic.

Dunn, Rita. (April 1997). "The Goals and Track Record of Multicultural Education." EDUCATIONAL LEADERSHIP 54, 7: 74–77 Reprinted with permission of the Association for Supervision and Curriculum Development.

- *Culturally based learning styles.* So long as such programs include reasonable provisions for language and cultural differences, they can help students make the transition into mainstream classes. In that sense, they may be considered similar to other compensatory programs that are not multicultural in their emphasis. As a researcher and advocate of learning styles, however, I would caution against attempting to identify or respond to so-called cultural learning styles. Researchers have clearly established that there is no single or dual learning style for the members of any cultural, national, racial, or religious group. A single learning style does not appear even within a family of four or five (Dunn and Griggs 1995).
- *Bilingual or bicultural approaches.* Attention to cultural and language differences can be done appropriately or inappropriately. Bi- and trilingualism in our increasingly interdependent world are valuable for, and should be required of, all students. An emphasis on bilingualism for only non-English-speaking children denies English-speaking students skills required for successful interactions internationally. Today, many adults need to speak several languages fluently and to appreciate cultural similarities and differences to succeed in their work.

    Another problem arises in those classrooms in which bilingual teachers speak English ungrammatically and haltingly. Such teachers provide a poor model for non-English-speaking children, who may remain in bilingual programs for years, unable to make the transition into English-speaking classes. Ultimately, this impairs the ability of these children to move into well-paying professions and careers—the ultimate goal of most of their parents.
- *Selective cultural programs.* Building on the language and culture of selected groups and not of others suggests bias and bigotry. Parents should teach their children to appreciate and respect their native cultures; schools should teach children to appreciate and respect all cultures. If the need exists to expand attention to more cultures, let us do that. But let us stop promoting one culture over another with the inevitable result of dividing our children and diminishing their sense of belonging to the dominant culture that is uniquely American—intentionally a combination of the best of all its citizens.
- *Minority- and gender-based grouping for math and science.* Emphasizing math and science specifically for minority or female students may be based on good intentions, but it ignores the fact that minority students and female students all learn differently from one another and differently from their counterparts—whether those be high- or low-achieving classmates. Providing resources and methods that help all students learn rapidly and well should be the focus for teaching math and science—and every other subject. Are there not males and majority students who fail those subjects? The answer is to change how those subjects are taught, not to isolate certain groups and teach them as though they all have the same style of learning.

Sensitizing Ourselves to Social Agendas

Some multicultural education programs are specifically designed to increase cultural and racial tolerance and reduce bias. These are intended to restructure and desegregate schools, increase contact among the races, and encourage minorities to become teachers; and they lean heavily on cooperative learning (Banks 1994). Sleeter and Grant (1993) describe these programs as emphasizing human relations, incorporating some compensatory goals and curricular revisions to emphasize positive contributions of ethnic and cultural groups, and using learning styles to enhance students' achievement and reduce racial tensions.

Some of these programs emphasize pluralism and cultural equity in American society as a whole, seeking to apply critical thinking skills to a critique of racism and sexism. Others emphasize multilingualism or examine issues from viewpoints other than those of the dominant culture.

In my judgment, these focuses are more political than educational or social. Critical thinking is a requirement for all—not a select few. In addition, whose thinking prevails in these programs, and what are their credentials? Being a minority member or having taken a course does not automatically make a person proficient in teaching minority or female students, or in critiquing social issues. Political debate is helpful to developing young minds; one-sided, preconceived viewpoints are not.

Curriculum and Multicultural Achievement

In the debate over New York's "Children of the Rainbow" curriculum, the ideas of multicultural education captured almost daily headlines. Opponents argued that curriculum change would not increase student achievement, whereas proponents insisted that culturally diverse students performed poorly in school because they could not relate to an American curriculum.

Drew, Dunn, and colleagues (1994) tested how well 38 Cajun students and 29 Louisiana Indian students, all poor achievers, could recall story content and vocabulary immediately and after a delay. Their recall differed significantly when they were instructed with (1) traditional versus multisensory instructional resources and (2) stories in which cultural relevance matched and mismatched students' identified cultural backgrounds. Each subject was presented with four story treatments (two culturally sensitive and two dominant American) and tested for recall immediately afterward and again one week later. The findings for Cajun subjects indicated significant differences between instructional treatments, with greater recall in each multisensory instructional condition—Cultural-Immediate, Cultural-Delayed, American-Immediate, and American-Delayed. The main effect of instructional treatment for Louisiana Indian subjects was significant as well. Recall scores were even higher when they used multisensory materials for American stories. No significant main effect emerged for test interval with either group.

This study demonstrated that what determined whether students mastered the content was *how* the content was taught, not the content itself. The culturally sensitive curriculum did not produce significantly higher achievement for these two poorly achieving cultural groups; the methods that were used did.

What determined whether students mastered the content was how the content was taught, not the content itself.

Teaching Methods and Multicultural Achievement

Other studies of teaching methods revealed even more dramatic results. Before being taught with methods that responded to their learning styles, only 25 percent of special education high school students in a suburban New York school district had passed the required local examinations and state competency tests to receive diplomas. In the first year of the district's learning styles program (1987–88), that number increased to 66 percent. During the second year, 91 percent of the district's special education students were successful, and in the third year, the results remained constant at 90 percent—with a greater ratio of "handicapped" students passing state competency exams than regular education students (Brunner and Majewski 1990).

Two North Carolina elementary principals reported similarly impressive gains as a result of their learning styles programs. In an impoverished, largely minority school, Andrews (1990) brought student scores that has consistently been in the 30th percentile on the California Achievement Tests to the 83rd percentile over a three-year period by responding to students' learning styles. Shortly thereafter, Stone (1992) showed highly tactual, learning disabled (LD) elementary school students how to learn with Flip Chutes, Electroboards, Task Cards, and Pic-A-Holes while seated informally in rooms where levels of light matched their style preferences. The children were encouraged to study either alone, with a classmate or two, or with their teacher—based on their learning style strengths. Within four months, those youngsters had achieved four months' reading gains on a standardized achievement test—better than they ever had done previously and as well as would have been expected of children achieving at normal levels.

Many professional journals have reported statistically higher scores on standardized achievement and attitude tests as a result of learning style teaching with underachieving and special education students (Dunn, Bruno, Sklar, Zenhausern, and Beaudry 1990; Dunn, Griggs, Olson, Gorman, and Beasley 1995; Klavas 1993; Lemmon 1985; Perrin 1990; Quinn 1993). Indeed, a four-year investigation by the U.S. Office of Education that included on-site visits, interviews, observations, and examinations of national test data concluded that the Dunn and Dunn Learning Styles Model was one of only a few strategies that had had a positive effect on the achievement of special education students throughout the nation (Alberg, Cook, Fiore, Friend, and Sano 1992).

What Have We Learned?

Research documents that underachieving students—whether they are from other cultures or from the dominant U.S. culture—tend to learn differently from students who perform well in our schools (Dunn and Griggs 1995; Milgram, Dunn, and Price 1993). As indicated in the examples cited earlier, schools with diverse populations reversed academic failure when instruction was changed to complement the children's learning style strengths.

In our book, *Multiculturalism and Learning Style* (Dunn and Griggs 1995), my coauthor and I summarize research findings on each of the major cultural groups in the United States—African Americans, Asian Americans, European Americans, Hispanic Americans, and Native Americans. The research clearly shows that there is no such thing as a cultural group style. There are cross-cultural and intracultural similarities and differences among all peoples. Those differences are enriching when understood and channeled positively.

Given this information, I believe it is unwise for schools with limited budgets to support multicultural education in addition to—and apart from—regular education. Instead, schools need to make their instructional delivery systems responsive to how diverse students learn (Dunn 1995).

Educational programs should not separate young children from one another. Any separation becomes increasingly divisive over time and is likely to produce the opposite of what multicultural education is intended to accomplish. Segregated children begin to feel different from and less able than the larger groups of children they see—but are apart from. These feelings can lead to emotional insecurity and a dislike of others.

The United States was founded as a nation intended to absorb people from many nations. Monocultural education in the guise of multicultural education offends the cornerstone of those intentions. The melting pot concept does not diminish one's heritage. It unites the strengths of many cultures into a single, stronger blend of culture to reflect the best of all.

References

Alberg, J., L. Cook, T. Fiore, M. Friend, and S. Sano. (1992). *Educational Approaches and Options for Integrating Students with Disabilities: A Decision Tool.* Triangle, Park, N.C.: Research Triangle Institute.

Andrews, R.H. (July–September 1990). "The Development of a Learning Styles Program in a Low Socioeconomic, Underachieving North Carolina Elementary School." *Journal of Reading, Writing, and Learning Disabilities International* 6, 3: 307–314.

Banks, J.A. (1994). *An Introduction to Multicultural Education.* Boston: Allyn and Bacon.

Brunner, C. E., and W. S. Majewski. (October 1990). "Mildly Handicapped Students Can Succeed with Learning Styles." *Educational Leadership* 48, 2: 21–23.

Drew, M., R. Dunn, P. Quinn, R. Sinatra, and J. Spiridakis. (1994). "Effects of Matching and Mismatching Minority Underachievers with Culturally Similar and Dissimilar Story Content and Learning Style and Traditional Instructional Practices." *Applied Educational Research Journal* 8, 2: 3–10.

Dunn, R., J. Bruno, R.I. Sklar, R. Zenhausern, and J. Beaudry. (May–June 1990). "Effects of Matching and Mismatching Minority Developmental College Students' Hemispheric Preferences on Mathematics Scores." *Journal of Educational Research* 83, 5: 283–288.

Dunn, R., S. A. Griggs, J. Olson, B. Gorman, and M. Beasley. (1995). "A Meta-Analytic Validation of the Dunn and Dunn Research Learning Styles Model." *Journal of Educational Research* 88, 6: 353–361.

Dunn, R. (1995). *Educating Diverse Learners: Strategies for Improving Current Classroom Practices.* Bloomington, Ind.: Phi Delta Kappa.

Dunn, R., and S.A. Griggs. (1995). *Multiculturalism and Learning Styles: Teaching and Counseling Adolescents.* Westport, Conn.: Praeger Publishers, Inc.

Klavas, A. (1993). "In Greensboro, North Carolina: Learning Style Program Boosts Achievement and Test Scores." *The Clearing House* 67, 3: 149–151.

Lemmon, P. (1985). "A School Where Learning Styles Make a Difference. *Principal* 64, 4: 26–29.

Milgram, R. M., R. Dunn, and G. E. Price, eds. (1993). *Teaching and Counseling Gifted and Talented Adolescents: An International Learning Style Perspective.* Westport, Conn.: Praeger Publishers, Inc.

Perrin, J. (October 1990). "The Learning Styles Project for Potential Dropouts." *Educational Leadership* 48, 2: 23–34.

Quinn, R. (1993). "The New York State Compact for Learning and Learning Styles." *Learning Styles Network Newsletter* 15, 1: 1–2.

Schlessinger, A., Jr. (1991). "Report of the Social Studies Syllabus Review Committee: A Dissenting Opinion." In *One Nation, Many Peoples: A Declaration of Cultural Independence,* edited by New York State Social Studies Review and Development Committee. New York: Author.

Sleeter, C.E., and C.A. Grant. (1993). *Making Choices for Multicultural Education: Five Approaches to Race, Class, and Gender.* 2nd ed. New York: Merrill.

Sobol, T. (1990). "Understanding Diversity." *Educational Leadership* 48, 3: 27–30.

Stone, P. (November 1992). "How We Turned Around a Problem School." *Principal* 71, 2: 34–36.

Article Review Form at end of book.

Why are the attitudes of preservice teachers toward multicultural education so important? What is the teacher's role in developing and implementing an effective multicultural education program?

Teachers' Role in Multicultural Education

Setting the stage for preservice teachers

Leslie H. Irwin

Leslie H. Irwin is a faculty member of the College of Education at Arizona State University West, Phoenix. He teaches courses in multicultural education and classroom management.

Though multicultural education has had great coverage—seemingly to the point of exhaustion—in the numerous studies, books, articles, and media generated talk in the public, preservice student teachers are still asking questions and making statements that call for a review of their roles as teachers in multicultural education. This information needs to be reiterated so that these preservice teachers can internalize it for assistance in making crucial professional decisions and planning appropriate teaching strategies in the classroom. This article, therefore, proposes to address the issue of the teacher's role and attitude toward multicultural education, and to clarify the concept for preservice teachers in order to assist them in establishing goals congruent with desirable current classroom practices.

Teaching in today's diversified educational institutions requires that teachers who carry the responsibilities of a classroom acquire the knowledge of and sensitivity to the variety of cultural representation in the classroom. According to Gollnick and Chinn (1994, p. 29), ". . . they need the knowledge and skills for working effectively in our culturally diverse society." This calls for teachers to employ "culturally sensitive strategies and content to ensure equitable opportunities for academic success, personal development, and individual fulfillment for all students" (Chisholm, 1994, p. 46).

Multicultural education by design is supposed to teach students to recognize, accept, and appreciate cultural, ethnic, social class, religious, and gender differences (Manning and Baruth, 1996). Classroom teachers play a central role in this endeavor. This role does not dilute the teacher's primary mandate of focusing on academics, but incorporates the socio-cultural uniqueness of the individual student within the mosaic of the classroom. Within this context, every child will feel appreciated and wanted and the classroom becomes a welcoming environment for all students.

Preservice teachers need to be mindful that their attitudes and behaviors undeniably will impact on students' attitudes and behaviors. Even though knowledge, skills, and attitudes are paramount in curriculum goals, attitudes of teachers toward diverse groups often fall short in the realm of activities and expectations that enhance equity and equality in educational attainments.

Traditionally, certain teachers have been known to be uncomfortable, unhappy, and have exhibited low productivity in classrooms with students from varying cultural backgrounds or who have handicaps (Sims &

de Martinez, 1981). These are negative attitudes whose concomitant behaviors may correspondingly result in negative nonproductive experiences for culturally diverse students. This eventually culminates in low productivity, alienation, and eventual dropping out of these students. Teachers make a difference in the classroom, and with a conscious effort, this malaise can be remedied. Justiz and Darling (1980) noted that just as modeling behavior affords a means of transmitting culture in informal settings, the teacher in the formal environment of the school affects students in the same manner. Students are constantly watching and evaluating teachers' behaviors and responding accordingly in either negative or positive ways, depending on their perceptions of teachers' demeanors or attitudes toward them. They live and react in accordance with these perceptions, especially those that appear to be in consonance with teachers' expectations.

Students often seek the approval of teachers, coaches, and others whom they respect and whose behaviors, attitudes, and beliefs they invariably tend to emulate. To a large extent, these students will internalize the philosophies and beliefs of these significant persons in their lives. Teacher attitudes and acceptance can effect considerable change in students' own perceptions through educational programs that reflect the virtues of diversity. Tiedt and Tiedt (1995) indicated that the teacher is invaluable in the success or failure of any program, and what he or she does in the classroom is of primary importance from the moment children enter the classroom. The teacher, after all, is the final arbiter in the classroom and, therefore, has within his/her power whether or not and to what extent to initiate and/or infuse cultural awareness in the classroom and across the curriculum.

In adopting a standard to deal with multicultural education, the National Council for Accreditation of Teacher Education (NCATE) had previously acknowledged a need to provide preservice teachers with some degree of exposure to and knowledge of minority groups (Olstad et al., 1983). A teacher's initial encounter with issues of cultural diversity and culturally diverse children, therefore, should not be in the classroom with pupils but during college preservice teacher preparation. This experience will in all likelihood minimize the unexpected cultural shock upon encountering the diverse and what may seem an unfamiliar composition of today's classrooms. The classroom is a microcosm of the American cultural mosaic, its diversity, and expectations. A preservice teacher's early exposure to this representative population in the preparation program would develop an appropriate sense of recognition and behavior appropriate to the setting that he or she will encounter.

The role of classroom teachers is vital in the success or failure of multicultural education.

Signs of apprehension, uncertainty, and a semblance of intolerance to diversity issues in the classroom may result from a lack of adequate preparation of teachers in the area of awareness toward diversity in the pre-service training. An obvious vital starting point is for teachers to become aware of their own biases. Teachers need an understanding of the implications of culture in general and the ramifications of negative attitudes of dominant cultural groups toward diversity in other areas of society. By examining and becoming aware of how schools inadvertently or in subtle ways retain and embody traces of institutionalized discrimination, teachers can avoid becoming agents in maintaining these behaviors.

As important points in multicultural education, Banks (1994) reiterates the necessity for preservice teacher training to include the use of multiethnic materials together with a general attitude change. Very often, teachers are not aware of the existence of multicultural resource materials available in their schools, and those who seem to be aware of them may have limited or no knowledge of how to utilize these materials effectively to promote the spirit of multiculturalism in their classrooms (Irwin, 1988).

Implementing multicultural education and addressing diversity issues and awareness across the curriculum calls for teachers to equip themselves with pertinent knowledge, skills, and attitudes that are congruent with behaviors indicative of acceptance, respect, and awareness. Knowledge, understanding, and appreciation of experiences and contributions of various racial, cultural, or minority groups in American society, together with the recognition of the causes of discrimination, prejudice, and inequality, are elements that teachers can and should familiarize themselves with to enhance multicultural education in schools (Appleton, 1983).

When teachers are cognizant of the impact of socio-cultural factors on the learning style preferences of students from diverse backgrounds, they will be able to design their teaching styles to meet these needs. Teachers' understanding of the effects of attitudes, values, and expectations on the motivation and performance of students, particularly those from low socio-cultural backgrounds, is an asset in transcending socio-cultural biases. The school as a social institution and teachers as its agents are charged with expediting changes that are reflective of the trend in American society. Swisher (1982) has reiterated that an understanding and support of significant people, particularly teachers, is essential for effective change to occur.

Teachers may misrepresent the true concept of multicultural education if they continue to deal with its essential elements as isolated units to be conjured from the back shelves when the necessity arises. This approach treats multicultural education flimsily as a 'graft-on' program or a palliative that is employed to conveniently fit into an agenda. For multicultural education to succeed, the classroom teacher will have to make it an integral part of the whole curriculum. This is an effort whose capability is not beyond the teacher. A smooth transitional approach to infusion can be achieved with the classroom teacher venturing beyond the restrictive superficial stereotypical representation of various cultural groups in American society, dwelling specifically on such mundane items as ethnic foods and costumes. A teacher's emphasis on substantial aspects of culture that increase awareness of similarities between groups will elicit a positive understanding and acceptance among students, thus creating that desired atmosphere of belonging and acceptance in the classroom.

The role of classroom teachers is vital in the success or failure of multicultural education. Teachers have the authority and the means to create a classroom climate that will enhance positive attitudes, values, beliefs, and positive expectations among all students. Equal treatment, respect, and positive acknowledgment of each student regardless of any differentiating human factors would alleviate anxiety, fear, and uncertainty that minority students often harbor in their relationships with members of the dominant culture in schools. The teacher's efforts will also create a safe and nonthreatening atmosphere for growth and cooperative learning, resulting in the building of bridges among the diversities of students in the class. Multicultural education is definitely a classroom teacher's charge, and it behooves the preservice teacher to be aware of this role in the classroom.

References

Appleton, N. (1983). *Cultural Pluralism in Education—Theoretical Foundations.* New York and London: Longman.

Banks, J. (1984). *Multiethnic Education—Theory and Practice.* 3rd Edition. Boston: Allyn and Bacon.

Chisholm, I. M. (1994). Preparing Teachers for Multicultural Classrooms. *The Journal of Educational Issues of Language Minority Students.* Vol. 14. Winter 1994.

Gollnick, D. M., & Chinn, P. C. (1994). *Multicultural Education in a Pluralistic Society.* 4th Edition. New York: Merrill.

Irwin, L. (1988). *Attitudes of Southern Alberta Elementary School Teachers Toward Multicultural Education.* Brigham Young University. Doctoral dissertation.

Justiz, M. J., & Darling, D. W. (1980 Spring). A Multicultural Perspective in Teacher Education. *Educational Horizons,* 58.

Manning, L. M., & Baruth, L. G. (1996). *Multicultural Education of Children and Adolescent.* Boston: Allyn and Bacon.

Olstad, R. G., Goster, C. D., & Wyman, R. Jr. (1983). Multicultural Education for Pre-Service Teachers. *Integrated Education,* 21(6).

Sims, W. E., & de Martinez, B. B. (Eds) (1981). *Perspectives in Multicultural Education.* Washington D.C. University Press of America.

Swisher, K. (1982). *Attitudes of Parents and Teachers of American Indian Children Toward Multicultural Education.* New York City. ERIC ED 225 764.

Tiedt, P. L., & Tiedt, I. M. (1995). *Multicultural Education—A Handbook of Activities, Information, and Resources.* 4th Edition. Boston: Allyn and Bacon.

Article Review Form at end of book.

How can community service projects promote understanding of multiculturalism? What are characteristics of effective community service projects? To be effective, community service projects must be integrated into the academic curriculum. How can this integration be accomplished?

Community Service in a Multicultural Nation

Sandra J. LeSourd

Sandra J. LeSourd is associate professor of education and human development at California State University, Fresno.

In recent years, community service ideals have been promoted in the national political agenda. The commitment demonstrated by the enactment of the federally funded National and Community Service Trust Act provided impetus for action at the local level throughout the nation (Quinn, 1993). Educators followed by instituting model programs and entertaining conceptual discussion of appropriate purposes and methods for fulfilling service to community.

In the following discussion, I consider the fundamental nature of human commitment to, and participation in, the common good in a diverse, democratic society. Service programs offer promises for realization of the vital human traits that are needed in a society that seeks to sustain a good life for all its members. I believe planned interaction across social barriers is necessary to develop essential personal and intellectual qualities of citizenship for a pluralistic nation.

Definition of Service

Service is defined as an act done for the public good in which an individual or group voluntarily helps other individuals or groups (Gorham, 1992). According to this definition, the enactment of service depends upon a commitment to the public good that is intense enough to inspire action and that is not undertaken for the sake of advancing one's private interests. This criterion of humanness cannot be assumed to be easily or automatically developed in people without serious, focused educational planning.

In addition, the definition implies that a type of society that best represents the public good or public welfare can have an authentic existence that is achievable. Citizens in such an ideal society must exercise constant vigilance and willingness to act in accordance with defensible moral judgment. In a pluralistic society, definition of the public good is fraught with ethical challenges that emerge from value differences.

Connectedness to Others

Both the central intention and primary outcome of community service programs must be the development of human traits that distinguish the integrity of those who serve. Let us begin by examining a quality called connectedness to others that is embedded in scholarship from a range of perspectives. The following discussion is based on research (Oliner & Oliner, 1988), philosophical value positions (Greene, 1993), political commentary (Buckley, 1990), and pedagogical models (NCSS Task Force, 1992).

LeSourd, Sandra J. (1997). Community Service in a Multicultural Nation. THEORY INTO PRACTICE, 36, 157–163. (Theme issue on "Community Service Learning").

Through extensive interviewing of individuals who voluntarily took action to rescue Jews during World War II, and individuals who declined to actively assist, Oliner and Oliner (1988) created a composite of personal traits associated with altruistic persons. They concluded that rescuers, that is, those who were motivated to act despite threat of danger to self or family, had placed a high value on connectedness to other people throughout their lives. They were able to translate their concern for victims into action because the value of human relationship had always been central to their interpretation of quality in life.

In sum, a strong commitment to relationship with others was the underlying commonality shared by those who took the risk of saving Jewish lives. Their moral courage grew from the routine connectedness inherent in their entire pattern of living rather than from the urgent needs of an extraordinary circumstance. In respect to the topic of community service, the Oliners' findings point out that the impetus to serve is more likely to thrive in a social setting based on strong habits of commitment to relationship rather than in a context focused on advancement of individual interest.

An emphasis upon relationship is prominent in analyses of multicultural education (Greene, 1993; NCSS Task Force, 1992). The primary goal is to help individuals function easily and effectively with different others—the members of other racial, ethnic, and cultural groups. Participation in the actual life experience of various ethnic and cultural groups is recommended for achievement of this goal. When placed in intercultural contexts that are not immediately clear to them, participants have the opportunity to amass information that causes them to confront the disparities between their own and others' values. The more continuous and authentic personal encounters can be, the more likely participants will learn to value one another in spirit of true connectedness, rather than resorting to an instrumental view of different others.

Greene posits that a sense of community in a pluralistic nation is dependent upon maintenance of meaningful personal relationships across sociocultural barriers. Even Buckley (1990), a popular, politically-conservative observer of American life, includes the need for creating genuine human bonds in his interpretation of a quality society. He speculates that shared experience is the foundation for true friendship and the antidote for racism.

Earnest appeals for greater commitment to connectedness with others, especially different others, arouse sympathy. However, systematic analyses of operational mechanisms to accomplish this goal in service programs are lacking. It seems that programs are often created with the expectation that human relationships will strengthen naturally. Positive social contact between diverse groups, primarily in the course of servers providing assistance to the group perceived to be in need, is treated as an assumed project component. Possibly, the lack of defined implementation procedures is related to the difficulties of specifying concrete criteria in the realm of human relations. On the other hand, perhaps the process of building humane capacity through connectedness to others is incredibly delicate and intricate. The challenge of bringing this goal to focus and actualization may require far deeper conceptualization and more rigorous planning than currently imagined.

Humane Qualities

To suffuse a service ethic in a pluralistic nation, relationships must have the power to teach people to place genuine value upon the worth of each human being, extend moral consideration to all groups, and determine to act in the interest of others. Learning to value the inherent worth of individuals requires people to overcome the tendency to categorize others on the basis of qualities believed to make them different from oneself (Engle & Ochoa, 1988). Categorization, followed by evaluation of others' qualities as right or wrong, superior or inferior, jeopardizes the potential for genuine relationship (Oliner & Oliner, 1988). Group differences in cultural values and socioeconomic characteristics become reasonable and explainable when individuals befriend each other and learn one another's unique qualities.

An example of a generalization that interferes with positive human interaction is the suspicion that character flaws, rather than circumstances, account for the problems of the needy. Person-to-person connections between the privileged and the needy are necessary to teach that character is not completely predetermined by background (Greene, 1993). Reciprocal experiences that permit people to cross social barriers and attempt to understand how other members of the community perceive their personal reality are vital (Gorham, 1992).

Recognition that one's own worldview is not universally shared and that others have views that are profoundly different has traditionally been a basic goal of global education (Hanvey, 1982). The ability to view ideas and ways (including one's own) from multiple vantage points is indispensable for international or intercultural effectiveness. Wilson (1993) presents a detailed discussion of how the experience of living outside one's own country contributes to gains in perceptual understanding, including enhanced critical reflection, perspective consciousness, and open-mindedness.

Cross-cultural experience within the nation also provides opportunity for learning about human diversity. Logically, an ability to interpret decisions from alternative points of view necessitates thorough knowledge of the beliefs, realities, and experiences of diverse groups. Even though individuals perceive most deeply through their own language and worldview, total ignorance of any other perspectives is dangerously confining in the public realm of a plural society.

The extension of moral consideration to all groups is a mandate of democratic life in which the welfare of all is prized. Stability and community in a multicultural democracy depend upon citizens who learn to perceive the human character of persons outside their immediate social group. Brandhorst (1991) perceives a current tendency to emphasize the well-being of those inside one's own social group, and ignore the welfare of other groups, as a threat to societal cohesion in America. When the human character of members of a different social class, ethnicity, or language is unknown, they can be ignored easily. Recall that altruistic persons, who took action even in circumstances of potential danger, had a strong sense of responsibility for the welfare of those outside their own social circle (Oliner & Oliner, 1988).

Finally, citizens in a multicultural nation must have the determination to take action. Often, those who develop genuine relationships across social barriers do not receive enthusiastic conventional approval. They must have the courage to be exceptional, receive criticism, and risk vulnerability. It is unlikely that drastic circumstances or principles of justice will prompt individuals to action on behalf of others unless they are predisposed to place a high value upon their connectedness with others. Clearly an absence of sustained, reciprocal relationship among diverse people carries no promise for action.

Serow's (1991) survey of student volunteers in service projects supports the idea that relationship is actually the core of a service ethic. Students reported great satisfaction from the opportunity to assist others through participation in the concrete experiences of their lives. They were more inspired to help solve the problematic challenges of others' lives than by the opportunity to uphold principles of justice. The finding that servers generally receive notable satisfaction from having done something good for someone is important. Perhaps the national predilection to accept individual rewards with no thought of obligation to a greater cause can be eroded and an ethos of giving to society through helping relationships can be cultivated through service programs (Buckley, 1990).

Constructing the Public Good

Recall that service is defined as an act done for the public good. Definition of the public good requires interpretation of how democratic principles should be exemplified in a society with cultural, linguistic, and economic divisions. The people have the responsibility of constructing a viable political entity from many socially-divergent elements.

The most basic value tradition of American democracy is respect for human dignity—protection of the life and well-being of each person (Engle & Ochoa, 1988). Additional ideals, such as justice, liberty, and equality provide the moral themes for sorting out the fundamental dignity that should be extended to all people in all social groups. Rights and freedoms are defined by decisions made in the course of attempting to resolve case-by-case value conflicts across social divisions. Discourse that takes place in the process of interpretation should become a basis for solidarity rather than deepening divisions among groups (Aronowitz & Giroux, 1991).

Postmodern writers believe that the presence of different voices, languages, histories, and ways of viewing and experiencing the world is a deeply political issue (Aronowitz & Giroux, 1991; Greene, 1993). The ideals of democratic life cannot encompass all members of the national community until people of different traditions listen to the voices of others. All individuals have the right to participate and dissent in matters of public debate. A society open to plurality will come about when people inhabiting different realities have a genuine and reciprocal impact upon one another.

Perspective taking is the intellectual ability that is germane to affirmation of differences for clarification of the public good. In the public realm, diverse groups have to work together effectively to address problems even if their value differences are profound (Boyte, 1991). For wise evaluation and revision of the common institutions that should represent the public collectively, citizens need to be able to see others' position in relation to those institutions (Gorham, 1992).

In addition, participants in a pluralistic democracy need the courage and skill to be critics. Democracy survives as a dynamic force responsive to the people only because questioning and critical introspection are tolerated and, in fact, necessary. An important responsibility of education in a democracy is to teach citizens to practice critical thinking and speaking (Engle & Ochoa, 1988).

Aronowitz and Giroux (1991) use the term "language of morality" to describe a public way of thinking and communicating about the forms of life and conduct that are most appropriate morally. If people are to have the moral courage to correct injustice, they must have a disposition to exercise criticism. They must also have the skill to reason about instances of value conflict, articulate values to be sought, and make decisions even if information is ambiguous or incomplete (Newmann, 1989).

Successful conflict resolution is another requirement for citizen participation. Negotiation, bargaining, the just exercise of power, and decision making by common counsel are processes that make possible a balance of political control in a free society (Boyte, 1991; Engle & Ochoa, 1988). To contest issues and still maintain a peaceable political environment, individuals are called upon to treat others with respect, tolerate differences, engage in collective deliberation, and seek resolution of problems without repression or discrimination (Gorham, 1992).

It is important to be reminded that the resolution to conflict situations is not a matter of adherence to a single definition of a decent, humane life. In effect, Aronowitz and Giroux (1991) argue that subordinate groups have been marginalized in the past because their interests have not been recognized in processes of public deliberation. All the interpretations of a conflict must be scrutinized if the outcome of deliberations is to fairly represent the people. Both perspective taking and courageous criticism are conflict-resolution ingredients.

Service Experience

Service projects, in which students take action for the public good by voluntarily helping others, offer the opportunity for experience with great educative potential. The moral courage and intellectual skills required for citizen participation in a multicultural democracy can be honed through powerful, direct experience in the community.

The service experience must evoke intense emotion because it is imperative that students learn values of the heart as well as intellectual acumen (Schultz, 1991). It is unlikely that an intense personal commitment to compassion for the common good will develop in the absence of deliberate planning for sustained human interaction. As already observed, the moral courage to care for the common welfare and take subsequent responsible action requires a strong sense of connection to others. The personal relationships that develop between server and served must be full and direct to allow authentic knowledge of one another. Knowledge of the other must be sufficient to support perspective taking and transcend the persistent human tendency to stereotype and judge prematurely.

Reciprocal experiences, such as shared work projects in which participants of diverse sociocultural heritage or economic status have the same goals, provide the opportunity for discovering authentic knowledge of the other. Service programs should offer both server and served the opportunity to know people who would normally be excluded from their circle of conventional social contacts. Following are synopses of two experiments in human connectedness.

In a Queens College service program, college students were paired with homeless children in a deliberate effort to establish Big Buddy mentoring relationships (Salz & Trubowitz, 1992). Each weekend for an entire year, the pairs spent a full day together, exploring educational, cultural, and recreational attractions. In addition to enriching the children's experience and improving their school performance, another goal was to help them develop a greater sense of trust and improved self-esteem.

The program is reported to have succeeded in each of these goals. Improvement in the children's trust and self-esteem was attributed to the strength of the consistent, positive human relationship nurtured through the sustained, shared project experiences. It is also reported that the college students gained a sense of fulfillment and meaning from their personal commitment to children less fortunate than themselves. Thus, a program with human connectedness at its core was judged to have an impact on both the served and the server.

A different program involving cross-cultural interaction did not strengthen connectedness with others (Silcox, 1993). A group of American high school students traveled to Russia to work with Russian counterparts in an urban environmental monitoring project. The goals were to teach environmental education through a direct work experience and to build interpersonal connections and tolerance between cultures. American and Russian students shared daily life on the job and lived together in the private homes of participating Russian families for a 3-week period. Posttest findings showed increase in both groups' sensitivity to environmental issues and in their perceptions of their roles as change agents. On the other hand, neither group increased their cross-cultural tolerance or their willingness to accept one another's beliefs and ideas.

Different findings from two programs, both created, in part, to nurture a sense of connectedness, raises questions. In the Big Buddy program, urban college students and homeless children gained in ways that fulfilled their personal needs. However, it is not known if positive interaction between the social groups continued beyond program time limits, or exactly how either group of participants contributed subsequently to a stronger society. The interpersonal relationships created by program experiences had value, but the long-range social effect cannot be interpreted from available information.

The Russian-American experiment in cross-cultural immersion did not effect greater acceptance of different others. At first glance, it seems plausible that the short duration of the experience was a program weakness. Perhaps specific conditions, such as physical setting, language disparities, or needs of participants and the manner of their induction into the program influenced the disappointing outcome. Clearly, more empirical work in the area of building human connectedness through service is needed.

Academic Complements

To make service truly educative, participation in service projects needs carefully designed, full, simultaneous integration into an academic structure. Let us consider some important features of correlated academic curriculum components. In the intellectual domain, understanding of the classical foundations of democracy is imperative (Gagnon, 1991). The historical narrative that discloses how people have struggled to construct a society based on democratic processes of responsibility and caring provides the background for current moral action. Since moral decisions made in the national realm are a subset of guiding universal principles of humanitarian content, academic study must also include opportunity to consider universal principles of justice and liberty (Oliner & Oliner, 1988). Thus, formal, intensive study of literature that explicates the roots of U.S. political history and illustrates the universality of the human condition is an integral part of the process of education for democratic citizenship.

In addition, the correlated curriculum must focus on serious study of the social history of the cultural and linguistic groups of U.S. society. Citizens need sufficient knowledge of alternate life histories to be able to accurately explain the realities of life from different points of view. Classroom conversation should nurture the capacity to talk honestly and seriously about the human dimension of experiences encountered in the community no matter how disturbing or emotionally challenging the process (Newmann, 1989).

Rigorous analysis of how to best defend principles through actual participation in public affairs is another vital academic complement to service. While service projects provide experiential involvement, simultaneous academic curriculum should provide disciplined study of democratic action (Boyte, 1991; Bragaw, 1991). Organized, supervised social action projects that place students in local settings and give them roles that require participation in processes of influence and negotiation are necessary.

Correlated study and discussion of the actions required to initiate and support social change is also required. Students will discover that the charge to create a just democratic society is carried out in a disorderly and confusing manner. Even though situations may be ambiguous, decisions must be made using the knowledge and thinking skill that can be applied at the time. The formal curriculum should require students to examine and articulate values, their own, those that are in conflict, and those that are to be sought (Newmann, 1989). Then there is opportunity for open and honest reasoning guided by value commitments.

Finally, students engaged in service must learn about the substance of public policy issues that they naturally encounter in their work. A lifelong interest in the vital public issues that are intertwined with the life of the community can be cultivated by sophisticated data gathering and analysis during service work. It is important that the personal knowledge gained through connection with others be correlated with a formal knowledge underpinning the debatable questions that affect the quality of life. For political impact far beyond the duration of their assignments, service participants must develop a feeling of civic efficacy (Bragaw, 1991). The trust that a just and responsible community can be constructed by informed and participating members will have to be built carefully in the academic classroom and in the community laboratory.

Conclusion

Profound value differences arising from the pluralistic nature of our society must be accommodated in the democratic processes that allow for continuous transformation of the political realm. Citizens must be prepared to uphold principles of respect for human dignity while striving to include all voices in the life of the democracy. This article offers a brief exploration of some human qualities that undergird citizens' commitment to the common good in a diverse, democratic society. These qualities include a strong sense of relationship or connectedness to others, a belief that all persons deserve moral consideration, an ability to see and understand others' realities and interpret their perspective, and commitments to skilled criticism and conflict resolution.

I propose that community service experiences nurture the needed human qualities primarily by fostering person-to-person interaction across social barriers. Service programs that offer the opportunity for the server and the served to develop an intense relationship are recommended. Experience must be complemented with a suitable academic curriculum. For adherence to the citizenship education needs of a democratic society, students should study the substance of democratic principles, participate in real public decision-making processes, and learn about the social history of the various groups that make up the nation.

References

Aronowitz, S., & Giroux, H.A. (1991). *Postmodern education: Politics, culture, and social criticism.* Minneapolis: University of Minnesota Press.

Boyte, H.C. (1991). Community service and civic education. *Phi Delta Kappan, 72,* 765–767.

Bragaw, D. (1991, January). Expanding social studies to encompass the public interest. *NASSP Bulletin, 75*(531), 25–31.

Brandhorst, A. (1991). The social psychological perspective: Social contexts, processes, and civil ideologies. In R.E. Gross & L.T. Dynneson (Eds.), *Social science perspectives on citizenship education* (161–183). New York: Teachers College Press.

Buckley, W.F., Jr. (1990). *Gratitude: Reflections on what we owe to our country.* New York: Random House.

Engle, S.H., & Ochoa, A.S. (1988). *Education for democratic citizenship: Decision making in the social studies.* New York: Teachers College Press.

Gagnon, P. (1991, December). Balancing multicultural and civic education will take more than social stew. *The Education Digest, 57*(4), 7–9.

Gorham, E.B. (1992). *National service, citizenship, and political education.* Albany: State University of New York Press.

Greene, M. (1993, January–February). The passions of pluralism: Multiculturalism and the expanding community. *Educational Researcher, 22*(1), 13–18.

Hanvey, R. (1982). An attainable global perspective. *Theory Into Practice, 21,* 162–167.

National Council for Social Studies Task Force on Ethnic Studies Curriculum Guidelines. (1992). Curriculum guidelines for multicultural education. *Social Education, 56,* 274–294.

Newmann, F.M. (1989, October). Reflective civic participation. *Social Education, 53,* 357–360.

Oliner, S.P., & Oliner, P.M. (1988). *The altruistic personality: Rescuers of Jews in Nazi Europe.* New York: The Free Press.

Quinn, J.B. (1993, August 9). The new youth brigades. *Newsweek, 122*(6), 45.

Salz, A., & Trubowitz, J. (1992, March). You can see the sky from here: The Queens College Big Buddy Program. *Phi Delta Kappan, 73,* 551–556.

Schultz, S.K. (1991, March). Whither civic education: Classics or community service? *The Education Digest, 56*(7), 56–60.

Serow, R.C. (1991, Fall). Students and voluntarism: Looking into the motives of community service participants. *American Educational Research Journal, 28,* 543–556.

Silcox, H.C. (1993, May). Experiential environmental education in Russia: A study in community service learning. *Phi Delta Kappan, 74,* 706–709.

Wilson, A.H. (1993). *The meaning of international experience for schools.* Westport, CT: Praeger Publishers.

Article Review Form at end of book.

WiseGuide Wrap-Up

- Theory and practice are mutually supportive.
- Teacher preparation programs should encourage preservice teachers to evaluate classroom effectiveness and make changes as needed.
- Effective multicultural education programs are fused throughout the curriculum.
- Preservice teachers should acquire not only knowledge and skills but also attitudes and behaviors to promote understanding and acceptance in a multicultural society.
- Community service projects can enhance an academic curriculum by promoting interaction and collaboration among diverse groups.
- Preservice teachers should prepare themselves to meet the diverse academic and social needs of their students.

R.E.A.L. Sites

This list provides a print preview of typical **coursewise** R.E.A.L. sites. There are over 100 such sites at the **courselinks**™ site. The danger in printing URLs is that web sites can change overnight. As we went to press, these sites were functional using the URL provided. If you come across one that isn't, please let us know via email to: webmaster@coursewise.com. Use your Passport to access the most current list of R.E.A.L. sites at the **courselinks**™ site.

Site name: Family Education Network

URL: http://familyeducation.com/index.asp

Why is it R.E.A.L.? With a focus on families and other caregivers for children with special needs, this site includes up-to-date information on policy issues, best practices, special needs, and current state initiatives.

Key topics: students with special needs, learning disabilities

Activity: After reading the section on current state initiatives, describe activities or issues affecting your state.

Site name: Expect the Best from a Girl: That's What You Get (Women's College Coalition)

URL: http://www.academic.org/

Why is it R.E.A.L.? This site focuses on the relationship between expectations and achievement of females and on other gender-related issues. Issues related to the home environment, achievement in mathematics and sciences, and career exploration are specifically discussed.

Key topics: career exploration, mathematics and science achievement, gender equity

Activity: The site name is insightful and revealing. Discuss the message that it is intended to convey to audiences.

Site name: National Information Center for Children and Youth with Disabilities

URL: http://nichcy.or/

Why is it R.E.A.L.? With links in Spanish and English, the site is an information/referral center for disability-related issues. Target audiences include families, educators, and other professionals associated with children and youth with disabilities. Topics addressed include specific disabilities, Internet resources, individual education plan, professional organizations and conferences, and educational rights.

Key topics: students with special needs, learning disabilities, student rights

Activity: Identify rights of students with special needs that are often violated.

section 4

Assessing Our Position: Participating in Reflective Conversations on Selected Issues

Learning Objectives

After reading the articles in this section, you will be able to:

- Identify key issues currently causing debates among educators, community members, and others involved in educational processes.
- Discuss values education from a historical perspective.
- Define the concept of core knowledge.
- Discuss the pros and cons of national education standards.
- List reasons for and against voucher systems.
- Discuss the impact of school choice on public education.
- Give examples of educational services delivered via private contracts.

Effective teaching does not occur in isolation. In reality, it is a complex social activity influenced by many variables. Teachers, therefore, should be aware of and understand the diverse influences and controversial issues affecting the profession and its clients. When they have such an understanding, teachers can select the most appropriate instructional strategies to meet the needs of all students. Without such an understanding, teachers risk teaching content, not students.

No one can predict the hot topic of the day. Almost with certainty, however, key educational issues share common sources: lack of communication, personal rights vs. public rights, curricular concerns, governance structures, political decisions, changing roles of parents and educators, funding, and education reform movements. Preservice teachers must have opportunities to identify, discuss, and evaluate these issues; to form their own professional conclusions based on the facts; and to understand how each issue interfaces with the local community and state.

To address all of the issues currently facing educators and educational systems would require volumes of materials. The readings in this section, however, are representative of current issues. The first three readings—"The New Moral Classroom," "Making Schools Ad-Free Zones," and "The Jargon Jungle"—illustrate the diversity of issues as focus shifts from values education to commercialism to communication. The fourth reading, "The Core Knowledge Curriculum—What's Behind Its Success," is indicative of curricular concerns, whereas the fifth reading, "National Standards Threaten Local Vitality," focuses on governance structures and the role of the federal government in school reform. Societal issues and their impact on public education is the theme of the sixth reading, "Violence in the Classroom: Where We Stand." The final five articles—"The Empty Promise of School Vouchers," "Is School Choice Working?" "Considering Nontraditional Alternatives: Charters, Private Contracts, and Vouchers," "New Options, Old Concerns," and "School Choice: To What End?"—all focus on school choice and its impact on public school systems.

Questions

Reading 16: How have societal changes contributed to the emergence of values education in the classroom? What are some current strategies for incorporating moral education into the classroom?

Reading 17: What are the key arguments in support of commercialism in public education? What characteristics should school personnel consider when evaluating potential in-school advertisements?

Reading 18: What is the "jargon jungle" discussed in this article?

Reading 19: What is the philosophy supporting the core knowledge movement? According to selected research findings, why is the core knowledge initiative successful?

Reading 20: How would you characterize the opponents to national education standards? What should be the federal government's role in establishing national standards?

Reading 21: What are the most common strategies educators use to counteract violence in classrooms?

Reading 22: What does Edd Doerr see as some disadvantages of implementing a voucher system to allow for school choice? What has led to the broad-based support of voucher systems?

Reading 23: Overall, how do participants in school choice programs evaluate the effectiveness of school choice? What are strategies for improving school choice programs, especially in the areas of equity and student achievement?

Reading 24: What are the contrasting viewpoints related to school choice? What are charter schools, contracts, and voucher plans?

Reading 25: What are the arguments for and against school choice?

Reading 26: According to Tony Wagner, what should be educators' attitude toward school choice programs?

How have societal changes contributed to the emergence of values education in the classroom? What are some current strategies for incorporating moral education into the classroom?

The New Moral Classroom

All over the country, schools are using new methods to teach kids old values.

Eleanor Smith

Eleanor Smith lives in Oakland, CA, and writes on the sciences and social sciences.

A generation ago, American public schools began to walk away from their role as moral educators. Schools feared they would be accused of imposing religion or "indoctrinating" children, so they stuck to academics, leaving moral instruction to parents and the community.

But the traditional family was changing and television became our favorite babysitter. Many children of the 1960s and 1970s grew up believing that there are no universal values.

School administrators fretted over the situation; parents clamored for them to get back to teaching the difference between right and wrong. However, parents and supporters of moral education were not well organized and did not enjoy the support of their elected officials. All that is changing.

Today, leaders from Ronald Reagan to Mario Cuomo have been calling for schools to pay more attention to students' moral development. In response to the groundswell of enthusiasm for moral education, educators in schools from inner-city Chicago to upper-class Massachusetts are developing programs to foster "prosocial values," "character development" and "democratic virtues" in schoolchildren.

A second-grade teacher gathers her students around her and asks, "What is share?" When no one responds, she picks up a hand puppet and says, "Okay, let's see what 'share' means." She designates the children on her left as the "sharing group" and asks them to show the others how to share the puppet. A little girl plays with it briefly, then hands it to the boy next to her. He tries it on, then, giggling, turns it over to the boy next to him, and so on.

"Good!" the teacher exclaims. "That's sharing. Now look at their faces," she says, pointing to the smiling children on her left. "Are they happy or sad when they share?" "Happy!" the children exclaim.

This is an example of the many approaches being used to teach morals to children in hundreds of classrooms around the nation. But such approaches stir passions among those who oppose any discussion of values in the schools. Some argue that children come from so many different cultural, ethnic and religious backgrounds that it is difficult to agree on which values to teach. Others say that even if they could agree on values, they don't know how to teach ethics outside of a framework provided by religion.

"Part of the job of moral education," says Thomas Lickona, a developmental psychologist at the State University of New York at Cortland, "is teaching people the distinction between private morality [religion] and public morality—those kinds of things that are universal values to which we are all obligated, like it or not." Still, educators often meet opposition from those on the extreme left or the extreme right.

Some Christian fundamentalists, for example, take great exception to anything that smacks of "secular humanism," a philosophy derived largely from humanistic psychology. They are concerned not only about the teaching of evolution and sex education but also about social studies curricula that take a "global" as opposed to a strictly American perspective. The Christian right supports the efforts of schools to teach children values as long as they are traditional American Christian values.

Many school districts skirt the activist element by inviting members of their communities to come together to work out an acceptable approach. Mary Ellen Saterlie of Maryland's Baltimore County describes how her large, diverse school district developed its approach to moral education. First, a district-wide task force made up of educators, parents and other representatives from the black, middle-class white, Jewish and elderly communities met to examine how the county was already handling the teaching of values. They worked out a long list of values to include in a more deliberate program.

"We concluded that no one wants to be told what their values are or what they should teach," Saterlie says. The task force received a long letter from a fundamentalist minister asking what moral framework it was using to select its values. "So we decided to base our list of values on those found in the Constitution," she says. Eventually, the group came up with 24 "core values," including compassion, courtesy, freedom of thought and action, honesty, human worth and dignity, respect for others' rights, responsible citizenship, rule of law, and tolerance.

Participants in this renaissance of moral education seem to share the sentiments of California Superintendent of Public Instruction Bill Honig. In addition to helping children develop their scholastic aptitudes, he argues that "we must also encourage the full flowering of each child's humanity. Not every child is going to be smart, but every child has the potential to be good."

One of the more progressive programs is unfolding in San Ramon, a suburban community about 40 miles east of San Francisco. Here the Child Development Project (CDP), in three elementary schools, embraces an approach based on cooperation, which, along with fostering character development, is one of two major models for moral education.

A typical cooperative lesson might go like this: Second-graders meet in groups of four to solve several math "thought" problems together.

At one table, Susan, the reader, raises an index card and reads, "Portia and Freddy bought a pizza. The pizza man cut it into eight pieces. 'Would you cut it into 16 pieces, please?' Portia asks. 'We are really hungry.' Would cutting it into 16 pieces help?"

"It's the same!" exclaims John. "It's still the same."

"Yeah, because the pizza doesn't grow," says Susan. "That's stupid."

"What's the same?" asks Rachel.

John replies, "The pizza is still the same. There isn't any more if you make 16 pieces."

"Because the pieces will be smaller," adds Susan.

"Oh, yeah," says Rachel. "They don't get any more."

Toby asks, "Does everyone agree?"

Everyone nods, and John writes the group's answer: "No, because the pieces will be smaller."

Cooperative learning, a hot trend in education, involves small groups of children working on a common, usually academic task to promote cooperation, problem-solving skills and the ability to see other points of view. "We think it's important for kids to know there are these values—caring, fairness, helpfulness, concern for others and individual responsibility—and that they are widely and deeply shared within the culture," explains Eric Schaps, a social psychologist and CDP director. "But we think it's also important to provide kids with the direct experience of those values."

As for discipline, the San Ramon project takes the long view. "We view the child as a developing being, not a finished product," says Sylvia Kendzior, CDP senior program associate and veteran elementary school teacher. "We're trying to develop an awareness in them of desirable behavior and the skills necessary to carry it out." The method also invites children in making decisions, such as establishing rules of conduct, that affect their lives at school.

Schools, of course, never completely abandoned moral education. In fact, they provide moral education even when they don't intend to. The ways teachers treat students and each other, the physical and social atmosphere of the school and the degree of tolerance toward such problems as vandalism and student violence all tell students how respect, responsibility and other values are regarded.

The guise of overt moral education has changed dramatically during the last 30 years. In the 1950s, schools were expected to reflect the best values of their communities. In the traditional approach to "character development," as it was called then, teachers explained in no uncertain terms the difference between right and wrong; they told stories illustrating the virtues of hard work and loyalty; and they unselfconsciously preached the superiority of the American way of life. At least in retrospect, it seems that students flocked to school assemblies, competed for awards and understood what was expected of them. They respected adults and acknowledged the rules, even if they didn't always follow them.

Then, with the upheaval of the late 1960s and the 1970s, teachers lost their assumed right to respect and authority, says Kevin Ryan of Boston University. At the same time, the idea of America as a "melting pot" gave way to the view of society as a pluralistic pot of stew where, apparently, no one set of values was common to all.

A number of new approaches to moral education cropped up. One program, "values clarification," conceived by psychologist Louis Raths and his colleagues in the late 1960s, gained widespread popularity. The method, designed to help students make reasoned value decisions based on careful thinking and democratic principles, was supposed to be "values-neutral." Teachers were not to impose their own values on the students, merely to help students expose and act on their values.

Some oppose discussion of values in the classroom.

Critics and parents, however, found much to dislike about values clarification. They especially didn't like the way the teacher's passive, neutral posture led students to believe that there was no such thing as right or wrong. Rather than being values-neutral, parents and critics claimed, values clarification promoted the worst form of moral relativism. The technique is no longer widely used, but vestiges remain.

A Stress on Conduct, Not Theory

Despite the advent of new approaches to moral education, most educators and communities today, however, eventually center on the traditional model of character development. This strategy, whose advocates include former Secretary of Education William Bennett and California schools chief Honig, attempts to develop a student's character through direct instruction in positive social values, coherent school policies, a recognition system for students and schools that demonstrate good citizenship, and a consistent and firmly enforced system of discipline. "Even mentioning the moral character of education sounds like religious proselytizing to some," Honig says. "But core values have always been at the center of the school experience in the United States."

Character development is part of the "great tradition" that originated in ancient and primitive cultures, explains University of Illinois education professor Edward Wynne. "The tradition was concerned with good habits of conduct as contrasted with moral concepts," he wrote in *Educational Leadership*. How students act from day to day is more important than their ability to reason through a moral problem. The mundane specifics range from being polite to telling the truth when it's easier to lie, as George Washington did in the cherry tree fable.

In this light, the traditional approach to character development is thriving in the Clovis Unified School District near Fresno, California, in the heart of the state's farm belt. Clovis's Fort Washington Elementary exemplifies Wynne's approach to character development, using the second major model for moral education—competition.

Student participation is crucial to the program's success. Fort Washington is known for high academic achievement. The school offers a wide range of "co-curricular" activities from athletics and student government to music, speech and drama.

Fort Washington students compete with themselves by setting specific scholastic and citizenship goals. Classrooms compete for the Patriotic Classroom Award by keeping their classrooms tidy and returning library books on time. The incentive for all this competition, says principal Richard K. Sparks, is the desire to improve oneself.

Fort Washington draws on some of the principles of the philosophy known as "assertive discipline." This approach requires teachers to clearly express their expectations for classroom behavior from the start. When children make bad decisions, they are taught that they must suffer the consequences, Sparks says. "We use detention, restrict kids from recess, things like that. As problems escalate, we involve the parents and write up a behavior modification contract with them and the student, to target specific behaviors that we want changed."

Does Moral Education Change Children?

The big question, of course, is whether any of these programs influence how caring, principled and responsible elementary schoolchildren become over time. The cooperation-orientated San Ramon project is engaged in an 11-year study of its effectiveness. Researchers are evaluating a group of children who started the program in kindergarten and are now in the sixth grade. The same measures are applied to a comparison group of children in three schools that do not receive the program. On socioeconomic levels and baseline test scores, children in the two groups are "remarkably similar," Schaps says.

It's too soon for final conclusions, but the Community Development Project seems to be working. Schaps notes that there is more spontaneous helping and cooperation among program children. Although there is no more negative behavior in the group of children not participating in the program, the program children are more likely to feel that they share responsibility for adhering to class rules. They also cling more strongly to certain democratic values. They are more likely to defend their opinions, for instance, even when it might not make a difference. In many areas, such as academic achievement, there is no difference between the groups. But as the students in the CDP mature, they are more adept at resolving conflict and solving social problems. "This is impressive," Schaps says, "since the two groups were identical in this measure at kindergarten."

In a somewhat less ambitious project, California State University at Fresno professors Jacques Benninga and Susan Tracz are evaluating the moral development of students at Clovis. Their study focus is similar to that used for San Ramon, making it easier to compare the two divergent approaches.

"Stark differences" exist between Clovis and San Ramon when one looks at how teachers and students interact, Benninga says. And minor differences appear on various other measures. But when one considers the broad perspective, the distinctions blur.

"Our general conclusion is that these philosophically different curricular approaches do not result, over time, in differences in how children relate to and think about others." He adds that at the second-grade level, children in both programs expressed a greater preference for resolving conflicts verbally rather than physically; helping others, even if it means sacrificing something themselves, making up for some wrongdoing; and thinking independently, than children who were not in the programs.

"The key is motivation," Benninga says. "In Clovis, the kids are motivated to success, both social and academic, by competition. In San Ramon, the children are motivated to success by cooperation. As long as the program is well-thought out in terms of what's best for children, either model can work." Benninga suggests that a synthesis of the two may even be more effective than any single one.

After a generation of dissension and confusion, schools have turned their attention back to the moral fiber of their young charges. The high costs of neglect have become unbearable. Cortland's Tom Lickona describes his dream of a moral generation: "We'd see less materialism and greed, which are the driving forces behind the public scandals. People would be able to take responsibility for their actions, such as accepting blame when they make mistakes. Employees wouldn't steal so much from their employers, students would cheat less." People would have more self-respect and would abuse drugs and alcohol less; people would feel less alienated. "There would be less violence," he adds, "and greater participation in our democratic government."

As support for moral education grows, more schools will join the movement. They have no choice. "There is a hunger for morality in the land," Lickona says. "People really do want to create a society where they can count on their neighbors to be decent human beings. The schools can't ignore them and the families know they can't do it alone."

Article Review Form at end of book.

What are the key arguments in support of commercialism in public education? What characteristics should school personnel consider when evaluating potential in-school advertisements?

Making Schools Ad-Free Zones

Advertisers spend billions to market so-called educational products, services, and points of view to vulnerable young consumers. It's time to stem the tide of commercialism that is enveloping our schools.

Rhoda H. Karpatkin and Anita Holmes

Rhoda H. Karpatkin is President, and Anita Holmes is Assistant Director of Education Services, Consumers Union, 101 Truman Ave., Yonkers, NY 10703.

> I'm ticked at ads where people bite a Twix and don't feel so stressed. It can cause weight problems if people think food can make them feel better.
>
> —Andrew Bean, Mount Vernon, Indiana, *Zillions* magazine (1994)

> Collect labels/proofs from these Campbell products . . . and redeem them for valuable school equipment.
>
> —Campbell's advertisement aimed at teachers and children

Each year, kids see some 30,000 print, broadcast, and other ads. Advertising is everywhere—boldly displayed in magazines and newspapers, billboards, and direct-mail brochures; blaring from radios and TVs; hiding as product placements and advertorials; placed decoratively on clothing, book bags, and sneakers; and disguised as games, comics, and TV cartoon shows.

Like Mary's proverbial little lamb, ads are also following kids to school. School buses display large 7-UP ("the uncola") signs. Algebra books sport bright Nike covers (Cover Concepts reports that its book cover ads reach more than 16 million kids).

Advertisers are bound by few restrictions on—and fewer qualms about—*what* and *how* they advertise to kids. They also have few if any limits on *where* they advertise. More and more of education is becoming ad-financed, with equipment and even hard cash being "given" to schools, courtesy of advertisers with something to sell to students or their families.

The Bottom Line

Why is this happening? Because kids of all ages are a large and growing market, and school is where they spend 20 percent of their time. Not only are there a lot of kids (more than 54 million between the ages of 3 and 17), but with their allowances, gifts, and part-time jobs, they spend a lot of money. Children from 6 to 12 spend about $11 billion annually; teenagers have an additional $57 billion of their own money to spend and $36 billion of their families'. Moreover, the youth population is expected to increase by about 10 percent over the next 10 years (Consumers Union 1995a).

Kids spend most of their billions of dollars on food and beverages, video and electronic products, toys and games, movies and sports, and—oh, yes—clothes and sneakers (Guber and Berry 1993). And no wonder: they're egged on by the tens of thousands of commercial messages aimed at them daily.

In addition to spending their own money, kids directly influence about $160 billion of the money their parents spend annually (Consumers Union 1995a). Many kids have a say in where the family eats out and goes on vacation, what car the family drives, and, of course, what the family eats and drinks (Guber and Berry 1993).

Finally, kids are "consumers in training." They have a lifetime of spending before them (Jacobson and Mazur 1995). As a result, marketers spend their marketing dollars not only trying to develop brand loyalties for products kids want and buy now, but also in developing consumer attitudes, habits, and loyalties that will affect kids' future spending behavior.

A number of forces are converging to pressure teachers and administrators to accept these ads and other promotional materials. In addition to the growing competition among corporations for the burgeoning youth market and the growing commercialism in all sectors of society, there is the chronic school budget squeeze.

Most of the arguments in support of in-school commercialism rest on schools' financial needs and the assumption that administrators and teachers can counteract any adverse affects of the ads. No one contends that in-school commercialism per se is desirable; rather, it's regarded as a means to an end. Clearly, though, there would be no such debate if schools weren't seriously underfunded and forced to accept help from companies willing to give it.

In addition to spending their own money, kids directly influence about $160 billion of the money their parents spend annually.

Strings Attached

In a new report called *Captive Kids,* Consumers Union (1995a) documents how the nation's chronically underfunded schools have become ad vehicles for companies eager to sell to this captive audience. The report is a follow-up to *Selling America's Kids* (Consumers Union 1990), which surveyed marketing strategies used to prey on the psyches and purses of our youngest and most vulnerable consumers.

As *Captive Kids* shows, school ads often take subtle and sneaky forms. They may be disguised as sponsored educational materials (BIC's "Quality Comes in Writing," Domino Pizza's "Encounter Math"); as contests (Oxy 10's $10,000 Scholarship Contest," Sears Optical's "The Eyes Have It"); or even as reading incentive programs (McDonald's "All-American Reading Challenge," Toys 'R Us's "Geoffrey's Reading Railroad").

Place ads appear in classroom magazines, such as *Weekly Reader* and *Scholastic*. In fact, the two biggest developers of corporate-sponsored educational materials and programs, Scholastic Inc. and Lifetime Learning Systems, claim to reach 88 and nearly 100 percent of the nation's schools, respectively. (The latter organization has distributed nutrition information packets for preschoolers with more than 1 million samples of General Mills' snack food, Fruit Roll-Ups. These products are just the tip of the iceberg.

Commercials have also infiltrated in-school radio and TV programs, such as the ad-sponsored daily classroom news program, Channel One. The 12-minute program, which claims to reach 8 million students in grades 6–12, includes 2 minutes of commercials. (By contrast, the other main daily classroom news program, CNN Newsroom, is 15 minutes long with no commercials.)

Here is a sampling of the ad messages (and innuendoes) that Channel One broadcast to students from April 4–8, 1994—with the implied endorsement of teachers and principals:

- "CareFree bubble gum is bursting with flavor." (Kids who chew it have great fun.)
- Clearasil's medicated formula "leaves no oily residue." (Gorgeous, clear-skinned, fun-loving kids use it.)
- "Drink Pepsi. Have fun." (Pepsi drinkers are cool and hip.)
- Secret deodorant is "strong enough for him (handsome teenager) but pH balanced just for you (female teenager)." (Girls who use Secret attract guys.)
- Snickers candy bars can "stop the hunger inside you" (and help you win big in sports).

In *Captive Kids,* we evaluated more than 100 educational and so-called educational materials, contests, and other programs sponsored by businesses and trade groups. We found that more than half were commercial or highly commercial. And we found that nearly 80 percent of the teaching kits and packets contained biased or incomplete information, promoting consumption of the sponsor's product or service or a position that favors the company or its economic agenda.

Among the more blatantly commercial and biased:

- *A Proctor & Gamble educational packet,* "Decision: Earth," which taught that clear-cut logging is good for the environment ("It mimics nature's way of getting rid of trees") and that disposable diapers are better for the environment than are cloth ones. So blatantly commercial and biased was this material that a coalition of environmentalists organized by the cloth diaper industry asked attorneys general in 11 states to investigate the kit's truthfulness.

Proctor & Gamble, the country's largest manufacturer of disposable diapers, had financed the study that produced those results. The company stopped distributing the kit in early 1994, but it continues to distribute another packet, *Planet Patrol*, which is nearly as biased.

- *Campbell's "Prego Thickness Experiment,"* designed "to help your students become aware of the many situations in which scientific thinking plays a part." The experiment quickly degenerates into a way for kids to prove its ad claim—that Prego spaghetti sauce is thicker than Ragu spaghetti sauce.
- *National Live Stock and Meat Board teaching kits* plugging pro-meat viewpoints into almost every curriculum area. "Digging for Data," which ostensibly teaches methods of scientific inquiry, provides data and actually leads students to deduce that early American settlers were short because they didn't eat enough meat.
- *Kellogg's "Kids Get Going With Breakfast"* program presents fat content as the sole concern when choosing a breakfast food; sugar and sodium content aren't mentioned. The program also prominently displays the Kellogg's logo and one of its cereals.

An Easy Mark

Because kids are more impressionable than adults, less sure of themselves, and less capable of sorting out fact from fiction, advertising can affect their thinking and behavior. Young children, in particular, have difficulty distinguishing between advertising and reality in ads, and ads can distort their view of the world.

Although older kids have some ability to see past the hype and manipulation, most haven't fully developed those skills. And even kids who have become media savvy can fall prey to ads that play on their insecurities. At the very least, sneaky advertising can spur kids to waste money on things they don't really need. It can encourage kids to become materialistic, giving them a desire for expensive products or leading them to equate consumption with happiness. Ads can influence values and contradict the lessons parents and teachers are trying to teach kids, leading to struggles with parents over buying and consumption.

Clearly, there would be no such debate if schools weren't chronically underfunded and forced to accept help from companies willing to give it.

Countless ads play on kids' insecurities. They imply that if kids lack certain products, they're losers; if they aren't skinny and beautiful or strong and muscular, they're nothing. Such ads can lead to feelings of dissatisfaction and low self-esteem. They can even promote desires for harmful or unhealthful products and lifestyles, or make unhealthy behaviors seem normal (Consumers Union 1990, Center for the Study of Media and Values 1993, Jacobson and Mazur 1995, Molnar in press).

A 1992 study by the Center for Science in the Public Interest found that 9 out of 10 food ads on Saturday morning TV were for candy bars, sugary cereals, salty chips, or other nutritionally flawed foods. Researchers have found links between TV commercials and obesity and elevated levels of cholesterol in children (Jacobson and Mazur 1995).

In the March 1995 *Consumer Reports*, we describe how effectively cigarette marketing tactics influence young consumers. In fact, the more money spent advertising a particular cigarette brand to young consumers, the more popular that brand is among smokers under 18. For example, in the late 1960s, Virginia Slims were introduced—the first cigarette targeted (and heavily advertised) to women. Also in the late 1960s, there was a sharp rise in the percentage of teenage girls (but not boys) who started smoking (Consumers Union 1995b).

Because fewer than 10 percent of smokers start smoking *after* turning 20, kids are the only new fertile ground for the tobacco industry. The tobacco industry claims it has no intention of marketing to youngsters, but its ad campaigns show otherwise. Tobacco ads appear in magazines popular with teenagers and on billboards in places they're likely to be—at sporting events and on the way to school, for example.

Beer and other alcoholic beverages are similarly marketed. According to the Center for the Study of Media and Values (1993), if you're not a heavy drinker by age 25, you aren't likely to become one. Although the makers of alcoholic beverages deny it, a survey of ads by the center shows that many target young people.

Have It *Your* Way

A number of education groups, including the Association for Supervision and Curriculum Development, the National Parent Teacher Association, and the National Education Association, have taken strong stands against commercialism in schools and have developed guidelines for accepting advertising in schools.

In addition, two consumer interest groups, the Society of Consumer Affairs Professionals in Business (SOCAP) and Consumers International (formerly International Organization of Consumers Unions), have prepared voluntary guidelines for education materials sponsored by businesses. The SOCAP guidelines represent the best corporate thinking on the subject. Both sets of guides say materials should be

- accurate
- objective
- complete
- clearly written
- non-discriminatory, and
- noncommercial.

Although Consumers Union believes schools should be ad-free zones, we support the standards called for in the SOCAP and Consumers International guidelines (SOCAP 1989, IOCU 1989). We have called on business leaders, educators, parents, and government to work together to embrace practical, responsible approaches that will protect the educational integrity of our school systems.

To prevent classrooms from becoming purveyors of commercial messages or influences, the education community should take the following steps:

- Require sponsored programs and materials to undergo the same review and meet the same standards as other curriculum materials, using SOCAP or Consumers International guidelines.
- Reject the idea that allowing advertising in the school is an ethical way to acquire materials or finance education and instead pursue noncommerical partnerships with business.
- Educate children about how to deal with propaganda and commercial messages—a lifelong tool—by helping them analyze ads, demythologize products, evaluate sources of information, and clarify alternatives in the marketplace. This media literacy and consumer education should begin in the elementary grades.

Nurturing Media Literacy

Consumers Union developed *Zillions* magazine (formerly *Penny Power)* and a classroom program based on the magazine as a way to help kids become media-literate. Our threefold objective:

- To help kids see past product hype and detect false and inflated advertising claims.
- To help kids manage their money wisely—to become thoughtful consumers.
- To advise kids on dealing with peer pressures and other problems they face each day.

As readers of *Zillions* can tell you, marketers have some pretty sneaky ways of advertising to kids. Nine- to fourteen-year-old-subscribers send in lots of examples, including nominees for the magazine's annual ZAP aware (as in "Zap it off the air, please"). The more rotten the ad, the more Zs in its ZAP. Recent winners (or should we say losers) included ads for the Real Power Tool Shop, Gymnast Barbie, and Frosted Flakes ("ZAP Awards" 1993–94, 1994–95). What was wrong with these and other ads?

- *Many were misleading.* Some claimed or implied that using the product would make kids more competent or even more popular.
- *A large number contained half truths or outright lies.* Some misrepresented the size and appearance of the product; some omitted important information that would make the claims made seem implausible; some failed to show products being used in a normal setting; some used sneaky techniques to make products seem to do what they couldn't.
- *Many used advertising techniques designed to hook kids by playing on their emotional vulnerabilities and insecurities*—celebrity endorsements, sex appeal, cute pets, pop music, fast-paced action, fun, joy, romance.

Consumers Union's concerns go beyond the school environment to address the larger issue of the ethics of marketing to kids. We believe promotions that target kids must meet higher standards than those aimed at adults. They should clearly identify themselves as advertising and should not pitch unhealthful products or exploit kids' trustfulness, inexperience, and vulnerabilities. Living up to these standards is a responsibility not only of sellers, but of publishers and broadcasters as well.

Finally, we believe children need to learn that not every product can be wanted, not every want can be a need, and not every need can be met. Indeed, as many adults have discovered, the most important needs in life usually can't be met by products but are more profound—needs for affection, self-esteem, good relationships, and the satisfaction of being responsible citizens.

Helping kids grow into sensible and fulfilled adults entails helping them to learn to manage their wants, their needs, their money, their health, and their values and dreams. No easy task for teachers or parents—and a task made more difficult by the growing commercial pressures on kids. Teachers, who are aware of commercial techniques and how to help children deal with them, have an important role to play.

References

Center for the Study of Media and Values. (1993). *AdSmarts: A Media Literacy Curriculum.* Los Angeles: Scott Newman Center.

Consumers Union Education Services. (1995a). *Captive Kids: Commercial Pressures on Kids at School.* Yonkers, N.Y.: Consumers Union.

Consumers Union Education Services. (March 1995b). "Hooked on Tobacco: The Teen Epidemic." *Consumer Reports.* Yonkers, N.Y.: Consumers Union.

Consumers Union Education Services. (1990). *Selling America's Kids: Commercial Pressures on Kids of the 90s.* Yonkers, N.Y.: Consumers Union.

Guber, S., and J. Berry. (1993). *Marketing To and Through Kids.* New York: McGraw-Hill.

International Organization of Consumers Union (IOCU). (1989). *IOCU Code of Good Practice and Guidelines for Controlling Business-Sponsored Educational Materials in Schools.* London: IOCU.

Jacobson, M. F., and L. A. Mazur. (1995). *Marketing Madness: A Survival Guide for a Consumer Society.* Boulder, Colo.: Westview Press Inc.

Molnar, A. (In press). *Giving Kids the Business: The Commercialization of American School Reforms.* Boulder, Colo: Westview Press Inc.

Society of Consumer Affairs Professionals in Business (SOCAP). (1989). *Guidelines for Business-Sponsored Materials.* Alexandria, VA.: SOCAP.

"ZAP Awards." (December 1993/January 1994, December 1994/January 1995). *Zillions: From Consumer Reports for Kids.* Yonkers, N.Y.: Consumers Union.

Authors' note: For the complete text of *Captive Kids*, send $3 to Consumers Union Education Services. Also available: *Tips and Guidelines for Evaluating Sponsored Educational Materials.*

Article Review Form at end of book.

What is the "jargon jungle" discussed in this article?

The Jargon Jungle

In new books, two veteran educators spell out very different visions for the public schools.

Barbara Kantrowitz

It's that time of the year when dazed and confused parents of school-age children try to find their way through the jargon jungle. Portfolio assessment, critical thinking, multiple learning styles, metacognitive skills, whole language—after a few classroom conferences, parents must begin to wonder whether some of these teachers ever speak standard English. Fortunately, two long-time guides through the pedagogical wilderness—E. D. Hirsch Jr. and Theodore Sizer—have weighed in with new books that should help education consumers work past the middle.

Ideological opposites, the two authors have vastly different prescriptions for education. In *The Schools We Need* (317 pages. Doubleday. $24.95), Hirsch, author of the 1987 best seller "Cultural Literacy," argues persuasively for a national core curriculum supplemented by subjects of local or regional significance. (In an influential series of books he has outlined grade-by-grade suggestions for such an approach, beginning with "What Your Kindergartner Needs to Know.") A national curriculum, Hirsch says, would help even the playing field for poor kids, who often don't get the educational jump-start at home—books around the house, trips to museums—that is part of the child-rearing agenda in many middle-class families.

Sizer, who has focused on secondary education in two previous books, "Horace's Compromise" and "Horace's School," finds the greatest promise in grass-roots reform efforts that involve active consortiums of administrators, teachers and parents. In *Horace's Hope* (198 pages. Houghton Mifflin. $22.95), the last volume of the trilogy, Sizer revisits what he describes as "typical" high schools as well as members of the Coalition of Essential Schools, a national reform group he chairs.

Of the two, Hirsch's is the more useful map for parents. Despite his admitted bias against what he calls "progressive education," Hirsch provides an illuminating history of more than five decades of reform. The bottom line: much of what's purported to be new is actually quite old and has never been proven effective. Again and again, he points out that teaching methods based on "new research" can trace their roots to theories first proposed generations ago. His targets include: "developmentally appropriate" education that results in a dumbed-down curriculum for elementary-school children and an overemphasis on "individual learning styles" that leads to meaningless grade inflation.

The final section, a "Critical Guide to Educational Terms and Phrases," is worth the price of the book all by itself. It's an alphabetical glossary explaining the mysteries of such topics as "culturally biased tests," hands-on learning," "multiple intelligences," "student-centered education" and "thematic learning." Hirsch, a professor at the University of Virginia, is clearly struggling to maintain some objectivity despite his personal preferences. But a careful reader will detect a rather droll tone to some of the definitions. Take, for example, his discussion of the "promise of technology." It's a particularly effective deflation of the gee-whiz view of all things digital. "Caution is called for," Hirsch writes. Later, he notes that "there is no evidence that a well-stocked and well-equipped mind can be displaced by 'accessing skills'"—a popular way of describing the ability to look things up on a computer.

Diminished Expectations

Hirsch's arguments are fueled by his passionate belief in universal high-quality education as the key to democracy. Sizer, a professor emeritus at Brown University, exhibited that same energy in his earlier books. But this time out, Sizer and Horace—his fictional amalgam of veteran high-school teachers—appear to be hopeful only because they've lowered their expectations. Sizer finds schools that work, but in most cases, that success stems from the creativity and dedication of a particular principal or a group of teachers or parents and is frustratingly hard to replicate on a wide scale. How do you copy the talent of a dynamic principal like Dennis Littky, whose transformation of New Hampshire's Thayer Junior-Senior High School was so dramatic it became the subject of a TV movie? Horace finds hope, Sizer says, in the great maelstrom of ideas circulating in the past few years. So what if some have turned out to be less than advertised? Ideological turbulence, Sizer writes, is a healthy development, the first step in real reform. Perhaps, but in the meantime, we must mourn for the students who get only one shot at an education and suffer terribly if fate has placed them in the wrong trend at the wrong time.

What's missing in too many progressive curricula is an emphasis on the accumulation of actual facts—what used to be considered the foundation of a good, basic education. As Hirsch points out, learning *how* to think is meaningless without something challenging to think about. All that jargon in the jungle hides the light.

Article Review Form at end of book.

What is the philosophy supporting the core knowledge movement? According to selected research findings, why is the core knowledge initiative successful?

The Core Knowledge Curriculum

What's behind its success?

To achieve excellence and fairness in education, an elementary school needs to teach a body of shared knowledge, grade by grade. The Core Knowledge Foundation offers some guidelines.

E.D. Hirsch, Jr.

E. D. Hirsch, Jr., is a Professor at the University of Virginia in Charlottesville. He is the founder of the Core Knowledge Foundation, 2012-B Morton Dr., Charlottesville, VA 22901.

The Mohegan School, in the South Bronx, is surrounded by the evidence of urban blight: trash, abandoned cars, crack houses.The students, mostly Latino or African-American, all qualify for free lunch. This public elementary school is located in the innermost inner city.

In January 1992, CBS Evening News devoted an "Eye on America" segment to the Mohegan School. Why did CBS focus on Mohegan of several schools that had experienced dramatic improvements after adopting the Core Knowledge guidelines? I think it was in part because this school seemed an unlikely place for a low-cost, academically solid program like Core Knowledge to succeed.

Mohegan's talented principal, Jeffrey Litt, wrote to tell me that "the richness of the curriculum is of particular importance" to his students because their educational experience, like that of "most poverty-stricken and educationally underserved students, was limited to remedial activities." Since adopting the Core Knowledge curriculum, however, Mohegan's students are engaged in the integrated and coherent study of topics like: Ancient Egypt, Greece, and Rome; the Industrial Revolution; limericks, haiku, and poetry; Rembrandt, Monet, and Michelangelo; Beethoven and Mozart; the Underground Railroad; the Trail of Tears; Brown v. Board of Education; the Mexican Revolution; photosynthesis; medieval African empires; the Bill of Rights; ecosystems; women's suffrage; the Harlem Renaissance—and many more.

The Philosophy Behind Core Knowledge

In addition to offering compelling subject matter, the Core Knowledge guidelines for elementary schools are far more specific than those issued by most school districts. Instead of vague outcomes such as "First graders will be introduced to map skills," the geography section of the *Core Knowledge Sequence* specifies that 1st graders will learn the meaning of "east," "west," "north," and "south" and locate on a map the equator, the Atlantic and Pacific Oceans, the seven continents, the United States, Mexico, Canada, and Central America.

Our aim in providing specific grade-by-grade guidelines—developed after several years of research, consultation, consensus-building, and field-testing—is *not*

From EDUCATIONAL LEADERSHIP, May 1993, pp. 23–29. Reprinted by permission of the author.

to claim that the content we recommend is better than some other well-thought-out core. No specific guidelines could plausibly claim to be the Platonic ideal. But one must make a start. To get beyond the talking stage, we created the best specific guidelines we could.

Nor is it our aim to specify *everything* that American schoolchildren should learn (the Core Knowledge guidelines are meant to constitute about 50 percent of a school's curriculum, thus leaving the other half to be tailored to a district, school, or classroom). Rather, our point is that a core of shared knowledge, grade by grade, is needed to achieve excellence and fairness in elementary education.

International studies have shown that *any* school that puts into practice a similarly challenging and specific program will provide a more effective and fair education than one that lacks such commonality of content in each grade.[1] High-performing systems such as those in France, Sweden, Japan, and West Germany bear out this principle. It was our intent to test whether in rural, urban, and suburban settings of the United States we would find what other nations have already discovered.

Certainly the finding that a school-wide core sequence greatly enhances achievement *for all* is supported at the Mohegan School. Disciplinary problems there are down; teacher and student attendance are up, as are scores on standardized tests. Some of the teachers have even transferred their own children to the school, and some parents have taken their children out of private schools to send them to Mohegan. Similar results are being reported at some 65 schools across the nation that are taking steps to integrate the Core Knowledge guidelines into their curriculums.

In the broadcast feature about the Mohegan School, I was especially interested to hear 5th grade teacher Evelyn Hernandez say that Core Knowledge "tremendously increased the students' ability to question." In other words, based on that teacher's classroom experience, *a coherent approach to specific content enhances students' critical thinking and higher-order thinking skills.*

I emphasize this point because a standard objection to teaching specific content is that critical thinking suffers when a teacher emphasizes "mere information." Yet Core Knowledge teachers across the nation report that a coherent focus on content leads to higher-order thinking skills more securely than any other approach they know, including attempts to inculcate such skills directly. As an added benefit, children acquire knowledge that they will find useful not just in next year's classroom but for the rest of their lives.

The most significant diversity faced by our schools is *not* cultural diversity but rather, diversity of academic preparation.

Why Core Knowledge Works

Here are some of the research findings that explain the correlation between a coherent, specific approach to knowledge and the development of higher-order skills.

Learning can be fun, but is nonetheless cumulative and sometimes arduous. The dream of inventing methods to streamline the time-consuming activity of learning is as old as the hills. In antiquity it was already an old story. Proclus records an anecdote about an encounter between Euclid, the inventor of geometry, and King Ptolemy I of Egypt (276-196 B.C.), who was impatiently trying to follow Euclid's *Elements* step by laborious step. Exasperated, the king demanded a faster, easier way to learn geometry—to which Euclid gave the famous, and still true, reply: "There is no royal road to geometry."

Even with computer technology, it's far from easy to find short-cuts to the basic human activity of learning. The human brain sets limits on the potential for education innovation. We can't, for instance, put a faster chip in the human brain. The frequency of its central processing unit is timed in thousandths rather than millionths of a second.[2] Nor can we change the fundamental, constructivist psychology of the learning process, which dictates that we humans must acquire new knowledge much as a tree acquires new leaves. The old leaves actively help nourish the new. The more "old growth" (prior knowledge) we have, the faster new growth can occur, making learning an organic process in which knowledge builds upon knowledge.

Because modern classrooms cannot effectively deliver completely individualized instruction, effective education requires grade-by-grade shared knowledge. When an individual child "gets" what is being taught in a classroom, it is like someone understanding a joke. A click occurs. If you have the requisite background knowledge, you will get the joke, but if you don't, you will remain puzzled until somebody explains the knowledge that was taken for granted. Similarly, a classroom of 25 to 35

Jeanne Storm

Jeanne Storm is a Teacher at Three Oaks Elementary School, 19600 Cypress View Dr., Ft. Myers, FL 33912.

Nine years ago, as a second-year teacher, I was surprised to discover that my 5th graders didn't know the 50 states and their capitals. I made it my personal goal to teach them about the states that make up their country. My colleague next door didn't share my concern. She wanted to ensure that *her* students knew the names and faces of every U.S. President.

Today I can't say there is anything wrong with the content we used to teach. The point is: it isn't fair to our students that some learn one thing while others learn something else. We must *agree* on some core of specific content and resolve to teach it at the appropriate levels.

Three years ago my school, Three Oaks Elementary in Fort Myers, Florida, began implementing the Core Knowledge curriculum. As an educator I've never been more excited about teaching than I have been since using this program. The *Core Knowledge Sequence for Grades 1-6* provides a model of grade-by-grade content that all children can build upon year by year. This content includes literature, American and world civilization, science and technology, fine arts, and mathematics.

In the beginning we formed a committee of teachers and administrators to discuss how we could integrate Core Knowledge into our curriculum. We met through the 1990 spring semester and the following summer. Even for our young staff, change wasn't easy: many of us were already comfortable with the teacher's editions and the units we had taught in the past. But as we delved into Core Knowledge, we realized that the content proposed was the "good stuff" that we all ought to be teaching.

In our many meetings, the committee began putting the specific content into monthly theme-based units. After much discussion—and several confessions of our own ignorance about some of the topics—we came up with a scope-and-sequence centered around schoolwide themes that we all could live with. With this rough plan in hand, the committee members called meetings with their grade levels and worked out any remaining kinks.

That summer teachers went to work developing new units for nearly every month of the year. If we hadn't shared the work, it would have overwhelmed us. Still, there were times when many of us wondered, "Why are we killing ourselves over this anyway?"

Then school began, and our questions were answered as our children's enthusiasm for learning skyrocketed. That first September the 3rd grade team taught a unit on Native Americans. Though I had nearly always taught about Native Americans, I now had specific content to cover: beliefs, culture, daily life, and locations of nations in the Iroquois Confederacy.

The teachers on my team had chosen to teach Core Knowledge from a whole-language approach (Core Knowledge gives teachers the freedom to make pedagogical choices). Our study began with the balance of nature in science, comparing how the Native Americans respected their land with how it is treated today. Using the content specified for 3rd grade, we discussed such terms as *ecologists, fossil fuels, acid rain, greenhouse effect,* and *ozone layer.*

The Core Knowledge Curriculum has convinced me that teaching meaningful content is far more rewarding that teaching vague skills and ambiguous units.

This unit was easily integrated across the curriculum. In social studies, we used Venn diagrams to compare and contrast culture, beliefs, and daily lives of Eastern Woodland Tribes. Students also constructed replicas of the longhouse, chickee, and wigwam.

In language arts, students discovered examples of the four types of sentences through "The Quillwork Girl and Her Seven Brothers" and other Native American creation myths. Then they wrote their own creation myths and checked one another's work for inclusion of statements, questions, commands, and exclamations.

After reading "The Earth on Turtle's Back" from *Keepers of the Earth: Native American Stories and Environmental Activities for Children* by Michael Caduto and Joseph Bruchac, students made mock turtle rattles out of recycled sandwich containers. Then, outside, students took turns being blindfolded, testing their listening abilities to identify the location of the shaking rattle as it imitated the sound of a rattlesnake.

I taught a literature lesson on simile and metaphor using the Paul Goble story, "The Girl Who Loved Wild Horses." Even in September, student writing was more exciting and detailed than I had ever remembered. At the conclusion of the unit, 8-year-old Jessica wrote:

> My Wild Horse
>
> I have a horse her name is Prince.
> I love her very much.
> She is beautiful.
> Her skin sparkles like the rain.
> Her tail flows with the trees.
> Her legs let her run with the sun.
> She is the prettiest of all.

The Core Knowledge Curriculum has convinced me that teaching meaningful content is far more rewarding than teaching vague skills and ambiguous units. As E. D. Hirsch, Jr., has said: children from every ethnic and economic background should have access to a shared core of knowledge that is necessary to reading, understanding, and communication.

Following a unit on the Norsemen and their legends, one of my students was intrigued with finding out about the character Loki, a trickster. Matthew enthusiastically piped up, "That guy is in my comic books. He can change his form and play mean tricks! Do you think the comic book people got him from the Norsemen?"

Ah, to be literate! It makes my job meaningful.

children can move forward as a group only when *all* the children have the knowledge that is necessary to "getting" the next step in learning.

Studies comparing elementary schools in the United States to schools in countries with core knowledge systems disclose a striking difference in the structure of classroom activities.[3] In the best-performing classrooms constant back-and-forth interaction among groups of students and between students and the teacher consumes more than 80 percent of classroom time. By contrast, in the United States, over 50 percent of student time is spent in silent isolation.[4]

Behind the undue amount of "alone time" in our schools stands a theory that goes as follows: Every child is a unique individual; hence each child should receive instruction paced and tailored to that child. The theory should inform classroom practice as far as feasible: one hopes for teachers sensitive to the individual child's needs and strengths. The theory also reveals why good classroom teaching is difficult, and why a one-on-one tutorial is the most effective form of instruction. But modern education cannot be conducted as a one-on-one tutorial. Even in a country as affluent as the United States, instruction is carried out in classes of 25 to 35 pupils. In Dade County, Florida, the average class size for the early grades is 35. When a teacher gives individual attention to one child, 34 other pupils are left to fend for themselves. This is hardly a good trade-off, even on the premise that each child deserves individual attention.

Consider the significance of these facts in accounting for the slow progress (by international standards) of American elementary schools. If an entire classroom must constantly pause while its lagging members acquire background knowledge that they should have gained in earlier grades, progress is bound to be slow. For effective, fair classroom instruction to take place, all members of the class need to share enough common reference points to enable everyone to understand and learn—though of course at differing rates and in response to varied approaches. When this commonality of knowledge is lacking, progress in learning will be slow compared with systems that use a core curriculum.

Just as learning is cumulative, so are learning deficits. As they begin 1st grade, American students are not far behind beginners in other developed nations. But as they progress, their achievement falls farther and farther behind. This widening gap is the subject of one of the most important recent books on American education, *The Learning Gap* by Stevenson and Stigler.

This progressively widening gap closely parallels what happens *within* American elementary schools between advantaged and disadvantaged children. As the two groups progress from grades 1-6, the achievement gap grows ever larger and is almost never overcome.[5] The reasons for the parallels between the two kinds of gaps—the learning gap and the fairness gap—are similar.

In both cases, the widening gap represents the cumulative effect of learning deficits. Although a few talented and motivated children may overcome this ever-increasing handicap, most do not. The rift grows ever wider in adult life. The basic causes of this permanent deficit, apart from motivational ones, are cognitive. Learning builds upon learning in a cumulative way, and lack of learning in the early grades usually has, in comparative terms, a negatively cumulative effect.

We know from large-scale longitudinal evidence, particularly from France, that this fateful gap between haves and have-nots *can* be closed.[6] But only one way to close it has been devised: to set forth explicit, year-by-year knowledge standards in early grades, so they are known to all parties—educators, parents, and children. Such standards are requisites for home-school cooperation and for reaching a general level of excellence. But, equally, they are requisites in gaining fairness for the academic have-nots: explicit year-by-year knowledge standards enable schools in nations with strong elementary core curriculums to remedy the knowledge deficits of disadvantaged children.

High academic skill is based upon broad general knowledge. Someone once asked Boris Goldovsky how he could play the piano so brilliantly with such small hands. His memorable reply was: "Where in the world did you get the idea that we play the piano with our hands?"

It's the same with reading: we don't read just with our eyes. By 7th grade, according to the epoch-making research of Thomas Sticht, most children, even those who read badly, have already attained the purely technical proficiency they need. Their reading and their listening show the same rate and level of comprehension; thus the mechanics of reading are not the limiting factor.[7] What is mainly lacking in poor readers is a broad, ready vocabulary. But broad vocabulary means broad knowledge, because to know a lot of words you have to know a lot of things. Thus, broad general

Core Knowledge: How to Get Started

Bruce Frazee

Bruce Frazee is Associate Professor of Education, Trinity University, Box 83, 715 Stadium Dr., San Antonio, TX 78212.

Since 1990, when Three Oaks Elementary in Fort Myers, Florida, became the nation's first "Core Knowledge" school, more than 50 schools across the country have taken pioneering steps to teach the curriculum. Having had the opportunity to work with a number of these schools, I can offer a few observations about what it takes to turn Core Knowledge from theory into practice. Though there is no single model for success, Core Knowledge schools follow some common guidelines.

It takes, first, understanding, acceptance, and involvement among the school community. In the early stages it is important to involve administrators, school board members, and parents in becoming informed about Core Knowledge and in reaching agreement about plans and expectations. Educators who are accustomed to curriculum defined as broad skills and objectives will need to become familiar with the specific guidelines in the Core Knowledge curriculum, as well as the reasons they are so specific. This is also the time to confront any misunderstandings and objections.

Having had the opportunity to work with a number of "Core Knowledge" schools, I can offer a few observations about what it takes to turn theory into practice.

One of the primary tasks of a school considering the *Core Knowledge Sequence* is to align it with the skills and outcomes required in local and state guidelines. Doing so allows educators to develop a consensus about curriculum consistent with the school's vision. It's also an important step in gaining commitment: teachers often see that there is much in the *Core Knowledge Sequence* that they already teach, that there are exciting new topics to explore, and that they now have explicit guidelines to help them cohere as a professional community.

Next, teachers face the task of bringing Core Knowledge to life in the classroom. To accomplish this difficult but rewarding work, teachers need time to collaborate and share experiences at their grade levels, across grade levels, and among schools. Those who think of Core Knowledge as "rote learning of isolated facts" are simply misinformed or have too little faith in teachers. I have enjoyed working with many teachers as they brainstorm about grade-level or schoolwide interdisciplinary themes. Through a variety of strategies—for example, webbing or guided questions—teachers can organize content from the *Core Knowledge Sequence* into thematic units of their choosing; they can also select strategies and resources conducive to in-depth learning. Assessment of progress can be accomplished through student writing, bulletin boards, projects, performances, portfolios, and much more.

To write curriculum based on the *Core Knowledge Sequence*, teachers sometimes must prepare to teach something they might know little about; for example, medieval African empires or Homer's *Iliad*. In such cases, teachers become models of the lifelong learning that schooling should inspire.

All of this may seem familiar: the difference is, with specific content guidelines, teachers can collaborate more effectively and feel confident that they are helping students build upon prior knowledge from year to year. The Core Knowledge curriculum gives students from different regions and economic backgrounds a common language with which to produce shared knowledge (Lutz et al. 1992, Kierstead and Mentor 1988, Patrick 1991). One has only to observe the excitement and involvement in Core Knowledge schools to see that teachers can devise active, interdisciplinary ways to help all students, regardless of background, become culturally literate.

References

Kierstead, J., and S. Mentor. (1988). "Translating the Vision Into Reality in California Schools." *Educational Leadership* 46, 2: 35-40.

Lutz, J. P., C. Jones, and E. LaFuze. (January 1992). "Core Knowledge: Now It Can Be Taught." *Principal* 71, 3: 13-15.

Patrick, J. (April 1991). *Student Achievement of Core Subjects of the School*. Washington, D.C.: Office of the Educational Research and Improvement.

knowledge is an *essential* requisite to superior reading skill and indirectly related to the skills that accompany it.

Superior reading skill is known to be highly correlated with most other academic skills, including the ability to write well, learn rapidly, solve problems, and think critically. To concentrate on reading is therefore to focus implicitly on a whole range of educational issues.[8]

It is sometimes claimed (but not backed up with research) that knowledge changes so rapidly in our fast-changing world that we need not get bogged down with "mere information." A corollary to the argument is that because information quickly becomes obsolete, it is more important to learn "accessing" skills (how to look things up or how to use a calculator) than to learn "mere facts."

The evidence in the psychological literature on skill acquisition goes strongly against this widely stated claim.[9] Its fallacy can be summed up in a letter I received from a head reference librarian. A specialist in accessing knowledge, he was distressed because the young people now being trained as *reference specialists* had so little general knowledge that they could not effectively help the public access knowledge.

His direct experience (backed up by the research literature) had caused him to reject the theory of education as the gaining of accessing skills.

In fact, the opposite inference should be drawn from our fast-changing world. The fundamentals of science change very slowly; those of elementary math hardly at all. The famous names of geography and history (the "leaves" of that knowledge tree) change faster, but not root and branch from year to year. A wide range of this stable, fundamental knowledge is the key to rapid adaptation and the learning of new skills. It is precisely *because* the needs of a modern economy are so changeable that one needs broad general knowledge in order to flourish. Only high literacy (which implies broad general knowledge) provides the flexibility to learn new things fast. The only known route to broad general knowledge for all is for a nation's schools to provide all students with a substantial, solid core of knowledge.

The only known route to broad general knowledge for all is for a nation's schools to provide all students with a substantial, solid core of knowledge.

Common content leads to higher school morale, as well as better teaching and learning. At every Core Knowledge school, a sense of community and common purpose have knit people together. Clear content guidelines have encouraged those who teach at the same grade level to collaborate in creating effective lesson plans and schoolwide activities. Similarly, a clear sense of purpose has encouraged cooperation among grades as well. Because the *Core Knowledge Sequence* makes no requirements about *how* the specified knowledge should be presented, individual schools and teachers have great scope for independence and creativity. Site-based governance is the order of the day at Core Knowledge schools—but with definite aims, and thus a clear sense of communal purpose.

The Myth of the Existing Curriculum

Much of the public currently assumes that each elementary school already follows a schoolwide curriculum. Yet frustrated parents continually write the Core Knowledge Foundation to complain that principals are not able to tell them with any explicitness what their child will be learning during the year. Memorably, a mother of identical twins wrote that because her children had been placed in different classrooms, they were learning completely different things.

Such curricular incoherence, typical of elementary education in the United States today, places enormous burdens on teachers. Because they most cope with such diversity of preparation at each subsequent grade level, teachers find it almost impossible to create learning communities in their classrooms. Stevenson and Stigler rightly conclude that the most significant diversity faced by our schools is *not* cultural diversity but, rather, diversity of academic preparation. To achieve excellence and fairness for all, an elementary school *must* follow a coherent sequence of solid, specific content.

1. International Association for the Evaluation of Educational Achievement (IEA), (1988), *Science Achievement in Seventeen Countries: A Preliminary Report*, (Elmsford, N.Y.: Pergamon Press). The table on page 139 shows a consistent correlation between core knowledge systems and equality of opportunity for all students. The subject is discussed at length in E. D. Hirsch, Jr., "Fairness and Core Knowledge," *Occasional Papers 2*, available from the Core Knowledge Foundation, 2012-B Morton Dr., Charlottesville, VA 22901.
2. An absolute limitation of the mind's speed of operation is 50 milliseconds per minimal item. See A. B. Kristofferson, (1967), "Attention and Psychophysical Time, *Acta Psychologica* 27: 93-100.
3. The data in this paragraph come from H. Stevenson and J. Stigler, (1992), *The Learning Gap*, (New York: Summit Books).
4. Stevenson and Stigler pp. 52-71.
5. W. Loban, (March 1964), *Language Ability: Grades Seven, Eight, and Nine*, (Project No. 1131), University of California, Berkeley; as expanded and interpreted by T. G. Sticht, L. B. Beck, R. N. Hauke, G. M. Kleiman, and J. H. James, (1974), *Auding and Reading: A Developmental Model*, (Alexandria, Va: Human Resources Research Organization); J. S. Chall, (1982), *Families and Literacy, Final Report to the National Institute of Education:* and especially, J. S. Chall, V. A. Jacobs, and L. E. Baldwin, (1990), *The Reading Crisis: Why Poor Children Fall Behind*, (Cambridge, Mass: Harvard University Press).
6. S. Boulot and D. Boyzon-Fradet, (1988), *Les immigrés et l'école: une course d'obstacles*, Paris, pp. 54-58; Centre for Educational Research and Innovation (CERI), (1987), *Immigrants' Children At School*, Paris, pp. 178-259,
7. T. G. Sticht and H. J. James, (1984), "Listening and Reading," In *Handbook of Reading Research*, edited by P. D. Pearso (New York: Longman).
8. A. L. Brown, (1980), "Metacognitive Development and Reading," in *Theoretical Issues in Reading Comprehension*, edited by R. J. Spiro, B. C. Bruce, and W. F. Brewer, (Hillsdale, NJ: L. Earlbaum Associates).
9. J. R. Anderson, ed., (1981), *Cognitive Skills and Their Acquisitions*, (Hillsdale, NJ: L. Earlbaum Associates).

Article Review Form at end of book.

How would you characterize the opponents to national education standards? What should be the federal government's role in establishing national standards?

National Standards Threaten Local Vitality

Marilyn Gittell

Marilyn Gittell is a professor of political science at the Graduate School and University Center of the City University of New York, New York City. The author of fourteen books, she is presently editing a book on school finance and reform for Yale University Press.

Given the current overwhelming support for national standards, one wonders why it has taken so long to make the creation of standards a national priority. But, in fact, strong opposition to such standards persists and continues to come from both the right and the left. Above all, such opposition points to the weakness of a federal strategy for educational reform that deviates from our national commitment to educational equity. That deviation, and how it can be corrected, is the subject of this article.

I will first, however, describe nine positions in opposition to national standards, show what these points of view have in common, and demonstrate how they can contribute to our thinking on educational equity.

Opposition to Standards

Opposition to national standards comes from people with a variety of points of view:

- People who honor and cherish the tradition of local control of education, particularly at the school district level, question why the national government considers itself competent to establish national standards.
- People who give priority to equity and equitable financing of education question the commitment and follow-through of national politicians. They are pessimistic about how a national curriculum can serve these ends.
- People who focus on the role of the states (which provide 50 percent of the funding for education and are legally responsible for providing equal education) and who have spent considerable energy reforming and enhancing state education efforts view the effort to create national standards as undermining the states.
- People who see American federalism as the most effective means of retaining a decentralized and democratic political system question the need for national education standards, which deny the vitality of local responsiveness to local needs.
- People who value and encourage diversity in all aspects of American society question how national standards can encompass that diversity.
- People who question the value of the extensive testing in American schools (and challenge the validity of the tests themselves) wonder how the implementation of national standards will be evaluated. What tests, they ask, will be used and how will they affect teaching and learning?
- People who lead school reform efforts—building alternative school models, small-sized

From The Clearing House, Vol. 69, No. 3, pp. 148–150, Jan./Feb. 1996. Reprinted with permission of the Helen Dwight Reid Educational Foundation. Published by Heldreff Publications, 1319 Eighteenth St., N.W., Washington, D.C. 20036–1801.

schools, and new curricula based on the inquiry method—oppose any national standards that contradict or undermine their efforts.

- People who do not think that foreign school systems are exemplary models of education ask why we would want to emulate systems that use assessments as a means of exclusion.
- People who worked on the national history curriculum or the New York social studies proposal, and have faced the wrath of colleagues who disagree with their suggested standards, predict the difficulty, if not the impossibility, of reaching agreement on the content of national standards across several subject areas.

The common thread running through most of this opposition is this belief: National standards move the federal government from its long-held position of minor partner in American elementary and secondary education into that of an enforcer, without fundamentally changing its role in finance or governance.

I argue that the federal government, rather than focusing on standards and assessment, should concentrate on what it can uniquely contribute to American education—namely, producing greater equity in funding and in compensatory education.

Progressive Federalism

The politics of education in America reflect the competing values that exist in the larger political culture. Americans struggle to balance the need to preserve an inclusive, participatory, and democratic policymaking process with the drive to attain efficiency and economy through professional centralization of decision making. Our federal system allows us to retain local controls and responsiveness through the states and localities while using federal leadership to sustain the values of equity and fairness. Only at the higher levels can we guarantee equity; thus a natural division of roles persists.

The federal government should concentrate on producing greater equity in funding and in compensatory education.

In *Choosing Equality: The Case for Democratic Schooling,* I outlined a theory of *progressive federalism* based on this division of power.[1] Progressive federalism embraces local governance of local schools, while significantly broadening the participation of stakeholders. It supports public ownership in education that requires "a democratic process guiding the governance process, which goes beyond the election of school boards or public officials." It calls for expanded public discourse. Because states control the largest portion of education funding and institutional resources, progressive federalism views them as the center of political activity and the focal point for reform; they are potential "[agencies] for redistributing school resources and control and for mediating the direction of national and local action."[2] Progressive federalism thus "affirms that government action is the central instrument for achieving egalitarian goals" and holds that it is the duty of the national government to provide leadership to work toward those goals.[3] Plans for national standards reflect many of the key features of progressive federalism; they part with progressive federalism, however, by declining to assert the federal government's legitimate pursuit of egalitarian goals.

American education can only achieve its full potential under a dynamic federal system that encourages all levels to work together to achieve its most important goals. Equality is the essential goal. An emphasis on standards and performance will not necessarily produce equality, as the past fifteen years of education reform have demonstrated. State school reform in the 1980s, so highly acclaimed, did not reduce educational inequities; it improved quality for those who were already advantaged. The results of the educational reforms of the 1960s contrast with the results from the 1980s: those earlier reforms asserted equality as the major priority and achieved quality as a part of that effort.

Sustained support of the democratic process requires greater and continuing public discourse on education goals and standards in an expanded and more inclusive political arena. The federal government's leadership in engaging parents and community in that discourse and in the school decision-making process should be reinforced and enhanced. Only through broad-based participation will the combined goals of equity and excellence be appropriately balanced.

Equity as a Goal

The equity function was initially assumed by the federal courts, first in *Plessy v. Ferguson* when the Supreme Court stated that separate was equal,[4] then dramatically in the 1954 decision *Brown v. Board of Education of Topeka* when it recognized that separate was unequal.[5] Later, in the early 1960s, the national education title acts formulated federal compensatory programs to redress the inequities in school systems. Federal dollars, although never more than 8 percent of education funding nationally, symbolized the commitment to the positive goal of equality. The legislation included financial incentives, but more important, it provided federal leadership and direction to the states. Those programs, and others like them initiated in the decades of the 1960s and 1970s, significantly reduced the gaps in learning opportunities for a broad cross section of the society. Outcomes were certainly essential to program evaluation, although standards and testing were not priorities. Federal support and direction worked well with local programs that were designed specifically to respond to local populations. Some programs, however, such as Head Start, demonstrated the need for other elements, such as compensatory funding and parent participation.[6]

A significant aspect of the educational agenda of that era was the recognition of the political arena in which education decision making takes place. The Elementary and Secondary Education Act (ESEA) supported mandatory and voluntary parent and community participation in school decisions. The 1975 Education for All Handicapped Children's Act, a landmark in the federal role in education, established detailed requirements that prescribed how schools must make decisions for the future education of children with special needs. The law requires a plan to be prepared jointly by parents, teachers, counselors, and psychologists; parents are integral to the decision-making process, and no decision can be made without their approval. Federal law guarantees that all parents, rich or poor, black or white, will be respected in their judgments of what is educationally sound for their children. This legislation moved the concept of opportunity to learn to another level. Educational standards were henceforth to apply to a population formerly excluded, and the importance of a parental role in the decision-making process was recognized in federal legislation.

Although educational equity is clearly within federal legislative intent, the compensatory priority of federal aid is sometimes undermined by implementation at all levels. Because federal regulations and lack of oversight allow federal dollars to be distributed according to state formulas, federal grants programs can reinforce state inequities. Chapter 1 funding is the most pointed example of a federal policy gone awry. The General Accounting Office (GAO) finds that many wealthy schools benefit from Chapter 1 while schools with considerably higher proportions of poor students are underfunded.[7] Funds appropriated for poor students are routinely distributed to wealthy districts. In Illinois, for example, the formula means that only 64,000 of Chicago's 150,000 officially poor children are served; Chicago has ineligible schools with poverty rates as high as 53 percent. Meanwhile, schools with a 4 percent poverty rate in Schaumburg, a northwest Chicago suburb, receive Chapter 1 funding.[8] In New York, schools in the Oneonta system, which has a district poverty rate of 6 percent, receive $1,612 per Chapter 1 student, while schools in the Edmeston system, which has a district poverty rate of 34 percent, receive only $761 per Chapter 1 student.[9] Most critics conclude that if Chapter 1 funds were directed to schools instead of to individual children these inequities would be prevented. Better standards for establishing financial equity in those school systems would go a long way toward improving the quality of education, especially in low-income areas.

American education policy should recognize three goals: equity; expansion of public discourse and participation in school decision making; and excellence. The federal emphasis must be on equality. With our strong tradition of federalism and community-based education, we should be defining standards locally. The vitality of our educational goals can best be assured by promoting vigorous public discourse, rather than looking to Washington as the sole source of standards and assessment. Although proponents of national standards sometimes claim that standards that apply to all in the same way will produce equity, or that opportunity-to-learn standards encompass equity goals, there is no evidence to support these claims.

Improved governance, broader participation, higher standards, more equitable funding, and encouragement of public debate among a broad cross section of stakeholders should be part of the role of the federal government, which must be straightforward about its priorities. An essential part of the federal role is its assertion of national leadership in confirming social values and priorities. Equitable funding of schools and school districts is basic to our commitment to equality and key to raising systemwide performance. Encouraging these goals through higher state standards would demonstrate the vitality of the federal system.

Notes

1. See A. Bastian, N. Fruchter, M. Gittell, C. Greer, and K. Haskins, *Choosing Equality: The Case for Democratic Schooling* (Philadelphia: Temple, 1986), especially chapter 6, "Governance and Funding: Toward Progressive Federalism," 134ff.
2. Bastian et al., *Choosing Equality,* 145.
3. Bastian et al., *Choosing Equality,* 134ff.
4. *Plessy v. Ferguson,* 163 U.S. 537, 1896.
5. *Brown v. Board of Education of Topeka, Kansas,* 347 U.S. 483, 1954.
6. See Bastian et al., *Choosing Equality;* also U.S. Department of Health and Human Services, *A Review of Head Start Research Since 1970* (Washington, D.C.: Office of Human Development Services, HSHSS, 1983); Nancy Mallory and Nancy Goldsmith, *The Head Start Experience,* 1991. ERIC PSO19322; and Paul Peterson, "Background Paper," in *Making the Grade,* by the Task Force on Federal Education Policy (New York: Twentieth Century Fund, 1983).
7. See U.S. General Accounting Office, *Remedial Education: Modifying Chapter 1 Formula Would Target More Funds to Those Most in Need,* 1992 (GAO/HRD–92–16); The Commission on Chapter 1, *Making Schools Work for Children in Poverty: A New Framework,* 1992.
8. Michael Selinker, "Battle Heating Up over Funding Formulas," *Catalyst* (February 1993), 4.
9. Education Policy Unit, Department of Public Policy. The Community Service Society of New York. Work in progress.

Article Review Form at end of book.

What are the most common strategies educators use to counteract violence in classrooms?

Violence in the Classroom

Where we stand

The authors provide an overview of this special issue on preparing administrators and teachers to handle violence and problematic behaviors in schools.

William N. Bender and Phillip J. McLaughlin

William N. Bender, PhD, taught in a junior high school resource room for several years and is now an associate professor at the University of Georgia. Phillip J. McLaughlin, EdD, is an associate professor of special education and a director of the interactive teaching network at the University of Georgia. He has developed internationally acclaimed staff development teleconferences on inclusive schools and teaching the tough-to-teach. Address: William N. Bender, 549 Aderhold Hall, University of Georgia, Athens, GA 30602.

This issue of Intervention in School and Clinic *focuses on the topic of violence in the classroom. In addition to acquainting our readers with this area, the various articles also present curriculum and teaching models that can be used in integrated settings. I am pleased that Professors William N. Bender and Phillip J. McLaughlin, who have assembled an outstanding blend of both authors and topics, agreed to serve as guest editors of this issue. We are honored that* Intervention *is able to showcase the outstanding work of so many talented individuals. We hope you enjoy reading the articles, and we welcome your comments.—GW*

Sometimes one is confronted by the unexpected, with very little insight as to how to respond. This is where schools across the nation today are with respect to violence in the classroom. Metal detectors and other security measures are appearing throughout the nation in our secondary schools, and visitors are scrutinized at every primary and elementary school in order to decrease the likelihood of violence against our children. The children themselves report that they are extremely nervous about (or downright afraid of) going to school.

Some of this involves perceptions; although most citizens believe there has been a drastic increase in juvenile crime, there has actually been a reduction in the last 20 years (Sautter, 1995). However, the increasing severity of violent acts in schools, coupled with the lower age of the perpetrators of these violent acts, has resulted in schools that are much less safe today than previously.

The Array of Approaches to Violence Prevention

Because of the growing problem, we felt that a practitioner-oriented journal would be an appropriate venue to pull together what we now know about interventions for decreasing violence and disruptive behavior in the schools. To date, schools have adopted a wide array of strategies for decreasing violence, and selecting the right approach or combination of approaches for a particular school is a challenging task.

In an effort to make sense of the morass of strategies, Waite (1995) provided a tri-level organizational structure that encompasses the broadest array of strategies possible. Specifically, he delineated three different classes of strategies schools have considered. First, for prevention and/or reduction of violence, teachers and schools can initiate a number of strategies within the context of their normal operations, with relatively little cost. In fact, teachers can implement many of these strategies in their own classroom, for example, more structured behavior management, buddy systems, use of crisis teachers or counselors, and initiation of procedures for dealing with violence when and if it occurs. These types of strategies constitute the least intrusive level of violence prevention because they are relatively low in cost, require little in terms of personnel and equipment, and do not compromise civil liberties. In short, teachers and administrators can be better prepared to manage problematic behaviors in the school context simply by stronger preparation in effective behavior management strategies. This is, after all, the job of every educator.

With that option stated, however, some problem behaviors seem to be unresponsive to behavior management strategies. For these, Waite (1995) identified a second tier of strategies that focus on assisting the individual student relate to and understand his or her behavior in a new way via peer collaboration, or cooperation strategies. Adult mentorship strategies, discussed by Katz (this issue), also fall into this category. For example, should a school undertake specialized training for selected staff members in peer mediation, and then provide a peer mediation class? This approach would represent some degree of expenditure and could result in improved behavior throughout the school. Several other strategies presented herein fall into this category. These involve helping kids understand their own behavior, as well as some additional expense for staff training and staff time (e.g., the Kimmie's Kids model, PeaceBuilders, and the bully-proofing strategies described in the following articles).

Waite's (1995) third tier involves the most intrusive strategies, which also tend to be the most expensive. This tier would include such things as metal detectors, school security cameras, and employment of schoolbased police officers. These strategies are expensive not only in monetary terms but also in terms of the loss of privacy for students and teachers alike. In addition, the community's perception of a school is likely to be somewhat less positive when severe security measures are utilized.

Intervention Strategies

With this tri-level hierarchy in mind, understanding the emphasis behind the various strategies presented herein is relatively straightforward. Several of the articles (i.e., those by Bender & McLaughlin, Embry, Katz, and Walker & Gresham) present overviews of numerous strategies for interventions based on what has been tried successfully throughout the nation. Wherever possible, highly specific detail is provided to enable teachers to apply the guidelines and strategies discussed. For example, very few teachers ever have to face a fully developed hostage situation in the classroom, but having some background information such as that provided by Bender and McLaughlin (this issue) would be crucial should such a situation arise. Most teachers do not receive this type of information in their preservice or inservice education.

"To date, schools have adopted a wide array of strategies for decreasing violence, and selecting the right approach or combination of approaches for a particular school is a challenging task."

The other three articles in this issue focus directly on particular interventions developed to prevent or reduce violence (Abery & Simunds; Garrity, Jens, Porter, Sager, & Short-Camilli; Tomlinson & Bender). These strategies clearly fall into what Waite (1995) viewed as the peer support or collaboration approach. These articles—most of which are from practitioners who confront this potential violence problem every day—will enrich your arsenal of responses in dealing with violence.

What We Do and Don't Know

After gleaning this information from the relevant literature, we did want to indicate the similarities among the strategies that are available, as well as what we did not find in our efforts to bring this issue to fruition. First, although a "get tough" policy is often discussed in the national press (e.g., zero tolerance for weapons, school security cameras, campus-based policing, etc.), theorists consistently asserted that this approach alone was insufficient. Such highly intrusive strategies are appropriate in many cases and can alleviate some of the violence problems, but most theorists (see Walker & Gresham, or Embry, this issue) doubt that use of these intrusive tactics alone will significantly reduce violence over the long term. Rather, they urge adoption of a full range of tactics (Walker & Gresham, this issue; Waite, 1995). This is interesting in view of the fact that school security measures seem to be the first option imposed by school administrations when a violent incident has occurred.

Next, several theorists seemed to approach the violence issue from the perspective of risk/resiliency (see Katz, and Walker & Gresham, this issue). In other words, identification of factors that place students at risk for violence as well as the factors that increase their resiliency seems to be an emerging theme in this literature. Embry (this issue) emphasized the intentional construction of a social environment based on nonviolence as one method to increase resiliency. Katz suggested a number of factors schools can consider to become a sanctuary for kids in a violent world. This emphasis on risk/resiliency thinking seemed to permeate the extant literature on violence interventions.

Still, numerous aspects of this literature are not clear. First, we found very little solid research on any of the violence prevention or violence reduction strategies. Thus, although all of the suggestions, guidelines, strategies, and programs presented in this issue provide anecdotal data that suggest positive results, little empirical research is available on any of these strategies or techniques. This may reflect the fact that the field of violence prevention and violence reduction strategies is relatively new, but we urge researchers to explore—using solid research designs—these strategies in the context of public school classrooms.

Second, after reviewing a number of approaches and strategies that might have been included here, we found that very few of the strategies represented a truly systems-wide perspective. Specifically, when a school or school district wishes to "do something!!!" about a violence problem, that district is likely to implement an array of strategies on a number of fronts—installation of metal detectors, initiation of peer mediation programs, staff development training on weapons violations, community disciplinary committees for community involvement, and so forth. Needless to say, these interventions would be more effective if they were developed in conjunction so that they would be mutually supportive of one another. However, none of the readily available strategies presented herein addressed such a broad array of tactics. The strategies, rather, seem to focus on only one or two specific tactics (e.g., peer mediation, mentorship programs, or strategies for dealing with a hostage situation). For example, the bully-proofing strategies described by Garrity et al. (this issue) have been applied in numerous schools, and anecdotal evidence suggests the validity of this set of strategies. However, the tactics deal with reducing bullying, and little is said about gang-related violence, or appropriate use of school security measures. Likewise, the Kimmie's Kids program has been used to revitalize the student body and to empower students as a group to reduce violence, but this strategy does not suggest any integration with efforts to curb gang activity. Thus, in this developing field, there seems to be little systems thinking as yet, and we would encourage development of systems thinking that includes a wide array of interlocking and mutually supportive strategies.

Specifically, theorists encourage broad applications of combined efforts (e.g., Embry, or Walker & Gresham, this issue), but few of the available interventions provide a structure for conceptualizing combination approaches. We would urge these theorists and others to consider including a systems-wide perspective in development of the interventions; that is, tell the superintendent what school security measures to purchase and specifically relate that rationale to the types of professional development provided to the staff on peer mediation, or weapons responses, and so on. Only through a wide integration of combined approaches can a school district realistically expect to reduce the likelihood of violence.

Finally, several important research questions have not been addressed in this developing literature on interventions for reducing violence. For example, what, if any, relationship exists between the presence of men on the faculty and the incidence of violence in a school? The data do indicate that the vast majority of perpetrators of violence in schools are males. And, although educators have historically called for more men in education, no coordinated effort for recruiting has been made. Katz (this issue) presented information on mentoring programs, and there is some general appeal to the notion that male students might be able to relate more appropriately to male teachers, thus reducing the frustration that has been linked to increased violence (see Walker & Gresham, this issue). In particular, several programs around the nation have tried to provide appropriate male role models for African American males (e.g., Black Men of Atlanta, discussed by Bell, 1995).

Still, the relationship between effective male role models in the school and violence reduction has not been adequately demonstrated, nor have any of the strategies presented herein focused on this factor. In short, we simply don't know if this factor makes a difference.

Likewise, we are uncertain what the relationship between effective discipline and violence reduction is. Specifically, in a departmentalized secondary school where every individual teacher in his or her classroom is an effective disciplinarian, violence may still occur—between classes, in bathrooms, and so on. Further, not all areas of any school can be closely monitored at all times. Thus, the age-old question as to when a teacher's policing functions begin and end. Are teachers responsible for hallway monitoring, lunchroom monitoring, or bathroom monitoring?

Conclusions

With these observations and cautions noted, we present the strategies and tactics gathered in this issue of *Intervention.* These approaches have received wide acclaim from the various schools and school districts in which they have been implemented, and thus, these represent the state of knowledge in the field. In almost every case, additional information on particular strategies is available, and readers are urged to contact the authors directly should further information be desired.

From a broader perspective, we sincerely hope that this effort can lead schools to increase the efforts aimed at making our nation's schools safer environments. As parents ourselves, this is one of our most important concerns regarding our children's education. We expect schools to help our children reach to the stars academically, but even more fundamental is the school's responsibility to keep our children safe.

References

Bell, E. (1995, April 10). An interview with the Atlanta chief of police on violence reduction in the schools. In W. N. Bender & R. L. Bender (Eds.), *Options for violence prevention* (Teleconference produced by the Teacher's Workshop, Bishop, GA).

Sautter, R. (January, 1995). Standing up to violence. *Phi Delta Kappan* (Special Report), pp. k1–k8.

Waite, D. (1995). Strategies available for violence prevention. In W. N. Bender & R. L. Bender (Eds.), *Violence prevention* (Teleconference produced by the Teacher's Workshop, Bishop, GA).

Article Review Form at end of book.

What does Edd Doerr see as some disadvantages of implementing a voucher system to allow for school choice? What has led to the broad-based support of voucher systems?

The Empty Promise of School Vouchers

"Cream-skimming" of the best students by nonpublic schools would leave public schools with little but poorer performing pupils.

Edd Doerr

Mr. Doerr, Religion Editor of USA Today, *is executive director, Americans for Religious Liberty, Silver Spring, Md.*

In early 1996, the appropriations bill for the District of Columbia was held up repeatedly as Senate Republicans sought to use it as a vehicle for introducing an "experimental" plan for tax support of nonpublic schools through tuition vouchers. The attempt was blocked by Senate Democrats with the aid of a few Republicans.

Two years earlier, the Senate defeated a proposal by Bob Dole (R.-Kans.), Dan Coats (R.-Ind.), and Joseph Lieberman (D.-Conn.) to set up a Federally funded voucher experiment. Impassioned speeches by Chris Dodd (D.-Conn.) and Ted Kennedy (D.-Mass.) helped kill the bill. Currently, limited voucher plans in Milwaukee and Cleveland are being tested in the courts.

These are but the latest skirmishes in a seemingly never-ending war over proposals to provide public funding for nonpublic elementary and secondary schools. Over the past three decades or so, the issue repeatedly has been battled over in the halls of Congress, many state legislatures, Federal and state courts, statewide referenda, scholarly journals, and the media.

This issue involves many billions of dollars in public funds, the education of tens of millions of American children, hot-button religious matters, fundamental constitutional arrangements, and, indeed, the very future of the nation. Accordingly, the controversy over vouchers and other plans for public support for nonpublic schooling demands attention and close scrutiny.

It should be noted at the outset that much of the impetus for voucher plans is fueled by an endless barrage of criticism of public education, creating doubts in the minds of many about its efficacy and value, as well as stirring interest in so-called "free market" remedies for widely heralded school problems. In *The Manufactured Crisis: Myths, Fraud, and the Attack on America's Public Schools,* David C. Berliner, professor of education, University of Arizona, and Bruce J. Biddle, professor of social research, University of Missouri, trace much of the disinformation to efforts by Reagan and Bush Administration officials who misled the media and the public about the problems of American education, diverted attention from the schools' real problems, and promoted phony "solutions." It should be added that, beginning during the Nixon Administration, Republican Party officials adopted a policy of promoting tax aid to nonpublic schools as a way of pulling votes away from the Democrats in certain parts of the country.

Berliner and Biddle maintain that what appears to be a decline in SAT scores actually is the result

From USA TODAY, Vol. 125, No. 2622, March 1997, pp. 89–90. Reprinted by permission of The Society for the Advancement of Education.

of the great expansion of the testing process to include vast numbers of less-advantaged students They show that SAT scores tend to be directly proportional to family income and angrily reply to the critics of public education that "We have little sympathy . . . for critics who run down America's schools for their putative failures when the ongoing accomplishments of those schools are manifest and the society they serve is deteriorating. When school achievements are steady or even improve in a society that is falling apart, we think that educators have pulled off a miracle. It is time to celebrate the public schools of the nation, not to blame them."

The authors further point out that the data do not support the widespread view that average student achievement and performance are declining, students are "dumber" than they used to be, and American schools in general fail badly in international comparisons. Rather, the data show that the U.S. spends proportionately less money on elementary and secondary education than most other industrial countries, that money does make a difference in the quality of education, and that sharp increases in school spending are due primarily to the high costs of providing for "special circumstances" children, who are found in disproportionately far higher numbers in public than in nonpublic schools.

Berliner and Biddle attribute much of that "manufactured crisis" to propaganda campaigns by the religious and secular radical right and to media sloppiness and irresponsibility. They explain succinctly why voucher plans would harm, rather than help, education.

They further note that many educational problems are related to the worsening distribution of income and wealth—less equitable than in any other democratic industrial nation—and to the fact that this country allows a larger percentage of children to live in poverty than is the case anywhere else in the developed world. Even more scandalous than the toleration of high levels of child poverty are the gross discrepancies in spending between public school districts, a situation largely nonexistent in other advanced democracies.

Disputing Claims

Much of the public argument for vouchers ("certificates," "educational opportunity grants," "Junior G.I. Bills," etc.) centers around the notion that they, "educational free markets," and "school choice" somehow will improve performance. However, comprehensive studies of school choice by the pro-voucher Bush Administration's Department of Education (1992); the Carnegie Foundation (1992); political scientist Jeffrey Henig (1994); and researchers Kevin B. Smith and Kenneth J. Meier in *The Case Against School Choice* (1995) do not support such claims. The Carnegie Foundation concluded that "choice can be a tremendously expensive reform to implement and sustain," and that "where choice has been implemented and studied in other countries, the results have been mixed or disappointing."

Smith and Meier found that, because nonpublic schools usually are selective academically and in other ways, "cream-skimming" by nonpublic schools, whether aided by vouchers or not, tends to have a negative effect on public school performance. They write that selecting or giving preference to the best students may occur in choice plans confined to public schools and thus "exacerbate the already considerable inequities among school districts."

Henig shows that even expanding choice among public schools may give some students more options, while reducing them for others. Moreover, he makes clear that such widely touted "solutions" as magnet schools cost about eight percent more to operate than regular schools and that transportation services for magnet schools run about 27% more than for regular schools.

Voucher supporters frequently argue that nonpublic schools deserve public support because they are superior to public schools. However, *Money* magazine concluded in October, 1994, that students in the best public schools outperform most nonpublic school students; the average public school teacher has stronger academic qualifications than the average nonpublic teacher; the best public schools offer a more challenging curriculum than most nonpublic schools; and public school class sizes are no larger than in most nonpublic schools.

A significant development in the controversy over vouchers for nonpublic schools occurred in Canada in September, 1995, but mostly was ignored in the U.S. Voters in the province of Newfoundland, who never have known anything but a sort of universal voucher plan—no public schools and four tax-supported religious school systems (Roman Catholic, Pentecostal, Seventh-Day Adventist, ecumenical Protestant)—chose to scrap their inefficient system in favor of U.S.-style public schools. The Toronto *Globe and Mail* hailed the vote, which was larger than the province's original vote to join Canada, as a money saver and an important step toward improving the province's "lamentable record of scholastic performance."

Behind the lofty rhetoric of school "reform" used by advocates of voucher plans lies the simple desire of many nonpublic school operators, most of them religious bodies, to get tax support for their institutions. Let us look, then, at the case against school vouchers.

One major objection is that vouchers—at least as applied to sectarian schools, which account for about 85% of nonpublic enrollment—violate the church-state separation principle in the U.S. and most state constitutions. In *Lemon v. Kurtzman* (1971), the Supreme Court held unconstitutional Pennsylvania and Rhode Island laws that provided state aid to denominational schools. In that case, the Court spelled out the test for constitutionality: a law must have a primary secular purpose, may not advance or inhibit religion, and may not result in "excessive entanglement" between church and state. Two years later, in *Committee for Public Education and Religious Liberty v. Nyquist*, the Court struck down a New York scheme, similar to vouchers, that reimbursed parents for denominational school tuition. Vouchers surely would run afoul of the *Lemon* and *Nyquist* rulings, though changes in Supreme Court personnel make predictions with absolute certainty impossible.

All of the state constitutions except three (Maine, North Carolina, and North Dakota) bar tax aid to sectarian schools and/or institutions. The constitution of the Commonwealth of Puerto Rico, adopted by the territory and approved by Congress in 1952, reiterates the language of the First Amendment and adds: "there shall be complete separation of church and state." The island's highest court ruled a voucher plan unconstitutional in 1995. Efforts to remove state constitutional barriers to vouchers and similar "parochiaid" plans have been rejected uniformly by voters.

Vouchers would undermine religious liberty. By the time the Constitution and Bill of Rights were written, a consensus had developed favorable to the concept of separation of church and state. This view, articulated by James Madison in his 1785 "Memorial and Remonstrance Against Religious Assessments," held that support for religious institutions should be wholly voluntary, not coerced through taxation, whether some churches were favored or all were treated equally. By routing public funds directly or indirectly to sectarian schools, vouchers would violate every citizen's fundamental right to contribute voluntarily only to the religious institutions of his or her free choice.

Vouchers are opposed by most Americans. Between 1966 and 1993, statewide electorates from coast to coast have had to vote on voucher plans or other proposals to provide or allow public funding for nonpublic—primarily sectarian—schools. The aggregate vote in these 20 referenda showed voters opposed to any diversion of public funds to nonpublic schools by a 66.9 to 33.1% margin. This aggregate vote is close to the 65-33% opposition registered in the 1995 Gallup/Phi Delta Kappa poll.

Supporters of vouchers have pointed to polls that show opinion slightly favoring vouchers or breaking somewhere near even. Examination of the poll questions, however, reveals that they generally mix choice among public schools inextricably with tax aid for nonpublic schools. Separating the two issues shows people favoring more choice among public schools while opposing tax aid to nonpublic schools.

Pluralism vs. Special Interests

Some economists who favor vouchers seem to regard providing education as being the same as manufacturing widgets or gizmos, with buyers making decisions much the same as when they buy cars or choose a brand of cigarette. Education is not widgets, though. Public education is pluralistic, religiously neutral education under public control and open to all children.

Nonpublic education, on the other hand, may be described fairly as special-interest education. It is not under meaningful public control; does not have to play by the same rules as public education; may discriminate in admissions, faculty hiring, and curriculum selection and design in ways that would be considered intolerable in public education; and, for the most part, is sectarian. It is not generically religious or similar to public education with a dollop of religion stuck on at the end of the day. Instead, it is pervasively sectarian education in the main.

Given the heavily sectarian nature of most nonpublic education, vouchers would mean tax support for the kinds of selectivity and discrimination common in nonpublic schools. The issue of school choice is not so much about parents selecting schools for their kids but, rather, concerning nonpublic schools choosing which students to admit, the sort of teachers to hire, and the faith or ideology that should permeate the curriculum.

Private schools choose their students and faculty actively through admission and hiring policies and passively through the nature of their program. For instance, Orthodox Jewish schools do not attract Catholic families; Nation of Islam schools do not attract white Christian families; and expensive college prep schools are not likely to attract (or accept) poor children with handicaps. Any voucher plan that seeks to compel nonpublic schools to play by the same rules as public schools will not get much support from the nonpublic school sector.

Vouchers mean tax support for the horizontal dividing of children, families, and communities along social class lines and vertically along religious, ideological, ethnic, and other lines. Poor and handicapped children generally will be the losers. The constituency for public education and its improvement and adequacy will fade, a phenomenon already visible in some areas of the country.

Albert J. Menendez's study of fundamentalist school textbooks, *Visions of Reality: What Fundamentalist Schools Teach,* found that the most popular ones in use "promote sectarian separatism, religious intolerance, anti-intellectualism, disdain for the scientific spirit, and right-wing political extremism." Vouchers would compel all taxpayers to subsidize such instruction.

Voucher plans would cost a great deal of money, which invariably would come from higher taxes, cutbacks in public education funding, or both. As the goal of most voucher advocates is some rough parity between public funding for public and nonpublic schooling, with per capita public school spending running about $5,500 per year and with nearly 5,000,000 students in nonpublic schools, such a plan would cost approximately $30,000,000,000 per year.

That figure does not include increased spending for school transportation. After all, if students can not get to school, choice (such as it might be) would not mean much. As nonpublic schools tend to serve more widely scattered constituencies, nonpublic school transportation costs, as already has been demonstrated in Pennsylvania and Ohio, would rise astronomically.

Vouchers for nonpublic education would be bad public policy. They would harm, rather than help, education. They violate fundamental constitutional principles, run counter to well-established public opinion, fragment communities, shift schooling from education toward indoctrination, and increase educational costs.

Article Review Form at end of book.

Overall, how do participants in school choice programs evaluate the effectiveness of school choice? What are strategies for improving school choice programs, especially in the areas of equity and student achievement?

Is School Choice Working?

Is different better? Not necessarily, say researchers studying the effects of choice. But their findings can help us design programs that increase achievement and better serve diverse families and students.

Bruce Fuller

Bruce Fuller is Associate Professor of Public Policy and Education, University of California, Berkeley, School of Education, Tolman Hall 3659, Berkeley, CA 94720. He formerly taught at Harvard University and codirected, with Richard Elmore and Gary Orfield, the School Choice and Family Policy Project, funded by the Lilly Endowment.

Choice serves families at opposite ends of the social-class spectrum in America: about 15 percent of low- and high-income parents opt to exit their neighborhood school for a public or private school of choice (NCES 1995). More than 20 states have now approved charter school legislation. Publicly supported voucher programs operate in Milwaukee and, beginning last month, in Cleveland. The private sector supports voucher or scholarship programs in 20 cities nationwide (Moe 1996).

But rising enthusiasm over school choice has far outpaced careful attempts to assess the concrete effects of choice experiments: charters, magnets, and voucher programs. Harvard University recently sponsored a three-year-long seminar series attended by researchers who are evaluating choice programs. Are these experiments working? Which children benefit, and which ones get overlooked? Can we make choice fairer for all students? The empirical results of these studies appear in *Who Chooses, Who Loses? Culture, Institutions, and the Unequal Effects of School Choice* (Fuller and Elmore 1996).

Three Questions

Our project examined three questions that empirical evidence can help answer—with an eye on how to improve the design of choice programs.

1. *Which families exit their neighborhood school and exercise choice?* Choice programs are enormously popular, especially in low-income and working-class communities, where parental dissatisfaction with local schools is the greatest. Yet even within these neighborhoods, better educated parents and those already involved in their children's schooling participate more frequently in choice programs. This is not surprising. What's notable is that this self-selection and sorting, based on social class and family practices, occurs even among low-income and working-class families.

In Milwaukee, even though three-fourths of all participating students come from female-headed households, maternal education levels vary, as does the extent to which mothers supervise their children's homework. More than half of the parents who participated in the choice program had attended college, compared with just 30 percent of those who did not participate.

How children are selected by choice schools can exacerbate the inequality between participants and nonparticipants. In the San Antonio voucher program, for instance, administrators use the child's prior academic performance in determining access to a limited number of slots

Fuller, Bruce. (October 1996). "Is School Choice Working?" EDUCATIONAL LEADERSHIP 54, 2: 37–40. Reprinted with permission of the Association for Supervision and Curriculum Development.

in the bicultural choice schools. The reading scores of students admitted to these schools are twice as high as those of children who do not apply to choice schools. This creaming-off of the strongest students serves to concentrate high-achieving students in new choice schools and leaves behind lower achievers in neighborhood schools.

Choice does little to desegregate schools or to break down ethnic enclaves of families. It can even reinforce racial separation. In Milwaukee, several of the nonsectarian community schools now supported by vouchers are ethnocentric in their identity and their curriculum. Nearly 100 percent of students enrolled in Milwaukee's Urban Day and Harambee School are black, and the student population at Bruce-Guadalupe Community School is nearly all Hispanic. This unanticipated resegregation effect is troubling.

2. *Do a thousand organizational flowers bloom under liberalized school markets?* Pro-choice financing structures, under some conditions, do stimulate the creation of innovative schools. We know that charter schools, magnets, and voucher-supported community schools differ from typical neighborhood schools. Yet we have no evidence that choice schools boost children's achievement. We simply do not know enough about what is happening in the classroom. In short, there is no reason to assume that different is necessarily better. As we see in the marketplace every day, products and companies fail. We can expect the same with schools. The difference is that it is much easier to write off a lost investment than a lost educational opportunity for children.

One curiosity is that choice schools, despite their rebellion against school bureaucracy, are usually founded on publicly financed organizations. In Milwaukee, for example, the 15 community schools that now accept voucher students grew out of preexisting youth centers, preschools, or nonprofit community action organizations. California's 93 charter schools reflect a related pattern. The most common force behind these schools is a small cluster of public school teachers or an activist principal who has grown dissatisfied with bureaucracy.

What's troubling is the lack of any compelling evidence that entry into a choice school actually results in measurable achievement gains.

3. *Does school choice improve student performance or boost parents' commitment to their child's development?* If parent satisfaction were a reliable indicator, the answer would be an emphatic yes. A recent U.S. Department of Education study found steady growth in parental demand for magnets and waiting lists for these schools in many urban districts. More textured data gathered from the Milwaukee voucher program show that parental satisfaction does rise after one's child enters a choice school, and this is reflected in parents' pressure to expand the program (Witte 1996).

What's troubling is the lack of any compelling evidence that entry into a choice school actually results in measurable achievement gains. In Milwaukee, reading gains during the first year were somewhat higher among choice students than among a control group of similar low-income students. But in the second and third years, results were quite inconsistent, especially in mathematics achievement. One weakness of the Milwaukee data is that they are aggregated for all choice students. We need to look at individual schools and classrooms to assess the success of actual school management and classroom practices. In contrast, the first-ever longitudinal study of achievement (over three years) in magnet schools, completed earlier this year at the University of Wisconsin, shows significant gains in high school compared with students attending neighborhood schools (Witte 1996).

In San Antonio, choice participants did display markedly higher learning curves during the first year, relative to their counterparts who remained in neighborhood schools. These encouraging gains appear to be significant even after taking into account children's family background and prior achievement. It is difficult, however, to distinguish improvements resulting from better schooling from prior effects that result from the selection of those students with the best record of prior achievement.

We have no direct evidence on what happens to the performance of children left behind in neighborhood schools. We do know that the parents of these youngsters are less educated and less involved in their children's schooling. Earlier research has identified the problem of negative "peer effects" on classroom performance: When low performers are concentrated in the same classroom, they tend to suppress one another's achievement (for example, Bryk and Raudenbush 1992).

Evidence emerging from the preschool arena—a vibrant mixed

market of 48,000 small organizations serving 5 million children—offers important lessons for the future of school choice. As with the Milwaukee program, most preschool subsidies go to low-income families, either directly through parental vouchers or indirectly as per-capita grants to nonprofit child-care organizations, including church-affiliated institutions. This strategy, which can be characterized as "choice with equity," appears to be largely successful. In the space of three decades, access to preschooling has become fairly equitable, reaching about half of all 3- to 5-year-olds from low-income and middle-class families, including programs based in public schools (Fuller et al. 1996). The related issue of whether preschool quality is distributed fairly is more difficult to answer.

Toward Greater Equity

What we've learned thus far can help us rethink how to better harness school choice in order to yield more consistent gains in children's learning and ensure greater equity. Findings to date point to the risks of rushing headlong down the path of unrestrained school choice programs. In general, these tend to reward parents who are already most committed to their youngsters' education, leaving behind children who receive the least help and encouragement from their families. Achievement is likely to rise for those in the choice schools and fall for those left behind in the neighborhood schools. No evidence yet demonstrates that choice sparks inventive changes inside classrooms.

Democratic government must certainly create incentives that reward parents who work hard to push their offspring up the ladder of economic and social mobility—without harming children whose parents are less committed or unaware of how to attend to their youngster's schooling. And political leaders continue to search for reforms that will truly touch the day-to-day management of schools and the vigor and rigor of classroom life.

Toward these ends, can we modify the design and implementation of choice programs to lead to more impressive and equitable gains?

One positive step would be to encourage all parents within a town or city to actively consider their school options and express a discrete choice. In Cambridge, Massachusetts, for example, each year all families must list their top three schools. Public authorities then balance these individual choices against the state's interest in preventing overcrowding and in providing ethnic diversity within each school.

A simpler option is to randomly select from among families requesting choice schools, rather than use students' prior achievement or parents' initiative as criteria. Using prior school achievement to select "choice students" does just that: it skims off the most able and isolates kids who are receiving the least amount of support from their parents and teachers.

Better information about school options and employing media that are particularly effective in reaching different ethnic groups may broaden interest in school choice to a wider set of parents. In Montgomery County, Maryland, one study found that Hispanic parents were half as likely to understand their magnet school options, compared to white parents.

Choice schools should have clear plans for how they will alter classrooms and the teaching-learning process.

In addition, choice schools should have clear plans for how they will alter classrooms and the teaching-learning process. Cosmetic factors have been enormously important in selling charters, small schools, magnets, and voucher schools. But their leaders should be accountable for explaining precisely how they will enliven the classroom process as should public educators.

We must evaluate concrete effects on children and families. As the school choice movement has gained political adherents, tough questions about real effects are being asked less frequently. We have promised poor and working-class families lots of things since the 1960s. Choice is being advanced as another medicinal panacea for the ills linked to poverty. For a small investment, we can build additional evidence on which types of local programs yield what kinds of effects on parental commitment and children's achievement.

One fact is clear: The sprouting of choice initiatives in education and family policy offers a vibrant response to the increasingly pluralistic character of American society. Whether pro-choice policy fundamentally alters realities at the grass roots remains to be seen. Choice, ideologically, advances our Jeffersonian attraction to decentralized government as a way to advance rugged individualism. But Thomas Jefferson also viewed the common school as a balance wheel that would nurture shared values and a richer understanding of difference and human diversity. If the common school cannot provide this balance, we must find common ground through new forms of schooling.

Most fundamentally, real progress will occur only when two crucial, human-scale organizations, the classroom and the family, make gains. Effective education and the careful upbringing of children stem from subtle interactions among child, teacher, and parent. School choice proponents are just beginning to look into this core and ask how we can approach teaching and child development anew.

References

Bryk, A. and S. Randenbush. (1992) *Hierarchical Linear Models.* Beverly Hills: Sage.

Fuller, B., and R. F. Elmore, with G. Orfield, eds. (1996). *Who Chooses, Who Loses? Culture, Institutions and the Unequal Effects of School Choice.* New York: Teachers College Press.

Fuller, B., S. D. Holloway, and I. Bozzi. (1996). "Evaluating Early Childhood Education Programs." In *Early Childhood Education Yearbook,* edited by B. Spodek and O. Saracho. New York: Teachers College Press.

Moe, T., ed. (1996). *Private Vouchers.* Stanford Hoover Institution Press.

National Center for Educational Statistics. (1995). *Use of School Choice.* Education Policy Issues series. NCES 95–742R. Washington, D.C. NCES.

Witte, J. F. (1996). "Who Benefits from the Milwaukee Choice Program?" In *Who Chooses, Who Loses? Culture, Institutions, and the Unequal Effects of School Choice,* edited by B. Fuller and R. F. Elmore, with G. Orfield, pp. 118–137. New York: Teachers College Press.

Article Review Form at end of book.

What are the contrasting viewpoints related to school choice? What are charter schools, contracts, and voucher plans?

Considering Nontraditional Alternatives

Charters, private contracts, and vouchers

Julia E. Koppich

Julia E. Koppich, Ph.D., is a San Francisco-based education consultant, and a visiting professor at the Claremont Graduate school.

Abstract

Charter schools, vouchers, and contracts with private agencies providing educational services all reflect the belief that a substantial part of educational budgeting, decision making, and accountability should be based at the level of individual schools, rather than at the school district level. Though states are moving quickly to set up charter schools, and some states and districts are debating the merits of vouchers or experimenting with private contracts, in fact there is little information about the educational effectiveness of these innovations.

Charter schools face substantial challenges in financing and business operations; many state charter school laws provide no start-up or capital funds and only limited operational funds. In addition, many charter school laws are vague on key questions of authority and school-district relations. Contracting with private agencies presents a wide range of options, many of which have been tried in only a few locations. The most publicized contracts with private agencies to run multiple schools have included some highly visible disappointments and no clear successes as yet, though experience is too limited to draw conclusions about contracting in general.

Vouchers that may be used at private schools are extremely controversial for several reasons. Because private schools can decide which students they will accept, opponents are concerned that extensive use of vouchers may dramatically change the composition of the public school student body. It is also unclear whether vouchers to religious schools (which comprise 82% of all private schools in the United States) violate the constitutional requirement for separation of church and state.

The 1983 release of *A Nation at Risk*, the report of the National Commission on Excellence in Education, shifted the debate about education in American from a focus on equity (defined as a legal obligation to provide substantially equal educational resources for all students), which had occupied reformers in the 1960s and 1970s, to a focus on excellence (that is, ensuring that ever larger proportions of the school-age population reach higher levels of achievement). Despite more than a decade of national, state, and local educational reform efforts, the American public continues to express deep concern about the public school system as a whole.

A clear expression of that concern is the increasing level of support for publicly funded alternatives to existing schools.

Source: Koppich, J.E. Considering Nontraditional Alternatives: Charters, Private Contracts, and Vouchers. The Future of Children (Winter 1997) 7, 3: 96–111. Reprinted with permission of the Center for the Future of Children of the David and Lucile Packard Foundation. The Future of Children journals and executive summaries are available free of charge by faxing mailing information to: Circulation Department (650) 948–6498.

This article will describe three of these emerging alternatives—charter schools, contracts under which outside agencies provide educational services, and voucher programs. Each of these alternatives represents a fundamental shift from the norm. Moreover, each is rooted in a simple yet profound idea: individual schools, rather than aggregations of schools called districts, should be the locus of most educational budgeting, decision making, and accountability.

This article first addresses the historic shift from individual school site control to control by school districts. The article then summarizes, to the extent available, evaluative data on charters, contracts, and vouchers. In this regard, it is important as well to raise an issue that is, at least, reason for caution. Much, indeed most, of the research on charters, contract schools, and vouchers has been conducted and reported on by partisans, groups or individuals who are known to hold particular perspectives and whose research results corroborate their views. The findings themselves may be valid, but rarely are they arrived at by means of dispassionate (that is, agenda-neutral) research and evaluation.

The Common School and the Development of Districts

The American system of public education has its roots in the common school. The descriptor was not meant to imply that the school was for commoners; rather, that it would be common to all people. The common school was, moreover, to be available at no cost, provide students from diverse backgrounds with a common educational experience, be totally supported and controlled by the common effort of the entire community, and contribute to rendering social and economic class boundaries permeable.[1]

The framers of the American education system did not anticipate the development of the large public bureaucracies many school systems have become. Currently, nearly 45 million students in the United States attend grades K–12 in almost 80,000 public schools, organized into nearly 15,000 school districts.[2] The 100 largest of these districts, including New York City with more than one million enrollees and the Los Angeles Unified School District with upwards of 600,000, are responsible for educating 23% of all public school students.[3] The reasons for this consolidation into increasingly large districts are numerous and historic: Larger districts were believed to benefit from economies of scale; collecting and distributing tax revenue over a larger area would sometimes solve problems of school-to-school funding inequities. In Florida and Nevada, for example, school district boundaries are aligned with county boundaries, resulting in several very large districts.

The early framers of the public education system also did not anticipate the twentieth century's increasing expectation that all children be educated for an increasing number of years and to a much higher degree of academic competency. As educational expectations rise, so does the obligation to deal in a specialized way with a widening range of student needs. In the nineteenth century, common schools provided their students with rudimentary literacy and numeracy skills, after which many students left school without serious negative consequences. Today, many families demand specialized services such as vocational education, advanced college placement, foreign language competency, accommodations for unusual learning styles or behavioral or emotional challenges, child care on the school site, and education reflecting multicultural or specific ethnic history. Many feel that common schools cannot respond to all of these demands in sufficient depth and that more specialized public schools are needed. Much of the current demand for school site control reflects local desire for these kinds of schools committed to addressing individualized preferences.

Owing in part to size, many school districts have developed as tightly controlled centralized bureaucracies. Observers have frequently noted that the principal job of district headquarters staff is to ensure that schools hew faithfully to local, state, and federal rules, regulations, statutes, and procedures. This bureaucratic structure, claim its critics, is inherently antagonistic toward innovation, efficiency, and entrepreneurship.

Collective bargaining agreements between teachers' unions and school district management also serve often to reinforce the bureaucratic nature of educational decision making. Contracts apply to districtwide template to teachers' employment conditions, implicitly assuming that all teachers and all school settings are identical. In addition, industrial-style collective bargaining assumes a lack of commonality between the needs and responsibilities of labor and those of management, an assumption that further impedes flexibility and innovation. While a few districts and their teachers' unions have begun to alter collective bargaining to decentralize and customize decision making (for example, through joint union-district committees or contract waiver provisions), examples of these efforts are limited.[4]

Proponents of the schooling options explored in this article assert that these plans offer the freedom and flexibility which allow schools to tailor their programs to the needs of individual students and will result in higher levels of achievement. Opponents contend that implementation of charter schools, contract schools, and vouchers will produce elitist schools which will enroll the best students from conventional public schools, leave conventional schools with diminished budgets, create an education system segregated by race, income, and philosophy, and abandon the goal of a common American schooling experience.

Box 1 States with Charter School Legislation by Year of First Enactment, as of June 1997

1991	Minnesota
1992	California
1993	Colorado, Georgia, Massachusetts, Michigan, New Mexico, Wisconsin
1994	Arizona, Hawaii, Kansas
1995	Alaska, Arkansas, Delaware, Louisiana, New Hampshire, Rhode Island, Wyoming
1996	Connecticut, District of Columbia, Florida, Illinois, New Jersey, North Carolina, South Carolina, Texas
1997	Mississippi, Pennsylvania

Sources: For years 1991 to 1996: Office of Educational Research and Improvement. *A study of charter schools: First year report 1997*. Washington, DC: U.S. Department of Education, 1997; for 1997: Schnaiberg, L. State charter laws get new round of attention. *Education Week*. June 25, 1997, p. 10.

California and Arizona together account for 57% of charter schools and 59% of charter school students.

Charter Schools

Charter schools are *public* schools which are freed from many local and state regulations in exchange for increased accountability for student achievement results.[5] As of November 1, 1996, there were 481 charter schools in operation nationally, enrolling 105,000 students. California and Arizona together account for 57% of charter schools and 59% of charter school students.[6] Charter schools include elementary, middle, junior high, senior high, and comprehensive K–12 schools.

As public schools, charter schools are required to be nonsectarian and are precluded from charging tuition. They may be organized by individuals or by groups, such as teachers, parents, and colleges and universities, who are granted a charter by the designated public agency specified in state law (generally a state board of education or local school board) to operate the school. The charter delineates what resources the school will receive, how the school will be managed and governed, what the curriculum will be, how achievement will be measured, and what student outcomes are anticipated. Charter schools operate as schools of choice; that is, enrollment in them is voluntary.

The charter school movement is still quite new. Minnesota enacted the first charter school law in the nation in 1991. Since then, 26 other states have similar laws, as shown in Box 1. State statutes vary widely regarding matters such as the number of schools that are allowed to become charter schools, the agencies that approve charters,[7] who is eligible to seek a charter, and the amount of operating autonomy granted a charter school.[8] As illustrated in Table 1, some state laws allow wide autonomy to charter schools, while others have been said to create "charters in name only," under strict control by the school district. For example, if teachers in a charter school remain employees of the district, rather than of the school, district control of the school's program may be largely maintained.

Most of the nation's charter schools have been in operation less than three years; almost half began in 1996–97. Preliminary data are just beginning to emerge regarding the kinds of programs charter schools offer and the students they serve. Most charter schools emphasize a particular academic philosophy, some concentrating on "back to basics," while others pursue newer pedagogical approaches such as "integrated interdisciplinary curriculum."[8,9] Many report they make considerable use of educational technology.[8] Some charter schools have affiliated with nationally known programs and organizations, such as Accelerated Schools, the

Table 1 Charter School Laws as of August 1996

	Stronger Laws (likely to yield larger numbers of autonomous schools)												
	AZ (94)	DE (95)	NC (96)	FL (96)	NH (95)	SC (96)	MA (93)	MI (94)	TX[a] (95)	IL (96)	CA (92)	DC (96)	NJ (96)
Nonlocal board sponsor available	X	X	X				X	X	X			X	X
or appeal process exists[d]			X	X	X	X					X		X
Individuals or groups from outside the public school system can organize a charter proposal	X	X	X	X	X	X	X	X	a	X	X	X	e
Automatic exemptions from most state laws/rules and local policies	X	X	X	X	X	X	X		X	X	X	X	
Fiscal autonomy; School has complete control over funds generated by student count (including salaries)	X	X	X	X	X	X	X	X	X	X	f	X	e
Legal autonomy (for example, teachers are employees of school, not local district)	X	X		X	X		X	X	X	X		X	e
or the charter (not the law) determines the level of legal autonomy			X			X					X		
No (or very high) limits on the number of charter schools that can be formed (compared with total population)	X	X	X	X	X	X		X		X			X
Some percentage of noncertified individuals can teach at charter school (without having to seek a waiver or alternative certification)	X	h	X	X	X	X	X	i	X	X[j]	X	X	
Total "Stronger" Components	7	7	7	7	7	7	6	6	6	6	6	6	5

Notes: Highlighted columns are the six most recently passed charter school laws. The general strength of these laws reflects a trend toward stronger legislation. Since August 1996, Mississippi and Pennsylvania have passed charter school laws.

[a] Based upon "open enrollment" charter school portion of Texas' charter school bill. Eligible organizers are limited to public or private higher education institutions, a nonprofit, or a governmental entity.

[b] Connecticut's legislation has a state-sponsored charter school component that reflects the analysis included in this chart. The state also has district-sponsored charter schools that are considerably less autonomous and not included in this analysis. Existing private schools are not allowed to apply for a charter. For-profit organizations may not apply for a charter but are free to contract with successful charter applicants. Parents or groups of parents who home school their children may not apply for a charter to continue such activities. The fiscal independence of the school depends on the terms of its charter.

[c] In Wisconsin, charter schools are automatically exempt from most state laws and rules, not local board policies. Also, recently enacted provisions strengthen the law for potential charter schools within the Milwaukee district only in that such schools can become legally and financially autonomous and have access to an appeal process involving the new state secretary of education. In Wisconsin, the district gets to determine whether to accept any applications at all. Once a district decides to accept applications, a group of parents or community members may apply.

International Baccalaureate, the Coalition of Essential Schools, and the New American Schools Development Corporation. Private and for-profit organizations have established charter schools as well. The Renaissance School in Boston is a cooperative effort of the for-profit Edison Project and the Horace Mann Foundation. Some charter schools focus on particular segments of the student population. Options for Youth is a dropout recovery charter school in San Bernardino, California. Jingletown is a charter middle school for limited- and non-English-speaking students in Oakland, California.

A 1995–96 in-depth survey of 35 charter schools in seven states conducted by the Hudson Institute found that nearly two-thirds (63%) of the charter

Table 1 (continued) Charter School Laws as of August 1996

	Weaker Laws												
	MN (91)	CO (93)	LA (95)	CT[b] (96)	WI[c] (93)	HI (94)	WY (95)	NM (93)	RI (95)	GA (93)	KS (94)	AR (95)	AK (95)
Nonlocal board sponsor available *or* appeal process exists[d]	X X	 X		X				X	 X				
Individuals or groups from outside the public school system can organize a charter proposal	X	X	X	X	X		X				X		X
Automatic exemptions from most state laws/rules and local policies	X		X		c	X							
Fiscal autonomy: School has complete control over funds generated by student count (including salaries)	X	g	X	X		X							
Legal autonomy (for example, teachers are employees of school, not local district) *or* the charter (not the law) determines the level of legal autonomy	X	g	X	X									
No (or very high) limits on the number of charter schools that can be formed (compared with total population)		X			X	X	X			X		X	
Some percentage of noncertified individuals can teach at charter school (without having to seek a waiver or alternative certification)			X										
Total "Stronger" Components	5	5	5	4	3	3	2	1	1	1	1	1	1

[d] "Stronger" charter school law components are those that are most true to the charter school concept, challenge the status quo aspects of the system, and theoretically may lead to broader student impacts and ripple effects. Component #1 (availability of nonlocal board sponsorship or appeal) is considered a vital component to get an adequate number of charter schools started. The strength of appeals processes varies from state to state. Some analysts argue that the recent bills in Florida and South Carolina include appeals processes that will allow local districts to veto charter applications. Legislation in many states allows a wide variety of individuals and organizations to apply for charters, but no states allow religious schools to apply.

[e] In New Jersey, any teacher or parent within a district may themselves, or in conjunction with any in-state higher education institution or private entity, establish a charter school; such schools are eligible for at least 90% of the local levy budget per pupil; and district collective bargaining provisions automatically apply to converted public schools, while salaries within new charter schools must fall within the range established by the district in which the school is located.

[f] California's charter schools are allowed by law to be legally and fiscally autonomous, but this depends upon the provisions of a given school's charter.

[g] Legally, Colorado's charter schools are to remain a part of the local school district and to receive at least 80% of their funds from it; in practice, however, many are operating quite autonomously.

[h] In Delaware, up to 35% noncertified teachers may be utilized if no qualified alternative certification program exists (and presently there is no such program in the state).

[i] In Michigan, the issue of automatic law exemptions is still unclear, and certification is required except in university-sponsored schools wherein higher education faculty can teach.

[j] Noncertified individuals need not apply for an alternative certification, but the Illinois legislation spells out conditions for employment of noncertified individuals which are similar to requirements of formal alternative certification in other states. The state's cap on charter schools is 45, and the legislation includes regional subcaps as well. These two qualifications suggest that the Illinois legislation may be "weaker" than it appears.

Source: Reprinted with permission from Education Commission of the States. *Clearinghouse notes: Charter schools.* Denver, CO: ECS, August 1996.

schools' students were members of minority groups, a "large number" of whom were economically disadvantaged.[10] The charter schools, not surprisingly, attracted primarily students who were not satisfied with their own public schools. The majority (81%) of these students transferred to the charter school from their existing public schools, and the remainder came from private schools, had previously been home schooled, or had dropped out. The survey authors described many of the students as "square pegs" who were not comfortable in the "round holes" available in conventional schools. Indeed, they found that charter schools also tended to attract unconventional teachers, many of whom relished the challenge of meeting special needs.

It is too early for reliable student achievement data, and conceptual problems with assessment make it unlikely that clear data will be available soon.[11] A compelling argument on behalf of charter schools is that they will be responsible for demonstrating results. But accountability systems in charter schools, thus far, are little better than those in other public schools. Many charters do not have in place measurable performance expectations, and charter-granting agencies have not yet insisted in rigorous accountability systems.[12] Available student data are largely self-reported and related more to inputs (number of students, types of courses, availability of technology) than to outcomes. Additionally, many charter schools assess student outcomes in nonstandardized form, such as through samples of student work collected in portfolios, thus making comparisons between charter schools and other public schools difficult.

At this time, the impact of charter schools on student outcomes is largely unknown. In any event, given the diversity of educational approaches and student needs encompassed by charter schools, it is highly likely that outcome data will provide mixed results, with charter schools being shown to have both positive and negative attributes and results. At this point, what is clear is that those who seek to establish charter schools face a number of financial, legal, and technical challenges.

Financial Challenges

Charter schools are funded through their "home" school districts. Some state laws require that all operating dollars be disbursed directly to the charter schools; others do not. For example, charter schools in Wisconsin receive from their districts whatever funds they can negotiate. California charter schools are entitled to the district-determined average for the type of school (elementary, middle, or high school) and then must negotiate for a share of categorical funds.

A more immediate concern is that charter schools will drain operating funds—particularly discretionary funds—from regular public schools.

No definitive data about the cost of charter schools have yet been compiled. However, the most complete assessment of the fiscal issues confronting charter schools is contained in a 1996 report prepared by the Education Commission of the States.[13] The researchers found that charter schools are challenged by:

- *No start-up funds.* Most charter schools must begin operation, including leasing space, hiring staff, buying materials and equipment, and securing appropriate kinds of insurance, with only the start-up capital school operators can scrape together from donations or out of their own pockets.
- *Limited (or no) access to local operational and categorical funds.* As of May 1996, the Education Commission of the States found that "with the exception of charter schools in Massachusetts, only a handful of currently operating charter schools receive 100% of the combined state and local operations funds."[12] In the majority of states, districts are empowered to withhold from charter schools part or all of the district's local tax revenues for day-to-day operations. Similarly, access to categorical funds is often limited for charter schools. Because most federal funding and a significant share of state funding for schools is categorical (that is, restricted to specific purposes such as special education or bilingual education), this can constitute a substantial share of the school's funding.
- *No capital funds.* Charter schools have no access to local funds for capital improvement and no authority to issue bonds. They must thus use operating funds for capital expenditures. Recognizing this problem, Arizona in 1997 approved state aid for capital/facilities expenditures for charter schools.[14]
- *"Seat time" funding.* Virtually all school districts receive money from their states on the basis of average daily attendance. States make few adjustments for schools that configure

instruction in nonconventional ways. For example, a charter school that does not require daily attendance might receive less funding for a comparable number of students.

Emerging anecdotal evidence suggests that resourceful charter schools can overcome some fiscal barriers. The executive director of Fenton Avenue Charter School in Los Angeles, for example, points to the opportunity to "make fast, economical decisions," such as hiring a local contractor to install and repair light fixtures for $1,475, rejecting the district's offer to do the job for $5,000.[10]

Regulatory, Governance, and Management Challenges

State laws governing charter schools remove some, but not all, regulatory requirements. A certain minimum of laws and regulations regarding health, safety, and nondiscrimination is clearly needed and is required by charter statute. However, some state statutes retain many additional limitations, only some of which are described in Table 1. For example, in Arizona, charter schools must conform to the state's detailed Uniform System of Financial Records, though amendments in 1996 eased this requirement somewhat.[10]

State laws often fail to specify the legal status of charter schools. It may be unclear whether a charter school has independent legal standing, allowing that school to sue and be sued, or to enter into contracts with vendors without district approval.

In the Hudson Institute survey, coordinators in two of the eight states indicated that governance problems posed the greatest immediate threat to charter schools. Typically, governance problems involve conflicts between the school's board and its staff. In other instances, charter parents of staff split into warring factions. Such disputes can sink a fledgling school.

Management challenges in a new charter school are similar to those in a new small business—for example, obtaining suitable facilities and insurance, and hiring and managing staff. Establishing and maintaining a charter school require both business and education expertise, and the typically small staff of a start-up charter school may lack critical technical skills. Most states do not provide technical assistance for start-up charter schools even though they do make such assistance available for new small businesses.[13] A limited amount of technical assistance is provided by the U.S. Department of Education through its charter school Web site.[15]

Some private firms are currently managing 20 schools, serving 14,900 students, in 7 states.

The Impact of Charter Schools on School Districts

From a policy perspective, charter schools must be judged not solely on the basis of client satisfaction or even student outcomes, but by the totality of their impact on the public school system. This impact, however, is largely speculative at this point. Critical issues to consider are whether charter schools lead to changes in enrollment patterns in public schools and their fiscal impact on public schools.

The small size of the charter school population relative to the total public school population (105,000 versus 45,000,000 students, in 481 versus 80,000 schools) does not allow firm projections of enrollment patterns. The Hudson survey found anecdotal evidence that, contrary to projections, some charter schools tended to attract the most "difficult" students. It would be premature, however, to conclude that this will always be true.

A more immediate concern is that charter schools will drain operating funds—particularly discretionary funds—from regular public schools. Virtually all schools and districts have substantial fixed costs, irrespective of student enrollment. If students move to charter schools, causing enrollment at regular schools to drop, the district may be unable or unwilling to decrease those fixed costs (at least in the short run) and, consequently, may be forced to cut back drastically in the "discretionary" areas where much of the district's more creative and innovative efforts occur, such as training to improve pedagogy or grants to individual teachers for innovative projects.

Are charter schools the wave of the future or a passing fad? It is too early to tell. Ultimately, the success of charter schools will rest on the degree to which they are able to resolve the many fiscal, governance, and management issues described here, as well as to construct reasonable accountability systems and demonstrate improved student achievement.

Contract Schools

Contracting in education (sometimes referred to as "privatization") involves the use of government funds to purchase services from either for-profit or not-for-profit organizations in the private sector. Contracting can take many forms. Districts (or schools) may contract with outside firms for particular services, such as maintenance or transportation, or even for specific courses of study. Two elementary schools in Miami, Florida, for example, contracted with Berlitz to provide foreign language instruction for their students.[16] Other districts have long contracted for compensatory education, special education, or remedial instruction services. A few districts have begun to contract for the services of their chief executive officer.

The form of education contracting that has been the subject of the greatest controversy involving hiring for-profit firms to manage entire public schools.[17] Private firms, such as Minnesota-based Education Alternatives Incorporated (EAI), the New York City–based Edison Project, and Alternative Public Schools operating out of Nashville, Tennessee, currently are managing 20 schools, serving 14,900 students, in 7 states.[18] The impulse for contract schools is much the same as that for charter schools: In exchange for accountability for results, schools are freed from some of the rules and regulations that are said to hamstring innovation.

Baltimore's Experience

The most widely studied contracting experiment involves EAI in Baltimore, an urban district with classic urban district problems—low achievement, high dropout rates, and poorly maintained facilities. The Baltimore school board contracted with EAI in 1992 to operate nine of the city's public schools. EAI was paid $26.7 million and reported gross profits of $1.9 million in the first contract year.[19] The contract was canceled after three and one-half years of its expected five-year run. The EAI Baltimore experience provides an opportunity to examine the challenges of contracting entire school operations.

EAI is a public corporation which sells stock to finance its business. The company's ability to make a profit—and return some of that profit to its investors—is directly tied to EAI's success in cutting costs in the schools it is contracted to run. Baltimore awarded the contract to EAI on a noncompetitive basis. The company promised to remedy many of the schools' problems, including substandard facilities and inefficient management practices, and guaranteed that students would post test score gains in the first year. School personnel would remain school district employees but under EAI's direction.[20] EAI brings to the schools its own patented educational program, called Tesseract. The program stresses parental involvement, personalized education plans for each student, cross-disciplinary instruction, and the inclusion of "real life experiences" as part of the curriculum.

After the first year of the program, reading and mathematics scores of EAI students (as compared with those of a control group of students in non-EAI schools) declined.[21] Scores for EAI students declined again in the second year; control group scores rose. By the third year, test scores for EAI students had caught up with those of their control group counterparts. A University of Maryland Baltimore County (UMBC) evaluation of the EAI experience found that "the management expertise that the private sector should be able to bring to bear on a public enterprise has not been sufficient for the expected level of transformation of the [EAI] schools in Baltimore City."[22]

The researchers praised the Baltimore school board for risk taking (hiring an outside firm to manage some troubled schools), said they observed some modest change in teachers' instructional practices in EAI schools, and lauded the program for reducing the number of pull-out programs which removed students from regular classes during the course of the school day. But in comparing EAI-run and district-run schools, the researchers also found that EAI schools cost 11% more per pupil, parent involvement levels did not differ, class sizes were the same, schools were comparably clean and maintained, and the overall effectiveness of teaching was the same. The UMBC study concluded that "the promise that EAI could improve instruction without spending more than Baltimore City was spending on schools has been discredited."

Finally, EAI's refusal to produce a public budget aroused skepticism about the company's reported profit and loss levels.[23] EAI's founder and president, John Golle, has since announced that the firm no longer will attempt to work in urban school systems but, instead, will confine its efforts to the suburbs.[24]

The Edison Project

Another national for-profit firm in the contract education business, the Edison Project, has contracts to manage schools in Colorado, Florida, Kansas, Massachusetts, Michigan, and Texas.[25] Edison's curricular program includes extended instruction in mathematics and reading; instruction in music, art, physical education, and Spanish (often considered "frills" in financially strapped public school districts); and heavy emphasis on technology (the program aims to provide each student with a personal computer), all packaged into an extended school day. The Edison Project schools, some of which operate as charter schools, have been functioning a year or less, not long enough to be able to report student achievement results.

Because private schools can select which students they will accept, opponents are concerned that vouchers may serve primarily those least in need.

Lessons Learned

The General Accounting Office (GAO) recently completed a study of some of the for-profit education arrangements, including Public Strategies Group, Inc., and it supervision of Minneapolis schools, and EAI's Baltimore, Dade County, and Hartford experiences.[19] The GAO study concluded that "contract services [have] yielded some benefits for students. . . . Private management companies have served as catalysts for districts' rethinking of the status quo." However, the study also found that, while management firms have sometimes achieved cleaner buildings, greater access to computers, and more individualized instruction, they have not yet shown academic improvement.

Contracting the management of entire schools is quite a new phenomenon. Yet experience points to at least three issues that must be carefully considered as districts entertain this form of educational reform. First, school boards must develop means by which to ensure that private firms maintain public accountability for educational goals and financial management.

Second, appropriate balances need to be struck between the business and educational expertise required to operate a school successfully. Building on these different kinds of expertise in a collaborative and professional manner is critical.

Third, the locus of decision-making authority must be explicitly spelled out. It is difficult to hold contractors accountable for performance if they do not have authority over such critical matters as personnel management, budget, and curriculum.[26]

Voucher Plans

Vouchers are government payments to households, redeemable only for tuition payments at authorized private schools.[27] Parents choose which school their child will attend, subject to any admission requirements or selection procedure the school may have established. Vouchers are controversial for several reasons, two of which are especially central to the debate. First, because private schools can select which students they will accept, opponents are concerned that vouchers may serve primarily those least in need, leaving public schools the province of only the most economically and educationally disadvantaged. Second, it is unclear whether vouchers to religious schools violate the constitutional requirement of separation of church and state.[28]

The *Lemon* decision and other key federal cases indicate that the Supreme Court is moving in the direction of being more accommodating of government funding that affects religiously affiliated schools.

On the other hand, voucher proponents charge that public schools operate as monopolies, holding captive students who, though not receiving adequate educations, have few educational options because private schools are beyond their financial means.[29] Finally, this section discusses the limited evidence concerning the outcomes of the nation's first publicly supported voucher program, in Milwaukee, Wisconsin.

Who Will Be Served by Vouchers?

Voucher proposals run along a continuum. Pure free marketers, such as economist Milton Friedman, would provide every family with school-age children a voucher redeemable at any private or public school.[30] Those who champion this approach assert that supply would take care of demand, in other words, that voucher-redeeming schools would exist in appropriate locations and with appropriate educational approaches to meet a wide range of students' educational needs.

The other end of the voucher continuum is anchored by proposals such as those advanced by UC Berkeley law professors Jack Coons and Steven Sugarman. While they accept much of the market argument (such as that supply and demand would be in equilibrium), they advocate that voucher plans be targeted to students most disadvantaged by the current public education system, particularly those in inner cities.[31,32]

A critical variable in different voucher plans is whether voucher-accepting schools can charge tuition which exceeds the voucher amount. Critics charge that "partial vouchers" will disproportionately benefit middle- and upper-income families, who can afford to pay the remainder of the tuition bill.

The Constitutionality of Vouchers

The first amendment to the Constitution states that "Congress shall make no law respecting an establishment of religion, nor prohibiting the free exercise thereof." The first half of this sentence, commonly referred to as the establishment clause, creates a prohibition against the establishment of religions or religious organizations by the federal government, and, through the Fourteenth Amendment, by state governments as well. The second half of the sentence, or free exercise clause, guarantees the right of individuals to practice their religions freely.

It is the tension between these two clauses that frames much of the discussion regarding the constitutionality of vouchers. Is, for example, the use of tax dollars to support church-affiliated schools through a voucher program a violation of the establishment clause? When does ensuring against the "establishment" of a government-sanctioned religious organization infringe on citizens' rights to practice their religion freely? The issue is a critical concern in the voucher debate because 82% of private schools are religiously affiliated.[33]

Both federal and state courts have grappled with these issues in school-related cases for decades.[34] In 1925, the U.S. Supreme Court upheld the right of parents to send their children to private—including church-affiliated—schools.[35] In 1947, the Court held that it is not a violation of the Constitution for local governments to fund public transportation of students to religious schools if they are also funding transportation of students attending public schools.[36] However, in 1971 the Court decided in *Lemon v. Kurtzman*[37] that state aid to parochial schools was a violation of the establishment clause. (The *Lemon* case dealt with Rhode Island and Pennsylvania statutes that provided for direct payment of salary supplements by the state to teachers of secular subjects in religiously affiliated schools.) The court devised a three-pronged test for determining whether financial subsidies to private schools are constitutional. Financial contributions from the state must (1) have a secular purpose, (2) not have the principal effect of advancing or inhibiting religion, and (3) not result in excessive government entanglement with religion.

The *Lemon* decision has been used by courts in subsequent cases to decide the constitutionality of financial assistance plans involving private schools. However, the application of the *Lemon* test has resulted in very different court decisions for similar cases. For example, in 1973 the Supreme Court considered a New York statute that provided tax deductions and some tuition reimbursements to low-income parents who enrolled their children in private, including religious, schools.[38] In this case, the Court held that the New York law violated the second prong of the *Lemon* test because it, in effect, advanced religion. However, in 1983, the Court ruled that a Minnesota statute which created a tax deduction program for private, religiously affiliated education did not violate the *Lemon* test because the program included both public and private school families.[39] In two more recent cases, the Court held that (1) a state could provide funds for vocational rehabilitation services for a blind student to attend a Christian college[40] and (2) a school district can provide a sign language interpreter to a deaf student attending a Catholic high school.[41] Most recently, the Court made it easier for federal Title I programs to be conducted on site in religious schools.[42]

Overall, it is not yet clear whether Milwaukee's voucher-redeeming schools offer a significant improvement over public schools.

The *Lemon* decision and other key federal cases seem to indicate that the Supreme Court is moving in the direction of being more accommodating of government funding that affects religiously affiliated schools, particularly when that funding goes to the student or student's parents and does not directly benefit the religious school itself.[34] However, how the Court will decide future cases remains unclear.

The Milwaukee Experiment

Much of the debate regarding the pros and cons of vouchers is academic as only two voucher plans are operational.[43] Milwaukee is the home of the first publicly financed voucher program, which initially included only nonsectarian private schools. Its intended expansion to religious schools has sparked a found of court battles.

The Milwaukee Plan was promoted principally by African-American legislators, community activists, the city's mayor, and Wisconsin's governor, who believed the public school system was educationally short-changing minority students in particular. When the legislature authorized the plan, it was quickly challenged and then upheld on a 1992 five-to-four decision by the state supreme court.

Under the Milwaukee Plan, public school students may attend private (currently nonsectarian) schools. Each participating school receives an amount per pupil equal to the average paid by the state to public schools. The program, geared specifically to disadvantaged students, was originally limited to 1% of the public school population (fewer than 1,000 students); in 1996, it was expanded to 3,500 students. It imposes little government oversight on participating schools. In 1995, the Wisconsin legislature amended the authorizing statute for the Milwaukee Plan to include religious schools.[44] A new suit challenging the program's constitutionality was filed, and proponents and opponents await the court's decision.

A study of the Milwaukee program by University of Wisconsin–Madison Professor John Witte found that achievement gains (as measured by scores on standardized tests) are spotty, at best, proving neither proponents' assertions that performance gains would be readily apparent nor opponents' claims that the program is a failure. Moreover, stated Witte, definitive achievement results are complicated by the fact that students need several sustained years in a school to test the program effects, and the participating voucher schools have experienced a high rate of attrition.[45]

However, a new study of the same achievement data by researchers from Harvard and the University of Houston declares Witte's study "methodologically flawed." This analysis, say the researchers, shows that vouchers make a significant achievement difference, that after three or four years in the Milwaukee program, reading scores of low-income minority children in voucher schools were 3 to 5 percentile points higher than reading scores of comparable public school students and mathematics scores were 5 to 12 points higher.[46]

The U.S. Supreme Court is likely at some point to hear another voucher case, and even constitutional lawyers are hard pressed to predict the outcome.

Overall, it is not yet clear whether Milwaukee's voucher-redeeming schools offer a significant improvement over public schools. The related question of whether Catholic schools (which enroll more than half of all private school students nationally) offer a significant educational advantage to economically disadvantaged students is addressed in Appendix C in this journal issue.*

Cleveland's Voucher Program

Cleveland's voucher program, which took effect at the start of the 1996–97 school year, was enacted into law by the Ohio legislature in 1995. Overseen by the state board of education (the district was put in receivership in March 1995), the program provides vouchers worth $2,500 for low-income parents to send children in grades K–3 to private sectarian and nonsectarian schools. Money to fund the voucher program comes from the state education budget.

When the program was announced, 6,000 families applied; 2,000 children, more than a quarter of whom (27%) were already attending private schools, were selected by lottery to receive the vouchers.[47] Of the 48 participating voucher schools, 37 are religiously affiliated, prompting an immediate court challenge.

In the initial trial, the Ohio court ruled that the voucher program does not violate either the state or federal constitution: "This court is persuaded that the nonpublic sectarian schools put in the scholarship [voucher] program are benefited only indirectly and purely as the result of the genuinely independent and private choices of aid recipients."[48] However, on May 1, 1997, a three-judge panel of the Ohio 10th District Court of Appeals unanimously struck down Cleveland's voucher program. The court ruled

*Does not appear in this publication.

that the state's experiment with school vouchers is unconstitutional because it "provides direct and substantial non-neutral government aid to sectarian schools." The case is now on appeal to the Ohio Supreme Court.[49]

Vouchers remain controversial. Continuing court challenges are virtually assured. The U.S. Supreme Court is likely at some point to hear another voucher case, and even constitutional lawyers are hard pressed to predict the outcome. Achievement data remain indeterminate.

Conclusions

The reforms reviewed in this article—charter schools, contract schools, and vouchers—focus on schools as the central "units of production." Each, implicitly or explicitly, conveys in its method of organization the understanding that school- or classroom-based diagnosis of and adaptability to individual students' learning needs are a critical component of a successful education program. Having said that, it is important to note that scant empirical data are yet available on which to make sound judgments regarding the efficacy of any of these reforms.

Half the states have ventured into experiments with charter laws, though some allow only limited delegation of authority to the charter operators. Those who open charter schools face major challenges of finance, governance, and management.

Contracting with private agencies to run entire schools may be an important innovation. No clear successes have yet been demonstrated, and some highly visible contracts have been cancelled, but the national experience with contracting is still much too limited to draw conclusions about the viability of this option.

Vouchers still face important federal and state constitutional challenges, as well as strong political opposition. Their efficacy is, as yet, unclear.

1. Cremin, L. *The American common school: An historic conception.* New York: Teachers College, Columbia University, 1951.
2. U.S. Department of Education, National Center for Education Statistics. *Digest of education statistics, 1996.* Washington, DC: U.S. Government Printing Office, 1996, pp. 12, 96.
3. Bose, J. *Characteristics of the 100 largest public elementary and secondary school districts in the United States.* Washington, DC: National Center for Education Statistics, June 1996.
4. Kerchner, C., Koppich, J., and Weeres, J. *United mind workers: Unions and teaching in the knowledge society.* San Francisco: Jossey-Bass, 1997.
5. However, charter schools must abide by federal statutes, such as civil rights laws.
6. Education Commission of the States. *Clearinghouse notes: Charter school statistics.* Denver, CO: ECS, March 1997, p. 7.
7. California, for example, allows only local school boards to grant charters. Michigan empowers local boards as well as universities and community colleges to do so. Wisconsin and Minnesota authorize the state board of education to approve charters. Arizona has established a separate board for charter schools.
8. Education Commission of the States. *Charter schools: What are they up to?* Denver, CO: ECS, 1995.
9. Integrated interdisciplinary curricula incorporate different disciplines into one theme or project. For example, the study of local waterways could incorporate local history, science, math, and writing.
10. States included in the survey were Arizona, California, Colorado, Massachusetts, Michigan, Minnesota, and Wisconsin. Partial data were collected on an additional 8 charter schools, bringing the total studied to 43. Finn, C. E., Jr., Manno, B. V., and Bierlein, L. *Charter schools in action: What have we learned?* Washington, DC: Hudson Institute, August 1996, pp. 27, 37–41, 90–91.
11. The U.S. Department of Education in 1996 began a four-year study of charter schools designed to examine their implementation, impact on students, and effect on public education. The study will include yearly telephone interviews with all operational charter schools nationally, plus field visits and longitudinal assessment of student achievement in a sample of charter schools. Office of Educational Research and Improvement. *A study of charter schools: First year report 1997.* Washington, DC: U.S. Department of Education, 1997.
12. Bierlein, L. *Charter schools: Initial findings.* Denver: Education Commission of the States, March 1996.
13. Bierlein, L. A., and Fulton, M. F. *Emerging issues in charter school financing.* ECS Policy Brief. Denver, CO: Education Commission of the States, May 1996.
14. Schnaiberg, L. State charter laws get new round of attention. *Education Week* (June 25, 1997) 16,39:10,16. Available online at http://www.edweek.org.
15. The U.S. Department of Education's charter school Web site is located at http://www.uscharterschools.org.
16. Kerchner, C. T., and Koppich, J. E. *A union of professionals: Labor relations and education reform.* New York: Teachers College Press, 1993.
17. Charter schools also represent contracting arrangements when a private firm operates the school.
18. Toch, T. Do firms run schools well? *U.S. News and World Report.* January 8, 1996, pp. 46–49.
19. U.S. General Accounting Office. *Private management of public schools: Early experiences in four school districts.* GAO/HEHS-96-3. Washington, DC: GAO, April 1996. The GAO study did not examine Edison or Alternative Public Schools.
20. Because teachers in Baltimore remained employees of the school district, EAI had only a contract to *manage* schools, not to *operate* them. An important feature of an operating contract is the ability to control the selection of employees. The concept of operating contracts for public schools is explored in depth in Hill, P., Pierce, L., and

Guthrie, J. *Reinventing public education.* Chicago: University of Chicago Press, 1997.

21. EAI attempted to claim that first-year test scores had risen, but when an analysis showed they had not, EAI was forced to take back this assertion.
22. University researchers evaluated seven EAI-managed schools and seven "matched" public schools. Williams, L. C., and Leak, L. E. *The University of Maryland Baltimore County evaluation of the Tesseract Program in Baltimore.* Baltimore: Center for Education Research, University of Maryland Baltimore City, August 1995.
23. An independent audit criticized EAI for "booking" school budgets as corporate revenue even though most of the money was liened.
24. EAI was also hired to manage the South Pointe Elementary School in Dade County (Miami). A study of that experience concluded that "South Pointe students did not improve their academic skills beyond what they would have achieved had they attended a regular Dade County public school." Abella, R. *Evaluation of the Saturn Project at South Pointe Elementary School.* Miami: Dade County Public Schools, July 1994. The contract was not renewed. EAI's contract to manage all 11 public schools in Hartford, Connecticut also was terminated.
25. The Edison project has been plagued by money problems. Unable to raise sufficient capital to implement its original ambitious goal of opening its own schools, Edison has instead opted to manage existing public schools.
26. These points are discussed in greater detail in Hill, P. T. Contracting in public education. In *New schools for a new century.* D. Ravitch and J. Viteritti, eds. New Haven: Yale University Press, 1997.
27. Privately funded voucher programs are not treated here.
28. For additional arguments against vouchers, see Lowe, R., and Miner, B., ed. *Selling out our schools: Vouchers, markets, and the future of public education.* Milwaukee, WI: Rethinking Schools, 1996.
29. Chubb, J., and Moe, T. *Politics, markets and America's schools.* Washington, DC: Brookings Institute, 1990.
30. Friedman, M. Public schools: Make them private. *Wall Street Journal.* February 19, 1995, at C7.
31. Coons, J. E., and Sugarman, S. D. The private school option in systems of educational choice. *Educational Leadership* (December 1990/January 1991) 48,4:54–56.
32. Coons, J. E., and Sugarman, S. D. The scholarship initiative: A model state law for elementary and secondary school choice. *Journal of Law and Education* (Fall 1992) 21,4:529–67.
33. National Center for Education Statistics. *Private schools in the United States: A statistical profile, 1990–91.* NCES 95-330. Washington, DC: U.S. Department of Education, Office of Educational Research and Improvement, 1995.
34. Even if the Supreme Court finds vouchers to be constitutionally permissible, a state court may find them to be a violation of the state constitution's establishment and/or free expression clauses. Some state courts have already done so. Kemberer, F. R., and King, K. L. Are school vouchers constitutional? *Phi Delta Kappan* (December 1995) 77,4:307–11.
35. *Pierce v. Society of Sisters,* 268 U.S. 510 (1925).
36. *Everson v. Board of Education,* 330 U.S. 1 (1947).
37. *Lemon v. Kurtzman,* 403 U.S. 602 (1971).
38. *Committee for Public Education and Religious Liberty v. Nyquist,* 413 U.S. 756 (1973).
39. *Mueller v. Allen,* 463 U.S. 388 (1983).
40. *Witters v. Washington Department of Services,* 474 U.S. 481 (1986).
41. *Zobrest v. Catalina Foothills School District,* 113 U.S. 2462 (1993).
42. *Agostini, et al. v. Felton, et al.* 117 S.Ct. 1997 (1997); *Chancellor, Board of Education of the City of New York, et al. v. Felton, et al.* 117 S.Ct. 1997 (1997).
43. Voters in California, Colorado, Oregon, and Washington have rejected voucher initiatives.
44. Nonsectarian private schools in Milwaukee currently are at capacity. Nearly 90% of private schools in the city are religious.
45. Forty percent of voucher students left voucher schools in the first year of the program.
46. Greene, J. P., and Peterson, P. E. Methodological issues in evaluation research: The Milwaukee school choice plan. Paper prepared for the program in Education Policy and Governance, Department of Government and Kennedy School of Government, Harvard University, August 29, 1996. Available at http://hdc-www.harvard.edu/pepg/op/witte2.html.
47. The program also provides $500 grants for tutoring for children on the voucher waiting list.
48. Walsh, M. Court clears Cleveland's voucher pilot. *Education Week* (August 7, 1996) 15,4:1,20. Available online at http://www.edweek.org.
49. Skertic, M., and Theis, S. Ohio court finds voucher illegal. *The Cincinnati Enquirer.* May 2, 1997. Available online at http://enquirer.com/editions/1997/05/02/oc_vouchers.html.

Article Review Form at end of book.

What are the arguments for and against school choice?

New Options, Old Concerns

We are witnessing an explosion of interest in creating new types of schools and giving parents the power to choose among them. But how will this affect our traditional democratic notions of public education for the common good?

John O'Neil

John O'Neil *is Senior Editor of* Educational Leadership.

Magnet schools, alternative schools, charter schools. Intra-district choice, inter-district choice, open enrollment. Back-to-basics schools, technology academies, schools designed for young African-American males.

In the past two decades, support has built for increasing the variety of options within public education, and for giving parents more power to decide which option suits their child best. Advocates say that greater variety among schools will increase the likelihood that parents will find a school that matches their educational values and their child's learning needs. By having a choice, moreover, parents are more likely to be involved in and committed to the school they've chosen than they would be if it had been assigned by school authorities. Further, the demand for schools of different types and quality could spur school officials to create more schools that "consumers" favor, or close or revamp programs with little support, some advocates say.

But even as the number of options grows, questions are increasingly being raised about the ultimate impact of the trends toward greater school variety and parental choice. Will choice result in more responsive, higher-quality schools and happier parents? Or will the proliferation of options further sort students and families by race, social class, and special interest, eroding our traditional democratic notions of a common school experience for all?

"If we are to take seriously the role of the public school in actualizing democratic mandates, the development of schools and school experiences cannot be left to the vagaries of consumer and family demand," Peter Hlebowitsh, associate professor of education at the University of Iowa, warns in a recent issue of the *NASSP Bulletin.* "The common school ideal, and its accompanying common causes, are made optional in a climate of choice and variety, where anything goes as long as there is client interest in it" (Hlebowitsh 1995).

Charter Schools Emerge

Public schools have always offered some variety, of course, but the push for options and choice has greatly intensified recently. In 1991, for example, Minnesota became the first state to pass a law allowing charter schools.[1] Now, 25 states and the District of Columbia have charter school laws, and 226 charter schools serve 28,000 students around the nation, according to a new report (American Federation of Teachers 1996).

The presumed benefits of charters are similar to those claimed for other choice programs. In well-conceived and well-run choice plans, "You create a school that *stands* for something substantively or pedagogically or both, and then you allow people to . . . select themselves to be there," says Mary Anne Raywid, professor emerita at Hofstra University and a longtime choice advocate. This allows both par-

O'Neil, John. (October 1996). "New Options, Old Concerns," EDUCATIONAL LEADERSHIP 54, 2: 6–8. Reprinted with permission of the Association for Supervision and Curriculum Development.

ents and teachers to commit to a common mission or focus of a school, rather than being assigned for strictly bureaucratic reasons. Raywid also believes that choice offers a ticket out for students stuck in low-performing schools. "It gives students a chance to attend a school of quality that they otherwise might not be able to attend, and it gets them out of poor schools." Because well-to-do families have always had the choice of moving where the best schools are, choice plans can give less advantaged families similar options.

Creating different school programs and offering parents choices among them makes sense because there is no "one best school" for every child, supporters say. Choice can support educational innovation, they say, by encouraging practioners to develop alternatives to the typical school program.

Creating different school programs and offering parents choices among them makes sense because there is no "one best school" for every child.

Increased Sorting?

Other experts warn that choice creates new problems or intensifies old ones. The most common concern is that, far from leveling the playing field, choice can exacerbate inequities. When schools must compete for students, "the kids who are the most desirable . . . are going to have an edge, and they're going to win those competitions," says Amy Stuart Wells, associate professor of educational policy at the University of California at Los Angeles. Adds Willis Hawley, education dean at the University of Maryland, "The people who will benefit are those who are the most aggressive, the most resourceful, and the most committed." The end result, some experts believe, is that the "best" students and the most involved parents will flee neighborhood schools for magnet programs or other specialized schools. Neighborhood schools will have difficulty sustaining such a loss.

In an article appearing in *Education Week,* Hawley (1996) argued that, "For many parents, the social, racial, and ethnic characteristics of a school's students are more important than a school's curriculums or its academic effectiveness in their selection of a school." School choice, Hawley wrote, "will reduce the opportunities that students of different racial and ethnic backgrounds have to learn from and about one another."

Other experts disagree, saying that the best choice plans are designed to mitigate such harmful effects. Raywid says that *all* schools in a district can be set up as distinctive schools of choice, so that certain schools aren't seen as second class. So-called "controlled choice" plans factor race and ethnicity into school assignments to ensure that parents' choices don't increase racial isolation. Transportation is provided to ensure students' access to a range of schools. And successful choice plans also include measures to inform parents of their options, such as school tours, parent liaisons, and choice fairs where schools publicize their offerings, Raywid says.

Private or Public Good?

Others, however, are concerned that the trends toward more options and greater choice represent a shift with dangerous philosophical overtones. More and more, they say, education is seen as a *private* good, with parents positioned as consumers of whatever public education best suits their needs. Losing credence is the argument that public education is provided for the *common* good, and that students should share some common experiences in common settings. Can this be achieved when schools hew largely to the demands of the market?

"What happens to democratic process and collective debate, including the voices of nonparents, when parents control the system as autonomous consumers?" writes David Tyack (1992), professor of education and history at Stanford University. "What happens to common purposes when the goal is individual satisfaction, to children with special needs when many schools are not required to deal with them, and to balanced academic standards when schooling is deregulated?"

Even supporters of choice have some nagging doubts. "I have some concerns that if schools become defined as belonging just to their immediate constituents, then it raises the question of why the rest of us should support them," says Raywid.

The prospect of voucher plans—which some see as the ultimate form of parental choice, but which many advocates of school choice staunchly oppose—tinges the discussion about options and choice. Are vouchers, which parents could use to send their children to a private school, the logical next step for school choice, or will vouchers continue to be limited to a handful of experimental programs involving low-income families? Most experts predict the latter. "The history of voucher propositions is that it will be very hard to find a coalition of people who support public funding going to private schools," says Tyack.

By having a choice, parents are more likely to be involved in and committed to the school they've chosen than they would be if it had been assigned by school authorities.

Ironically, the threat of vouchers may result in *more* support for choice, but choice limited to the public school system. "Public choice is probably getting a better hearing today, in part because people are very frightened by vouchers," says Raywid. It seems clear that, far from running out of steam, the trend toward more options and parental choice is as strong as it has every been.

1. Although states differ substantially in their specific laws, charter schools are essentially public schools that operate independently of their local school district.Typically, charter schools are started by groups of parents and teachers who want to create alternatives to the programs offered by the local district. They are granted a charter by (depending on the state) the local school board,the state, or another entity. Charter schools receive public funding and, to maintain their charter, they must meet agree-upon performance goals.

References

American Federation of Teachers. (1996). *Charter School Laws: Do They Measure Up?* Washington, D.C.: American Federation of Teachers.

Hawley, W. (April 10, 1996). "The Predictable Consequences of School Choice." *Education Week* XV, 29: 47, 56.

Hlebowitsh, P. (September 1995). "Can We Find the Traditional American School in the Idea of Choice?" *NASSP Bulletin* 79, 572:1–11.

Tyack, D. (Fall 1992). "Can We Build a System of Choice That Is Not Just a 'Sorting Machine' or a Market-Based 'Free-for-All'?" *Equity and Choice* 9, 1: 13–17.

Article Review Form at end of book.

According to Tony Wagner, what should be educators' attitude toward school choice programs?

School Choice

To what end?

The fulfillment of free market fantasies, Mr. Wagner opines, should not be the primary objective of school choice.

Tony Wagner

Tony Wagner, a former teacher and principal, is president of the Institute for Responsive Education, Boston; a visiting associate professor at Northeastern University, Boston; and the author of a study of school reform, How Schools Change: Lessons from Three Communities *(Beacon Press, 1994).*

We all want more choices. It has become a part of the American consumer dream. So we all want some form of school choice. But as with so many things in our shopping mall paradise, there is a great deal of hype about school choice—interspersed with a few facts.

This said, I still favor school choice as a strategy for making fundamental educational change. The problem is to distinguish the free market fantasies from the realities of what is needed to make school better.

Fantasy 1. We can create a privatized, "free market" education system. Unless you're running a specialized service or a school for would-be truck drivers, beauticians, or computer technicians, there is very little money to be made in the "schooling" business.

The economic facts are simple. About 85% of the cost of both public and private schools is devoted to personnel. Education is a labor-intensive business. If you want to cut costs, you either have to pay workers much less or hire fewer of them. The former is being tried—with little success to date. And with regard to the latter, having fewer teachers means increasing class size. But all the current research suggest that smaller classes are a key to higher student achievement. So how can private companies promise both to raise student achievement and to make money at the same time?

The promising is easy. The delivery isn't. Education Alternatives, Inc., is on the verge of going out of business. And the Edison Project has been scaled down radically. Remember the idea of franchising hundreds of new schools around the country and giving every student a computer at home? These things aren't happening. (The older students in one Edison school I recently visited were finally getting their computers, eight months after the school opened, but the school library had almost no books on the shelves!) Remember the promise to provide a better education for the same money—about $5,500 per pupil? Here in Boston, Edison's flagship school is struggling to make ends meet with a very favorable building lease from the state and more than $7,200 per pupil in district funds.

Edison may make some bucks on its slick new curricula. But it is worth noting that much of the Edison approach to teaching and curriculum came from the nonprofit sector—gratis! Edison borrows heavily from the work of Theodore Sizer, Howard Gardner, and James Comer, though they are not given any credit for their contributions of intellectual capital.

There is another reason why there will never be a "free" market in education, and it is an economic reason as well: lack of sufficient venture capital. Starting a new school is a very expensive proposition. I serve on the board of a Boston charter school—City on a Hill—which has raised about $350,000 in start-up money. That money has gone for planning and curriculum development, computers, books, supplies, a pilot summer program, and so on. City on a Hill's classroom and athletic facilities are very modest and come through a lease arrangement with the local YMCA. If the school loses its lease, it will face serious difficulties. These days, only middle-class public school communities and elite private schools with well-heeled alumni can afford to buy or build new facilities.

Early indications are that many charter schools around the nation are finding it difficult to raise start-up money. So where is all the capital going to come from to start thousands of new schools? Good question—especially when we don't yet know where we're going to get the estimated $113 billion needed just to repair existing public school facilities.

Fantasy 2. Greater choice of schools will automatically create better schools. At the moment, public school choice in many communities resembles the "choices" we had in cars during the Fifties. The name plates, the bells, and the whistles differed from one model to the next, but all the cars self-destructed in a couple of years, and people died in them at about the same rate. It's also not unlike the choice between major competitors in the soft drink industry. We have a choice between Coke and Pepsi, but neither one of them is particularly good for us. A "free" market isn't always free, and it certainly doesn't guarantee a better product.

I live in Cambridge, Massachusetts, a city that has had controlled choice among its 13 K-8 schools for nearly 15 years. School choice, by itself, has not produced significant improvements in these schools. The majority of the 13 seem virtually interchangeable and are mediocre. Several of the schools enjoy good reputations that stem in large part from the effective leadership of dynamic principals. But these schools are oversubscribed. Parents do not often get their first choice of school, and the most innovative principals have told me that they have to continue to fight the central office to maintain their programs. So what has school choice accomplished in Cambridge?

The key questions for the school choice movement, then, are questions of purpose. Is the goal to scare educators into doing more with dire threats of increased competition? Or is the goal to placate parents with the illusion of greater consumer "freedom"? If it is either one of these, the results will be very disappointing. People can be frightened or fooled only for so long—especially as students continue to be poorly educated. As a social policy, school choice must be linked to a vision of real educational change rather than to fantasies of a free market.

Reality 1. We need "skunk works" schools to do research and development. To create new products, investment in R&D—research and development—is essential. If we want a dramatically better product from our education system, then we must provide opportunities and incentives to our brightest educational entrepreneurs.

An R&D strategy used increasingly in the business world is to spin off a small working group of innovators—often called a "skunk works." This group is given additional resources and the autonomy to develop new products or to improve processes. If it is successful, then that group leads the way in transforming the rest of the organization.

We need lots of new "skunk works" schools of choice to perform the same functions for American education. The new schools in New York City and Philadelphia, the "pilot schools" in Boston, the schools sponsored by the New American Schools Development Corporation, and some members of the Coalition of Essential Schools are doing important R&D. But every large school district in the country should be engaged in similar efforts.

Some of the charter schools are also committed to doing R&D. To guarantee that more charter schools serve this function, the application process in many states could be replaced by a "Request for Proposals" that would require applicants to explain what "best practices" they will explore, how they will ensure that they have a representative sample of students with equal access, how they plan to assess outcomes, and how they plan to disseminate results.

Assessment will be complicated. Comparative studies will probably show that students who attend charter schools achieve more. But these outcomes may have little to do with charters per se. Smaller size and consensus about a school's mission are likely to be the most important ingredients for success. Which leads me to my next point.

Reality 2. Public education must be reinvented, not merely reformed; we need a greater diversity of small schools in which students, teachers, and families agree on a shared mission and work together closely. A central lesson of the Industrial Era in American education is that the assembly-line approach to learning produces a standardized product in high volume, but of low quality. School choice among varieties of assembly-line schools is no choice at all. One size clearly does not fit all. All learning must be personalized. Allowing people to create or to choose from a greater variety of small schools will permit better matches between teachers, students, and families. Smaller schools will also give teachers more opportunities to individualize learning for all children.

It is increasingly clear as well that significant improvements in learning for all students require closer collaboration between schools and families. People working together in smaller schools can build strong relationships and come to agreement more readily on their unifying mission and core values. Perhaps more important than new state charter school legislation are the new district policies and flexible funding strategies in New York, Boston, and Philadelphia that encourage groups to start small, semi-autonomous schools within existing public school buildings.

By itself, school choice is not a meaningful reform. It is but one strategy for encouraging new approaches to teaching and learning and for building a greater sense of community in our schools. It is a way of creating the preconditions for change, so that the truly difficult and important work of reinventing American education can move forward.

Article Review Form at end of book.

WiseGuide Wrap-Up

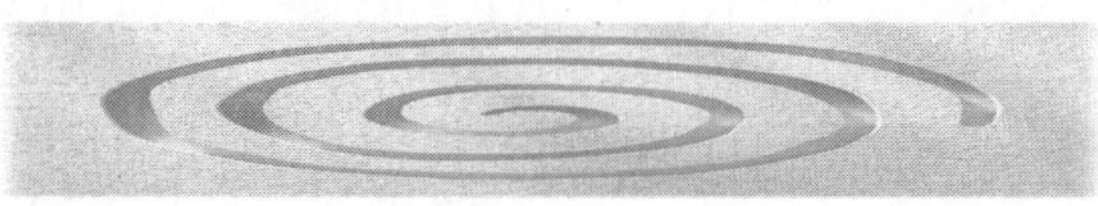

- Controversial educational issues often stem from the tension between public and private education and from societal problems (for example, violence).
- A variety of educational options exist, with three of the most popular being charter schools, voucher systems, and private contracts.
- Contemporary curricular issues center around the core knowledge movement, national education standards, and specialized content (for example, values clarification, moral education).
- Educators must communicate effectively with colleagues, parents, students, and other noneducators.

R.E.A.L. Sites

This list provides a print preview of typical **coursewise** R.E.A.L. sites. There are over 100 such sites at the **courselinks**™ site. The danger in printing URLs is that web sites can change overnight. As we went to press, these sites were functional using the URL provided. If you come across one that isn't, please let us know via email to: webmaster@coursewise.com. Use your Passport to access the most current list of R.E.A.L. sites at the **courselinks**™ site.

Site name: Pathways to School Improvement—North Central Regional Educational Laboratory

URL: http://www.ncrel.org/sdrs/pathwayt.htm

Why is it R.E.A.L.? This site is a comprehensive reference for information on common educational issues, including assessment, at-risk students, early childhood education, governance of public schools, achievement in mathematics, preservice teacher education, professional development, and technology.

Key topics: educational issues, assessment, preservice education, professional development, technology, at-risk students

Activity: Choose one of the issues addressed at the site, and write a summary of the concerns or controversial components of the issue.

Site name: Developing Educational Standards

URL: http://putwest.boces.org/Standards.html

Why is it R.E.A.L.? This site includes comprehensive information on the philosophy supporting educational standards and on existing standards.

Key topics: educational standards

Activity: Request a copy of state standards for your certification area from your state Department of Education.

Site name: Violence in the Schoolhouse: A 10-Year Update

URL: http://www.townhall.com/townhall/spotlights/9-11-95/is94e5cr.html

Why is it R.E.A.L.? Information and updates on classroom violence focus on trends established during the past 10 years, the impact on public school classrooms, the nature of violence, types of classroom violence, characterizations and victims of violence, strategies to address classroom violence, and causes of violent behavior.

Key topics: classroom violence

Activity: After interviewing a local high school principal, write a newspaper article about the number and types of violent acts at that high school in the past year.

Assessing Our Position: Participating in Reflective Conversations on Selected Innovations

Learning Objectives

After reading the articles in this section, you will be able to:

- Identify some of the most popular innovations being implemented in today's classrooms.
- Discuss the role of authentic assessments in teacher preparation programs.
- Discuss the role of full-service schools in meeting the needs of public school students.
- Explain why students prefer a balance between distance education and on-site course delivery methods.
- Discuss the benefits of belonging to a learning community.

Educators must be risk takers. They must be willing to experiment with new models, new strategies, and new paradigms that are built on a solid, or at least emerging, knowledge base. They must be willing to adjust their attitudes and actions as the needs of their students and the learning community change. They must have a desire to contribute to the knowledge base by applying new strategies and then sharing the results with colleagues. All of these predispositions describe innovative teachers who are leaders within their school systems.

Just as teachers should be innovators, so should school systems. Systemic change is often necessary to ensure that the needs of teachers, students, parents, and community members are adequately met. Effective innovations at the organizational level require large-scale support and collaboration. To ensure appropriate acceptance of and participation in innovations, preservice teachers must understand the role of innovation in individual classrooms, the role of the classroom teacher in an innovative school system, and the relationship between research findings and innovative practice.

The readings in this section are representative of the wide variety of educational innovations, with an emphasis on teacher productivity and student achievement. The first reading, "Semantics, Psychometrics, and Assessment Reform: A Close Look at 'Authentic' Assessment," discusses the role of authentic assessment in a comprehensive evaluation plan. The next reading, "Full-Service Schools," examines schools that provide comprehensive programs aimed at meeting the academic, social, and physical needs of all students. Innovative formats—specifically, block schedules—are the focus of the next reading, "Steps for Improving School Climate in Block Scheduling." The fourth reading, "Distance Education: Does Anyone Really Want to Learn at a Distance?" is representative of innovations in course delivery strategies. Learning communities, as discussed in the last reading, "Creating Intentional Learning Communities," are new models for professional communication and support.

Questions

Reading 27: According to James Terwilliger, what is the role of authentic assessments within an overall evaluation plan? Why do empiricists question authentic assessments?

Reading 28: What are full-service schools? What are two major reasons for the increasing number of full-service schools?

Reading 29: Before deciding to implement block scheduling, building faculty and administrators must consider a variety of issues. Which issues have the greatest impact on a decision to move to a block schedule?

Reading 30: What is perhaps the one crucial element that ensures success of distance education programs?

Reading 31: How do learning communities differ from traditional organizations?

According to James Terwilliger, what is the role of authentic assessments within an overall evaluation plan? Why do empiricists question authentic assessments?

Semantics, Psychometrics, and Assessment Reform

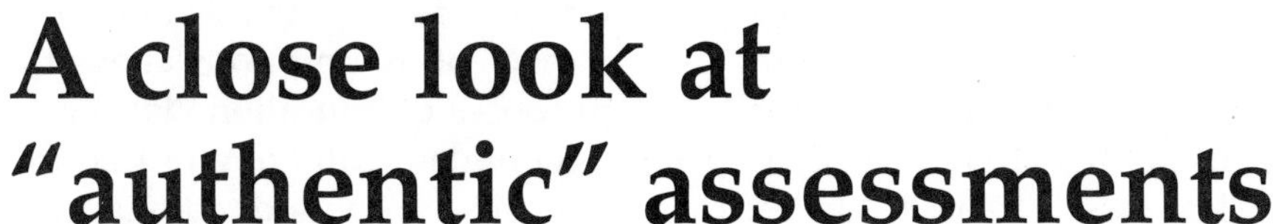

School reform advocates have argued that "authentic" classroom assessments are complex performances or exhibitions that "are designed to be truly representative of performance in the field." The use of "authentic" implies that such assessments are superior to more conventional assessments. However, proponents of "authentic" assessment rarely present data, evidential or consequential, in support of the validity of "authentic" assessments. Further, as typically conceived, "authenticity" denigrates the importance of knowledge and basic skills as legitimate educational outcomes despite substantial evidence to the contrary. It is suggested that "authentic" be discontinued in future scholarly discussions of classroom assessment.

It is obvious to even the most casual reader of the literature on educational assessment that the field is currently undergoing a fundamental and profound transformation. The traditional concepts and methodologies associated with assessment are being questioned by a variety of critics including school reform advocates, subject matter experts, cognitive theorists, and others. In general, advocates for change recommend the assessments of achievement should be designed to reflect more precisely complex "real-life" performances and problems than is possible with short-answer and choice-response questions that characterize many teacher-made tests.

The purpose of this article is to raise question about the claims that are frequently made by advocates of assessment reform. My critique focuses on the work of Wiggins (1989a, 1989b, 1993), who first introduced the concept of "authentic" assessment and who is one of the most influential critics of traditional assessment approaches. However, it is clear that the notion of "authenticity" has widespread appeal. A computer search of the ERIC database reveals 96 journal articles or papers published since 1989 with the phrase "authentic assessment" in the title. Several journals have devoted special issues to the topic, e.g., *Educational Leadership* (December 1996/January 1997), *Journal of Secondary Gifted Education* (vol. 6, no. 1), and *Middle School Journal* (vol. 25, no. 2). Darling-Hammond and her colleagues at Teachers College have produced a book (Darling-Hammond, Ancess, & Falk, 1995) and numerous technical reports

From EDUCATIONAL RESEARCHER, Vol. 26, No. 8, Nov. 1997, pp. 24–27. Reprinted with permission of American Educational Research Association.

on the use of "authentic assessment" in the New York schools.

I wish to make it clear at the outset that I do not oppose some of the ideas that have been put forth by advocates of "authentic" assessment. In fact, I agree that assessment practices are in need of reform. However, I believe that, as is often the case, the rhetoric of the reformers is misleading and largely unsupported by data. (This point was made several years ago by Beck (1991) but seems to have been ignored.) I fear that there is a danger that perfectly useful and appropriate assessment methods will be discarded in a rush to adopt a variety of other techniques of unknown psychometric and educational quality. I believe that alternative assessment procedures should be adopted in combination with more traditional forms of assessment as evidence of the educational and psychometric value of such alternatives becomes available.

Word Magic and Assessment Reform

The *American Heritage Dictionary* gives the following definitions of "authentic":

> 1. a. Worthy of trust, reliance, or belief: *authentic records.* b. Having an undisputed origin: genuine.
> 2. Law. Executed with due process of law: *an authentic deed.*

Synonyms are listed as "real," "genuine," and "authoritative." Obviously, terms like these have a decidedly positive connotation. Therefore, objects or products to which these terms are applied are likely to be viewed as more desirable or of better quality than objects or products that are not so described. That is why these terms appear so frequently in commercials and advertisements in the popular media, e.g., statements such as "Coke is the *real* thing!," "*Genuine* factory auto parts," and "*Authentic* French cuisine." A bakery chain in the Twin Cities has recently introduced Renaissance breads with the slogan, "Authentic handmade breads in the European tradition."

It seems that the word "authentic" has an almost mystical power. Phrases such as "authentic instruction," "authentic performance," and "authentic outcomes" are appearing with increasing frequency in the educational literature. (One can only speculate about forms of instruction, performance, and outcomes that might be labeled "inauthentic.") One of the more memorable titles in the Teachers College series is "An Authentic Journey: Teachers' Emergent Understandings About Authentic Assessment and Practice" (Einbender & Wood, 1995).

A variety of books with titles such as *Authentic Assessment in Action* (Darling-Hammond et al., 1995) and *Assessment of Authentic Performance in School Mathematics* (1992) have been published. Lesh and Lamon, the editors of the latter book, provide the following interesting definition:

> Stated simply, authentic mathematical activities are those that involve: (i) real mathematics, (ii) realistic situations, (iii) questions or issues that might actually occur in a real-life situation, and (iv) realistic tools and resources. (p. 18)

There are two problems with this definition. First, as previously noted, words like "real," "realistic," and "real-life" are synonymous with the word "authentic." Therefore, the definition is circular. Second, and more fundamental, what constitutes "realistic" or "real-life" situations and "realistic" tools and resources are frequently open to debate. What appears to be "realistic" to one individual often seems to be "unrealistic" to another. One way to "objectively" define "real-life" questions and situations would be to construct a database that could be employed in defining the likelihood that a student would encounter specific questions, problems, and the like in nonschool settings. Lacking such a database, test designers typically rely on individual (or, perhaps, team) judgments of what is "realistic."

Educational assessment is a complex process that is built on a variety of assumptions about the purposes of education along with a set of data-gathering procedures that need to be judged against a series of both practical and technical standards. The use of labels that impute special status to a specific set of data collection procedures only serves to obscure fundamental assessment questions that must be addressed. For example, questions concerning the validity of assessment techniques help to focus discussion on relevant data instead of arguments about "authenticity." Therefore, terms like "authentic," "genuine," and "real-life" should be reserved for advertising copy and avoided in scholarly discussions of educational assessment.

Origins of "Authentic" Tests

The term "authentic" was first introduced in reference to tests by Wiggins (1989b) in an article in *Educational Leadership,* a journal for school administrators and general educators. Wiggins defined "authentic" tests in terms of complex

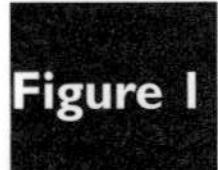

Figure 1 An example of a test of performance. Courtesy of Albin Moser, Hope High School, Providence, RI. To obtain a thorough account of a performance-based history course, including the lessons used and pitfalls encountered, write to Dave Kobrin, Brown University, Education Department, Providence, RI 02912. (From Wiggins, 1989b, p. 44.)

An Oral History Project for Ninth-Graders

To the student:

You must complete an oral history based on interviews and written sources and then present your findings orally in class. The choice of subject matter is up to you. Some examples of possible topics include: your family, running a small business, substance abuse, a labor union, teenage parents, and recent immigrants.

Create three workable hypotheses based on your preliminary investigations and four questions you will ask to test out each hypothesis.

Criteria for Evaluation of Oral History Project

To the teacher:

Did student investigate three hypotheses?

Did student describe at least one change over time?

Did student demonstrate that he or she had done background research?

Were the four people selected for the interviews appropriate sources?

Did student prepare at least four questions in advance, related to each hypothesis?

Were those questions leading or biased?

Were follow-up questions asked where possible, based on answers?

Did student note important differences between "fact" and "opinion" in answers?

Did student use evidence to prove the ultimate best hypothesis?

Did student exhibit organization in writing and presentation to class?

performances or exhibitions in which a student completes a report or makes a public presentation following an extended period of work on an out-of-class assignment. Wiggins presents the example shown in Figure 1.

Wiggins concludes his discussion of "authentic" tests as follows:

> In sum, authentic tests have four basic characteristics in common. First, they are designed to be truly representative of performance in the field; only then are the problems of scoring reliability and logistics of testing considered. Second, far greater attention is paid to the teaching and learning of the *criteria* to be used in the assessment. Third, self-assessment plays a much greater role than in conventional testing. And fourth, the students are often expected to present their work and defend themselves publicly and orally to ensure that their apparent mastery is genuine. (p. 45)

It is instructive to examine the example Wiggins gives in light of the four characteristics he claims all "authentic" tests share. First, what "field" is represented in the oral history project? Because the choice of topic is left to the student, the "field" must be history with special emphasis on techniques employed by historians who employ "first-person" sources in their research. In fact, this approach is hardly "truly representative of performance in the field" if the "field" is more broadly defined as history because the great majority of historians rely on written rather than "first-person" sources in their work.

Second, it is not clear that the criteria for evaluation of the project were shared with the students. (In fact, the example strongly suggests that the criteria were for the teacher only.) Therefore, how could they have been "taught and learned"? Even if the criteria were shared with the students in advance, what exactly would a teacher expect them to learn from them? Most students would use the criteria as a checklist to make certain they had satisfied the teacher's demands before turning their projects in for evaluation by the teacher! Because many of these criteria are very specific to the particular project, they appear to have limited value as general learning outcomes.

As an aside, it is not clear from the criteria presented exactly how they are to be employed in evaluating the projects. Because most of the questions posed can readily be answered "yes" or "no," it would be possible to devise a simple checklist. Obviously, a more elaborate scoring system could also be designed, but the example provides no clues if that is the case. As is the case in all examples he gives in his writings, Wiggins provides no data regarding the reliability of scoring (or the amount of time devoted to scoring) the "authentic" tasks he recommends. The lack of supporting data is a reflection of the secondary role Wiggins gives to such issues in his reference to "scoring reliability and logistics of testing" in the above quote.

Third, there is no indication that self-assessment is involved in the oral history project.

Finally, it is clear that the oral history project does involve an oral presentation to the class. Presumably, the oral presentation may also be followed by a discussion during which the presenter would have to answer questions and defend his or her work.

"Authenticity" and Validity

Several issues are highlighted through the detailed comparison of the oral history example with the criteria for "authentic" tests given by Wiggins. The same example and criteria for "authenticity" were presented in a follow-up article (1989a) that appeared in the *Phi Delta Kappan*. First, it is not entirely clear what is meant by the phrase, "designed to be truly representative of performance in the field." What exactly is the "field" in this example? Who decides what is "truly representative" of the field? This raises questions regarding test *validity*. In his follow-up article, Wiggins's only reference to validity of "authentic" tests is the comment, "Far greater attention is paid throughout to the test's 'face' and 'ecological' validity" (1989a, p. 712). To focus on face validity is to concentrate only on the surface features of an assessment. To do so misses the point that the validity of an assessment device is fundamentally linked to how well the device reflects an underlying construct, e.g., analytical reasoning ability.

Messick (1994) has discussed at length issues associated with the validation of performance assessments. He cites the classic treatment of performance test by Fitzpatrick and Morrison (1971) in which they state, "there is no absolute distinction between performance tests and other classes of tests" (p. 238). Using this as a point of departure, Messick states

> Hence, performance assessments must be evaluated by the same validity criteria, both evidential and consequential, as are other assessments. Indeed, such basic assessment issues as validity, reliability, comparability, and fairness need to be uniformly addressed for all assessments because they are not just measurement principles, they are *social values* that have meaning and force outside of measurement wherever evaluative judgments and decisions are made. (p. 13)

With regard to special claims of "authenticity," Messick notes

> The portrayal of performance assessments as *authentic* and *direct* has all the earmarks of a validity claim but with little or no evidential grounding. That is, if authenticity is important to consider when evaluating the consequences of assessment for student achievement, it constitutes a tacit validity standard, as does the closely related concept of directness of assessment. We need to address what the labels authentic and direct might mean in validity terms. We also need to determine what kinds of evidence might legitimize both their use as validity standards and their nefarious implication that other forms of assessment are not only indirect, but inauthentic. (p. 14)

As previously noted, Wiggins presents *no* validity data, evidential or consequential, in any of his writings on "authentic" assessment.

Assessment and Educational Philosophy

A theme that runs through conceptions of "authentic" testing is an emphasis on performances that are designed to assess "higher order" outcomes. Wiggins (1989b, p. 45) lists several characteristics of "authentic" tests. Tests that are "authentic" should include tasks that are contextualized and complex, involve a student's own research, emphasize *depth* more than breadth, and involve somewhat "ill-structured" problems. He specifically disavows any interest in "atomized tasks," corresponding to "isolated outcomes," "mere recall," and "plug-in skills." Such pejorative terms make it clear that Wiggins has little respect for the assessment of knowledge or basic skills.

Wiggins (1993, pp. 222–225) gives examples of a variety of "roles and situations through which students can perform with knowledge." He argues that such roles could serve as "templates" for better test design because, "These roles and situational challenges are common to professional life" (p. 222). Wiggins claims it is a "logical fallacy" to argue that students must be given "drills" and "tests concerning their mastery of drills" before requiring performance in professional roles and situations. "Drill testing" is a means to an end, and "it is certainly not to be confused with the important performance itself" (p. 222).

Wiggins ignores the possibility that most "roles and situational challenges common to professional life" involve an extensive knowledge base. Individuals who lack the knowledge base have little or no chance of performing successfully in the "real-life" roles that he describes. For example, an historian typically specializes in a particular time period and geographical region for his or her research, e.g., Colonial America during the period 1650–1770. In order to make a useful contribution to the literature on this topic, the historian must first become familiar with a vast amount of work previously published by other historians working on this and related topics.

Knowledge and Expertise

The fundamental role played by knowledge in "real-life" is well documented in the extensive body of work on the nature of expertise. Chi, Glaser, and Farr (1988) have edited a series of papers that summarize much of the work in this field. In their overview of this work, Glaser and Chi list several "key characteristics" of the performance of experts. The first characteristic they cite is that expertise generally is restricted to specific domains of performance and does not transfer from one domain to another. They state

> The obvious reason for the excellence of experts is that they have a good deal of domain knowledge. This is easily demonstrated; for example, in medical diagnosis, expert physicians have more differentiations of common diseases into disease variants (Johnson et al., 1981). Likewise, in examining taxi drivers' knowledge of routes, Chase (1983) found that expert drivers can generate a far greater number of secondary routes (i.e., lesser known streets) than novice drivers. (1988, p. xvii)

Knowledge and Literacy

Wiggins's emphasis on roles "common to professional life" reflects a very narrow view of educational outcomes. Hirsch (1987) is critical of attempts to dismiss knowledge in favor of more lofty educational goals. He argues that the denigration of "mere facts" by advocates of instruction in "higher order" skills creates a false dichotomy.

> The polarization of educationists into facts-people versus skills-people has no basis in reason. Facts and skills are inseparable. There is no insurmountable reason why those who advocate the teaching of higher order skills and those who advocate the teaching of common traditional content should not join forces. No philosophical or practical barrier prevents them from doing so, and all who consider mature literacy to be a paramount aim of education will wish them to do so. (1987, p. 133)

Proponents of educational reform who stress "critical thinking" and similar "higher order" thinking skills should consider Hirsch's advice seriously when planning classroom instruction and assessment.

Conclusions

The promotion of "authentic" assessment, however well intentioned, is flawed in several respects. First, "authentic" is misleading and confusing. The term inappropriately implies that some assessment approaches are superior to others because they employ tasks that are more "genuine" or "real." This claim is based largely on an appeal to face validity, a concept that has been abandoned by modern psychometric theorists. Second, it is a mistake to deny the role of knowledge in the assessment of educational outcomes. To do so ignores a substantial body of theory and ample empirical evidence that supports the central role of knowledge in many domains of performance.

References

Beck, M. D. (1991, April). *"Authentic assessment" for large-scale accountability purposes: Balancing the rhetoric.* Paper presented at annual meeting of American Educational Research Association, Chicago.

Chi, M., Glaser, R., & Farr, M. (Eds.). (1988). *The nature of expertise.* Hillsdale, NJ: Lawrence Erlbaum Associates.

Darling-Hammond, L., Ancess, J., & Falk, B. (1995). *Authentic assessment in action: Studies of schools and students at work.* New York: Teachers College Press.

Einbender, L., & Wood, D. (1995). *An authentic journey: Teachers' emergent understandings about authentic assessment and practice.* New York: Columbia University, Teachers College National Center for Restructuring Education, Schools, and Teaching.

Fitzpatrick, R., & Morrison, E. (1971). Performance and product evaluation. In R. L. Thorndike (Ed.), *Educational measurement* (2nd ed., pp. 237–270) New York: American Council on Education/Macmillan.

Hirsch, E. D. (1987). *Cultural literacy: What every American needs to know.* New York: Houghton-Mifflin Co.

Lesh, R., & Lamon, S. (Eds.). (1992). *Assessment of authentic performance in school mathematics.* Washington, DC: AAAS Press.

Messick, S. (1994). The interplay of evidence and consequences in the validation of performance assessment. *Education Researcher, 23*(2), 13–23.

Wiggins, G. (1989a). A true test: Toward more authentic and equitable assessment. *Phi Delta Kappan, 20,* 703–713.

Wiggins, G. (1989b). Teaching to the (authentic) test. *Educational Leadership, 46,* 41–47.

Wiggins, G. (1993). *Assessing student performance.* San Francisco: Jossey-Bass Publishers.

Article Review Form at end of book.

What are full-service schools? What are two major reasons for the increasing number of full-service schools?

Full-Service Schools

Schools in which quality education and comprehensive social services are offered under one roof have the potential to become neighborhood hubs, where children and their families want to be.

Joy G. Dryfoos

Joy G. Dryfoos is an independent researcher supported by the Carnegie Corporation. She can be reached at 20 Circle Dr., Hastings-on-Hudson, NY 10706.

In the library of the Salome Urena Middle Academy at Intermediate School 218, three-member teams are hard at work over Spanish lessons. Two members of each group—a student and a parent—are instructing a third member—a police officer from the local precinct. In return for lessons in the language of this Washington Heights neighborhood, the officers—mostly white and non-Hispanic—invite these families to visit the police station and to stay in touch. This mutually beneficial arrangement, which combines educational lessons with parental and community involvement, is the result of a collaboration between a school system and the Children's Aid Society in New York City.

All over the country, school and community people are putting the pieces together to help schools meet the varied needs of today's students and their parents. I call the product of these collaborative efforts "full-service schools," a term first used in Florida's landmark legislation (Department of Health and Rehabilitative Services 1991). The creation of one-stop centers where the educational, physical, psychological, and social requirements of students and their families are addressed in a rational, holistic fashion is attractive to both school people and social service providers. Community agencies can relieve schools of the burden of changing high-risk behaviors and have direct access to the students every day.

What's driving this movement? As anyone who works in a school knows, more and more children are arriving every day not ready to learn. Families who have difficulty clothing, feeding, and housing their children have little time for traditional family nurturing and enrichment. A second factor is the movement toward integrating programs. Everyone is fed up with categorical approaches that don't cure anything. One day it's substance abuse prevention, then teen pregnancy, AIDS, suicide, and, lately, violence. The demands for immunizations, pregnancy tests, mental health counseling, family counseling, and crisis intervention cannot possibly be met by existing school personnel.

Creating a Full-Service School

As the model in Figure 1 shows, full-service schools aim to provide both quality education and support services. Under the menu for *quality education* are various ingredients that the literature indicates are critical to revitalizing schools (Dryfoos 1994). These items generally fall into the educational domain, and schools systems assume fiscal responsibility for providing them.

Under *support services* are examples of health, welfare, recreation, and life-enhancing pro-

Dryfoos, Joy G. (April 1996). "Full Service Schools." EDUCATIONAL LEADERSHIP 53, 7: 18–23. Reprinted with permission of the Association for Supervision and Curriculum Development.

Figure 1 The full-service school.

Quality Education Provided by Schools

Effective basic skills
Individualized instruction
Team teaching
Cooperative learning
School-based management
Healthy school climate
Alternatives to tracking
Parent involvement
Effective discipline

Services Provided by Schools or Community Agencies

Comprehensive health education
Health promotion
Social skills training
Preparation for the world of work (life planning)

Support Services Provided by Community Agencies

Primary health services
Health screening
Immunizations
Dental services
Family planning
Individual counseling
Group counseling
Substance abuse treatment
Mental health services
Nutrition/weight management
Referral with follow-up
Basic services: housing, food, clothes
Recreation, sports, culture
Mentoring
Family welfare services
Parent education, literacy
Child care
Employment training/jobs
Case management
Crisis intervention
Community policing
Legal aid
Laundry

grams that are in place in various combinations in schools around the country. Most of these programs are operated by community agencies that bring their own funding with them.

Other services, such as social skills training and life planning, might be provided by either schools or community agencies. The real challenge here is how to create a one-stop unfragmented collaborative institution. The answer is: with great patience and fortitude.

Various models of full-service schools are emerging in communities and schools with the greatest needs and the most disadvantaged populations. In such settings, the principal often acts not only as the leader in the restructuring, but also as the prime facilitator for assuring smooth integration of outside partners into the school environment. Security and maintenance are important issues.

Successful programs also rely on a full-time coordinator or program director, who builds a team of personnel sensitive to issues related to youth development, cultural diversity, and community empowerment. In many locations, bilingual staff are essential. A designated space such as a clinic or a center in a school acts as a focal point for bringing in services from the community. Indeed, the most important outcome of entering into the full-service schools process may be providing a magnet for other resources.

A Look at a Full-Service School

A recent conference on School-Linked Comprehensive Services for Children and Families identified 22 exemplary programs (U.S. Department of Education 1995). Intermediate School 218, mentioned earlier, is one of them. Let's look at some more ways that this New York City school is trying to serve its students and their families.

It's 7 a.m., and Intermediate School 218 is open for breakfast. Before school officially begins, students play sports or attend classes in dance and Latin band. Located in a new building in Washington Heights, the school offers students a choice of five self-contained academies: Business, Community Service, Expressive Arts, Ethics and Law, or Mathematics, Science, and Technology. A store in the school's attractive lobby sells supplies for students.

At the Family Resource Center, parents receive social services, including immigration, employment, and housing consultations. Social workers and mental health counselors are also on hand to serve students and their families. A primary health and dental clinic is on the premises.

After the official school day ends, the building stays open until 10 p.m. for educational enrichment, mentoring, sports, computer lab, music, arts, and entrepreneurial workshops. Teenagers are welcome to use the sports and arts facilities and to take classes along with adults on topics like English, computer work, and parenting skills. The school also stays open weekends and summers, offering the Dominican community many opportunities for cultural enrichment and family participation.

Intermediate School 218 is a true settlement house in a school, made possible through a partnership between the Children's Aid Society and Community School District 6.

More Exemplary Models

Another promising school-community collaboration can be found in Modesto, California. To better serve students and their families, this school system has formed partnerships with many outside agencies—public mental health, social services, health, probation, police, housing, and drug and alcohol agencies, as well as nonprofit health and service agencies.

The Hanshaw Middle School is open long hours to serve the needs of a deprived, largely Hispanic neighborhood (Modesto City Schools 1995). With support from Healthy Start—California's comprehensive school-linked services program—Hanshaw created a family resource center on the campus. The family center provides a wide range of activities—from aerobics classes to computer workshops. The center also houses an interagency case management team and a primary health care and dental clinic. A mental health clinician, on site every day, provides long-term family therapy and crisis intervention. After-school activities include sports and mentoring, and neighborhood outreach involves parents with school programs.

Another example of educational and support services provided under one roof can be found in the Bedford-Stuyvesant area of Brooklyn. The Decatur-Clearpool School, which opened in 1992, was designed to incorporate the Comer School Development Program (Knowles 1994). To provide varied services to its students and their families, this K–8 school collaborates with Clearpool, Sponsors for Educational Opportunity (both nonprofit organizations), and the Edwin Gould Foundation. An extended day program offers after-school activities for students. The Family Center offers many activities including mentoring, job training, and parent workshops. And, at the school's Health Center, run by the Brooklyn Hospital Center, students and their families receive medical, psychological, and social care.

The most unusual aspect of this school is a 335-acre residential center in the woods, the original Clearpool camp, which has been adapted for day trips and overnight academic retreats for Decatur students and their families. The year-round, two-campus school expects to add an extra 60–75 days to the school year.

Barriers to the Process

Attempting to provide so many services in one place, not surprisingly, is an immense undertaking. From the experiences of these and other promising models, we can learn about some of the obstacles to success.

• *Governance.* As would be expected, the more complex the model, the more demanding the administrative arrangements. The mounting rhetoric calls for sophisticated collaborative organizations, whereby school systems and community agencies leave behind their parochial loyalties and pitch in to form a new kind of union (Melaville et al. 1993).

In reality, most emerging models are shaped by state and foundation proclivities. A grant goes either to a school system, which then subcontracts for services, or to a community agency (designated as the lead organization), which enters the schools through a memorandum of agreement. In neither case is governance changed.

New Beginnings in San Diego, which has completed its first evaluation, warns that it's "difficult to overestimate the amount of time collaboration takes" (Barfield et al. 1994). The New Beginnings collaborative center brings together five major service agencies to run a center in the Hamilton School, staffed with family advocates. Participants there discovered that it was easier to get agencies to make "deals" to sign contracts to relocate workers to schools than to achieve permanent widespread changes in how services are delivered to families in San Diego.

• *Turf.* Related to governance is turf: who owns the school building? When a whole new staff working for an outside agency moves onto school property, many territorial concerns arise. What role does the school nurse play in the school-based clinic? Why not hire more school social workers if family counseling and case management are needed? Issues arise over confidentiality, space, releasing students from classes, and discipline. It takes time and energy and, particularly, skilled principals and program coordinators to work through appropriate policies and practices.

• *Lack of continuity.* To succeed, full-service schools depend on a stable group of people committed to the process. For example, the Decatur-Clearpool School, noted earlier, has operated effectively for several years, but the collaborative is currently facing challenges because of changing leadership. The district has had three superintendents and the school has had three principals in four years. Teacher turnover has been endemic, and each new faculty member must be oriented to the holistic, family-centered approach of the school.

• *Controversy.* Another obstacle to creating full-service schools is communities and/or school boards that resist the idea of using the school building for anything but educational purposes. Experience throughout the country, however, has shown that this resistance has dissipated rapidly with the availability of state and foundation grants. A crucial aspect of launching full-service arrangements is to conduct extensive local needs assessments and planning prior to program development. In general, these early efforts equip parents and school personnel with the necessary data to convince decision makers and educate the media about the importance of integrating services in the school.

• *Funding.* The annual cost for full-service school models ranges from $75,000 for Kentucky's Youth and Family Service Centers to $800,000 for the most comprehensive community-school. School-based clinics cost on the average $150,000 per year, not including large amounts of in-kind and donated goods and services. The annual cost for a school-based clinic user is about $100 per year, while the cost per student in a more complex arrangement is about $1,000.

States are major funders of these initiatives and, even with looming budget cuts, are moving ahead to support more comprehensive school-based programs. Except for a recent initiative in the Bureau of Primary Health Care, no federal grants go directly to communities and schools for integrated services. The full-service school concept has been recognized, however, in new legislative endeavors such as the revisions of Title 1, Empowerment Zone grants, and the Crime Bill (but the funding for after-school services did not survive the cuts). Federal regulations could be changed to facilitate the increased use of categorical dollars for integrated services, for example, Drug Free Schools, HIV prevention, special education, and mental health programs.

Many schools are already gaining access to Medicaid funds—for example, the Farrell Area School District near Pittsburgh, Pennsylvania, another comprehensive service provider. This small (1,280 students), extremely disadvantaged district has invited 57 partners to help operate a Family Center and several school-based clinics, which arrange for Medicaid reimbursement.

Two difficulties in using Medicaid money are eligibility determination and reimbursement procedures. The advent of managed care adds to the complexity, with school service providers struggling to establish either fee-for-service or per capita payment contracts with managed care providers. Legislation should guarantee that school-based centers can become "essential community providers" so that enrollees in managed care plans can obtain preventive services, such as mental health and health education, within these plans.

As pointed out by Modesto's superintendent, "the proof of any program funded by grant monies is sustainability after the grant ceases" (Enochs 1995). The Modesto City Schools have demonstrated how programs can be institutionalized. When their large grant from California's Healthy Start (about $400,000 per year over four years) expired, the school system was able to obtain continuing support from county agencies and the local health center while using Community Development Block Grant and Title I funds for core support.

Does Full-Service Have a Future?

While support for the concept of full-service schools is strong, even the most ardent advocates want assurance that centralizing services in restructured schools will make a difference in the lives of the children and their families. Evaluation results are spotty, not surprising given the early stages of program development and the difficulties inherent in program research. Much of the research has been on autonomous components such as school-based clinics or family resource centers (Dryfoos et al. 1996). Several states—Florida, Kentucky, and California—are beginning to produce reports on the more comprehensive programs that they sponsor (Wagner et al. 1994).

In full-service schools with health clinics, clinic users have been shown to have lower substance use, better school attendance, lower dropout rates, and in a few places with targeted reproductive health services, lower birth rates. Students, parents, teachers, and school personnel report a high level of satisfaction with school-based services and particularly appreciate their accessibility, convenience, and confidentiality.

Early reports from the more comprehensive community-schools are encouraging. Attendance and graduation rates are significantly higher than in comparable schools, and reading and math scores have shown some improvement. Students are eager to come to schools that are stimulating, nurturing, and respectful of cultural values. Parents are heavily involved as classroom aides, and advisory board members, in classes and cultural events, and with case managers and support services. Property destruction and graffiti have diminished, and neighborhood violence rates have definitely decreased.

The full-service school is a home-grown product that can take many shapes: community schools, lighted school-houses called Beacons, school-based clinics, family resource centers. Relatively small investments by state governments and foundations are enabling innovative leaders to better use existing categorical resources to relocate personnel and devise more integrated delivery systems. Research will confirm that combining prevention interventions with school restructuring will create stronger institutions and schools will become neighborhood hubs, places where children's lives are enhanced and families want to go.

We know that the school's role is to educate and the family's responsibility is to raise the children. Many of today's parents need assistance in accomplishing that task. Full-service schools may be the most effective arrangement for achieving school, family, and societal goals.

References

Barfield, D., C. Brindis, L. Guthrie, W. McDonald, S. Philliber, and B. Scott. (1994). *The Evaluation of New Beginnings: First Report, February 1994.* San Francisco: Far West Laboratory for Educational Research and Development.

Department of Health and Rehabilitative Services and Department of Education. (1991). *Request for Program Designs for Supplemental School Health Programs, Feb. 1–June 30, 1991.* Tallahassee: State of Florida.

Dryfoos, J. (1994). *Full-Service Schools: A Revolution in Health and Social Services of Children, Youth, and Families.* San Francisco: Jossey-Bass.

Dryfoos, J., C. Brindis, and D. Kaplan. (1996). "Evaluation of School-Based Health Clinics." In *Adolescent Medicine: State of the Art. Health Care in Schools,* edited by L. Juszak and M. Fisher. Philadelphia: Hanley and Belfus.

Enochs, J. (August 21, 1995). "Report on Implementation of SB-620 Three-Year Healthy Start Operational Grants to Develop Coordinated School-Based Interagency Services." Memo to Modesto City (California) Schools Board.

Knowles, T. (1994). "The Decatur-Clearpool School: Synthesizing Philosophy and Management." Paper prepared for the annual meeting of the American Educational Research Association meeting in New Orleans.

Melaville, A., M. Blank, and G. Asayesh. (1993). *Together We Can: A Guide for Crafting a Profamily System of Education and Human Services.* Washington, D. C.: U. S. Government Printing Office.

Modesto City Schools. (1995). "Modesto City Schools: 1994–95 Healthy Start Report. Hanshaw Middle School." Modesto, California, City Schools.

U. S. Department of Education. (1995). *School-Linked Comprehensive Services for Children and Families.* Washington, D. C.: Office of Educational Research and Improvement and American Educational Research Association.

Wagner, M., S. Golan, D. Shaver, L. Newman, M. Wechsler, and F. Kelley. (1994). *A Healthy Start for California's Children and Families: Early Findings from a Statewide Evaluation of School-linked Services.* Menlo Park, Calif.: SRI International.

Article Review Form at end of book.

Before deciding to implement block scheduling, building faculty and administrators must consider a variety of issues. Which issues have the greatest impact on a decision to move to a block schedule?

Steps for Improving School Climate in Block Scheduling

Teachers and students will experience difficulties implementing a block schedule, the authors point out, but the positive outcomes make the initial struggles worthwhile.

J. Allen Queen and Kimberly A. Gaskey

J. Allen Queen is an associate professor in the Department of Middle, Secondary, and K-12 Education, University of North Carolina, Charlotte, where Kimberly A. Gaskey is a graduate student. They are the co-authors of The 4x4 Block Schedule *(Eye on Education, March 1998).*

As the mania for school reform continues to sweep the nation, educators enter the waters of change with a degree of trepidation. Change always sparks feelings of concern, but the fear of stagnation can be far greater. One innovation currently being instituted successfully in schools across the nation is block scheduling, which is revolutionizing the opportunities afforded high school students. The positive changes in the climate of schools on a block schedule stem in part from an increased ability to meet the needs of individual students. Smaller classes, a wider variety of subjects offered, and the opportunity for in-depth, hands-on study are all concrete outcomes of the use of extended class periods. As the diversity of the student population increases, the flexibility of block scheduling becomes ever more desirable.

Participating in the development of a block schedule and surviving its first year of implementation require an open mind, a flexible spirit, and a dedication to the success of the chosen schedule. Schools that reform their schedules can take comfort in the collective experience of educators who have already made such a change. Schools that have used block schedules are seeing their students become motivated toward exploration and discovery in their classes. But making a change of this magnitude requires the establishment of achievable goals or steps. The following points should help administrators and teachers consider the intricacies of the models and understand the plans that they must make in order to adopt a new schedule successfully.

Basics of Block Scheduling

A number of models of block scheduling exist, but they all share the goal of allowing schools to adopt flexible programs in a variety of ways, depending on the school and students' needs. The 4 x 4 model takes the format of two semesters of four classes, each 90 minutes in length. Modifications can be made to the schedule, such as an additional

Reprinted with permission from PHI DELTA KAPPAN, Vol. 79, No. 2, October 1997, pp. 158–161.

abbreviated period for remediation or for yearlong courses.

The A/B schedule is different in that students will take periods 1 through 4 on A days and then switch to periods 5 through 8 on B days. Another difference is that studies in specific subject areas continue over an entire school year, rather than lasting for just one semester. But there are possibilities for modification here as well.

Yet another option is microcourses, which make longer blocks of time available for certain classes. These classes last for several weeks or months and are paired with courses that follow a traditional yearlong schedule.

The choice of a particular model of block scheduling requires close analysis of the school, its teachers, and its students. Involving the school community in choosing a model and molding the schedule to meet the needs of the students helps to build a sense of ownership of the model.

Curriculum Alignment

After a school community has chosen a specific model of block scheduling, the curriculum must be modified by expanding course offerings, apprenticeship opportunities, postsecondary classes, and graduation requirements. Block scheduling allows for the addition of numerous electives in such areas as astronomy, mythology, technical writing, computer programming, and advanced foreign languages. On surveys, students have responded favorably to such proposed elective courses, and their subsequent enrollment in these classes has borne out their interest. The opportunity to take a wider range of vocational, art, and higher-level core classes energizes students and enables them to see positive possibilities for the future.

A new block schedule also creates opportunities for programs that take place off the school grounds. Apprenticeships, mentoring programs, and postsecondary study in a university or community college are all possibilities.

Remedial classes can be offered for students who have transferred in or for students who are falling behind in difficult core classes. These students can receive the individual attention they need to keep up with their agemates and graduate on time. Because of these second chances, the dropout rate in schools that use block schedules tends to fall rapidly. And because of the degree of flexibility in the schedule, students do not feel completely defeated if they fail a class, because they have time to try again.

The choice of a particular model of block scheduling requires close analysis of the school, its teachers, and its students.

When planning individual schedules of students and teachers, administrators and counselors should remember that it is probably a mistake to load all required courses into one semester and all electives into another. Balancing the load for both students and teachers is important so that teachers do not have more than two preparations per day or students more than two required courses.

Course Development and Unit Design

Once the classes and schedules have been arranged, teachers can begin aligning the instruction for each course they will teach. The development of "pacing guides" helps teachers plan the time to be spent on each topic in a course. Students also find such guides helpful in adjusting to the new schedule.

Instead of teaching five Shakespearean plays in the senior English class, for example, teachers will have to find new ways to cover the material. Teaching one full play and examining the differences in several scenes from other plays may better fit the new schedule. The students are still able to master the language and grasp the universality in Shakespearean drama. The classes are also conducive to programs such as writing across the curriculum, team teaching, teacher and student project exchanges, and so on.

The flexible nature of block scheduling carries over to the planning of courses and units. Short field trips can be scheduled that do not keep students away from the school for an entire day. Teachers have extended planning periods and thus can be more creative in designing instruction. Classes that are creatively constructed can be challenging for teachers and more interesting for students.

Developing Pacing Guides for Time Management

An initial pacing guide spelling out the number of days to be spent on certain topics will help teachers block out their time and organize their courses. Before teaching a course in the block schedule, teachers should take their initial pacing guide and create a daily guide for what they intend to cover. It is helpful to leave two to three blank days in the schedule for unforeseen events, for review, or for in-depth study. Pacing guides can also be used to plan for each individual class.

During the first month or so of teaching in the new schedule, it will be essential to plan almost every minute of a class period. Most teachers have been surprised by the extremely fast pace that students are able to maintain, given the extra class time. Therefore, it is helpful to have at least a week's worth of planning available in advance. Students thrive in this fast pace because they don't grow bored with repetition or tired of lessons that seem to last for days. Students can use the pacing guides in a cooperative group activity to plan their own time limits for achieving group goals. Pacing guides and detailed planning make survival possible during the first month of teaching in a block schedule. Teachers derive a high degree of comfort from the organization developed in a guide.

Instructional Strategies and Lesson Designs

Teachers who successfully use the block schedule move away from the introduction/lecture/review format and vary the presentation of materials. Students are capable of concentrating for the longer blocks of time, but the class structure should change every 20 to 30 minutes to maintain a high level of interest. An experience-based classroom focused on cooperative learning, critical thinking, process writing, and active learning will keep the pace brisk and the students involved. Indeed, teachers and students are often surprised by the positive changes in the classroom climate under a block schedule.

Teachers have also found clever ways to organize student movement in the classroom as a way to give relief from sitting for extended periods. Such movement does not have to take place in every class period, and all students don't necessarily have to move. Simply switching to a small-group format or assigning one student to pass out papers or locate writing portfolios that students will retrieve individually at some point during the class can help students who seem to be having difficulty staying focused.

A block schedule offers students flexibility and a voice in their education—creating a focused group of learners.

By varying lessons, teachers can present materials to a diverse population of students with numerous learning styles. Cooperative learning improves attitudes about self, school, and peers, and it can be used to foster open-mindedness and an appreciation for others if projects require interdependence, individual accountability, and specified objectives. Socratic seminars work well in a block schedule. These seminars redefine the role of the teacher as that of instructional facilitator rather than storehouse of knowledge. Teachers become seekers of knowledge and learn along with students. By employing a variety of lesson designs, along with interpretive and critical analysis, teachers can enable students to work actively with new information and become responsible for more than a simple regurgitation of facts.

Classroom Management and Improved Discipline

Evidence of an improved school climate can best be seen in the decline in the number of discipline problems reported and in the positive reports from teachers on the energized atmosphere of their classes. The students switch classes less often, which seems to help create a less frenzied atmosphere.

Schools that have adopted block schedules report a reduction in absenteeism and drastic reductions in discipline problems. Discipline will continue to be a problem for beginning teachers and for some individuals on any staff, and a detailed training program in classroom management should be a required part of the transition to block scheduling. However, students generally like the opportunities provided by the block schedule, and the varied teaching methods hold their attention. The students like the schedule because it works for them, and so they create fewer discipline problems. Moreover, they attend classes more frequently because cutting means missing a more substantial portion of the subject matter of a course.

Advanced Placement and Honors Classes

One of the concerns every school faces in the transition to a block schedule is voiced by teachers who prepare their students to take Advanced Placement (AP) exams each spring. The concern focuses on retention—or, more precisely, the lack thereof. Under most block schedules, students who take an AP class in the fall will have to wait until spring to take the test, and their teachers wonder about the impact of the delay on their scores.

Several solutions to this problem have been implemented successfully. Microcourses that extend over the entire school year maintain continuous instruction right up to the testing date. Postsecondary enrollment options in the spring would also keep students active in specific advanced areas. The simple scheduling of several spring AP classes, with careful attention not to overload students, also meets the concern about retention of content.

In other ways, though, a block schedule can be an excellent vehicle for AP and honors classes because the extended time allotted to class periods allows for the use of materials and activities that enable students to undertake advanced work. The new schedules allow for projects, for greater interaction between students, and for in-depth study in areas of special interest. Students can also actively participate in directing the AP and honors courses, as the schedule allows for a high degree of creativity. Advanced students flourish in a flexible schedule and are afforded the chance to take electives in areas that they could not have explored under previous schedules. Instead of ending foreign language studies after the second year, for example, students in a block schedule can continue to take a third and fourth year of a language.

Special Student Populations

Under a block schedule, students who have failed a course can repeat it again without falling an entire grade behind their agemates. This fact alone helps keep their morale high, and students who must retake a class do not feel as defeated. They can still graduate on time, thanks to the new schedule. Modified block schedules often provide an abbreviated period for club meetings that can be used for remediation, tutoring, writing lab reports, or obtaining individual help from teachers.

As we stated above, the dropout rate falls for schools on block schedules, and the absentee rate also drops. The second chances and individualized help available in a block schedule can give students the motivation to stay in school. Although missing a single class meeting puts students further behind their classmates, it is still possible for students to catch up when they have been ill, for the course load is reduced in a block schedule.

Practices associated with inclusion are also successful in block schedules. Students with special needs can be a part of the school and not be relegated to a small, isolated area of the building. Their social development is thus enhanced as their special needs are met.

Assessment and Evaluation

Just as teachers use varied methods to present materials in the classroom, they should also use varied methods of assessment. Alternative assessment may take such forms as compiling portfolios, doing group and individual projects, completing surveys, and giving oral presentations. Because of time differences in the block schedule, it is essential that students receive regular feedback with regard to their progress in a class. A course that lasts just one semester will be over before a student can make up work, retake tests, or study harder to improve grades.

It is also essential that the voices of teachers, parents, and students be heard as part of the evaluation of the schedule itself. Any modifications and improvements can become the property of the entire school community, but only if frequent reports are given about strides made, problems encountered and solved, and possibilities for future changes. Students, parents, and teachers should all be surveyed on several occasions to elicit their opinions and concerns. Such sharing will go a long way toward ensuring that a new schedule is successfully implemented and will also help energize the school by involving all stakeholders.

Know That the Next Semester Will Be Better

Teachers and students will suffer from fatigue when they begin the new schedule simply because it is new. After becoming accustomed to the new time frame and the varied course load, this fatigue will subside. If schedules are modified to ensure that all electives are not lumped into one semester and all required classes are not lumped into another, students will prosper from the balance.

Another helpful survival tool will be to schedule exams before the Christmas break so that the break will actually serve as a time to reenergize, not as a time to prepare for exams. Students will receive immediate feedback about the quality of their efforts while the course is still fresh in their minds. The Christmas break can then serve to revitalize teachers and to excite students, as they will often return in the new year to a completely new set of classes.

As with any new challenge, teachers and students will experience difficulties, but the block schedule offers students flexibility and a voice in their education. This voice empowers students and creates a focused and enthusiastic group of learners. School climate is dramatically affected by block scheduling because the schedule addresses individual needs and gives teachers greater opportunities to be creative. Schools that have implemented block scheduling have surveyed their communities, and most respondents say that they like the new schedules and would never want to return to a traditional schedule. The change has proved worth any initial struggles.

Article Review Form at end of book.

What is perhaps the one crucial element that ensures success of distance education programs?

Distance Education

Does anyone really want to learn at a distance?

Michael Simonson

Michael Simonson, a professor of curriculum and instruction and associate director for research for the Research Institute for Studies in Education, has written three books and 50 articles on instructional technology.

Research demonstrates that students prefer not to learn at a distance (Schlosser & Anderson, 1994). Certainly, there are times when the convenience of distance education outweighs other considerations, but if given a legitimate choice, students prefer sitting in a classroom, laboratory, or conference room with other learners and the instructor. Students report that they value the presence of a learning group, and that the informal interactions that occur before and after, and sometimes during, a formal class are valuable components of the total learning experience. Basically, learning at a distance is not what most students prefer (Schlosser & Anderson, 1994).

If students really do not want to be distant learners, then what is behind all the recent excitement about distance education? In the last five years, distance education has become a major topic in education (Hanna, 1995). In 1995, there were more than 30 conferences dealing with some aspect of distance education, and almost every professional organization's publications and conferences have shown a huge increase in the number of distance education related articles and papers (Simonson, 1996).

Technology in Education—An Earlier Debate

The discussion about distance education is somewhat reminiscent of the recent debate in the educational technology field that began when Richard Clark, a researcher and theorist, published a classic article containing his now famous "mere vehicles" analogy. Clark summarized over five decades of educational media research. It was obvious to him that many researchers were attempting flawed studies involving media. Clark believed that they did not understand the last 60 years of research about media and learning (Clark, 1983).

It was even more alarming (Clark, 1983) that many practitioners were making unrealistic claims about the impact of technology on learning. According to him, there was a large segment of the educational community who felt that mediated instruction was inherently better than teaching when media were not used.

> In 1983, Clark wrote in volume 54 of the *Review of Educational Research* that: the best current evidence is that media are mere vehicles that deliver instruction but do not influence student achievement any more than the truck that delivers our groceries causes changes in nutrition . . . only the content of the vehicle can influence achievement. (445)

Clark's article went on to convincingly claim that instructional media were excellent for storing educational messages and for delivering them almost anywhere. However, media were not responsible for a learning effect. Achievement was not enhanced merely because instruction was media-based. Rather, Clark contended that the content of the instruction, the method used to promote learning, and the involvement of the learner in the instructional experience were what influenced learning.

While many did not, and still do not, agree with Clark, (Kozma, 1994) his article caused a reassessment of how the field looked at the impact of media. Clark (1994) has continued to implore the education community to "give up your enthusiasm for media effects on learning," which was the theme of his most recent publication on this topic. "Give up your enthusiasm" has become a new rallying cry for those who do not believe there is a media effect. Educational technology researchers are increasingly examining the process of learning when technologies are used, and the capabilities of technologies to provide access to information, for example.

Technology: A Story

A second analogy by another great technology pioneer also has relevance to distance education. In the 1960s, Jim Finn from the University of Southern California talked about the stirrup as a technological innovation that changed society. He often told a story that went like this (Finn, 1964).

The Anglo-Saxons, a dominating enemy of Charles Martel's Franks, had the stirrup but did not truly understand its implications for warfare. The stirrup made possible the emergence of a warrior called the knight who understood that the stirrup enabled the rider not only to keep his seat, but also to deliver a blow with a lance having the combined weight of the rider and charging horse. This simple concept permitted the Franks to conquer the Anglo-Saxons and change the face of western civilization. Martel had a vision to seize the idea and to use it. He did not invent the stirrup, but knew how to use it purposefully.

Finn summarized the implications of his story as follows:

> The acceptance or rejection of an invention, or the extent to which its implications are realized if it is accepted, depends quite as much upon the condition of society, and upon the imagination of its leadership, as upon the nature of the technological item itself . . . The Anglo-Saxons used the stirrup, but did not comprehend it; and for this they paid a fearful price. . . . It was the Franks alone—presumably led by Charles Martel's genius—who fully grasped the possibilities inherent in the stirrup and created in terms of it a new type of warfare supported by a novel structure of a society which we call feudalism. . . . For a thousand years feudal. institutions bore the marks of their birth from the new military technologies of the eighth century. (Finn, 1964, p. 24)

Clark and Finn

What Clark strongly proposed with his "mere vehicles" and "give up your enthusiasm" arguments was that media and technology do not directly affect learning. He forcefully argued that educators should not claim that technology-based learning had any inherent advantage over other methods of learning. Like Finn, Clark proposed that technologies may provide ways of accomplishing tasks that are new and not readily obvious.

Finn advocated that practitioners should attempt to identify unique approaches for changing society by using new technologies in new ways. Finn's story explained that the stirrup not only made getting on and off a horse easier, but also made possible a new and previously unheard-of consequence: the emergence of the knight, and it was the knight that caused significant and long-lasting changes in society.

The implication of the arguments of these two educators was that when new technologies emerge, they often allow users to be more efficient. However, it is not technologies themselves that cause changes: rather, changes occur because of new ways of doing things that are enabled by technologies. The stirrup made riding horses easier and more efficient, but it was the knight that changed medieval society.

Distance Education Today and Tomorrow

Distance education is one of the most dramatic of recent technology-based innovations in education. Many educators are making grand claims about how distance education is likely to change education and training (Willis, 1994). Certainly, the concept of distance education is exciting, and recent hardware and software innovations are making telecommunications systems more available, easier to use, and less costly. Distance education has begun to enter the mainstream.

However, distance educators are being confronted by two conflicting pressures. First, *students do not really want to learn at a distance.* They prefer to meet with the learning group and the instructor in the lecture hall, the classroom, the seminar room, or the laboratory (Schlosser & Anderson, 1994). Second, *students are increasingly demanding to be allowed to learn at a distance.* They want to be able to supplement and even replace conventional learning experiences with distance education experiences (Hanna, 1995). This is because there are many other considerations than personal preferences that motivate learners, especially about where and when they learn.

These opposing forces pose a dilemma for the educational community. Should resources be dedicated to improving the traditional educational infrastructure of buildings, classroom laboratories, and offices, or should resources be used to develop modern and sophisticated telecommunications systems.

Because of advances in technology, effective educational experiences can be provided for learners, no matter where they are located. In other words, technologies are now available to develop cost-effective distance education systems, and there is considerable pressure to do so (Hanna, 1995). However, the limited availability of resources force educational leaders to make choices about whether distance learning is appropriate for their institution.

The practice of distance education has dramatically changed in the last five years. Traditional approaches to distance education based on the delivery of print and linear media technologies are no longer as relevant to the field as it is practiced in the United States (Simonson, 1996). As a matter of fact, a redefinition of distance education has occurred. Distance education is now often defined as:

> institution-based, formal education where the members of the learning group are separated geographically, and where interactive telecommunications systems are used to connect learners, resources, and instructors (Simonson and Schlosser, 1995).

This definition is based on a position about the correct practice of distance education. If distance education is to be successful:

> its appropriate application should be based on the belief that the more similar the learning experience of the distant student is to that of the local student, the more similar will be the desired outcomes of the learning experience (Simonson and Schlosser, 1995).

In other words, the successful incorporation of distance education into mainstream education will depend on providing learners with equivalent learning experiences no matter where they are located. The research clearly demonstrates that in general, distant learners achieve as well as local learners (Schlosser & Anderson, 1994). However, less is known about the differences of the learning processes of distant and local learners. Probably, distant and local learners employ different strategies for learning. For example, distant learners may study longer in order to assimilate course information (Jurasek, 1993). Certainly, more research is needed.

If distance education is to gain widespread acceptance, it should not be necessary for any group of learners to compensate for different, possibly lesser, instructional experiences. Thus, those developing distance educational systems should strive to make equivalent the learning experiences of all students no matter how they are linked to the resources or instruction they require. Institutions that can provide equivalent, or nearly equivalent, learning experiences for local and distant learners should pursue distance education. Those institutions that cannot, or will not, institute systems that provide equivalent experiences will ultimately be relegated to a secondary and peripheral place in the distance education field.

Conclusion

Separation of the student and the teacher is a fundamental characteristic of distance education. Increasingly, educators are using technology to increase the access of the distant learner to the local classroom and to make the experience of the remote student comparable to the experience of the local learner. Distance education is a dramatic idea. It may change, even restructure, education, but only if it is possible to make the experience of the distant learner as complete, satisfying, and acceptable as the experience of the local learner. If distance education is to be a successful and mainstream approach, then it is imperative that distance education systems should be designed to permit similar learning experiences for distant and local students.

Distance education using telecommunications technologies

is an exciting emerging field. Practitioners should not promote distance education as the next great technological solution to education's problems, nor make grand claims about the impact of telecommunications systems. Rather, those in the field should strive to use technology and technological approaches to make the experiences of distant and local learners positive and equivalent, at least until someone's genius identifies an approach to learning that uses telecommunications systems to change education, just as Charles Martel's use of the stirrup contributed to changes in society.

References

Clark, R. (1983). Reconsidering research on learning from media. *Review of Educational Research, 53*(4), 445–459.

Clark, R. (1994). Media will never influence learning. *Educational Technology Research and Development, 42*(2), 21–29.

Finn, J. (1964). The Franks had the right idea. *NEA Journal, 53*(4), 24–27.

Hanna, D. (1995). *Mainstreaming distance education.* Conference of the National Association of State University and Land Grant Colleges, Madison, WI.

Jurasek, K. (1993). *Distance education via compressed video.* Unpublished masters thesis, Iowa State University, Ames, Iowa.

Kozma, R. (1994). Will media influence learning: Reframing the debate. *Educational Technology Research and Development Journal, 42*(2), 7–19.

Schlosser, C. & Anderson, M. (1994). *Distance education: Review of the literature.* Washington, DC: Association for Educational Communications and Technology.

Simonson, M. (1996). *Reinventing distance education.* Presentation at the Annual Convention of the U.S. Distance Learning Association, Washington, DC.

Simonson, M. & Schlosser, C. (1995). More than fiber: Distance Education in Iowa. *Tech Trends, 40*(3), 13–15.

Willis, B. (1994). *Distance Education: Strategies and tools.* Englewood Cliffs, NJ: Educational Technology Publications.

Article Review Form at end of book.

How do learning communities differ from traditional organizations?

Creating Intentional Learning Communities

Organized across schools, districts, or states, educational reform networks offer teachers and administrators an opportunity to discuss their work and tackle problems in an atmosphere of trust and support.

Ann Lieberman

Ann Lieberman is Co-Director of the National Center for Restructuring Education, Schools, and Teaching, Box 110, Teachers College, Columbia University, New York, NY 10027.

Educational reform networks are fast becoming an important alternative to conventional modes of teacher and school development. At a time when educators feel that administrators and professional development staff are already overburdening and "developing" them, why would networks—seemingly shapeless and borderless and involving random collections of educators—become so popular?

Curious about this question, we first examined three networks created at the National Center for Restructuring Education, Schools, and Teaching (NCREST, Teachers College, Columbia University). We later expanded our study to include 13 other networks representing a range of purposes, locations, participants, and modes of operation (Lieberman and Grolnick, in press). What we saw helped to provide some answers to why and how reform networks have become such an important component in the reform of U.S. education.

Networks as Learning Communities

At the heart of members' involvement in reform networks, teachers and administrators label, share, and discuss their work experiences. In an atmosphere of trust and support, networkers contribute to and gain access to "just in time" learning (solving immediate problems of practice), as well as grapple with problems in greater depth and complexity:

> Eight assistant superintendents from neighboring districts gather in a members' boardroom for their monthly network meeting. As the others listen, one participant describes his district's efforts to implement a model of inclusion for special education students. "Please understand," he begins, "I'm here to tell you what works for us, but we also have some real problems and I'm hoping you can help." In the hour that follows, participants lean across the conference table to share their own experiences and insights. The discussion ranges broadly from issues of implementation and instruction to politics, ethics, philosophy, and the problems of change.

This kind of sharing has the effect of dignifying and giving shape to the substance of educators' experiences—the dailiness of their work, which is often invisible to outsiders yet binds insiders together. Networks are particularly good at helping school-based educators discuss and work on current problems, while exposing them to new ideas from peers in

"Creating Intentional Learning Communities" by Ann Lieberman from EDUCATIONAL LEADERSHIP, November 1996, pp. 51–55. Reprinted by permission of the author.

other schools and districts. Working across districts or even states, teachers and administrators find it easier to question, ask for help, or "tell it like it is," rather than to be the experts who, not wanting to appear inadequate, sit quietly, afraid to expose themselves by asking questions.

Although school-based educators may need to invent a great deal of reform knowledge (Darling-Hammond 1993, Little 1993, Lytle and Cochran-Smith 1992), norms that encourage invention are not yet part of the way most schools and districts operate. Because networks are a more flexible organizational form, they offer new ways of operating that can embrace the processes of teaching, learning, and leading as they really are—ambiguous, complex, unfinished—and thus tend to be more in tune with how school professionals live and view their lives. Networks offer people membership in a constructive community: a group of professionals engaged in a common struggle to educate themselves so that they can better educate their students.

Sharing has the effect of dignifying educators' experiences—the dailiness of their work, which is often invisible to outsiders yet binds insiders together.

Flexible Activities, Responsive Structures

In contrast to most traditional organizations, networks have the flexibility to organize activities first, then develop the structures to support those activities. This flexibility allows a network to create an activity, use it as long as it serves members' needs and purposes, and end it when members no longer perceive it as valuable. The responsiveness of the network provides for a more developmental approach to adult learning by empowering members to voice their approval or disapproval, by building commitment to the network rather than to a particular activity, and by encouraging a more personal and professional involvement of members in their own learning.

The flexibility of a network encourages the growth of new forms (cross-role groups, dinner meetings, study groups) when they seem appropriate and, in some instances, helps build the norms and functions associated with a particular network. In the Southern Maine Partnership, for example, "dine and discuss" is a home-grown idea that contributed to the growth of more egalitarian relationships among school and university-based partners:

> When the partnership started, we created "dine and discuss" conversations. Teachers, principals, and district office personnel chose topics of immediate concern and interest. We had 17 groups. Educators would come together for dinner, then read and discuss an article—much like a book club. Professors, teachers, and principals all talked together, thus reducing status differences. In time, "dine and discuss" was dropped as it no longer served the purposes of the partnership. But five years later, when someone asked what had happened to "dine and discuss," it was reinstituted.

Each network develops activities that reflect its own distinct culture. For example, Bread Loaf Rural Teachers' Network uses a summer retreat in Bread Loaf, Vermont, to socialize new members and an electronic network, Breadnet, to connect members and their students from Alaska to Mississippi. Both the Network of Progressive Educators—"for those who share values of progressive education"—and the League of Professional Schools— "a network of schools working on their own plans to promote democratic policies"—convene an annual conference that provides an opportunity for members to learn from and teach each other. The National Network for Educational Renewal, on the other hand, has used task forces when appropriate and has abandoned and reinstated them as the need arose.

Although their specific activities may differ, all networks offer forms of adult learning that support the needs of members who seek organizations that recognize and respect what they know and do.

A Culture of Continuous Inquiry

In addition to altering the formats for learning, networks also replace prescription and compliance with involvement in problem posing, sharing, and solving; discussions that concern actions and consequences; and a culture that encourages continuous inquiry. Networks advance goals for learning and professional competence that model and support a variety of modes of inquiry. Examples include task groups engaged in action research, teams writing school-based plans, teachers discussing assessment problems online, or networks assisting schools that are restructuring their approaches to teaching and learning. Many participants voice satisfaction with their involvement:

> My network's common values and principles form the basis for

> ongoing writings and dialog for many of us. Intellectually stimulating, educationally sound, and morally challenging! This is great stuff! This is hard stuff!
>
> Most of the real communication in my network is through informal contacts and conversation, . . . connections with people where trust is apparent.
>
> I teach in rural Vermont. I am the only middle school English teacher here. Fellow teachers in Breadnet help me to keep going and keep my sanity as well as extend my classroom and the quality of work the kids and I do.

Sharing information often becomes the focus of learning. Participants may prepare a report on some new aspect of teacher research or may exchange ideas about how schools are using rubrics. Others discuss ways their students are using the Net to communicate with other students as an audience for their work. In some cases, schools undergoing change help one another understand what they are doing and how the change process works.

Networks invite their members to help shape the agenda, which gives a voice to those who usually respond to the agendas of others. Successful networks organize their work so that members can be active participants rather than passive observers. But networks don't spontaneously know how to do all this. Leaders and facilitators must support, broker, and link school professionals together to encourage their participation in their own development.

Reinventing Leadership

One of the most important, yet least understood, aspects of reform networks is the role of leadership. Perhaps this is because much of network leadership is defined as facilitating, brokering, and linking, rather than leading. Leaders carry out such mundane activities as making phone calls, raising money, arranging meetings, brokering resources and people, and negotiating time commitments for university and school-based educators. Activities like these make possible the building and maintaining of collaborative models of learning, development, and change; the preservation of important ideals; and the advancement of new ideas.

Network leaders try to create "public spaces" where educators can work together across classrooms, schools, or districts. In locations free of the normal boundaries and cultural constraints of one's own organization, position, or place, it becomes possible to grow a culture of commitment to a new set of ideas and ideals. Helping to build a culture through activities that keep these ideas visible and integral to the work is an important part of leadership.

Although most networks have formal leaders such as regional directors, site coordinators, and partnership associates, they also provide numerous opportunities for leadership to emerge from the membership. Informal new categories—for example, teacher scholars, conference coordinators, and member-experts in the growing body of knowledge about teaching and learning—continue to expand. In fact, facilitators look for opportunities to create leadership, regardless of status or rank. This helps to strengthen members' commitment to the network, enlarges their vision of the possibilities for change, and broadens their personal and professional associations.

When the community grows and deepens, a network becomes an important catalyst for school renewal.

The linking of expectations with the opportunity to collaborate in the context of a warm and welcoming community legitimates a search for innovative solutions to complex educational problems that are often ill-defined and that have no simple or universal answers (Little 1993, Lieberman 1995, Darling-Hammond and McLaughlin 1995). Figuring out how to keep such a community growing as it deepens its knowledge and practice, while connecting the work of the network to its parent organizations, is a major concern of leadership. When the community grows and deepens, a network becomes an important catalyst for school renewal. This is no easy task—it is one that takes great skill, knowledge, and creativity.

Recurring Tensions in Networks

Throughout our study, we found several organizational tensions that occurred consistently. The dynamics inherent in the attempts to resolve these tensions—which involve personal conflict and organizational disequilibrium—appear to be central to the process of how networks organize, build new structures, learn to collaborate, and develop a sense of community. While the resolutions of these tensions were heavily influenced by the context and character of each network, the tensions themselves were common to all.

- *Negotiating between network purpose and the dailiness of activities.* No matter what the purpose of the network, the nature of the activities and the growth of relationships within the group are crucial elements in cementing the commitment of participants. A tension often develops between short-term activities and long-term purposes. Activities must be compelling enough to keep people coming back for more, no matter how meaningful or well-intentioned the long-term purposes. Networks can't hope to survive unless ways are found to build connections between larger or emergent meaning and the specific activities that together create that meaning.

- *Negotiating between "inside knowledge" and "outside knowledge."* Whatever the purpose, networks must decide what and whose knowledge should inform their work—specifically, when should which type of knowledge be influential, and to what extent? All network leaders agreed that, to be meaningful, the agenda must emerge from questions of practice. And the negotiation is constant: Who provides the information? How much of practice is "sharing ignorance"? How much generalized knowledge simply lacks a context? As one leader said, "The dilemma is when to push for further success on values or when to accept a practical adaptation."
- *Negotiating the centralization/decentralization problem.* A tension exists between taking either a "district office" approach, which often fails to involve the membership in shaping the work, or an arbitrary alternative approach, which might attract some committed members but usually fails to involve a larger number of participants. An effective network creates ways to engage participants directly in governance and leadership, while maintaining the flexibility to organize complex, far-reaching operations. Leaders need to design mechanisms, roles, and structures that achieve a greater degree of decentralization. Authority and control have often resided in universities and districts, leaving teachers with few opportunities to assume leadership roles. By contrast, a decentralized network encourages teachers to take on new roles and responsibilities, contributing to their own growth and development as well as that of the network.
- *Negotiating between informal/flexible and formal/rigid.* To develop collaboration across schools, districts, and role groups, a network must organize and facilitate activities and coordinate its work. As the network seeks ways to stabilize and expand, it may threaten the energy, initiative, peer support, and trust that developed informally (Miles 1978). The more success that networks experience, the more they reach out to other areas of work and the more pressure they feel to expand their bureaucracy. Protecting what makes the network special becomes more difficult as it grows, requiring time, effort, and, most of all, creative solutions to the problems associated with success.
- *Negotiating the tension between inclusivity and exclusivity.* Should a network restrict its membership to people with the same professional interests, values, and commitments? Or should membership be open to anyone who wants to join? Is it better to reach out immediately for a large membership, start small and expand later, or just stay small? Each choice has important consequences for the success of the network. Open networks need to satisfy constituents with different interests and levels of commitment, whereas networks that restrict membership tend to have a core of committed members (usually the first to join) who share a particular point of view and must concern themselves with how to socialize new members. These issues influence the structure of the network, the kinds of activities it provides, and the role that leadership plays—whether in deepening the work of the members of an exclusive network or in finding ways to involve members who are at different levels of sophistication in an inclusive one.

Networks, regardless of their unique qualities, have in common the ways in which they bring people together and organize their work. They all value knowledge that is both context-specific and generalized. Structurally and philosophically, they are more like a movement than an organization. In addition, agendas are more often challenging than prescriptive; work formats more collaborative than individualistic; attempts at change more integrated than fragmented; and approaches to leadership more facilitative than directive. At a time when schools are involved in reinventing themselves to serve a highly technological and multicultural world, these intentional learning communities are becoming an important and valuable force for changing education.

References

Darling-Hammond, L. (1993). "Reframing the School Reform Agenda: Developing Capacity for School Transformation." *Kappan* 74, 10: 753–761.

Darling-Hammond, L., and M. W. McLaughlin. (April 1995). "Policies that Support Professional Development in an Era of Reform." *Kappan* 76, 8: 597–604.

Lieberman, A. (April 1995). "Practices that Support Teacher Development: Transforming Conceptions of Teacher Learning." *Kappan* 76, 8: 591–596.

Lieberman, A., and M. Grolnick. (1996). "Networks and Reform in American Education." *The Teachers College Record* 98, 1.

Lytle, S., and M. Cochran-Smith, eds. (1992). *Inside-Outside: Teacher Research and Knowledge.* New York: Teachers College Press.

Little, J. W. (1993). "Professional Development in a Climate of Educational Reform." *Educational Evaluation and Policy Analysis* 15, 2: 129–151.

Miles, M. B. (1978). "On Networking." Unpublished manuscript. Center for Policy Research. Washington, DC: National Institute of Education.

Author's note: This paper is adapted from a study entitled "Networks and Reform in American Education" by Ann Lieberman and Maureen Grolnick (1996).

Article Review Form at end of book.

WiseGuide Wrap-Up

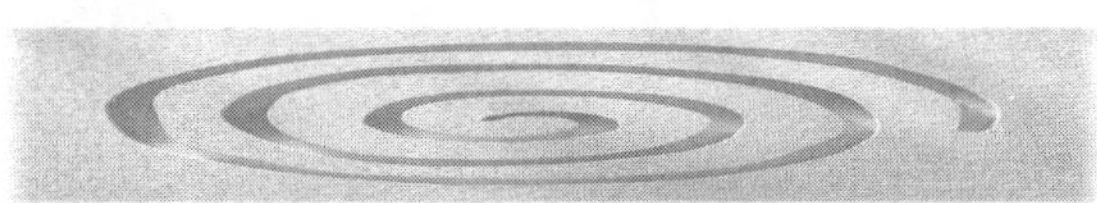

- Educational systems are dynamic and receptive to innovations that fulfill the academic, physical, and social needs of students.
- Preservice teachers benefit from field-based teacher preparation programs that allow them to become actively involved in the teaching-learning process.
- Authentic assessment procedures are only one component of a comprehensive evaluation plan.
- Societal influences and student needs have led to the establishment of full-service schools.
- Many schools are implementing alternative scheduling formats in an attempt to meet the needs of today's students and teachers.
- Learning communities are an effective means of support for teachers and administrators, including preservice and novice teachers.

R.E.A.L. Sites

This list provides a print preview of typical **coursewise** R.E.A.L. sites. There are over 100 such sites at the **courselinks**™ site. The danger in printing URLs is that web sites can change overnight. As we went to press, these sites were functional using the URL provided. If you come across one that isn't, please let us know via email to: webmaster@coursewise.com. Use your Passport to access the most current list of R.E.A.L. sites at the **courselinks**™ site.

Site name: North Central Regional Educational Laboratory Pathways to School Improvement

URL: http://www.ncrel.org/pathways.htm

Why is it R.E.A.L.? This site offers information on appropriate uses of authentic assessment procedures. Also included are discussions on the advantages and disadvantages of implementing authentic assessment plans.

Key topics: alternative assessment, evaluation

Activity: From the perspective of a preservice teacher, discuss ways that alternative assessments can be used in your teacher preparation program.

Site name: National Center for Research on Evaluation, Standards, and Student Testing

URL: http://cresst96.cse.ucla.edu/index.htm

Why is it R.E.A.L.? Sponsored by the U.S. Department of Education, this site contains recent reports on assessment issues, specifically at the K–12 level. Links to other sites and newsletters are included.

Key topics: assessment, evaluation, education standards

Activity: Select a report related to your content area, and write a summary of it.

section

Shaping Our Future: Becoming Visionaries

Societal changes and attempts to meet student and teacher needs have transformed public education systems during the past 50 years. Departures from tradition include, but certainly are not limited to, changes in organizational structures (for example, middle schools), school building designs, daily and yearly schedules, curricular offerings, and assessment plans. More specifically, ways of thinking about teaching and learning have changed, as reflected in today's educational systems.

The twenty-first century is approaching with new and different demands, and educational institutions must be prepared to meet those demands. K–16 (kindergarten through college) students will need the knowledge and skills requisite for success in an ever-changing global society. Only with shared visions and anticipation of the future can this objective be accomplished.

The readings in this section are relevant for preservice teachers and could potentially impact future directions of educational systems. The first reading, "Professional Development Schools Can Revitalize Teacher Education," discusses the role of field-based experiences in teacher preparation programs. The second reading, "Voices from Networked Classrooms'" examines the Internet as an instructional tool that links the world. Technological advances for twenty-first century schools are discussed in the next two readings, "Creating the Information Age School" and "Educational Electronic Networks." The last reading, "Learning Networks: Looking to 2010," illustrates the interconnectivity of schools, communities, regions, states, and nations via learning networks.

Learning Objectives

After reading the articles in this section, you will be able to:

- Discuss the role of professional development schools in teacher preparation programs.
- Identify obstacles that hinder the development and implementation of professional development schools.
- List recommendations for developing and maintaining successful professional development schools.
- Give examples to support the use of the Internet as a learning tool for K–16 students.
- Identify challenges faced by teachers who want to utilize the Internet as an instructional strategy.
- Discuss the importance of creating Information Age schools equipped for the twenty-first century.
- Define and give examples of learning networks.

Questions

Reading 32: What is the philosophy behind professional development schools? What obstacles may hinder the establishment and maintenance of professional development schools?

Reading 33: What are benefits of using the Internet as an instructional tool? What are some challenges faced by teachers who want to use the Internet as a tool for learning?

Reading 34: What does an Information Age school look like? What are some strategies for designing effective Information Age schools?

Reading 35: How have electronic networks had an impact on students' educational experiences? How can preservice teachers utilize the Internet?

Reading 36: What are learning networks?

What is the philosophy behind professional development schools? What obstacles may hinder the establishment and maintenance of professional development schools?

Professional Development Schools Can Revitalize Teacher Education

Educators finally are recognizing that hands-on, supervised field experiences are better preparation for prospective teachers than "book knowledge" taught in college classrooms.

Renee Campoy

Dr. Campoy is associate professor of elementary and secondary education, Murray (Ky.) State University.

Sometimes, stupid ideas persist in spite of common wisdom to the contrary. Because they are cheap and easy to administer, schools of education have perpetuated traditional teacher education programs whereby novice teachers are isolated on college campuses away from their purpose of study—real children in real schools. The professional development school (PDS) as a model of teacher education reform could change this with common-sense solutions to training the next generation of teachers.

For decades, demands have been made to reform the American education system. Usually, elementary and secondary education have been the objects of these efforts. For instance, in the 1980s, the Reagan Administration produced *A Nation at Risk* in an effort to create higher educational standards, and, in the 1990s, Presidents George Bush and Bill Clinton promoted Goals 2000 for the same end. More recently, higher education, particularly teacher education, has been targeted for reform.

Educators are beginning to realize that changes in kindergarten through 12th-grade education will not be effective when many novice teachers still are trained in traditional, campus-bound programs where course work has been separated from actual teaching experiences by time and distance. In some, this means that an education student may not work with children until the final semester of a four-year program for student teaching.

In comparable examples from industry and medicine, who would want to fly with a pilot who only had listened to lectures and taken tests without actually flying a plane? Who would want to be examined by physicians who lacked supervised experiences with patients as part of their training? Consumers would not stand for this, yet they tolerate the ineffective education of teachers. Expecting novice teachers to be qualified in the classroom is silly

From USA TODAY, Vol. 125, No. 2624, May 1997, pp. 68–69. Reprinted by permission of The Society for the Advancement of Education.

when their "book knowledge" can not be practiced and tested for effectiveness within a classroom. Educators finally are recognizing that common sense should prevail when it comes to including hands-on, extended, supervised field experiences in teacher education programs. Many teacher training institutions are taking a look at reform initiatives that may provide this.

The professional development school is one of the most prominent and compelling models of this type of teacher education reform. The PDS proposes to reorganize and renew teacher training programs by engaging specially selected public schools in a long-term relationship with a local college or university's teacher training. This type of synergy helps both institutions do more than each could do on its own. Many teacher training institutions across the country already are embracing this model. According to the ERIC Clearinghouse, more than 300 PDSs are operating across the country.

To those not in the field of education, it would seem obvious to conduct teacher training in schools. Often, though, new methods of teacher training are resisted by faculty members who prefer to teach on campus insulated from the practical realities of their profession. This notwithstanding, PDS programs are producing evidence that novice teachers learn more about teaching when their course materials are presented in conjunction with assignments working with children. It has been found that such a method provides powerful and effective feedback to the novice teacher during lessons when the pupils are bored, frustrated, indifferent, or happily engaged. In these cases, novice teachers do not have to be told that their lessons are poor; the children do that with their actions. Then, the teacher can move to the more complex problem of how to improve the lesson.

In addition to working with kids, novice teachers observe and interact with experienced classroom teachers. Many education students spend seat time at the university or college memorizing terms for tests without the experience or background knowledge needed to understand how or why teaching techniques will work in classrooms. The public is unaware how pervasive this type of education is in teacher training institutions and how poorly it serves the mission of developing competent teachers.

Some critics have suggested that the reality of school might frighten or discourage novice teachers. Instead, the opposite tends to be true. Experience in schools creates *realistic* expectations regarding student behavior and practical methods of instruction. Novices tend to believe that expert teachers simply follow a lesson formula that they have learned in college. They fail to understand—unless they observe, experience, and discuss it—that much of teaching is trial-and-error judgment, and the ability to be flexible, depending on the needs of pupils, is critical.

When novice teachers interact with youngsters and teachers in the school environment, their confidence increases. This serves to produce a teacher who is ready to deal with situations in today's schools. Teaching is a continuous learning process, not a static set of skills and knowledge taught in college and practiced until retirement. New teachers entering the field need to be flexible in acquiring skills to address a host of complex issues, including meeting the instructional needs of a variety of special education students, keeping pace with the informational and technological explosions, and dealing with difficult social issues such as violence and substance abuse. All of theses may manifest themselves in the classroom and usually can not be managed without prior experience and a practical framework for dealing with such situations.

Combating Conflicts

Given the national and local pressure to reform traditional educational programs, why haven't all teacher training institutions implemented PDS programs? One reason is that public school systems and teacher training institutions have their own reward procedures, funding sources, and governance structures. While each is charged by society with the responsibility of educating its citizenry, their means are often different, and the development of PDSs are hampered by a variety of institutional baggage. What seems to be common sense still is difficult to accomplish.

One critical issue to be addressed is that of governance and decision-making. Some decisions likely to be shared between the school and the teacher training institution would be the types of education courses that are placed in the school or choices about the education faculty members who work within the school. The PDS site and the teacher training institution should decide together what kinds of staff development programs to offer classroom teachers in order to improve their skills or if new types of instruction, such as in reading or science, should be tried. Both institutions have a stake in this. The teacher training institution wants the novice teachers to see current methods practiced by experienced, effective teachers, and the school seeks to provide the most beneficial methods of instruction for its pupils.

Time issues and reward systems are other critical items facing PDSs. Teachers who work at PDS sites often report that the additional responsibilities of supervising novice teachers have been added to their already overloaded schedules. University faculty find that courses taught off-site are treated the same as those taught on campus, even if they involve considerable additional travel and planning time. Few institutions have altered their policy and reward systems to compensate for changes made to the traditional teaching roles.

Funding often poses another problem. Many universities have been able to use grant funds to begin their projects so that they initially did not have to commit a portion of their operating budgets. This has been helpful in that it allowed the PDS—an often untested proposition—to become established. However, as projects mature and since many grants operate on three-year cycles, the PDS project must seek other funds. Institutionalizing PDSs—making their operations a normal, funded part of both the public school district and the teacher training institution—has been one of the biggest obstacles. Unless schools and teacher training institutions can redesign policy, generate funds, and create governance and reward structures supportive of PDSs, such programs are likely to become just another flash-in-the-pan educational trend.

Several years of trial-and-error development have taught educators that PDSs do not fit comfortably into the organizational structures of either the school district or the university. What is needed are hybrid organizational structures that reflect the unique combination of the public school and the teacher training institution. The faculty and administrators of this type of hybrid organization would have to design reward and policy structures supporting the combined work of the teacher training institution and the public school to create a higher-quality teacher education program. This new institution would produce teachers who work in schools as part of their early training and emerge ready to deal with children in the classroom because they have obtained much of their training in schools. As a result of this partnership between schools and teacher training institutions, common sense may prevail, benefiting society by better educating the next generation of students and teachers.

Article Review Form at end of book.

What are benefits of using the Internet as an instructional tool? What are some challenges faced by teachers who want to use the Internet as a tool for learning?

Voices from Networked Classrooms

Using the Internet and other technology can positively influence students' overall achievement. The motivation factor alone increases engagement, a goal of most classroom teachers.

Jean Brownlee-Conyers and Brenda Kraber

Jean Brownlee-Conyers is Assistant Superintendent of Curriculum and Instruction for Community Consolidated School District 93, 4 N 570 Old Gary Ave., Bartlett, IL 60103. Brenda Kraber is a teacher in the TREE at Glen Grove School in Glenview District 34, Glenview, Illinois. Patrick Baldwin, Heidi Fieselmann, Anthony Pesce, and Sean Robberson are 5th and 6th grade students at Glen Grove School. Glen Grove's Web site: http://gg.www.ncook.k12.il.us.

How Do We Use the Internet?

We use the World Wide Web and a variety of browsers and search engines to gather information and find experts. For example, when we read *The Hobbit*, we found a college professor who was interested in J.R.R. Tolkien. He answered our questions, and he gave us a place to link our Hobbit home page.

In another example, the Sports Interest Group needed to find the price of tickets, refreshments, and souvenirs for baseball games in diferent places around the United States. On the Web, they found the price of tickets, but not the prices of refreshments or souvenirs. Then the group found a number that they could call to get the information they needed.

The Web is also used to share information. A lot of students publish their final projects on the Web. Students who participate in mini-lessons and interest groups, such as the World Class Writers, publish home pages on the Web.

—*Heidi Fieselmann, grade 5–6*

In 1994, the Glenview, Illinois, Public School District, a K–8 district north of Chicago, created three technology-rich educational environments (TREEs) that use alternative methods of teaching and learning through networked communication technologies. Each environment consists of three teachers and about 75 students (ages 9–12) who work collaboratively in a flexible space the size of three classrooms. The students are heterogeneously grouped and include a range of learning abilities and cultural backgrounds representative of the district. In the TREE classes, teachers place great value on students' voice in their learning; and teachers and students work together to design individual problem-based projects that reflect students' interests. Keeping in mind the district curriculum requirements, teachers negotiate with the students the depth and breadth of their ideas, as well as the nature and quality of their final exhibitions. Teachers also offer mini-workshops and interest groups to supplement the students' learning.

Brownlee-Conyers, Jean and Kraber, Brenda. (November 1996). "Voices from Networked Classrooms." EDUCATIONAL LEADERSHIP 54, 3: 34–36. Reprinted with permission of the Association for Supervision and Curriculum Development.

Intensive Computer Environment—Networked

Each TREE group has enough computers to provide one for every three students. We acquired the computers through a recent reallocation of district funds, which places a priority on technology-rich environments and training. All students and teachers have direct access to the Internet, as well as software packages such as *Hyperstudio, Inspiration, ClarisWorks, MicroWorlds,* and *PageMill.* The computers are also connected on a local area network.

Teachers facilitate students' learning and keep track of their progress on curriculum outcomes, using personal digital assistants (small, hand-held, computerized notebooks). Students work individually and in groups, which are flexible across interests, needs, and ages. The success of the TREE groups depends on the availability of the extended learning community that the networked technologies and, in particular, the Internet provide.

After our first year, we found that TREE students had significantly higher achievement scores in inferential comprehension and writing skills than those of other students in the school. But what might be making the difference? Some suggestions emerge from the students' voices as they share with us how they are using the network, what they see as the pros and cons, and the challenges that we face in creating expanded learning communities. Four 5th and 6th grade students—Patrick, Heidi, Anthony, and Sean—have provided their perspectives on using the Internet, particularly the World Wide Web, in their studies (see boxes).

Challenges We Face on the Internet

Our patience has been challenged by the technology. It is not always easy to locate information or experts on the Web. For example, when too much information is loaded, the computer might "freeze" on us. We might have to restart the computer and start over from the beginning. Sometimes we can just wait, and usually the computer behaves.

We have learned to be clear with our questions, as well as to not give up and think of the Web as a maze. It is one of the neatest things to finally reach experts and for them to give us advice and treat us as a colleague, even if we're only 10 years old.

Sometimes we must go back to the old-fashioned way of learning. The network at various points "goes down." We have learned to be flexible and adjust our schedule to continue with our works. The Web isn't always a helpful source—and may lead us to inappropriate information. For example, if we do a search on batteries, someone on the Web might want to sell us batteries. If this happens, we might have to go to a book instead of the Web. Despite the challenge, the World Wide Web allows us to go beyond our classroom and school.

—Patrick Baldwin, grade 5–6

Benefits of Using the Internet

Searching the Web for information is more fun than checking out books and reading them at a table in a noisy room. Instead, we go to a computer and look through pages of information on the Web. We also can access sound recordings and mini-videos, such as a recording of a dolphin's sounds or a video of the discovery of the bow of the *Titanic*. The audiovisual applications often are more helpful and a lot more fun than books alone.

The Web enhances the quality of our work. For example, for a project on the theory of relativity, we will probably have problems trying to understand a college physics book. On the Web, we can find a FAQ (frequently asked questions) page or an expert to answer difficult questions.

I have also noticed that the Net can make us think differently about our projects. Instead of just reporting on the sinking of the *Titanic*, I searched the Web and found other options, such as learning how you might redesign the ship so it wouldn't sink, or writing a story from the point of view of a child. When we use the Web, it seems that anything is possible.

The Net can also give us current, accurate information for reports. For example, if a dolphin is killed by an unknown disease, there will probably be a home page put up in 24–48 hours. It could take months or even years to publish a book on the incident.

—Sean Robberson, grade 5–6

Challenges and Benefits of Networking

Challenges to Internet use—for both students and teachers—include dealing with possible abuse and inappropriate use of the Net, as well as planning for flexible use of technology. First, we have taken several steps to establish safeguards to protect students from inappropriate uses of the Net. In addition to requiring all students and their parents to sign an Appropriate Use form, we do not provide access to many chat rooms, adult sites, and dating rooms. Our network systems manager is also vigilant in monitoring what students download and save.

"The Net can give us current, accurate information for reports."

A Cautionary Note on the Internet

There are dangers on the Net—not dangers like stumbling on the Government's secret files on UFOs and having men in black coats at your front door the next day, but dangers like children finding things that should only be seen or read by adults. For example, chat rooms are a big problem. Chat rooms are places where people interact with others. Some children can find chat rooms on home pages that have something to do with television shows. Some students who use these areas inappropriately have been harassed and greeted by harsh language. In addition to chat rooms, adult magazines, inappropriate photos, and dating rooms can be found with little trouble. These avenues are certainly not appropriate for students.

—*Anthony Pesce, grade 5–6*

Moreover, we developed a document that establishes the rights, privileges, and responsibilities of everyone using the Net; and all students in the TREE sign it. (A copy of this document may be obtained from the authors.)

In the TREE classes, teachers place great value on students' voice in their learning; and teachers and students work together to design individual problem-based projects that reflect students' interests.

A second challenge is to create a learning environment that provides students and teachers flexibility in instructional practices and timely access to computers, phones, and the Internet. We use many kinds of activities and grouping arrangements to allow students maximum computer time. Of course, the initial challenge is to obtain the funding for all this hardware and software. Being able to show advances in students' achievements is essential in obtaining funds from any source or in acquiring a commitment of staff time.

The TREEs project has allowed us to use alternative methods of teaching, has opened our minds to the voices of our students, and has provided an environment that is enabled by technology. Our students have access to the world and, indeed, find school a great place to learn.

Article Review Form at end of book.

What does an Information Age school look like? What are some strategies for designing effective Information Age schools?

Creating the Information Age School

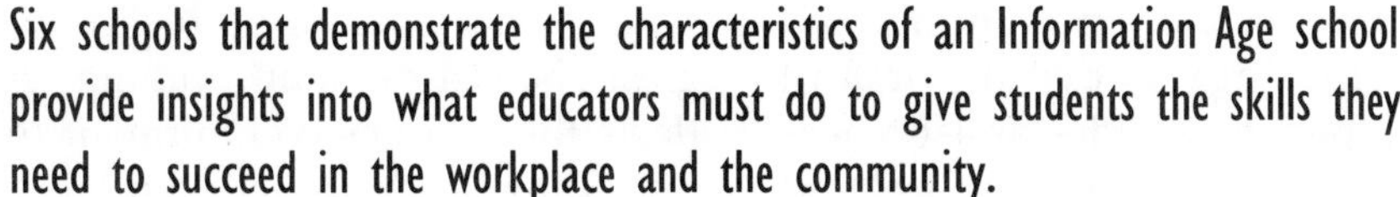

Six schools that demonstrate the characteristics of an Information Age school provide insights into what educators must do to give students the skills they need to succeed in the workplace and the community.

Vicki Hancock

Vicki Hancock is Director of New Ventures at ASCD (e-mail: vhancock @ ascd.org).

Most school-age children in the United States interact every day with a variety of information media—television, video games, multimedia computer systems, audio- and videotape, compact discs, and print. At the same time, workplaces are retooling with advanced technologies and acquiring access to complex, comprehensive information systems to streamline operations. Our youth have so much exposure to technological gadgets and information resources that one would think the transition from school to workplace would be second nature. Not so. According to recent projections, only about 22 percent of people currently entering the labor market possess the technology skills that will be required for 60 percent of new jobs in the year 2000 (Zuckerman 1994).

To eliminate this mismatch between schools and workplace, we need "Information Age" schools. But what does an Information Age school look like, and how do you begin to create such a school?

What It Looks Like

Researchers (Breivik and Senn 1994, Glennan and Melmed 1996, Cuban 1997) point to at least six attributes that characterize an Information Age school. The following descriptions of these attributes include examples of exemplary schools, along with contact information. I have "found" each of the schools by making site visits in my former role as an ASCD regional director and by serving as a judge in a variety of technology competitions.

Interactivity

In schools demonstrating interactivity, students communicate with other students through formal presentations, cooperative learning activities, and informal dialogue. Students and teachers talk to one another about their learning tasks in large groups, small groups, and one-to-one. Students have constant access to and know how to use print and electronic information resources to inform their learning activities. They recognize the value of the information in their own communities and interact with various community members, including businesspeople, social service staff, arts professionals, athletes, older adults, and volunteer workers, enhancing their curriculum studies with authentic information from primary sources.

At the Sun Valley Elementary School in Winnipeg, Manitoba, 4th grade students regularly participate in "keypals" activities to exchange cultural information with schools around the world. Students in grades 5 and 6 use resources from their school and community to develop "talking

Hancock, Vicki. (November 1997). "Creating the Information Age School." EDUCATIONAL LEADERSHIP 55, 3: 60–63. Reprinted with permission of the Association for Supervision and Curriculum Development.

books" that provide graphic, textual, and auditory lessons on animals, foods, weather, and other classroom topics for the 1st grade class. The librarymedia specialist helps students develop interactive multimedia projects for their classes and the community. One such project takes citizens on an adventure tour of Winnipeg.

The most probing questions come from the learners, who are curious about a variety of issues and intent on communicating what they discover.

Contact: Sun Valley Elementary School, 125 Sun Valley Dr., Winnipeg, Manitoba R2G 2W4, Canada; (204) 663-7664.

Self-Initiated Learning

When students initiate their own learning, they participate in productive questioning, probing for information they can use rather than waiting for the next question on a test or from a teacher. Information resources are central, not peripheral, in day-to-day learning activities. Students gather their own data to learn about topics, using a variety of sources and practicing effective research techniques. They are able to examine the large quantity of information they have gathered, synthesize it, and reduce it to usable quantities for their purposes. They can analyze and interpret information in the context of the problems or questions they have identified,and they can evaluate not only the quality of the information they've gathered but also the processes they've used to gather it.

The most important role for information technology at Taylorsville Elementary School in Taylorsville, Indiana, is to support a commitment to self-paced, individualized learning. Students participate in a program that emphasizes high expectations in core subjects and allows them to work at their own pace. Teachers use instructional strategies like multiage, multiyear groupings and team-based project work. Teachers facilitate, rather than direct, student learning, and they are comfortable using a variety of information technologies. Two days each school year are devoted to ongoing technology training, and a technology coordinator and three part-time aides assist teachers with their technology-related problem solving.

Contact: Taylorsville Elementary School, 9711 Walnut St., Taylorsville, IN 47280; (812) 526-5448.

A Changing Role for Teachers

To develop self-initiated learners in the Information Age school, the teacher's role must evolve away from dispenser of prefabricated facts to coach and guide. In this continuously changing role, teachers leave fact-finding to the computer, spending their time doing what they were meant to do as content experts: arousing curiosity, asking the right questions at the right time, and stimulating debate and serious discussion around engaging topics. In fact, every adult in the school community communicates the power of knowledge by modeling a love of learning. Preservice and inservice programs require the use of information resources and technologies as an integrated part of teachers' certification and recertification. Teachers create a community among themselves in which they are willing to plan together, share successes, resolve challenges, and model strategies for one another.

Professional development in information technologies is available daily at Adlai Stevenson High School in Lincolnshire, Illinois, in a specialized lab for teachers staffed by a full-time trainer. Proficiency with technology resources is a hiring requirement for teachers. All teaching staff have a three-year period to demonstrate proficiency with voice, data, and video technologies. The rigor of staff training reflects the school's commitment to providing students with an environment that promotes lifelong learning, provides opportunities to access global information and create knowledge, encourages participation from the community, and develops the skills of collaborative problem solving. Teachers and students use information technologies constantly for instruction, assessment, exploration, management, and the school's day-to-day operation.

Contact: Adlai Stevenson High School, One Stevenson Dr., Lincolnshire, IL 60069; (847) 634-4000; Internet: http://www.district125.k12.il.us.

Media and Technology Specialists as Central Participants

Media and technology specialists are critical in the Information Age school, and their role is twofold. Working with students, they are project facilitators. They can ask the initial questions that help students develop a focus for inquiry. They are thoroughly familiar with the school's and district's information resources and can direct students to multidisciplinary materials suitable for their investigations. With their technology skills, they can expose students to resources in a variety of media as well. They can assist students in their efforts to develop technology-enhanced products and presentations.

Working with teachers, they are instructional designers—partners in curriculum development and unit planning. Their expertise with information resources can inform teachers' exploration of curriculum topics and assist them in locating the materials they need. And, because ongoing professional development is an integral part of the work in an Information Age school, media and technology specialists contribute their expertise to the design and delivery of technology-enhanced inservice programs.

In the Information Age school, information skills are taught on an as-needed basis, and they are integrated throughout the curriculum.

Traditionally, students learned information skills in isolation as part of elementary- and middle-level "library skills" development. Technology "literacy" programs took place in computer labs during pull-out programs or in separately scheduled classes. In the Information Age school, such skills are taught on an as-needed basis, and they are integrated throughout the curriculum.

As a result of a districtwide effort to reform curriculum and instruction, the school day at Christopher Columbus Middle School in Union City, New Jersey, is organized into blocks of 90 minutes to two hours. Longer class periods have allowed teachers to create a project-focused, research-based curriculum that integrates the traditional subject areas with access to local and remote information resources through a variety of technologies. In addition to a central computer lab for whole-class instruction and walk-in use, each of the school's 12 classrooms has five computers, a printer, and a video presentation station. Students also have access to multimedia production equipment, computer video editing capabilities, and Internet connectivity from all PCs. Teachers receive three days of paid technology training each year, and a full-time technology coordinator conducts student computer classes, consults with teachers, and handles troubleshooting.

Contact: Christopher Columbus Middle School, 1500 New York Ave., Union City, NJ 07087; (201) 271-2085.

Continuous Evaluation

Everyone in the Information Age school recognizes the need for continuous evaluation not limited to scheduled standardized assessments. They engage in a high level of introspection, asking questions about the appropriateness of information resources, the efficiency of information searches, and the quality of information selection and evaluation. They also examine the quality of the products and presentations they use to share the results of their inquiries, as well as the communication process itself.

The Maryland Virtual High School of Science and Mathematics is a collaboration of 15 schools. They use information technologies to focus on computational science studies, accessing the Internet for mentoring, sharing projects, and assessing science resources. Students and teachers search and communicate online through local area networks (LANs) attached to each school's Internet hub. They use various software applications to create computational models of processes such as climate phenomena, animal population changes, and planetary motion. Teachers from the participating schools attend several three-day professional development sessions each year, as well as a five-day workshop at the end of each school year. Project staff are available for schoolwide training and outreach efforts in the various school communities.

Contact: Maryland Virtual High School of Science and Mathematics, 313 Wayne Ave., Silver Spring, MD 20901; (301) 650-6600; Internet: http://www.mbhs.edu.

A Changed Environment

An Information Age school has a different look and feel than a traditional school. Classroom methods link information retrieval, analysis, and application with strategies such as cooperative learning, guided inquiry, and thematic teaching. Information technologies are easily accessible, not locked away in media closets or labs. Student projects and products proliferate—not just as display items but as resources for other students and information for future investigations. Classrooms and hallways are frequently the scene of discussions and debates about substantive issues—topics important to both the curriculum and to the students investigating them. Most important, the most probing questions come from the learners, who are curious about a variety of issues and intent on communicating what they discover: How do you know that? What evidence do you have for that? Who says? How can we find out?

The curriculum at Patton Junior High School in Fort Leavenworth, Kansas, is "driven by students' needs to be productive members of an ever-advancing Information Age" (U.S.D. 207 Technology Initiatives brochure 1996). Instruction reflects the district's efforts to maintain high standards of achievement while encouraging learners to investigate a variety of topics in an exploratory environment. Students use technology tools and develop life skills in a 26-module program that includes topics such as robotics, audio broadcasting, maintaining a healthy heart, and becoming a confident consumer. The media center and classroom computers all provide Internet access. Teachers can use a centralized media management system to remotely schedule videotape, laserdisc, and interactive CD presentations without the need to check out and transport bulky equipment.

Contact: Patton Junior High School, 5 Grant Ave., Fort Leavenworth, KS 66027; (913) 651-7373; Internet: http://www.ftlvn.k12.ks.us.

How to Begin

To transform your school into an Information Age school, begin by using information technologies to encourage experimentation with the school's program. Focus on improving the connections between curriculum content and school process. Lengthen class periods. Consider multiage grouping. Experiment with interdisciplinary, problem-based, or thematic approaches to instruction. Develop individualized instructional plans for every student. Implement ongoing assessment measures that reflect students' continuous learning (portfolios, projects, performances). Encourage community members to regularly contribute their time and expertise throughout the school. Include them as part of decision-making groups for curriculum and technology planning. Provide incentives to teachers and administrators who demonstrate their willingness to try new methods and share what they've learned with their peers. Hire technology support staff with teaching experience to consult with teachers as well as troubleshoot equipment. Pay teachers to participate in professional development activities.

Rather than sitting back (like passive television viewers) marveling at the ever-increasing quantity of information and the rapidity of change, educators must lead students through a careful, cumulative acquisition of information literacy and technology skills. Teams of school professionals can plan integrated activities focusing on important content while encouraging students to practice these skills. Learners should engage from their earliest years in rich, complex, authentic experiences that provide a tension between creativity and utility. These experiences should also offer frequent opportunities for feedback and an environment of trust and open communication. This "orchestrated immersion" (Palmisano et al. 1993) can help ensure that students will leave their school years better prepared to participate actively and flexibly in their communities and the workplace.

References

Brevik, P., and J. Senn. (1994). *Information Literacy: Educating Children for the 21st Century.* New York, N.Y.: Scholastic.

Cuban, L. (May 21, 1997). "High-Tech Schools and Low-Tech Teaching." *Education Week on the Web* (http://www.edweek.org/ew/current/34cuban.h16).

Glennan, T., and A. Melmed. (1996). *Fostering the Use of Educational Technology: Elements of a National Strategy.* Santa Monica, Calif.: RAND

Palmisano, M., M. Barron, and L. Torp. (1993). *Integrative Learning System: Rationale, Overview, and Reflections.* Aurora, Ill.: Illinois Mathematics and Science Academy.

Unified School District 207. (1996). "Patton Junior High School Technology Initiatives." (Pamphlet). Ft. Leavenworth, Kan.: Author.

Zuckerman, P. (July 18, 1994). "America's Silent Revolution." *U.S. News and World Report* 117, 3:90.

Article Review Form at end of book.

How have electronic networks had an impact on students' educational experiences? How can preservice teachers utilize the Internet?

Educational Electronic Networks

Virtual field trips to Central American rain forests, global grocery price comparisons, NASA Hubble telescope images, community Web pages. Electronic learning networks are changing what happens in the classroom. What does the research say about ways to make sure network learning is meaningful to students?

James A. Levin and Cathy Thurston

James A. Levin is an Associate Professor in the Department of Educational Psychology, University of Illinois at Urbana-Champaign, 210 Education Building, 1310 S. Sixth Street, Champaign, IL 61820-6990 (e-mail: j-levin@uiuc.edu). Cathy Thurston is Director of the Office of Educational Technology, 32 Education Building, 1310 S. Sixth St., Champaign, IL 61820-6990 (e-mail: ethursto@uiuc.edu).

Electronic learning networks provide access to the riches of the world. Students in remote rural locations can reach the Library of Congress, classes in towns without museums can visit the Louvre, and students and teachers anywhere can communicate with content-area experts from around the world.

Networks also have made new forms of local and worldwide collaborative learning possible. They have helped to create writing communities (Bruce and Rubin 1993, Scardamalia et al. 1992), science communities (Learning Through Collaborative Visualization Project 1993, Newman and Goldman 1986–87, Ruopp et al. 1993), mathematics communities (Klotz 1996), problem-solving communities (Levin et al. 1987), and teacher education communities (Levin et al. 1994, Thurston et al. 1996).

These electronic communities bring together students, teachers, and adults from outside the education arena. For example, students have worked in communities to analyze and predict weather, to exchange measurements of the sun's shadow to figure the circumference of the earth, and to develop new solutions to local problems based on similar approaches used in distant places. Teacher education students have worked in communities to find or develop, evaluate, and electronically publish curriculum resources.

Students do most of their work off the network, and in many cases off the computer. Network-based learning, unlike word processing or programming, does not require vast numbers of computers and unlimited connection time. It can motivate students to become involved in a wide range of learning activities. And the computer and network infrastructure can be expanded as needed to allow for ever more powerful uses.

Research on the uses of electronic networks often starts with the exploration of innovative uses. Researchers then develop conceptual frameworks for such uses and look at barriers that may lead to difficulties and failure. Educators can use this information to make decisions about networks in their own settings.

One set of studies focused on the InterCultural Learning Network (Levin et al. 1987), where students collaboratively tackled water shortage problems in their communities, engaged in network-based analyses of cultural differences in holiday celebrations around the world, and contributed to a network-based newswire.

Levin, James A. and Thurston, Cathy. (November 1996). "Research Summary Educational Electronic Networks." EDUCATIONAL LEADERSHIP 54, 3: 46–50.

According to researchers, this kind of student writing is much more effective educationally than the electronic pen pal projects commonly advocated by network novices (Levin et al. 1989).

Cohen and Riel (1989) reported that writing for remote peers over a network produced better quality writing than writing for the teacher. This "audience effect" of network-based interactions can provide a powerful context for learning in many different areas. Researchers have found similar effects in science (Cervantes 1993, Ruopp et al. 1993), mathematics (Thalathoti 1992), and social studies (Levin et al. 1989).

Sharing Information with Society

Electronic networks are highly interactive. Information can flow in many directions. The research suggests that in the long term, the most significant impact of networks on education may prove to be the flow of information from educational institutions to the rest of society.

Many recent curriculum reform efforts have focused on problem-based and project-based learning. Networks allow students and teachers to draw from many fields, not just from education. And networks allow students and teachers to share their findings with the world at large. Thus, student work—while primarily oriented toward optimizing learning—can have a secondary benefit beyond the immediate learning context.

Networks allow students and teachers to draw from many fields, not just education. And networks allow students and teachers to share their findings with the world at large.

For example, networked students helped design recreational activities for space station astronauts (Cervantes 1993, Levin 1992). They developed concepts for transforming everyday sports and for creating new sports. NASA professionals had not tackled this task because the space shuttle is too small for such activities.

Students can, as part of their learning activities, contact adults in their communities to identify problems and challenges. They can use networks to access resources anywhere in the world and make them available to community members. For example, students in California, Illinois, Japan, Mexico, and Israel used a network to study a local water problem (Levin and Cohen 1985, Waugh et al. 1988). They used local resources to learn the specifics of the problem and the actions taken to solve it. The students relayed questions developed by local authorities to the distant students, who in turn asked their own experts. They exchanged information, and they analyzed it to identify actions that local authorities had not yet considered.

Much of the research to date has focused on overcoming the difficulties of using networks successfully in education.

Barriers to Using Electronic Networks

Much of the research to date has focused on overcoming the difficulties of using networks successfully in education. These barriers include lack of access and appropriate infrastructure, separation of telecommunications from the curriculum, lack of support for teachers attempting to work with innovative approaches, and lack of teacher expertise in telecommunications.

Infrastructure and Access

A number of studies indicate that it is important for teachers to have equipment in their classrooms (Harris 1994, Levin 1995, U.S. Office of Technology Assessment 1995). The Apple Classroom of Tomorrow research indicates that teachers should return from training sessions to classrooms equipped with the hardware and software on which they received their training (Ringstaff and Yocum 1994). Ideally, they should have access to telecommunications equipment at home and at school (Harris 1994).

Infrastructure—which includes wiring, modems or high-speed connections, and computer hardware and software—is a critical component of an effective network. Current estimates are that only 9 percent of the nation's classrooms are connected to the Internet (West 1996). In our experience with the Teaching Telapprentice-ships model, student teachers emphasized the importance not only of having hands-on training, but also of being "hooked up" or "wired" in their own classroom (Thurston et al. 1996).

Telecommunications and Curriculum

A second barrier to effective implementation of networks is the gap between network use and the curriculum. Studies show that networks are most effective when they are tied to the curriculum (Levin 1995, Thurston et al. 1996). Training is essential if teachers are to see telecommunications as a means to an end, not as an end in itself. For example, a high school French teacher developed a project where a large number of sites contributed recipes via the Internet. Her students then translated the recipes from French into English, which involved math as well as language skills. Then, they used desktop publishing software to create and illustrate a cookbook based on the project.

Using Networks Successfully

- The "audience effect" of network-based interactions can provide a powerful context for learning (Cervantes 1993, Ruopp et al. 1993, Thalathoti 1992, Levin et al. 1989).
- Teachers need to have telecommunications equipment in their classrooms (Harris 1994, Levin 1995, U.S. Office of Technology Assessment 1995).
- Networks are most effective when they are tied to the curriculum (Levin 1995, Thurston et al. 1996).
- Technical and administrative support is critical if teachers are to implement networks (National Association of Secondary School Principals 1996, Harris 1994, Levin 1995, Ringstaff and Yocum 1994).
- Teachers need appropriate and effective training, including hands-on experience and follow-up support (Benton Foundation 1995, Ringstaff and Yocum 1994).
- Districts should allocate 30–40 percent of their technology budget to teacher training (Benton Foundation 1995, Foa et al. 1996, Marshall 1995, U.S. Advisory Council on the National Information Infrastructure 1996, U.S. Office of Technology Assessment 1995).

Lack of Support

Another barrier to teacher implementation of networks is a lack of technical and/or administrative support. Very few schools have a full-time, on-site computer coordinator available to help teachers. *The Learning Connection* (Benton Foundation 1995) indicates that 60 percent of schools have no one to help, and it estimates that only 6 percent of elementary schools and 3 percent of high schools have a full-time computer coordinator.

The newly released Carnegie Report, *Breaking Ranks* (National Association of Secondary School Principals 1996), says such support is critical. In its "Priorities for Renewal," the report recommends that "every high school designate a technology resource person to provide technical assistance and to consult with staff to assist them in finding the people, information, and materials that they need to make best use of technology." Administrative support is as important as technical support (Harris 1994, Levin 1995, Ringstaff and Yocum 1994). In fact, the Apple Classroom studies show that the principal has a key role to play. The principal can control release time, provide access to hardware and software, promote team teaching or interdisciplinary study, and acknowledge efforts and provide recognition.

Lack of Effective Training

Research shows that many teachers have little or no experience with telecommunications or with technology in general (Benton Foundation 1995, Thurston 1990, U.S. Office of Technology Assessment 1995). In fact, lack of teacher expertise is probably one of the most significant obstacles to the effective implementation of networks. Teachers need appropriate infrastructure and access, opportunities to integrate technology into the curriculum, and technical and administrative support; but they also need effective training. And effective training requires hands-on experience and follow-up support (Benton Foundation 1995, Ringstaff and Yocum 1994).

Teachers need appropriate infrastructure and access, opportunities to integrate technology into the curriculum, and technical and administrative support; but they also need effective training.

Many experts believe it is a mistake to mandate telecommunications training for all teachers. Schools should support and recognize those teachers who are ready to move forward and learn (Foa et al. 1996, Harris 1994). Training should incorporate modeling or coaching in effective uses of technology (Benton Foundation 1995, Harris 1994, Ringstaff and Yocum 1994). The training should include face-to-face sessions followed by practice, then a return to follow-up coaching (Harris 1994). Teachers should work in pairs or small groups (Harris 1994, Ringstaff and Yocum 1994), so they have peer support when they return to their classrooms.

Studies show that districts should allocate 30–40 percent of their technology budget to teacher training (Benton Foundation 1995, Foa et al. 1996, Marshall 1995, U.S. Advisory Council on the National Information Infrastructure 1996, U.S. Office of Technology Assessment 1995). Typically, however, school districts allocate less than 15 percent for training (Benton Foundation 1995), and many have no budget at all.

Changing the Nature of Teaching and Learning

In summary, research has shown that the use of telecommunications in the classroom has the potential to change the nature of teaching and learning (Foa et al. 1996, Means 1994, Wilson et al. 1995). It can shift the focus from whole-group to small-group interaction; it can mark a shift from lecture to coaching; and it can enable teachers to do more one-on-one work with students. It can help shift the focus from test performance assessment to assessment based on products and progress (Wilson et al. 1995). And it can encourage teamwork, collaborative inquiry, and individualized instruction (Means 1994, U.S. Office of Technology Assessment 1995).

References

Benton Foundation. (1995). *The Learning Connection.* [Online] Available at http://cdinet.com/benton/goingon/learning.html.

Bruce, B., and A. Rubin. (1993). *Electronic Quills: A Situated Evaluation of Using Computers for Writing in Classrooms.* Hillsdale, N.J.: Erlbaum.

Cervantes, R. G. (1993). "Every Message Tells a Story: A Situated Evaluation of the Instructional Use of Computer Networking." Unpublished doctoral diss., University of Illinois, Urbana-Champaign.

Cohen, M., and M. Riel. (1989). "The Effect of Distant Audiences on Students' Writing." *American Educational Research Journal* 26, 2: 143–159.

Foa, L., R. L. Schwab, and M. Johnson. (May 1 1996). "Upgrading School Technology: Support the Zealots and Other Pointers for Entering a Strange New Land." *Education Week,* 52.

Harris, J. (1994). "Teacher Teachers to Use Telecomputing Tools." *The Computing Teacher* 22, 3: 60–63.

Klotz, G. (1996). *The Math Forum.* [Online] Available at http://forum.swarthmore.edu/build/prelim.prop.html. For more information send e-mail to klotz@cs.swarthmore.edu.

Learning Through Collaborative Visualization Project. (1993). *Learning Through Collaborative Visualization.* [Online] Available at http://www.covis.nwu.edu/. For more information send e-mail to bfishman@covis.nwu.edu.

Levin, J., and M. Cohen. (1985). "The World as an International Science Laboratory: Electronic Networks for Science Instruction and Problem Solving." *Journal of Computers in Mathematics and Science Teaching* 4: 33–35.

Levin, J., M. Waugh, D. Brown, and R. Clift. (1994). "Teaching Teleapprenticeships: A New Organizational Framework for Improving Teacher Education Using Electronic Networks." *Journal of Machine-Mediated Learning* 4, 2 and 3: 149–161.

Levin, J. A. (1992). *Electronic Networks and the Reshaping of Teaching and Learning: The Evolution of Teleapprenticeships and Instructional Teletask Forces.* San Francisco: American Educational Research Association.

Levin, J. A., M. Riel, N. Miyake, and M. Cohen. (1987). "Education on the Electronic Frontier: Teleapprenticeships in Globally Distributed Educational Contexts." *Contemporary Educational Psychology* 12: 254–260.

Levin, J.A., A. Rogers, M. Waugh, and K. Smith. (May 1989). "Observations on Educational Electronic Networks: Appropriate Activities for Learning." *The Computing Teacher* 16: 17–21.

Levin, S. R. (1995). "Teachers Using Technology: Barriers and Breakthroughs." *International Journal of Educational Telecommunications* 1, 1: 53–70.

Marshall, G. (July 1995). "Make It Count: How to Spend $1.5 Million in Technology Money Wisely." *American School Board Journal,* 26.

Means, B., ed. (1994). *Technology and Education Reform: The Reality Behind the Promise.* San Francisco: Jossey-Bass Publishers.

National Association of Secondary School Principals. (1996). *Breaking Ranks: Changing an American Institution.* Reston, VA.: NASSP.

Newman, D., and S. V. Goldman. (1986–87), "Earth Lab: A Local Network for Collaborative Science Classrooms." *Journal of Educational Technology Systems* 15, 3: 237–247.

Ringstaff, C., and K. Yocum. (1994). *Creating an Alternative Context for Teacher Development: The ACOT Teacher Development Centers* (ACOT Research Report Rep. No. 18). Cupertino, Calif.: Apple Computer, Inc.

Ruopp, R., S. Gal, B. Drayton, and M. Pfister. (1993). *LabNet: Toward a Community of Practice.* Hillsdale, N.J.: Erlbaum.

Scardamalia, M., C. Bereiter, C. Brett, P. J. Burtis, C. Calhoun, and N. Smith Lea. (1992). "Educational Applications of a Networked Communal Database." *Interactive Learning Environments* 2, 1: 45–71.

Thalathoti, V. (1992). "Teaching Exploratory Data Analysis Using a Microcomputer-based Telecommunications Network." Unpublished doctoral diss., University of Illinois, Urbana-Champaign.

Thurston, C. O., (1990). "Computers and Classroom Teacher: A Case Study of Staff Development and a National Survey of Technology Integration." Unpublished doctoral diss., University of Illinois, Urbana-Champaign.

Thurston, C. O., E. Secaras, and J. A. Levin. (1996). "Teaching Teleapprenticeships: An Innovative Model for Technology Integration in Teacher Education." [Online] *Journal of Research on Computing in Education* 28, 5. (http://www.educ.ksu.edu/Projects/JRCE/v28-5/Thurston/article/main.htm).

U.S. Advisory Council on the National Information Infrastructure. (1996). *Kickstart Initiative: Connecting America's Communities to the Information Superhighway.* St. Paul, Minn.: West Publishing Co.

U.S. Office of Technology Assessment. (1995). *Teachers and Technology: Making the Connection* (GPO Rep. No. 052-003-01409-2). Congressional Office of Technology Assessment. Washington, D.C.: U.S. Government Printing Office.

Waugh, M., N. Miyake, M. Cohen, and J. A. Levin. (1988). "Analysis of Problem Solving Interactions on Electronic Networks." Annual Meeting of the American Educational Research Association, New Orleans.

West, P. (May 22, 1996). "Schools, Libraries Seen Bridging Technology Gap." *Education Week,* 9.

Wilson, B. G., R. Hamilton, J. L. Teslow, and T. A. Cyr. (1995). "Teaching Methods and Technology." *ERIC Review* 4, 1.

Authors note: This material is based on work supported by the National Science Foundation under Grant No. RED-9253423. Any opinions, findings, and conclusions or recommendations expressed in this material are those of the authors and do not necessarily reflect the views of the National Science Foundation. Hardware and software support was provided by Apple Computer and by Microsoft Corporation. Sandy Levin assisted with this article.

Article Review Form at end of book.

What are learning networks?

Learning Networks

Looking to 2010

Thomas G. Tate

Thomas G. Tate is National Program Leader for the Communication and Information Technology Staff of the U.S. Department of Agriculture's Extension Service in Washington, D.C. He has been providing leadership to national and state information technology initiatives for more than 24 years. He has degrees from the Massachusetts Institute of Technology and the University of Missouri.

Abstract

Proposed learning network technology offers some alternatives to the way we currently carry out education and training. High schools, state land-grant universities, libraries, community learning centers, public information terminals in public buildings will all be affected by new innovations in information technology. Reinventing and conversion of our traditional educational institutions are feasible and plausible as a result of development in new learning network technologies. We are becoming a nation of community learning centers that cater to formal and informal training and educational needs. These learning centers will be used by a full range of learners: K–12 students during the regular school hours; students in after-school programs during the afternoon and early evening hours; and adults in labor, management, and the professions all during the day and night. This network of community learning centers will be linked by the new National Research and Education Network. Satellite as well as land-based educational networks will be involved. Information terminals at schools, libraries, community learning centers, public buildings, homes, farms, and firms will have access to and be linked by learning networks.

Crime in our city streets, declining farm prices, drug use and abuse, teenage pregnancy, decline in rural employment, obsolete industrial workers, home-bound senior citizens, soaring health costs, displaced military personnel, the handicapped—what do all of these challenges have in common? The answer is that in the year 2010 learning network technology will have a positive impact on them all.

We are living at an incredible crossroads in this world. How quickly everything is changing and turning over. The rules, the issues, the problems we are working on, and the tools that we have to work with all seem to be changing at an accelerated rate. Not only are we setting up demonstration farms in this country, but we are helping our new partners in the former Soviet Union to do the same.

We are recruiting teams of U.S. agricultural producers and advisers to go into Eastern Europe to help build a new understanding of market systems and democratic processes. We are beginning to exchange information with those new partners through telecommunication links.

Within our country, our primary and secondary school systems need revitalization. Our nation's small and intermediate-sized industrial and manufacturing firms have fallen behind many of their international competitors. Both arenas need modernizing.

How Do We Prepare for the Twenty-First Century?

What is the best way for us to prepare for the twenty-first century? One alternative is to begin living as though we were already there. For example, many residents in

From Thomas G. Tate, "Learning Networks: Looking to 2010" in ANNALS OF THE AMERICAN ACADEMY OF POLITICAL AND SOCIAL SCIENCE Vol. 529, September 1993, pp. 71–79.

rural America now have access to the same knowledge bases, experts, seminars, presentations, and course offerings as their urban cousins. Some may argue that they have better access, depending on the policy of the state they live in.

The Show-Me Network: Satellite Down-Links

In Missouri, high schools and junior high schools are now equipped with satellite down-link dishes that allow learners to participate in video teleconferences that are broadcast on the Missouri satellite network. Students who live in a small community that cannot justify having a calculus or physics teacher for the 4 students who are ready to learn can participate in the statewide high school video classroom in their own community. Students in schools throughout the state participate in the Missouri video learning network. The Missouri group also produces a guide to educational programs available via satellite. Their magazine and satellite program guide is called *Education SATLINK.*

How was Missouri able to afford this system? A modest 10 percent tax on the rental of videotapes in each video store in the state is earmarked for financing the state's video learning network. The taxpayers have been very accepting of this tax and feel good about the benefits that come to the state.[1]

1. For more information on the Missouri effort, contact Educational Satellite Network, 2100 I-70 Drive S.W., Columbia, MO 65201.

Learning Centers for Retraining Adults

In addition to the formal class work that students are able to accomplish, the community school is now positioned to be a round-the-clock learning center that can be used to retrain and reskill displaced military personnel, to upgrade the knowledge and skills of industrial and manufacturing workers and managers, as well as for continuing education for professionals.

Information Transfer between Learners and Teachers

With the addition of the National Research and Education Network (NREN) hookups that are on the way, learners, teachers, tutors, and coaches will be able to interact with each other.[2] Teachers and learners can transfer work in progress, mark papers, and engage in other learner-teacher feedback electronically via personal telecomputers connected to NREN. Then-Senator Al Gore sponsored the legislation to support the NREN. Perhaps the Clinton administration will support the expansion of the NREN for use by learners nationwide. Long-distance and local telephone companies, cable companies, and wireless communication firms will each provide appropriate telecommunication components, pieces of the patchwork quilt to support local learner access to national information resources.

2. The NREN and other civic networks will evolve into the National Information Infrastructure (NII). For more information on NREN and NII, contact CIT-ES-USDA, Room 3322, Washington, DC 20250-0900.

An Agricultural Learning Network

The nation's leading land-grant universities have joined to establish and operate a new agricultural information and instructional service called AG*SAT. By combining satellite, audio-video, and computer technologies, AG*SAT affiliates are able to share academic instruction, Cooperative Extension programming, and agricultural research information. Ultimately, all land-grant institutions will have the opportunity to participate in AG*SAT.

Learners are able to go to a Cooperative Extension service learning center in their community. Local citizens are encouraged to participate in the educational programs that are down-linked by the local receiving dish. Farms, ranches, homes, schools, and firms with a satellite signal receiving dish may also receive AG*SAT educational programming.

How does AG*SAT work? All AG*SAT institutions develop educational programming based on their strengths. Rather than reinventing the educational wheels, the member institutions plan programs that will have national applicability and increase the impact of shrinking funds available for educational programming. The Cooperative Extension system then alerts the educational community through its electronic program guide, which can be subscribed to on the NREN. Subscribers receive an electronic-mail version of the Satellite Calendar each time it is updated.

AG*SAT learners do not have to be passive viewer-listeners. AG*SAT learners may call in their concerns or questions via an 800 number, à la Larry King, or communicate their concern or question by electronic mail to the site that is originating the program.[3]

Distance Education: Place Shifting

"Distance education" is a term that is creeping into our vocabulary. It simply means learning methods where the learner does not have to be eyeball to eyeball with the knowledge provider. The Missouri learning network and AG*SAT are good examples of one type of distance education, satellite video teleconferencing. Similar interactive video classrooms can also be established through land-based cable. Telephone companies are investing now to link learners via telephone lines that will permit the learners to have two-way audiovisual interaction with a teacher who may be miles away from their learning location. These examples provide an important advantage to learners, place shifting. Place shifting is making the learning experience available to the learner at a place where the learner can participate.

Distance Education: Time Shifting

Another important element of distance education is time shifting. Time shifting is packaging the learning tool in such a way that the learner can access it at a time that is convenient to him or her. Current learning tools that have this characteristic are books, films, audiotapes, videotapes, videodiscs, compact discs, computer programs, and so forth. When the NREN is fully operational, the current learning tools will be retrievable from resource centers for use in schools, learning centers, farms, ranches, business firms, and homes. If the learner has a personal computer at home or in the workplace that is connected to the network, he or she will retrieve them from providers who will be available on the network 24 hours a day. Currently, CompuServe and Prodigy are two examples of commercial network providers that make learning tools available to remote personal computers connected over the telephone lines by modem.

Public Information Terminals

The federal government has tested the use of public information terminals that make federal information available to the public in public places, such as shopping malls and post offices. The U.S. Department of Agriculture, the U.S. Postal Service, the Veterans Administration, and the Social Security Administration are considering the possibility of public information kiosks that locally store a wide variety of information about the programs that these organizations offer. Applications range from changing one's postal delivery address to finding out how to control the pest attacking one's crops. These kiosks are a good example of time shifting and place shifting. These public information terminals will be connected to a national network that will be used to keep users, viewers, and listeners up to date on the latest information. Local input can be provided that will permit these public information terminals to serve as local community bulletin boards. These terminal will be equipped with printers to permit output to be taken away by the taxpayer. The terminals will provide audio, video, and textual information in response to buttons pushed on a control panel.

These public information terminals will be important assets to the community. For those individuals who do not yet have access to the public networks through their computer at home, school, or workplace, the public information terminal will ensure that information technology does not provide the technologically literate with unfair access to information. Publicly accessible information terminals are important to equality, ensuring that people can enter, on foot or by wheelchair, a library or post office and have open access to public information.

Learning at One's Own Pace: Pace Shifting

Imagine having your own personal portable television for your own entertainment as well as educational needs. Imagine being able to learn about whatever you want whenever you want from your own battery-operated interactive audiovisual compact disc player. Imagine being able to carry a national library collection with you wherever you go, being able to ask questions and get answers on the screen as text, still photographs, or audiovisual presentations. Imagine learning new skills, wherever you want, 24 hours a day. Imagine being able to use this learning tool whether your first language is English or Spanish. It is hoped that everyone in the United States, urban or rural, will take this for granted in 2010 as a

3. For more information on AG*SAT, contact AG*SAT, Box 83111, Lincoln, NE 68501.

birthright. In the meantime, national consumer electronics companies are producing edutainment—education cum entertainment—products such as those just described.

National Library in Your Pocket

New developments in information storage technology are creating new opportunities. Compact discs, popular throughout the world for distributing high-quality music entertainment, are now being used to store large quantities of data and information for retrieval onto display screen by learners. The CD-ROM (compact disc read-only memory) provides personal-computer users with convenient storage and retrieval of specialized collections of data and information.

The Grolier Encyclopedia company has just released *The New Grolier Multimedia Encyclopedia* on compact disc. It features all 21 volumes of the *Academic American Encyclopedia* on a single CD-ROM, with articles on everything from covered wagons to lunar landers. A host of new features makes the urge to explore virtually irresistible. The on-disc encyclopedia includes color photographs, illustrations, sounds, and motion sequences. Famous speeches, music, and more can be listened to. This development turns the personal computer into a multimedia learning center. There are now more than 1000 CD-ROM titles that have been released.

Interactive Television

How about those who do not know nor ever want to know how to use a personal computer? The latest development, compact disc interactive (CDI), will make them want to trade in their home audio compact disc player. The CDI players being introduced in 1993 provide educators and learners with a new set of options. The CDI player is connected to a television. The audio comes out of the speaker of the television—or it could be routed to come through a home entertainment center. A remote control unit is used to move the selector to items that appear on the television screen, similar to a jukebox selection panel. After two or three answers or options are selected from the screen, the action begins. The action is a learning sequence that demands the learner's involvement in order to progress. A dynamic mix of music, audio, and still and motion photography guide the learner to a knowledge destination that he or she determines. It is an interactive electronic game that teaches, not preaches.

Initially, the CDI product is being introduced with course options that range from learning how to play musical instruments to improving one's golf game. For the younger set, Sesame Street characters teach logic, letters, and numbers. There are tours of museums in Italy, Mexico, and the Untied States. Bell Atlantic is testing CDI as an alternative to the traditional Yellow Pages. If you want to build your own learning program, you can send your next roll of Kodak film to Kodak, and they will return your latest photo session to you on a compact disc that you can present to learners via the television screen. Portable units that are battery-operated will be introduced over the next couple of years.

In the test labs, these products have held adults and youths, rural and urban, spellbound and learning for hours. They are being introduced into the U.S. marketplace in the 1993–94 season.

Extension Community Learning Centers

Increasingly, institutions in the community are beginning to take on a more proactive role in providing self-improvement opportunities. Cooperative Extension offices located in public buildings such as courthouses and post offices are increasingly sharing their learning resource technology with other groups in the community. Computers in the local Extension centers are beginning to be connected to national networks that provide on-line retrieval access to knowledge and expertise stored in computers in the next county, state, or nation. Conference rooms in Cooperative Extension offices that are connected to satellite or land-based cable systems are being made available to a wide variety of groups throughout the community. This trend needs to spread to other institutions in the community that have facilities that could be shared as learning centers rather than sit idle or underused.

Reinventing the Land-Grant Institution

The problems of our society have become too complex to be solved solely by the resources available in our colleges of agriculture, natural resources, and home economics. The learning resources of every department of the college and university are needed to solve the problems of formal and informal learners.

For many years, two land-grant institutions, the University of Missouri and the

Massachusetts Institute of Technology, have made all of their subject matter departments available to business, industry, and labor clientele. Missouri has made its experts available through its Business, Industry, and Labor Extension Program, and the Institute through its Industrial Liaison Program. These models have been emulated by land-grant universities in other states. Perhaps it is time to accelerate these programs nationally.

Information and learning technology can broaden our access to the learning resource base of all subject matter departments, yet give us the power to narrow our focus to the specific problem and objective of the learner. If local citizens can understand and effectively tell the story, I believe that future national decision makers will allocate the resources necessary to permit the total land-grant university to work on improving schools and firms as well as farms. Industrial and educational units need the benefits of the learning systems that have made American agriculture the envy of the world.

Becoming a Learning Network

U.S. institutions are becoming a part of a learning network for firms, schools, families, and farms. The institutions and the individuals within them carry out multiple responsibilities as teachers, researchers, information providers, and problem solvers. We need to find new methods of breaking the linear teaching period of the traditional classroom location. Most learners are at the teachable moment at times and places other than where learning experiences tend to be offered. Most learners learn at a pace that is different from that of even other learners who are most like themselves. Can we convert our land-grant classrooms into interactive centers for learning and problem solving? Time shifting, place shifting, pace shifting: can information technology help us master these concepts? Can we become a connected network of learners, information providers, and problem solvers? Can we access and share learning resources across institutional, state, and national boundaries?

How can your own community begin to enjoy the benefits of these seemingly futuristic developments?

Learning institutions in your community are beginning to plan and implement some of these advanced learning technologies. In every state, the state land-grant university has established a major NREN terminal at the university's computer center. In most states, the outreach division of the university, the local county Extension offices, are becoming the first point in the community to have access to the learning resources on the NREN. To learn more about how to help with this effort, contact your local county Cooperative Extension office or Extension computer coordinator at your state's land-grant university.

Some communities have launched after-school programs that give young learners an opportunity to have semi-structured free time on computers in the school's learning centers. In many instances, these after-school programs are being supervised by volunteers. The volunteers are often parents or friends of students; they bring their professional skills and excitement to the learners in an informal atmosphere. The learners proceed at their own pace and often develop projects that are highly creative and lead to an improved interest in learning. The local 4-H club in many communities provides the program with structure, educational materials, and a supply of volunteers from the local community.

In some communities, volunteers are making their firms' computer training centers available to students' computer clubs on an after-school basis. In other communities, local firms are providing computers to school learning centers in exchange for grocery sales receipts collected by the students. Your local school board and local Cooperative Extension office are good contact points for getting involved in this movement.

Community Mobilization

If the computers in your community schools and libraries are not yet connected to the NREN, you may be the catalyst that can get the ball rolling. Why not identify others in your community who use information technology in their day-to-day work? You could contact them and organize a group that has a common vision to upgrade the tools that learners have access to in your local community. This action will strengthen your community. You will be empowering others to learn new ways of learning. You will help provide options for people to retrain themselves for new and different employment possibilities.

To help mobilize the resources needed for this educational transformation, you can contact your local chamber of commerce and its members for support. You can help them envision how these tools can strengthen the state and local work force and thereby the state and local economy.

Your local Cooperative Extension office is connected, or is in the process of being connected, to the NREN. Office staff can guide you to the experts in your community or state who will identify an individual who can provide advice and counsel on taking these steps toward the future. Close to 1000 local Cooperative Extension centers are now equipped with satellite down-link capability to bring education to learners in your community from providers all over the nation and around the world. The local Cooperative Extension center can also connect you to a network of more than 500,000 volunteers who are interested in advancing learning by young and old in rural and urban communities.

Help your elected officials understand how they can be part of the solution, not part of the problem. Tell them about the distance learning in Missouri. Make your community a member of the growing national network of community learning centers. It is your choice. Get involved.

Article Review Form at end of book.

WiseGuide Wrap-Up

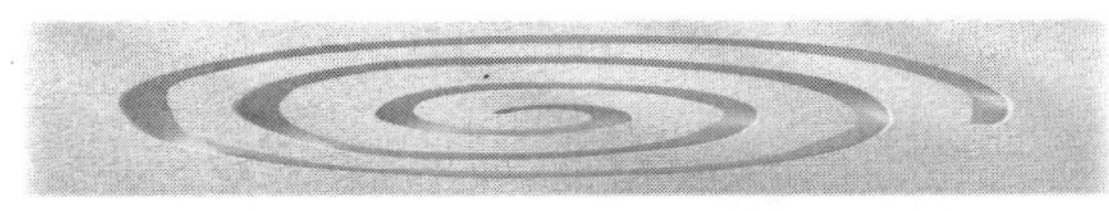

- Field experiences, internships, and field-based courses offered in professional development schools provide preservice teachers with excellent opportunities for becoming actively involved in the teaching profession.
- Establishing university/public school partnerships, including professional development sites, requires time and commitment from all stakeholders.
- To meet the present and future needs of students, educators must be proactive, visionary, and change-oriented.
- Technology will continue to emerge as a key ingredient in effective educational systems.

R.E.A.L. Sites

This list provides a print preview of typical **coursewise** R.E.A.L. sites. There are over 100 such sites at the **courselinks™** site. The danger in printing URLs is that web sites can change overnight. As we went to press, these sites were functional using the URL provided. If you come across one that isn't, please let us know via email to: webmaster@coursewise.com. Use your Passport to access the most current list of R.E.A.L. sites at the **courselinks™** site.

Site name: AcademicNet
URL: http://www.academic.com/
Why is it R.E.A.L.? This site presents strategies for using technology as an instructional tool.
Key topics: technology, teaching and learning
Activity: Plan and deliver a group presentation that uses technology as an instructional tool.

Site name: Parent's Guide to the Internet
URL: http://www.ed.gov/pubs/parents/internet/
Why is it R.E.A.L.? This site has a parents' guide to the Internet that includes a definition of the Internet, strategies for using the Internet, and suggestions for communicating cautions to children who use the Internet. The site also has links to other sites of interest to family and children.
Key topics: technology, Internet

Index

Note: Page numbers in *italics* indicate figures; numbers followed by *t* indicate tables; numbers followed by *n* indicate notes. Names and page numbers in **boldface** indicate authors and their articles.

A

B

C

D

E

F

G

H

O

P